Not the Love of my *Life*

A Story of Reclaiming One's Existence

Eric L. Di Conti

ISBN 978-1-959182-41-2 (paperback)
ISBN 978-1-959182-42-9 (hardcover)
ISBN 978-1-959182-43-6 (digital)

Copyright © 2022 by Eric L. Di Conti

All rights reserved. No part of this publication may be reproduced, distributed, or transmitted in any form or by any means, including photocopying, recording, or other electronic or mechanical methods without the prior written permission of the publisher.

Tower 9

Printed in the United States of America

CONTENTS

DEDICATION vii
PREFACE ix

1. NEW PATH 1
2. CAN I HELP YOU? 16
3. SHE'S TRYING TO REACH YOU 22
4. WOULD YOU MIND TAKING A LITTLE TEST FOR ME? 33
5. JESUS CHRIST! IT'S HOT! 38
6. HEY, FLY SHIT! 45
7. I'M THE LUCKIEST WOMAN IN THE WORLD 56
8. THE WRETCHED LIFE OF A PARASITE 58
9. LET ME TELL YOU GUYS SOMETHING 62
10. WE'RE IN ARIZONA 65
11. I HATE FLYING 73
12. THE RADIO EXPERIENCE 78
13. I'M SO GLAD WE'RE BACK TOGETHER 83
14. DO YOU WANT TO MEET ME FOR DINNER? 86
15. ORDER OF PROTECTION COURT CASE No. CC2006023696 89
16. HELLO, IS THIS ERIC DI CONTI? 100
17. WELCOME TO IN-TOWN SUITES 110
18. ARE YOU READY? 116
    Tiffany Nelson 120
    Susan Nelson-Stephanson 126
    Eric Di Conti 135
19. ARE YOU IN CALIFORNIA? 141

20. PAMELA CHAMBERS 149
21. THERE'S SOMETHING YOU NEED TO KNOW 157
   Ryanne Ritter Statement.. 167
22. YOU ARE NEVER GOING TO BELIEVE WHO I
   TALKED TO 188
   Judge Cuccurullo 190
23. DADDY, JIM IS BOTHERING US 195
   Request For Order Of Protection.................................... 199
24. HEARING FOR FINAL DISSOLUTION OF
   MARRIAGE 202
25. ARE YOU WITH THESE GUYS? 207
26. WE'RE WAITIN' ON SOME LOOT 215
27. CHRISTMAS IN MAUI 2006 220
28. THE KEENLAND YEARLING SALE? 229
29. STEVEN EVERTS, COUNSEL FOR TIFFANY
   NELSON 235
   Letter To Steven Everts 245
30. I'M GOING TO STICK AROUND FOR AWHILE 252
31. RISEN SAVIOR LUTHERAN CHURCH AND
   SCHOOL 257
32. CHURCHES ARE A STRANGE BREED OF PEOPLE.... 267
33. MY NAME IS LINDA PECANIC 271
34. HE WOULD HAVE EVENTUALLY BEEN CAUGHT ... 281
35. EMERGENCY MOTION TO REMOVE WITNESSES ... 290
36. WERE YOU INVESTIGATED BY CHANDLER
   POLICE? 298
37. DEFAMATION OF CHARACTER LAWSUIT 303
38. FRY'S FOOD AND DRUG 325
39. I'LL PUT YOU ON THE MAP MYSELF 341
40. STEVEN EVERTS REQUESTS ATTORNEY'S FEES
   TO BE PAID 350
41. WE NEED TO DISCUSS THE RESULTS OF. 358
42. WE'D LIKE TO EXTEND YOU AN OFFER 366

43. A SMALL DEGREE OF VINDICATION 382
44. JUST ONE TIME, YOU COULD STAND INSIDE
    MY SHOES 402
45. RESPONSE TO "NEW PATH" 406

EPILOGUE 411
FINAL THOUGHTS 413
AFTERWARD 417

DEDICATION

**To the TRUE Loves of My Life,
Kathryn Elisabeth and Megan Elisse.**

**I am so terribly sorry for the immeasurable
pain you two were made to suffer through and the
many times I was weak and far harder on you than I
should have been. I want both of you to know that
without the two of you, I never would have made it
through this turbulent time in our lives. Thank
you for being there for me when I was at my weakest
and needed to be reminded I had something to live for.
All my love; Pui di ieri, Meno di domani**

This book is also dedicated to all the fathers and mothers who have been wrongfully accused of horrific acts upon children, or each other, within the confines of each respective relationship. It is a sad day when one is accused of an act he, or she, did not commit, but that accusation remains fused to their name for eternity. Worse still is our judicial system will do nothing for you unless you have an attorney and are backed up with enough money to support that attorney for the better part of a year and, oftentimes, much longer. If you cannot, the miserable wretch making those accusations doesn't ever have to be held accountable.

"It's not a criminal act; it is a civil issue, sir," one judge told me. Really? It is a vicious cycle that doesn't appear will change anytime soon.

Additionally, I dedicate this work to those swindled by a man so adept at working the mortgage banking system and so genius in his planning that if it weren't for me believing in what's right, and having the moralistic instinct to stop him, he would still be out there cashing in on an already crippled banking industry. To the sub-contractors who were never paid and homeowners who lost everything, you are in my heart and I'm sorry I didn't see through him and react sooner than I did. To Dominique and Mark Acre (Lot 28 in Mirabel) and Tasha and Will Henstein (Lot 32 in Mirabel), who lost nearly everything they ever worked for, know that my prayers are with you.

"A society that loses its sense of outrage is doomed to extinction," as Honorable Edwin Torres, a Federal Judge in New York, once said. Much of what is contained in the following pages should be an outrage to many and due to our judicial system I fear Judge Torres may be a visionary in that respect.

To Fernando D. Vargas. Just one little call changed the course of nature. That one little call changed my life. Altered it forever. Though, had you *not* made that call it is true, I would not have had to endure the wrath of the court system, nor would I have lost so much of myself, but I would also have two huge voids in my life. I hope you are well, my old friend.

Finally, to Tiffany; I found a bottle of Chardonnay out of Mendoza, Argentina called *El Enemigo*. It's an amazing bottle of wine, but on the back is a quote that I wanted to add to this dedication page. Considering what you've done, it should resonate with you, because it sums up quite a bit; *"At the end of the journey, we remember only one battle: the one we fought against ourselves, the original enemy. The one that defined us."* El Enemigo translates to *"The Enemy."*

PREFACE

"There are lots of tangled knots within everyone's personality and sometimes being able to write helps me untangle some of them." – Robert Earl Keen

Nothing in this book is of importance to anyone, but me and two little girls. What is important is that I had to tell it, if for no other reason than to feel a sense of personal relief that my side of the story has been told . . . and people have heard it. Why did I write this then? To set the record straight. And to finally finish something I set out to do without stopping, midway through the task, and walking away. To let two little girls know I have not failed them.

Sometimes you hear stories and think to yourself, "There is no way this guy could have done *all* that, or had *that* much happen to him." Normally, that would be true, unless you consider this: ***"If you want to make God laugh, tell Him your plans."*** This quote comes from Louis Mandylor, a successful actor and director, whom I had the pleasure to meet and become friends with, in the early 1990 s. He said those words to me soon after we met and they have stayed with me ever since. I look at certain chapters in my life, realize I *did* share my plans with God, recall the words of Louis Mandylor, and cannot discount the strong probability that He *does* have a sense of humor. Some of His humor though, I would liken to, say, falling out of a car at sixty miles per hour and incurring a bad case of road rash. Some of His humor I didn't find very funny. Some of his humor lasted far too long.

The pages that follow have nothing to do with anything in my life but for five and a half years; the days between August of 2004 and early 2010. Everything you read that is outside this timeline is merely a precursor to things that came to happen, a result of things that happened, or for an informational background. What is contained on the pages that follow is true.

In reading this, some may view me as just a good Dad who loves his daughters and you would be right. I truly believe I *am* a good Dad and I *do* love my daughters. Conversely, there may also be several people out there who might suggest otherwise, and considering my record of accomplishments, prior to Katie and Megan, I would have to agree with them also. Prior to Kathryn and Megan entering my life, some may feel I was the furthest from a "good Dad" as one could be. At times, I *was* terrible and I admit it. As a father, some may believe I was as useless as shoes to a legless man. I continue to try to make up for some of those inadequacies. I may have fallen short many times, but the love for my daughters (all four of them) never wavered. This story, however, is about me and my two youngest daughters; Katie and Megan.

You may detect some anger and bitterness in my writing and if you do it is probably well warranted, but this was not written to lash out in anger or to "bash" anyone. This is merely my story and I am telling it exactly as it happened, how I felt as it happened, and with the hope that people might learn from what I went through. In that respect, nothing else really matters, as this book is to tell the story of a part of my life that was destroyed by one simple little statement made by a person, a "messenger," if you will. A statement that flickered as a small flame and may have been made innocently at first (or maybe not), but when it was realized people took notice, the statement was embellished upon until it became a raging forest fire with no means by which to extinguish it.

Normally, books start at the beginning and end when the story is over, but I wanted to begin this book with the ending so the reader can see early on, where my journey took me. From there I go back in time to the beginning, moving forward through my story, and finally circle back to the first chapter. With that said, this book begins with two e-mails one I received and the other is my response. They came toward the ***end*** of this particular journey and they were used as the first chapter to give you an idea of what follows in the book and the events that led up to those two e-mail.

Let me say that all of what follows is *almost* the absolute truth. Each insertion of correspondence, or court records, is inserted exactly as it was sent or filed in Superior Court. Nothing has been changed. I say "almost" the truth because some of the names of people had to be changed in the event that they didn't want to have their name/s in print, or I could not put their names in print due to the nature of their business. These people are merely some of the individuals with whom I happened to cross paths during this time in my life.

Some helped me and some did not, but for whatever reason God placed them in my life as either a beacon of hope or a test of my will and character. As is the norm, when dealing with the legal system, there are very few beacons, but rather a plethora of "tests" put before me. Roadblocks of different shapes and sizes and every one of them had an intricate combination of tasks, which I had to complete in order to get around the same. I do not know who coined the phrase, or if it's even the quote of a famous person, but it is so true; ***"In our life, only 10% consists of what happens to us, the other 90% is how we respond to it."*** This is a story of how those percentages are very different and the difficulty to respond— equally immense.

Mark Twain once said, ***"Write what you know about"*** and that is exactly what I have done, as the content of the pages that follow this one ***is*** what I know and ***is*** what happened.

My former wife used my extremely abusive upbringing, at the hands of my father, as the catalyst to her stories with the hope that people would hang on to the belief that abuse self-perpetuates; and did so in my case. Though it is true in many cases, abuse does self-perpetuate where the *abused* becomes the *abuser*. The fact is, I have never raised my hand to a woman, or a child, and it sickens me to think of such an act.

It has been a long, difficult, and painful road for me and for my two youngest daughters, but my girls and I have grown stronger with each "test" we are given. We have struggled beyond words, at times lived off what little we had, and appreciated the small things that we could call our own. Our resolve has never faltered, nor has our deep love for each other. Our bond is one that cannot be broken because of who we are and what we have become through this misery. They are my life and I am theirs. Ernest Hemingway once wrote, **"The world breaks everyone and afterward many are stronger at the broken places."** Even in its simplest form, I believe this statement to be true.

It is said that a relationship between a father and his daughter is of great importance in a young girl's life; I never knew what that meant until Kathryn and Megan became a part of mine and we traveled through a journey no child should be forced to travel. I knew much more about the importance of our relationship once we started our journey together, through the divorce process in Family Court, in the State of Arizona, County of Maricopa.

Everything we learn in our lives comes from a messenger of some kind. To some, it is an act of God. To others, it is a catastrophic event that takes place and changes their lives so dramatically. Still, others find their messenger to be a person they meet, brought together for no explainable reasons and through this person, their lives are altered forever. What I would glean from my life's changes was learned in the most brutal of ways. My "messenger" made me part of a disaster from which, under normal circumstances, only cockroaches emerge unscathed. That's probably the reason attorneys are so abundant. One person starts a disaster, attorneys take it and raise it to a catastrophic event and the only people left standing, in the end, are the attorneys; their pockets stuffed with cash. That's probably why they are referred to as "cockroaches;" and with good reason.

My "messenger" was like a mutating bacterium, spreading its poison throughout my body with only one mission in mind; to destroy the very essence of my existence. My messenger was the worst kind. There's nothing worse than a messenger who brings with them the unimaginable misery of telling brutal lies about someone and ultimately destroys that person's life by those same horrific lies. This messenger would be my wife, Tiffany; "The Love of My Life," and her vicious lies would bully themselves into my dreams nightly; they continue to this day. In your dreams; you can run but get nowhere. You can fight but never have the ability to hit your assailant. Worst of all, when you scream no sound can be heard and no one can hear silence. You are alone. I was alone.

Several years ago, I received a small spiral-bound book filled with blank pages. I write little quotes, or thoughts, in it from time to time. These writings are a window into who I am as a person and how I try to live my life. I have inserted several of these quotes into the pages of this book as I see them fit into the storyline. The first entry I ever wrote in the book was in 1996 and was the quote of a person unknown to me. It reads: ***"The most noticeable quality of humans is the manner in which hardship is endured."*** How ironic it was for me to have written this quote, as the first entry, so many years before I entered, what I feel was the Gates of Hell.

Another is from the book, Bridges of Madison County and describes, so closely, how I felt when I fell in love with the woman who would become *The Love of My Life*: ***"In a universe of ambiguity, this kind of certainty comes only once and never again, no matter how many lives-times you live."*** How miserably wrong I would find myself to be. How terribly amiss my *certainty* was.

How does a man fall into a pit of absolute chaos and come out unchanged? He doesn't; he is changed forever.

We all have stories to tell, but some stories - the private ones - will be told to only those whom we trust. Some stories are meant to be kept private and others should be told. Have to be told. Although much of it is private and should be kept that way, this story must be told. Has to be told. My existence was cruelly snatched away in March 2006. Pilfered by nothing more than a street urchin who, once exposed, displayed few noticeable redeeming qualities.

Why did I write this? To reclaim my existence.

Eric Di Conti

August 11, 2018

NOTE: This work contains a vast array of anecdotes laced with my opinion of the same. For the record, my opinions in no way reflect what, or who, the actual person I write about truly is. What I have written with respect to an incident that may have occurred is written exactly the way it happened and is the complete truth. Other than what is found in court documents and through public records, my perception of any given individual in this book is nothing more than my opinion of that person. Nothing more than my opinion. Also, in addition to some important background information and, to some, seemingly irrelevant background information, the pages in this book will carry you through that summer of 2004 and the many months, before and after, I spent struggling with my past, and who I really was as a person. Some sequences may appear vague with missing information, but if it isn't included in this book, it had very little, or no, bearing on the events described in the same and therefore was not included.

"NEW PATH"

"Optimism always; in spite of everything, even when the events do not seem to justify it." – Joseph Moccia, M.D., Inspirational/Motivational Speaker

Friday - February 13, 2009

On Monday, February 9, 2009, at 5:04 PM, I was driving south on the 101 Freeway in what is known as the East Valley, just outside Phoenix, Arizona. I had just left Scottsdale and was heading to my home in Tempe when my BlackBerry vibrated to let me know I had an e-mail. I pulled it from its case and saw that the e-mail had come from Tiffany, *The Love of My Life*. The Subject line read simply; *"New Path."*

I thought to myself, "New path? What the hell does she want now? I mean, she never makes contact unless she wants something," or she has had an epiphany that she believes can change the course of nature. By now, I normally found her correspondence fairly comical. Thoughts such as this are commonplace after what I had come to learn about the woman I had loved so deeply, so completely, and for so long.

I couldn't wait until I got home, so as I drove, I pressed the button to open the file and started to read. There were four words in the first sentence that made me realize this was one of her epiphanies; the sixth, seventh, eighth, and ninth words, to be exact.

NOTE: The following is the exact e-mail, in its entirety, as it was sent that day. Nothing has been changed.

"Eric:

The service today at church resonated deep within me and I am looking to follow a new path with you for the benefit of our girls.

Colossians 3:13-14 says: **'Bear with each other and forgive whatever grievances you may have against one another. Forgive as the Lord forgave you. And over all those virtues put on love, which binds them all together in perfect unity.'**

With that in mind, I am asking that today, Sunday, February 8, 2009, be the day we put our anger and hurt aside and put our love for the girls in the forefront. There have been real and perceived transgressions, real hurt, and true damage. However, the pain each of us has caused and felt pales in comparison to the love we both share for the girls and the love they share for us. I would do it all again, the good, the bad, the ugly, the fun, the painful-beyond-belief to once again be blessed with these daughters.

Effective today, I want to stop passing the girls off in parking lots like bags of groceries, and instead deliver them to the respective homes they share with each of us. I want them to bounce out of your doorway and jump into my car for our week together and do the same when it's time to come back to you. I want you to know that each Wednesday you are welcome to join us for dinner and I hope that you do, so we can talk about Megan's skating lesson and catch up on other news the girls have to share. I mean each and every word here and hope that your love for them outweighs your hurt and anger as mine does.

As a way to begin this new path, I want you to know that the $170 bill you had at Dr. Madrid's office has been paid in full by me. I want a new beginning and a new path to honor the girls we have been blessed with. I hope you will read the Colossians passage and take me up on the new beginning for the benefit of Katy **(SIC)** and Megan.

Tiffany

NOT THE LOVE OF MY LIFE

I was taken aback, and maybe even stunned, by this E-mail. As usual, I had a million different thoughts surging in my head. What made things worse (according to a renowned doctor in this field), is that I am afflicted with a severe form of ADHD which puts me in the top one percentile of all adults with this disorder and by 5 PM, my earlier dose of Ritalin had nearly metabolized; I was ready for another 20mg tablet. The diminishing amount of Ritalin in my system made trying to file my thoughts in an orderly fashion, difficult at best. In fact, without this drug, my thoughts, though they all make perfect sense, just slam into each other in about a disorderly fashion as one could imagine. I will go into the subject of Ritalin later on, so for now, don't get wadded up on the fact that I take it.

After reading Tiffany's E-mail, and what was even more usual, I questioned her motives. She had done things like this before, attempting to lure me into her little web of deceit, but when she flinched, for whatever reason, I was able to detect it and back away; probably saving myself some misery. Over the past few years, I had developed a keen sense of "somethin'-ain't-right-here." I taught myself to recognize it early, and I became pretty good at seeing the signs of a future beating. It kicked hard with this E-mail.

I called my good friend and confidant, Ryan Quinn, to tell him what Tiffany had just sent me. No answer.

"Damn it!" I said out loud, "God this bastard is hard to get a hold of!" Which he was.

If I didn't catch Ryan sometime during the day, it was rare I caught him after he went home. He rarely answered his phone after 5 PM; it didn't matter what day it was. I used to joke that once he got home he would crawl into his coffin and close the lid; not to be bothered until the next morning.

When Ryan got home he shut the world out and refused to deal with anything outside the walls of his home and when I jokingly questioned him about it one day, he confided in me that my true beliefs were not far off. Like me, he believes the world, for the most part, is good, but there is a safety zone inside your home; a place where no one can get to you. There is a sense of comfort in knowing we can put a wedge between the outside world and us by merely closing the front door. That three-foot by seven-foot, two-inch-thick obstruction, leaves the outside world right where it is supposed to be; outside.

All I wanted to do was to tell someone about the e-mail and I couldn't at that point. I forwarded it and then sent Ryan a text message to check his e-mail. When I did get a hold of him, his response was the same as mine; "Something isn't right."

Although, without having any Ritalin on board, I instinctively (or impulsively) wanted to respond right away; however, I waited for a day, or so, before I began to compose a response. I didn't want to act hastily and fire off an e-mail that was laced with barbs and condescension. If this was a real olive branch, I didn't want to ruin it.

I knew immediately that my response would need to be direct and concise and for that to happen, I needed time to think about what I would include in the response. I also decided that when she received my response, the girls could not be around to hear her reaction to it, or more importantly, have her read my response to them. In the past, she has done this with some of our correspondence, reading only the excerpts, or portions of the same, that would suggest, to little ears, I was not being very nice. It was Tiffany's way of showing the girls that I was "mean" to her and I was a "mean person." I've always called it *damage control* since, in a few years, she would be attempting to explain her actions during our divorce (and a great deal more) to the girls. The girls never bought any of the cheap crap Tiffany fed them. Though I never pushed, or questioned it I think, very early on, their loyalty was to me.

My first course of action was to pick up my Bible and read the verse that she referred. I wanted to make sure she didn't leave out (or add) any verbiage to benefit her new campaign. On many occasions, she has done this when quoting other documents and attempted to use it to her benefit, so I had to check. I have read, and reread, Colossians at length and even though, at only four chapters it is a short book, it contains a great deal of information about renewing one's faith in Jesus Christ and starting one's life all over; to be "Born Again," so to speak. Colossians give one the recipe for doing so.

Though she picked out a great verse from Scripture and as I suspected, she missed a great many more in the same chapter. In fact, she missed a great many more throughout that particular book.

I decided if this was going to work, and she was serious, there were several things that had to happen before we could move forward. It would have been impossible for me, if not reckless and irresponsible, to just accept what she said without ever questioning her motives. It didn't matter that she was now attending church, whereas before church was an inconvenience to her and she never took the girls. The only time the girls attended church services was when they went with me.

She had what some call a pseudo-faith, which reminds me of a story I had heard some time ago: One Sunday morning in a very large Church and just prior to the service starting, four gunmen in dark clothing and ski masks entered the building. One of them screamed, "Alright, anyone willing to die for Jesus Christ stay where you are. The rest of you get out! Now!"

There was a huge scramble for the doors. People pushing and shoving their way to the exits. People were falling all over themselves trying to get out of harm's way. In a little over a minute the church was nearly empty. All that were left were a few people in the choir, the preacher, and a handful of parishioners who were on their knees praying. The preacher, who was standing at the front of the church and holding his Bible, looked at the gunman, palms outward, as if to ask, "Why?"

At this point, the gunmen took off their masks and the leader, who gave the initial order to get out of the church, said to the preacher, "OK, Reverend, you can start your service now. I got rid of all the hypocrites."

I had my doubts about the sincerity of this olive branch, which *The Love of My Life* was extending

I started writing my response on Tuesday, February 10 and finished it two days later, Thursday, February 12. I wanted it written in a way that she would realize one cannot just wake up one day and decide that all is well, the flowers are blooming, life is beautiful and nothing in the past matters; because it does. This isn't the Junior Varsity Team anymore; it matters in a big way. The following is my response, in its entirety, and exactly as it was delivered to Tiffany Nelson. Nothing has changed. You will find that I am very verbose, but this letter had to be this long to get all my points on record. Please bear with it and each point will be answered as you read through the book.

ERIC DI CONTI
3031 SOUTH RURAL RD. #16
TEMPE, AZ 85282

February 10, 2009

TN,

*This is wonderful news, Tiffany! However, it's taken a couple of days to respond to your E-mail because, quite frankly, I'm still a little shocked by the words contained in it. There is so much I want to say and don't know where to start, but to say; I cannot help but wonder, given your past history, if there is actually an ulterior motive, or personal agenda toward which you are working. Additionally, on one hand, your words are something, of which, I have truly grown to be very wary. On the other hand, I know that in my heart you **want** this to go away; possibly, considering all that you've done, to finally feel better about yourself.*

Against my better judgment, I will cautiously accept this "offer" of yours, for the sake of the girls, with several stipulations. To be certain this cannot happen overnight and to be successful must be done in a series of stages, but I first want to address your reference to Colossians 3:13-14.

I guess the sermon you heard this past Sunday, if what you say is true, had a profound impact on you and I am thankful that something finally has.

The Book, Colossians, I am very familiar with, Tiffany, and though it's only four chapters I have read the book several times. The Verses 3:13-14 truly is profound and should "resonate deep within" all of us. However, this particular Book deals with accepting Christ and being a servant to Him at any and all costs; throwing your old life away and starting anew.

*Though one verse in a Scripture "resonates" deep within you, you cannot pick and choose, by which verses you wish to live; you must live by all of them. Maybe you missed the few Verses prior to 3:13-14. More specifically Verses 5-10, which reads; <u>"Put to death, therefore, whatever belongs to your earthly nature: **sexual immorality**, **impurity**, **lust**, **evil desires** and **greed**, which is idolatry. Because of these, the wrath of God is coming. You used to walk in these ways, in the life you once</u>*

<u>lived. But now you must rid yourself of all such things as these: anger, rage, **malice**, **slander** and filthy language from your lips. **Do not lie** to each other, since you have taken off your old self with its practices and put on the new self, which is being renewed in knowledge in the image of its Creator."</u>

These are the words that should "resonate" deeper than anything else you may have heard, or read, that day. Nearly three years ago, the Verses in this chapter made me understand what I needed to do to live as a better person and I try to live by them every day. If you are willing to cite Bible Verse such as the one you did, cite **ALL** of them and live by them. You cannot pick and choose.

To be honest, over the past three years I have become fairly familiar with The Bible, as a whole. Do not mistake me for saying I **know** The Bible, but rather I am more **familiar** with It than I have ever been. To narrow that statement down further, I have read the New Testament at length over the past few years, but one of the best Books of The Bible is Proverbs in the Old Testament.

As enticing as you may think your offer is, this is not a bandwagon I can just jump aboard and hope for the best. I would be doing myself a great injustice and my comfort level would diminish considerably, though the one thing that is drawing me toward this is your insistence you are extending this offer solely for "the girls." The consequences of a statement of this magnitude come with some sacrifice on your part that could, quite possibly, have an effect of exponential proportions.

If this truly **is** for the sake of the girls then you won't have any problem in agreeing with the following requests. Please note they are in order of absolute priority.

1) Move out of the house in which you live with Jim Norton. It is an extremely unhealthy living environment for the girls for a plethora of reasons. It always has been and will continue to be, as long as he is living under the same roof and sharing the same bed while you are not married. The incident where Katie was hurt by Jim's scissor lock, his drunken rages where the three of you locked yourself in a room until he fell asleep, etc., gives me cause to worry deeply about the safety of the girls. Further, and more importantly and according to The Bible, this is a sinful and immoral relationship. See Colossians

*3:5-10. If you are saying you are now putting the girls ahead of **EVERYTHING** and **EVERYONE**, then Jim Norton is of little consequence and it shouldn't be any problem at all to complete this simple task.*

2) Write a letter to The Chandler Police Department recanting the statement, and report, you filed on March 3, 2006. You will ask that your letter be attached to the original police report, so when a background investigation is conducted, it too will appear with the report that I was investigated for **"SEX CRIME-CHILD VICTIM,"** but they will also see that it was a lie.

3) Write a letter to the Gilbert Police Department recanting your statement that I kidnapped the girls during the trip we went to see my brother, upon his return from Iraq. The letter will state unequivocally that I **DID NOT** kidnap the girls and take them to California with the "intent of never returning" to Arizona; that your story was fabricated. You will also ask that the "arrest" which was made, in absentia, on me be expunged from my record.

4) Write a letter to the Maricopa County Supreme Court stating that the Order of Protection you obtained on March 2, 2006, was done so unlawfully, that your story was fabricated, and that you respectfully request that the Order of Protection be stricken from the record forever.

5) Write a letter to both DeeAn Gillespie and Michelle Kunzman stating their client, Eric Di Conti, never harmed, or abused in any manner either of his children and that the story was, in fact, a complete fabrication.

6) Write a letter of apology to me for **a)** maliciously destroying my name by making these horrible accusations. **b)** You will apologize for taking the girls away from me, for over a month, by your malicious act in lying and obtaining the Order of Protection. **c)** You will apologize for taking, without my permission, and distributing to all of our friends and acquaintances, the very private letter I wrote. You

*will also return each, and every, copy you made of the letter, as I believe you made many more than the pristine and unread copy you returned to me. I know that at least eight people read that letter and to see the letter, you claim is the only one remaining, to be in such good condition, I find it extremely difficult to believe you are no longer in possession of copies of the same. **d)** You will also include that you acknowledge, and apologize, that due to your actions I suffered great financial difficulties. **e)** You will apologize for your harassment of me at every turn over the past three years, INCLUDING having me taken into custody for not paying medical insurance premiums that I didn't even owe in the first place. You were the ONLY one who could have stopped me from being arrested that day and you did nothing to stop it. **f)** You will also write that the manner in which you have been collecting child support, for the past three years is a travesty, in that you planned to get a job with a law firm, and NOT stay working as a "real estate expediter" for $2800 per month, immediately after solidifying more support than you deserved. **g)** In the letter you will also include an apology for withdrawing every last penny out of our bank account, at the instruction of your attorney, Donna Jewett, on March 2, 2006. Finally, in your letter of apology to me, **h)** you will apologize for passing out copies of the Order of Protection at the girls' school, Our Lady of Mount Carmel in Tempe, which you unlawfully obtained by your lies.*

7) *You will write a letter to both Kathryn and Megan for making up the horrible lies you told to so many people and in it you will also apologize for taking over a month of their lives away from me, their father, due to the Order of Protection. In it, you will also apologize for lying to them, during the time the Order of Protection was in place, by telling them that I "didn't want to be their father anymore," so I "went back to California." What a horrible thing to tell a child. I will hold onto this letter and will turn it over to them when they are old enough to understand what you did and understand the damage your actions caused.*

8) *Write letters to each, and every, person whom you falsely informed I beat you, "one time, so badly, [you] could not leave the house for*

two weeks." These people would include but do not limit to Melissa Nordquist, Susan Collins, Tamara Gerbich, Scott Woodford and his wife Erin, etc.

9) Write a letter to the Sheppard and Ritter families apologizing for insinuating that their grandson/son, Brody, was molested by me and that you fabricated that story, as well.

10) Write a letter to Our Lady of Mount Carmel and apologize for lying to them by making all the plans of being a part of that school for this academic year and then, citing the divorce decree, boorishly yanking them out, so you, and/or your family members, didn't have to drive to Tempe to drop them off and pick them up.

The school the girls are now in, Imagine Schools in Gilbert, is a joke of an educational setting with immorality everywhere; Kids kissing in the hallways, Katie having her breast grabbed, a 5th grader with a naked photo of her "boyfriend" on her cell phone (taken by another 5th grader), Katie's teacher refusing to speak with me on any level above saying, "hello." Megan's teacher just doesn't speak to me at all. It's a freaking JOKE Tiffany and you took them out of a safe environment and put them in a place that better suits YOU. It had nothing to do with the girls at all, but rather had everything to do with the comfort of you and your family and you need to admit it. Mt Carmel has NEVER turned anyone away from an education there because they could not afford to pay. It had nothing to do with money because you were NEVER out-of-pocket, nor would you EVER be out-of-pocket and you must inform Mount Carmel of your selfishness and ask for their forgiveness. They would have received a better education from Mt. Carmel than anywhere else in this valley and you ruined any hope of a decent education for the girls. Further still is that they would never be accepted into a school like Xavier College Prep from a school like Imagine Schools of West Gilbert. They had a much better shot at it, had they gone to Mt. Carmel. Unfortunately, you dashed that hope; you need to realize that and admit it.

1) Write a letter of apology to my family, for the disparaging things you said about me, and let them know that everything you had stated

about me being abusive to you and the girls, and that the girls were afraid of me, was a complete fabrication and that you would like to be forgiven for the same.

2) Write a letter to the Court saying you are no longer owed any money by me; your attorney's fees have been completely satisfied and you will not seek to have them repaid now, or in the future. If it's about the girls, the money is completely insignificant and of no consequence. Certainly, if this task is a problem for you, it is where your priorities lay.

<u>NOTE: Each of the letters you write, and the language therein, will be approved by me and delivered by me, so as to ensure the letters actually get to the respective recipients and are not somehow misdirected. However, if you do not want to write these letters, I will write them for you (on your behalf). Once you have reviewed the letters you can sign them and we can have each notarized accordingly. We can even drop them in the mail together, if you'd like.</u>

3) Put together some kind of a plan in which you feel will best necessitate a reimbursement to me, of half of the funds you removed from our account over the last several years of our marriage. The total of those funds is somewhere around $330,000 and you need to show me where the money went and that I personally benefited from the same. Once you can show that I benefited from these monies, that amount can be deducted from the $330,000. Once we come to an amicable agreement as to how much money was "skimmed" we can decide how it is you intend to repay the same. The reference that is being made to "skimming" is in direct response to the offer you made to the several women that you could teach them how to "skim" funds from their marital accounts, so their respective spouses "would never know" and that "if the marriage doesn't work out, [they'll] have a nice little nest-egg at the end."

4) Put together some kind of a plan by which you feel will best necessitate a reimbursement to me, the funds you removed from our account the

night of March 2, 2006. By your own admission and testimony, you, at Jewett's direction, removed over $68,000 from our account and I wound up with what I remember to be $7,401. I think you would agree that this was not a fair and equitable disbursement of funds and it needs to be rectified accordingly.

Once the above has been accomplished we can talk about the girls "bouncing out of doorways and into cars." If you think about it, it's really not that much work, considering it's mostly a letter-writing campaign of at least fifteen letters and you can be done with it over the course of a weekend. The hardest part will be moving out of the place you live and finding a new place for you and the girls.

If your offer truly **IS** *about the love we each have for the girls, the above shouldn't take you too long to absorb and then agree to. Until then, I just cannot trust a thing you say, or trust a thing you say you will do. I believe in self-preservation and just jumping into this and taking a ride with you isn't in my best interest, nor is it in the best interest of the girls. I love them too much to just throw caution to the wind and hope for the best. I've done that more than once with you.*

I am a good man, Tiffany. I always have been and always will be. I made huge sacrifices for our family the ENTIRE time we were married and provided everything that you ever asked for. If there was ever even the slightest hint of any desire you may have had for something, I made sure you got it. You rarely wanted for anything. Your desire was to stay home and raise the girls and I made sure that was possible by working every waking hour that I needed to, so as to accommodate you and our family. I did all the cooking and made sure that every night, your feet were rubbed because that's what you enjoyed. I was NEVER unfaithful; however you cannot say the same. I took our vows very seriously, however you cannot say the same. In my life, I have never loved anyone as much as I loved you and you were able to completely destroy it in one day; destroy **ME** *in one day.*

I have lived in absolute misery for three years and due to your lies, have endured unspeakable prejudice and rejection from countless people. That includes people and parents at Our Lady of Mount Carmel Catholic Church! You should know that I had an enormous amount of trouble obtaining housing from those who ran background checks, *searching for sexual predators with the local police agencies. Why did I have trouble finding housing? Because that miserable little investigation kept surfacing; the one you keep saying I'm "being overly sensitive" about. When I **was** offered housing, the security deposit was so enormous (in one instance four times the amount of rent) I was unable to afford, move-in costs of over $5,000 in cash. I guess it was their way of saying "No" and letting me know I was unwanted; a pariah. All I was doing was looking for a place for our daughters to stay while they were with me, but because of your lies, I couldn't even do that. Can you imagine not being able to find a job, or a place to live, because someone told a vicious lie about you? I can speak with absolute confidence and expertise that it is a most humbling experience one could endure. Worse still is going to sleep at night and having nightmares of being homeless and then waking up to find you truly are. After all of this, I still don't know how, or why, someone could be so cruel, to another human being, in the manner you were to me.*

*Childcare. This is another misery I have had to deal with, but this is one I would do all over again. Who is it that I have in this state that could help me (at no cost) with the girls while I am at work and they have a day off, or early release from school? The answer to that would be; no one. My expenses have been enormous and even when **I** helped **you** with the girls, I was the one who paid for them to be with someone they enjoyed being with. I didn't do it for you; I did it for the girls. Make no mistake about that.*

*One statement you made that resonates deep within **MY** soul is also quite frightening to me. That you "would do it all over again, the good, the bad, and the ugly," chills me to the bone. Though I cannot imagine being without Kate, or Megan, if I had the foresight in August of 1997 and knew what was in store for me, and my two daughters, in March of 2006, I may have opted against having children at all and walked away from you. It scares me to think that you would be OK with knowingly putting children through what you did to them and then say you would do it again? This is frightening beyond words and imagination, Tiffany.*

In order for forgiveness to be obtained, you must first repent for those sins. If you are truly serious, then you will cast aside all of your self-righteousness, stop being prideful and show absolute humility to God and those around you. If you TRULY are sincere in what you are offering here, you can prove it by completing the tasks above. Know that the few things I am asking of you pale in comparison to what I have been through. Know also, that if you feel that you cannot do these things, then I fear the "message" you were given this past Sunday, February 8, 2009, did not really "resonate" as deeply within you, as you claimed it had. In light of an outcome where you feel I am asking for more than you can give, there is really nothing more to discuss until you face your own demons and defeat them.

If you want to learn how to live your life, read the Book of Proverbs. You can learn a great deal from it. **Proverbs 11:5** *says;* <u>*The righteousness of the blameless makes a straight way for them, but the wicked are brought down by their own wickedness.*</u> **13:3** *says;* <u>*He who guards his lips guards his soul, but he who speaks rashly will come to ruin.*</u> **15:4** *says;* <u>*The tongue that brings healing is a tree of life, but a deceitful tongue crushes the spirit.*</u> **19:5** *says;* <u>*A false witness will not go unpunished, and he who pours out lies will not go free,*</u> *and* **19:9** *backs it up with;* <u>*A false witness will not go unpunished, and he who pours out lies will perish.*</u> *Finally,* **Proverbs 19:28** *says;* <u>*A corrupt witness mocks at justice, and the mouth of the wicked gulps down evil.*</u>

Read also, **2ⁿᵈ Corinthians 2:5-11**. *This deals with "Forgiveness for the Sinner." It speaks about God forgiving those who have been forgiven by the person who was wronged, or sinned against.* **2ⁿᵈ Cor. 2:10** *reads,* <u>*If you forgive anyone, I also will forgive him.*</u> *You can ask God for forgiveness all day long, but there is still a "wrong" out there that needs to be corrected; it's what most people call penance.*

I want nothing more than to allow the girls to see us having a civil relationship, so **IF** *your "offer"* **TRULY IS** *about the girls then you can correct everything in a very short time and, quite frankly, it is time that you did. The girls have suffered long enough.* **SHOW** *me that you mean what you say. Show* **THEM** *that you mean what you say.*

Everything has a price, Tiffany, and by your actions, I have paid dearly, so now it's your turn to pay a little bit of it back and make things right. You have made a very bold statement that I pray you are able to back up with a little work. Until you can back up your words, it will be obvious that your "offer" wasn't about the girls at all, but rather all about **YOU** *and your need to once again feel better about yourself.*

Until then, I cannot hear what you are saying over the volume of your actions.

One can either live by The Bible, or die by it. Salvation lies within.

In light of the relatively painless tasks before you and because the above just isn't that complicated, I look forward to your positive response.

Eric

"CAN I HELP YOU?"

"Character is tested when you're up against it." – Dick Vermeil

Christmas Eve 1987

To give some background on what you just read and how I arrived at that point in my life, I must first take you back to a time in my life, a little more than twenty years before.

My paternal grandfather was one man I truly loved and given the fact that my own father had been absent, in one manner or another, from my life for so many years, I looked to him as my father and I'm sure he looked to me as his son. It always seemed he was trying to make up for his son's inadequacies and in doing so, took me under his wing and nurtured our relationship so I would never feel there wasn't a father figure in my life. "Nonno" was an integral part of my life and enabled me to connect with the basic fundamentals of caring about people. He taught me to love and not to be ashamed of who I was, although it wasn't until I was 40 some odd years old I finally let go of my past. My grandfather was my life and there was no better man on the face of the planet. Some who might think I worshipped [SIC] the man, could quite possibly be making their assumptions accurately.

I don't want to take too much away from my father because he *was* present in my life early on and to be sure, a force in it. Without going into too much detail; he didn't put up with much, so when he snapped there were bodies flying; he snapped a lot. There was a gang load of other more serious reasons that encouraged me to turn my back on my father, but violence is one that I can throw out there which everyone can accept with some degree of understanding. With good reason, I stopped speaking to him in 1977. But for the few times that we ran into each other at family functions, but spoke no more words than to say, "Excuse me," followed by an expletive as I passed, I never really spoke to him again. Any more than that and I'd be doing time in a state penitentiary.

I did make an attempt to give him a second chance at a relationship on Christmas Eve, 1987. I somehow, from someone, got an address of where he was living with his current wife, and son from that marriage, in Altadena, California. At the time I was married to a wonderful woman named JoAnn. She and I were expecting our first, and what would turn out to be our only child due to my being an idiot and a horrible husband. JoAnn's biggest problem was that she married a boy who didn't take our wedding vows with any seriousness. She would ultimately pay a big price for loving me.

That night JoAnn and I parked our car on the street and walked down the slight decline of the driveway leading to a house that appeared to be burning a few lights inside. I rang the bell associated with the address I was given. JoAnn stood in front of me and just to my right, my hand around her side. No one came to the door immediately.

I kind of hoped no one was home, so I didn't have to actually talk to him and also so I could tell my grandfather I had *tried* to see him but with no success. My grandfather wanted so badly for me and my father to make amends and have a relationship. I wasn't terribly interested in the first place and was only there because my grandfather asked me to reach out to his son.

"Your father misses you," he would say.

"Yeah, right," I thought to myself. "He missed, among other things, his punching bag."

Weighing my options I figured I'd have a better time spending a whole afternoon in a confessional and then repeating the hundreds of "Hail Mary's" and "Our Father's" I would undoubtedly be sentenced to. The front porch of my father's house was no place for disgruntled offspring to be. I wanted out of there and had no interest in continuing to stand there with the outside chance that prick would actually answer the door.

After a few moments, I glanced at JoAnn, shrugged, and for some ungodly reason, instead of grabbing her hand and running toward the car, I reached past her, knocked on the door, and waited some more. I'm not sure why I did this, because I wanted to leave so badly, but for whatever reason, I stayed glued to my post. I just stood there, on the darkened stoop of a home nestled at the foot of the San Gabriel Mountains in a small community, which borders Pasadena to the north, called Altadena.

Immediately after I knocked on the door and as I stood there, I felt a wave of anxiety wash over me and I recall my rate of inhalations increased along with my heart rate. I began to sweat. I hadn't seen this man, but maybe a mere three times, in the past ten years and now I was at his front door on Christmas Eve, with my wife who was at the end of a long pregnancy; one that seemed to rival that of the gestation of an elephant, which is right around two years. If I felt it was a long one, JoAnn was surely ready to expel our daughter and cut my throat for causing her such discomfort all these months.

Finally, there was some stirring from inside the house that was barely audible to me. "Shit!" I thought. The point of no return. There was no way I could turn, head back to the car, start it and drive away before the door opened. Had I been alone, by the time that door opened, I'd have been outta there and waiting for the light to turn green on Colorado Boulevard, some four miles away. Unfortunately, it's a little difficult to do when you have with you, a pregnant woman who continually leans back to counter the extreme weight in front of her and has the propensity of falling forward if she doesn't. Trying to make her run backward was completely out of the question although I thought about it for a brief second. We were stuck.

Inside I could hear footsteps approaching the door. They stopped and there was a pause as if someone was peering through the peephole. My anxiety was pegged and my heart rate jumped up to around a buck-eighty. The door opened and there stood the man I had hated for so many years. He looked at us in a confusing manner and then glanced down, noticing JoAnn's pregnant state. His eyes ra[n] back to our faces, swinging his eyes from JoAnn, then to me[,] then back again. My heart was pounding so hard I mused it could [be] heard as far away as the Rose Bowl.

"Damn it!" I thought, "Had I just left after the first time I knocked . . ."

He didn't speak for a few seconds and I remember thinking, "What the hell is wrong with this guy? Does he not know who I am?"

He finally spoke, "Can I help you?"

I thought to myself, "Can I *help* you? Are you fucking kidding me?" I realized he didn't even recognize me, his own son. I laughed to myself at how pathetic this man was.

I said to him, as I started to turn away, "We must have the wrong place. I'm really sorry to bo...."

"Eric?" He interrupted. Yes, I actually notated a "question mark" at the end of my name.

Before I turned back toward him I paused for a millisecond with one thought, my eyes squeezed shut and my teeth clenched, "Sonofabitch! Why the hell didn't I get the hell outta there when I should have?"

"Uh, yeah." I said as I turned back around.

"Oh my God! What are you doing here?" He asked with a bewildered smile on his face.

I kind of just shrugged my shoulders and muttered something that to this very day I'm not sure of, but it was probably something pathetically cliché and stupid, like, "We were in the neighborhood and thought we'd drop by."

He said, "Come in. Come in, please." By this time a very mousey and matronly woman appeared behind him, peering at us. His wife and my "stepmother," to whom I have never uttered a word in my life. I don't believe she ever spoke that night and I *know* I never addressed *her* in any manner.

I nudged JoAnn ahead of me and we were led into what I believe was his living room. I remember him commenting to JoAnn, "You're pregnant."

What an astute observation, Sherlock. We'll just call you, "Quick" from now on. I wanted to ask if he had any help in making

opted to just leave it alone. I didn't want any
back to my grandfather as I knew they would
my next visit to his house and I wanted no
ally settled down and my respirations went
breaths a minute.

hat my father was going on and on about
nnot tell you what subject matter was
discussed that night, nor can I tell you how long that visit lasted. It was a blur and all I can remember is that I wanted nothing more than to get the hell outta there and speed away from that house, down the hill, towards Pasadena. The good part is that I had appealed to my grandfather's wishes and he would be happy that I made the "attempt" however self-serving my visit was to strengthen an already strong relationship with my grandfather.

After leaving and as we were driving down the hill we didn't speak. When we hit Colorado Boulevard, I finally spoke, "That was a waste of time."

JoAnn let out a big sigh and concurred, "He's a little strange." I was relieved she saw it, too.

A few years later JoAnn and I would be separated and finally divorced for no other reason but for the fact she had a child for a husband. Of all the negative aspects of that split, I begged her to promise me one thing; No matter how much she hated me, no matter what she thought of me as a father, or husband, no matter how mad she got at me, I begged her to never allow our daughter, Analiese, to be left alone with my father. EVER.

She promised she would see that it never happened.

Of all our issues and ill feelings she had for me, she always kept that promise. I will be forever grateful to her for that promise kept and for that one promise I will always hold a place in my heart for her. JoAnn Di Conti is, by far, one of the finest mothers I have ever encountered in my life. She is truly what a mother should be when raising a child, with very little emotional help from me. She did a fabulous job and in my opinion, she should be considered for a seat alongside Mother Teresa.

Conversely, if you were to ask JoAnn where she thought I should be in those early years, she might opt for me a seat next to Charlie

Manson; on death row. Although it's taken a while, I've changed for the better; thankfully, she no longer holds those ill feelings toward me, I don't think.

On a side note, our daughter was due at the end of December, so with one week to go for a full-term pregnancy, one could imagine just how large JoAnn was. She was quite the spectacle doubling as a one-room condo for our child.

On another side note, for a joke (and this is a true story, I swear), because she was so big, I went to our local Post Office to see about getting JoAnn's boiler its own zip code. All I wanted was an obscure little number that would never be used, that could be associated with JoAnn's mid-section. I thought it would be a cool addition to the baby book, but what I obtained was a lot of stink-eye and pissed-off women. The federal employees weren't the least bit amused by my inquiry and, needless to say, I walked out empty-handed. It was the thought that counted. I never told JoAnn about it, but I'm sure she'll have a few words for me once she reads this.

Me and Nono – 1989

"SHE'S TRYING TO REACH YOU"

"In a universe of ambiguity, this kind of certainty comes only once and never again, no matter how many lives, or times you live." - From the book Bridges of Madison County

August 1997

    Tiffany Nelson, for whom this book is named, "The Love of My Life," and I met and began dating with fervor when my marriage to JoAnn came to an end. However I must add that it is true, and I am ashamed to admit, that our relationship started prior to JoAnn and I being formally separated. My infidelity was wrong and should have never happened, but it did and I am truly sorry for hurting JoAnn so deeply. She was the strong one and as I stated before, I was a child.

    During the three or four years Tiffany and I were together we had a wonderful relationship, but at times it was also a fiery one. It was one of passion that never seemed to ebb, but for the one problem I brought to the relationship, which was that I was too busy hiding from who I was. Embarrassed about my background, my family, and my world, I would say little about my background and allow those close to me to draw their own conclusions. My biggest problem was that I just never bothered to correct them, and quite frankly, I never really cared to correct them either.

Whatever sounded to be the best story, which was started by me then conjured up by others, I would run with and live that story however, each time the story changed I was reminded of the truth.

I hid behind everything that took me away from who I really was, and it wasn't until many years later I would finally face my demons, fight them, and rid myself of them. Those demons took me through what I believed to be hell and dragged me through misery so vile I sometimes wonder how I made it through without eating a bullet. Many more times, I thank God for the strength He gave me not to be weak and carry through with my brief desire to end my life. Years later, I would read about a man who survived an attempt to end his own life by jumping off the Golden Gate Bridge in San Francisco, California. He told the interviewer, "At the very moment, I let go of the railing and started to fall, I realized that all of my problems could be solved." I would learn that my problems were also solvable.

My life and background were a misery I refused to face for so many years because I was so damn afraid, but now that it's all over, I look back and wonder what all of the fuss was about. It goes back to the fear of the unknown; I believe there is a hell, but I don't **know** there is a hell. I can tell you with a pretty fair amount of confidence that I will never renounce my faith in God just to find out. I figure that the alternative to an eternity in Heaven would just plain suck out loud, so I'm hanging where I am.

"All lies and evil deeds stink. You can cover them up for a while, but they don't go away, and you'll have to face them sooner or later." I'm not sure who first used these words, but they sure have a bite to them.

Due to my hiding, Tiffany had had enough and one day it was over. I won't go into the trivial crap that goes along with relationships and all the repetitive reasons, of which everyone is well aware what causes them to fail. There's fault on both sides, but in this case, the fault, albeit not entirely, lies with me. Some failures in relationships are more distinct than others, but when relationships fail, it's never fun; and then sometimes, they just *fail*.

With Tiffany and me, one day, our relationship ended just like that. Game over. In the months following, I was distraught. And for the first nine months or so, I sat by my phone (the absolute truth) and hoped it would ring. It never did, and I had to move on.

I had a longtime friend in Fernando D. Vargas, whom I had met in the late eighties at a gym in Toluca Lake, California, called "Take 20." After our initial meeting, Fernando and I would become instant friends.

Fernando completed his undergraduate work at De[SIC] Paul University, a Roman Catholic University founded just prior to the turn of the 20th century and named after the philanthropist Saint Vincent de Paul. From there, Fernando traveled west to Sacramento, California and attended McGeorge School of Law where he received his law degree. After learning his occupation I would rarely refer to him by his given name, but rather as "counselor" for many years. He would call me "Count" as a reference to my Italian surname, meaning "of Count," or "the Count." Tracing my family tree back to some Countess, and though it meant nothing that she may have been the lowest form of royalty in her time, we were far from royalty in the modern food chain.

At the time Fernando drove a Corvette sporting a personalized license plate, which boasted an obvious oxymoron when considering the car. With a play on letters, it cleverly read, "Getting By." He would upgrade the car, a few years later, to a top-of-the-line BMW. As successful as I figure him to be, it wouldn't surprise me if Fernando had it displayed on a Bentley by now. I always smile when I think of him driving a high-dollar car with that pathetic misnomer hanging from each bumper, but that was Fernando's humor.

While, at that time and for many years prior, I was in construction, he worked in a law office, several floors above the street, tethered to a desk. In these years I worked for a company called Stumbaugh and Assoc., Inc., installing toilet enclosures, or "shitter splitters" as we so fondly called them, in public restrooms. I also installed all the accouterments that grace the walls of the same; toilet paper holders, ass gasket holders, paper towel dispensers, etc. You get the picture. I spent a lot of time in public restrooms. Being on my own for these installations I was free to work as quickly, or as leisurely, as I wanted. I worked quickly and as it was often, my day would end early; I would head toward his office, calling when I got close.

"Hey, Counselor, wanna grab a late lunch?"

"Count! Yeah, I can sneak outta here in about fifteen minutes. Where do you wanna go?"

"Hell, I don't care? Let's just find a place."

"I know a place we can go," he said. "It's right down the street."

A few minutes later, Fernando would emerge from the office building and within another five minutes, we were sitting in a little bistro called *Citrus*. During the time that Fernando was employed by this law firm, which will remain nameless, this would become our little hangout and late-lunch location. Actually, considering the number of times we frequented the joint, I think we may have been responsible for paying the restaurant's monthly electric bill.

Take 20, the gym where Fernando and I met, was one of those gyms that drew the "in crowd" from the movie industry in nearby Burbank, which was home to Disney Studios, Warner Bros., and NBC, and just over the hill, Universal Studios. I met and would become friends with many industry people and a few actors who *weren't* waiting tables between gigs. These were actual true working actors with no worry about paying the rent.

Fernando was, and still is, an attorney who deals in personal injury; the lowest form of life in the field of law. They are looked upon as bottom feeders with no morals, however, this person truly wanted to help those unable to help themselves. If someone truly needed him, Fernando would fight the big insurance companies to gain relief for his clients. Whereas many P.I. attorneys will take whatever, and whomever, comes their way, Fernando is one of the few who turns people away if he feels they are not being truthful.

I don't care what they say about the lawyers who practice in this arena; Fernando Vargas is a man with integrity and one of whom I have a great deal of respect. Although we don't see each other any longer, nor do we talk, I do know that as of this writing he is practicing in Upland, California. Ours was just one of those friendships that ran its course and when we got to that proverbial "fork in the road," we both traveled down different paths in life. I hope and pray he is doing well. As I write this chapter I am reminded of his comment when Tiffany and I broke up the first time; "Hey man, she'll be back.

You wait and see. I promise you, she'll be back." Those words would come back to haunt me.

In 1997 I was living in Newport Beach, California and had just ended a year-long relationship with a gal who will remain nameless. I had previously purchased a sailboat and was living aboard her. She was emblazoned with the name "Equinox III." She was previously owned by one of my closest friends, Wally Clark, who had moved to the Cayman Islands in that same year. He resides there today, on Seven Mile Beach. The story of how he got there is for another time, but the fact remains that he couldn't take his sailboat. To be completely honest, I bought her just because of her name.

An equinox only happens twice a year and it signals a time when the sun is directly over the equator and daytime and nighttime are of equal length everywhere on earth. It is a time of change. At the time I needed a change in my life and I thought the name, which graced her stern was a fitting and perfect one. Living on that sailboat was a wonderful and peaceful life for me; one that would change with one phone call from my old friend, Fernando Vargas.

I was at the courthouse, in Newport Beach, paying a traffic ticket when my pager went off. I remember looking down and seeing it was Fernando. I smiled and figured he wanted to tell me about some nut that walked into his office, wanting his services, but had the most bizarre story, and was turned away. Even though I hated using them I found a pay phone and dialed his number. The ability to speak on these payphones, without having your face pressed against the filthy headset is futile. The thought of mistakenly touching your lips to the receiver, which is undoubtedly home to the DNA of several thousand people, can exercise the gag reflex in a hurry. As I always did, I tried to hold the phone away from my flesh.

His secretary answered, "Oh, Hi, Eric! Fernando said you would be calling. Hang on."

"This is Fernando," he said, as if he didn't know who was calling.

"Counselor! What's up, bro?"

"Hey Count, what are you doing right now?" He asked.

I told him I was at court paying a ticket and asked why he had paged me.

He asked me, "Are you sitting down?"

"No, the goddamned cord on these payphones is only about three inches long, Fernando. What's up? I'm gonna lose my place in line."

An absolute euphony floated out of Fernando's mouth and through the receiver of the phone. "Eric, Tiffany called me. She's trying to reach you."

Time had just ceased to move; it had stopped. I was in a vacuum never before experienced. I was in one of those dreams where when you try to scream, no sound comes out, and the harder you try to scream the more suffocated you feel. However, I'm certain that if I had screamed there would have been a number of guns pointed at me, followed by the command, "Get your ass on the ground, asshole!"

There was a long pause before I answered. I was deciphering the words I just heard come out of his mouth, "Are you shitting me? Cause you better not be fucking kidding me, Counselor!"

"Eric," he says in a very calm and reassuring voice, "she called a few minutes ago and asked if I'd seen you lately, asked what you were doing, if you were dating anyone, yada, yada, yada."

I was stunned. "What did you tell her?"

"What do you think I fucking told her, idiot? Yes, nothing, no and 'he's been waiting for you to come back'."

"For Christ sakes, Fernando, why the hell would you tell her that?" I was pissed. "I don't want her to think I've been waiting around like some poor dejected dog that just wants his master to bend down and pet him."

"But you *are* that poor dejected dog. You've been waiting for her to come back, what, four or five years now?" He reasoned, "I told you she would be back, didn't I?"

"Well, yeah, but *she* didn't have to know that, you prick!" I thought for a moment. "Wait a minute! What? What did you just say? You *told* me she would be back?"

"Huh? Well, yeah, I told you she would be back. Don't try to deny that I was the one who said she would be back. I *was* the one who said it!"

"Oh, I'm not trying to deny it, Fernando. You *were* the one who made that very bold claim alright. You said, 'she'll be back, Eric, don't you worry,' but that was five fucking years ago, Fernando! Jesus!"

"Yeah?"

I was getting frustrated, "What? You wanna be called Nostradamus now? You're a visionary alright."

"All I'm saying is . . . ."

I cut him off, "What did she say?"

"She wanted me to give you her phone number." I could tell he was smiling.

"Holy shit, Counselor!" I said. "This isn't a joke, is it? Please, for the love of God and all things Holy, don't tell me you're joking."

He then says, "Do you have a fucking pen, or what? Jesus! Do you want me to drive down there and hand-deliver it to you? Make the call for you? Get a goddamned pen, Count, I'm busy!"

I borrowed a pen from a passing, fellow lawbreaker, who had just issued a check to the City of Newport Beach for speeding. Looking for a piece of paper to write on I noticed, hanging by a thin cable, the phone book beneath the black box, on which I was speaking to Fernando.

I thought to myself, "This thing is festering with so much bacteria it should be in a fucking Petri dish."

As is quite normal for me in situations like this, another random and possibly savant, thought came to mind. I don't know why I know these things, or where this knowledge emerged from, but Julius Petri, the guy for which the Petri dish is named, was a bacteriologist from Germany who died at the age of forty, in 1892. People were living into their seventies and eighties in those years, so I wondered; given his "job," I'm guessing he died some violent death at the hands of some viral, or bacterial, infection of some kind. Then I wondered briefly if they had pay phones back then. My mind does that to me all the time. I wish I could make it stop, but then I may not be that interesting, if I am at all.

I wrote Tiffany's number down on the corner of the cover, tore it off, and stashed it in my pocket before someone noticed I was damaging public property.

As much as I hated to admit it Fernando was right. I had been waiting for her to come back all those years and in fact, of the two women I dated in those years I told both of them that I would end our relationship immediately if the one person I truly loved ever came back and wanted to reunite. There was no gray area there.

NOT THE LOVE OF MY LIFE

They knew it would be over if Tiffany, "*The Love of My Life*," ever returned. Thankfully, Tiffany's timing was such that I didn't have to break anything off.

I made the call and a few days later we met for lunch in Century City. We just caught up on a few things and did all the small talk crap. The following weekend, I invited her to come to Newport Beach and onto my sailboat, a Catalina 36, on which we both have very different views. The Equinox III was docked at Newport Avenue and Pacific Coast Highway, right across from Bistro 201 restaurant. Directly across the street, on Pacific Coast Highway, was The Arches restaurant, which had been there for a million years and played host to some of the wealthiest people in Orange County.

I suggested that we meet the following Saturday, around ten in the morning, and then go to the Costa Mesa Fairgrounds, where every weekend the city holds a flea market, which draws a huge crowd. We would be just a couple of specs walking through it and reminiscing about the days we had spent together as a couple some four, or five, years prior. It turned out to be a wonderful day and I knew from that moment on my life would be changed forever. I had no idea, however, of just how drastic that "change" would be.

At about a quarter to ten that Saturday morning, I climbed the steps of The Equinox III and into the morning sunlight. The sun had already risen high enough where the morning shadows had shortened in length and the air was beginning to warm considerably. The halyards were banging away with the easy sway of the boat as the water raised her and set her back down under the little swells that traveled through the marina. I looked up and blinked at the sun, welcoming the warmth it brought to my skin, and enjoyed the wonderfully soothing way it warmed it. In anticipation of my visitor, I started cleaning up the deck and shifted things back to where they belonged and as I did, something caught my eye. I looked to my right, toward the small parking lot that accommodated the "live-a-boards" at the Harbor Tower Marina.

What I saw was a vision only seen in movies, or one could imagine in a dream. Tiffany had arrived only moments before and was out of her car and standing at the railing near the main gangway to the marina. The sun glistened and danced in her blonde hair that moved ever so subtly as a delicate breeze feathered it. Tiffany wore a brightly colored sundress, graced with red hibiscus that stopped just above her knees. It, too, would luft behind the slight westerly breeze and the sun shown through it as beautifully as ever, silhouetting her torso, hips, and incredibly long and slender legs. Though she didn't know what slip Equinox III was in, she was scanning the marina, looking for me, and my sailboat. She was an imposing figure standing there in the sunlight and she looked like an angel sent from God. The most beautiful woman I had ever laid my eyes upon was standing less than a hundred seventy-five feet from me and my breath was so completely taken away, I had to remind myself to breathe. Our eyes finally met and when her lips parted the most beautiful smile spread across her face. I know I gasped before I returned her smile. Her smile told me she was glad to be there and mine was telling her the same; I was glad we were back. I was so completely moved by that moment, it will never leave my mind.

As far as the Equinox III goes, Tiffany tells people it was a hovel in a constant state of listing, was about to sink, and that slept about three people, but anyone who knows sailboats can tell you a Catalina 36, sleeps many more than three people. She had a very wide beam, over ten feet, for most sailboats and in the cabin, a person can actually stand upright. I'm 6'1" (as is Tiffany) and can easily walk through the whole cabin without the need to duck down under any of the bulkheads. The roof of the cabin is about 6'2" above the finish floor. I think it was Tiffany's way of giving me a hard time and teasing me, that I didn't have a real home to live in, but one that is mobile.

I would find out later that while we were apart, she became used to much bigger and better and nicer than anything I ever had or could provide to her. Her description of Equinox III could have been a **RED FLAG**, but then it could also have been a way to have some fun at my expense. I would also find out later that she had a sick and twisted way of having fun at my expense.

It turns out that when we started seeing each other again, she was engaged to a guy named Christopher Ball, who just happened to be a trust fund baby for a very well-known and affluent, philanthropic family in Orange County, California. Yep. Engaged to someone else and now we were seeing each other. **RED FLAG!** Tiffany said he "smoked too much pot" and didn't think she could marry him because of this daily habit.

I'm thinking to myself, "PERFECT! Screw this guy." It then dawned on me that she could be set up for the rest of her life, and she's coming back to some poor slob with a vowel at the end of his name. There must be a God. I was dancing inside.

The matriarch of the Ball family was Chris' mother, Marion; and according to Tiffany, she ruled the roost. I was told Marion gave bags and bags of money to Hoag Memorial Hospital, schools, non-profit organizations, etc. In fact, she claimed that a street in Anaheim near Disneyland called "Ball Road" was named after the family. I'm not sure how true it is, nor did I have any inkling to verify it because I just didn't care, nor am I impressed with wealth, but you get the picture.

To make a long story short and so as not to bore you, she met me at my sailboat one evening and said she was going to break off the engagement to Chris. She said she would give back the sapphire engagement ring she had been given and would meet me back on the Equinox III, once it was done.

She returned that night to say she was unable to break it off, but eventually, somewhere down the road, she did return the ring and we started our life together. I couldn't have been happier . . . . at the time.

During that reunion, we caught up on the past several years, and even though we'd seen each other a few times, we had to start over and reintroduce our personal selves again.

But for the fact that she had married a couple of years after we stopped seeing each other, her story was fairly unremarkable, however, one little bit of information she furnished about that marriage was unnerving. She claimed that her husband, of only a few months as it turned out, "was abusive." He was, she claimed, an odd bird who was socially inept and would rather be out of her presence. The behavior of Ron Jenkins, she explained, was due to his failed professional football career as a wide receiver with the Dallas Cowboys.

He was *apparently* the recipient of a severe knee injury, from which he never recovered. I feel bad for athletes that have such a God given talent and can actually make it to "The Show" only to have their career ended by a freak accident on the field of play. As it was when I was growing up when the street lights came on I had better get my ass home and no matter how far into the game I was, I finished early. So was he. God works in mysterious ways.

So there I was feeling sorry for Tiffany and wanting to beat the piss out of Mr. Ron Jenkins for thinking it's OK to smack around a woman; particularly ***this*** woman. A woman of the most angelic proportions (in my eyes . . . at the time) to be abused in such a manner was inconceivable to me and I felt in my heart of hearts that this man should be punished. Thankfully I never ran into him, but trust me when I say, I had my radar up just in case he surfaced on the same street I happened to be on. Men who abuse women, in any way, are cowards and need a good, old fashion, beating themselves. Plain and simple. Years later, Ron Jenkins would take his own life. I would also come to realize and believe that Ron Jenkins never laid a hand on Tiffany. Ever.

Unfortunately, I would also come to realize something that would change my life in unimaginable proportions; I would learn that Tiffany was adept at portraying herself to other people, whatever was in her own best interest at any particular time. And what was amazing, she could hold that portrayal for very long periods of time; years, in fact.

"WOULD YOU MIND TAKING A LITTLE TEST FOR ME?"

"Do not go where the path may lead- Go instead where there is no path and leave a trail" - Ralph Wald Emerson

September, or October 1998. I think. Could have even been a different month altogether, but I'm pretty certain with the above. I think.

I have an addiction. Well, actually a few addictions, but thank God, they don't run concurrently. Before I continue, allow me to explain something to those of you who aren't aware of addictions and how they start, or for some, one ends to begin another. Before you cast me into the pit with the sodomites, or wish for a painful stoning for this indiscretion, allow me to give you some background.

I am afflicted with a highly recognized, little understood, but very real malady with a highly controversial treatment procedure . . . in children. As I am an adult, I am hammered with people's opinions on the subject ad nauseam. Some say it's complete bullshit; an illness conjured up so doctors and drug companies can make more money. Some say it is impossible to possess this malady as an adult; that a child grows out of it. The "malady" is Attention Deficit Hyperactivity Disorder, or ADHD to the layman out there, and let me assure you; it's real. Very real. In either late September or early October 1998, Tiffany was nearing the end of her pregnancy with our first child, Kathryn. We were at each other's throats and I didn't know if I wanted to continue the marriage. Actually, Tiffany had made comments to friends and family that she didn't think the marriage would work either, but I'm sure she was merely planting a seed for her future plan. I, on the other hand, was moody all the time, angered easily, and couldn't focus on much of anything.

I would forget everything from going to the store to buy milk, forgetting what I was at the store for, and coming home with bananas, only to be reminded, upon my return, that we needed milk (I'd head back to the store for milk). I could be at work and become so into a project there, forget to come home. You read that correctly; ***forget*** to come home. As would normally be the case, I was accused of having an affair, but the odd thing was, I was always reached by phone at work; in my office. Absolved of any wrongdoing, she thought I was there because I just didn't want to come home.

That's the way I lived for many years prior. I, of course, knew it wasn't *my* fault. In my untrained eye, Tiffany was just being bitchy because she was pregnant and extremely hormonal. Case closed. It got to be unbearable and I finally told Tiffany that we needed counseling. So we went. I couldn't wait to tell our respective stories and have our therapist explain to Tiffany that she was being irrational and that I was a great guy and that she was lucky to have me.

The therapist listened and listened and listened. When the hour was over she asked that I come back alone. Huh? I thought, "Okay, I'll play along. She wants me back for a visit and then she'll have Tiffany back for a visit and then we'll go back together for a final analysis and a fix to our problems. Perfect." I went back the following week.

The session went on for the usual hour and at the end, she asked that I come back the following week. Huh? Much like a dog does when something confuses him, I know I cocked my head sideways and looked at her.

"Would you mind?" She asked.

"Uh, Er. Hmm. Uh. No. No problem. Same time?"

I rationalized that it wasn't one visit each, she wanted to see me twice and then Tiffany twice, and ***then*** we'd come back together for the final analysis and a fix to our problems. That must be it.

The following week and after the session, she asked me to come back yet again!

I said, "Okay, hold on a minute here! What's going on, and why is it you want *me* to keep coming back? It's not *me* with the problem; it's my ***wife***!"

The therapist looked at me and said, "Well, that's not exactly the case. Would you mind taking a little test for me?"

She explained that the test, the three hundred-question variety, was to determine a level of brain activity with regard to the ability to focus on certain tasks for any given length of time. Huh? She went on to say that while she was no expert in the field, there was a doctor in the same office that could decipher the answers and put them into a diagnosis, if need be.

Reluctantly, I agreed to take her "little test."

The questions ranged from, as far as my memory serves me, if I like taking walks, to if I like people, to if I have friends, to my childhood, to how many jobs I've held in the past ten years, to how often I say things that aren't socially acceptable and if I feel badly for saying those things, to whether or not I say things before thinking about what I'm going to say, to if I have an oedipus complex, to how often I masturbate. Jesus! Is nothing sacred here? I answered all of them . . . . in about 5 freaking hours! That test was a bitch! I knew every answer and the real bitch was that I wasn't even getting graded on the damn thing! The first test I ever took and "aced," but received no grade. Where is the justice in that? I turned the test over to her and left, but not before securing yet another appointment with her for the following week. This was getting old in a hurry.

The following appointment was a blur. I walked into the office, signed in, sat down, and gave the pile of beat-up magazines sitting on the coffee table a good scrutinizing. There wasn't much that interested me, but I picked up a copy of Psychology Now, or a similar publication and thumbed through it. Something caught my eye as I whizzed through the magazine. I stopped on a page that had big letters which read: *Masturbation Can Cause Severe Depression In Some Men.* For the love of GOD and all things Holy! What is going on with this world? I tossed the magazine back on the table before anyone saw what I was looking at.

An impish little girl came out and called my name. I got up and as I approached the door she stepped aside for me to pass; she came up to my waste.

"Jesus, she's short," I thought. There may be a few kindergartners that would need her help to reach the faucet to wash their hands in a classroom, but I can't imagine there are very many she has any height on. She's not even as tall as my mother who stands a towering 4'9". God, help me if my mother reads this.

As I entered the office I noticed there was another person in the room. I gave no obvious signs that I noticed him. I greeted my "counselor" and then turned to the Asian gentleman and offered my hand. He introduced himself as Dr. Won Choi. Won I. Choi, to be exact. *One-Eye-Choi*? True story!

I just sat there and mused, "One Eye Choi? Are you kidding me?"

I sat down and listened to Dr. Choi for over an hour about the results of my "test" and his diagnosis was that I am afflicted with a "severe" form of ADHD and that I may be off the chart in some areas; top one percentile of adults afflicted with ADHD. My mouth was open I'm sure. He said that the medication of choice was Ritalin and that if I chose to go into a treatment program for ADHD I would probably be on it for the rest of my life. Beautiful! Again, I was thinking I would have more fun in a confessional telling a priest I masturbated and take the onslaught of Hail Marys and Our Fathers that would follow, but that wasn't going to help me in this office. I agreed to try it.

As it turned out Dr. Choi and I connected rather quickly and became friends in that office. I saw him just about every month for 8 years. He was a no-nonsense guy that pulled absolutely no punches when, early on, he'd rip my ass for various reasons that many times I thought would garner me some sympathy from him. I'd complain about Tiffany and he'd tell me what I was doing wrong. It was a symptom of ADHD and "thisa eees how you fixa dis probrem," he'd tell me.

I learned that he had come to the United States from South Korea a few years after serving as a medical doctor with the Korean Navy. After arriving here he became interested in Attention Deficit Disorder and was now one of the foremost experts on ADD, ADHD and various types of substance abuse and had been for over thirty years. I joke about him, but I don't know where I'd be if I had never walked into his office.

In the years that I saw him, he gave me some of the best advice and working tools to get through my day-to-day activities and I still use many of them to this day. I can't tell you how many people dump on me for taking Ritalin, saying, "It doesn't do anything," but I can assure anyone reading this, for some, Ritalin is a wonder drug. It completely changed my life and possibly saved it. It may not work for some kids and adults, but it works for me. I've found over the years of taking this drug that the only people who cry foul when this drug is discussed are people who don't know anything about the affliction this drug treats, or the drug itself. They're listening to that blithering idiot, Tom Cruise, give his tutorial about his vast knowledge of the drug. Take it from an expert on ADHD who **is** an expert on the drug; Tom Cruise and anyone else that feels it necessary to claim they know all about the evils of Ritalin is, very simply put; full of shit.

"JESUS CHRIST! IT'S HOT!"

"No good deed goes unpunished." - Unknown

APRIL 2004

My wife approached me and asked if I would mind helping her mother move in May. I've never turned anyone down that I was able to help and especially when someone needed help moving, besides, it was a few weeks away and I had some time to plan for it. I didn't really think about it, but the move would take me from Newport Beach, California to Chandler, Arizona in the dead of summer. And I wasn't thinking when I agreed to do it; however, even if I had thought about it, I would have still obliged my wife's request. I would do anything for her, at any time, for any reason. Even her slightest hints of wanting something or something done (from minor chores to remodeling a wall to include a pass-through and built-in bookshelf), she would have it handed to her. I think she figured out I had myself securely tied around her finger long before I ever knew what I was doing. I never imagined how incredibly destructive my "behavior," by loving her so deeply, would become.

The move would happen in May; May 15th, to be exact and how could I know it would be 115 degrees when I did it? Susan Nelson had a houseful of antiques sitting in Newport Beach, California and I **do** mean a *freaking houseful*.

I haven't seen such a large number of antiquities since being in a store, which sold these types of antique items. Her possessions could have been emptied and filled the heart of a dealer's store in Old Town Orange, California, where I believe at one time, had the largest number of antiquities dealers and stores, per capita than anywhere else in the country. I could be wrong, but that's what I heard.

One thing I didn't know was the fact that, with this move, I would be doing it alone. Solo. By myself. No help. Apparently, Susan's son, Tiffany's brother, my brother-in-law was just a little too busy to help his own mother move to another state. I think Tim had a NASCAR race to watch, or something. Whenever anyone in his family needed his help there was normally something more pressing on his agenda, especially if there was nothing in it for him. This spilled over to when his father, Brad, broke his ankle so severely he was unable to work again. Brad lived with Tiffany, me, and our very young daughters for what was supposed to be a couple of months, but lasted nearly two years. The day he broke his ankle, about six years prior, was the last day he worked until his death in 2006. To my knowledge, up until my last day with Tiffany, I had never known this loving son to lift a finger to help, physically, emotionally, or monetarily. Maybe there was an underlying issue that Tim had with Brad, but was never discussed. Whatever the case, it's a pretty sad state of affairs.

It was over 90 degrees and high humidity the morning I drove the biggest U-Haul truck made to a storage unit in Irvine and opened the roll-up door. I stood back with my mouth open; it was loaded to the ceiling, front to back.

"Jesus Christ," I thought to myself. "I am not in for a good time."

I looked at the visible pieces and began to piece together, in my mind, what items should be pulled out first and how they would fit in the truck; like a puzzle. For some reason, I have always been able to envision how a truck should be loaded, utilizing every inch of space I had available to me. Probably the reason I am always asked to help when someone moves. I'm always there.

I loaded the truck in about five hours.

Two things from this trip will remain with me for a long time; a cabinet and heat. There was one piece of furniture that I had never seen the likes of prior to meeting the Nelson Clan and haven't seen since. Nor do I ever want to see one again. Like ever. Susan's father was, from what I was told, but who knows, a very well-respected and successful dentist in Glendale, California.

To me, just that thought alone was odd, given the fact that Susan and her sister had mouths that looked as if their teeth were those of a crackhead, or plucked from the gums of someone you would find strolling down the streets of Any Town, United Kingdom. For some reason, residents of the UK have notoriously bad teeth and if you've ever been there and seen a flashing smile you'll know exactly what I'm talking about. If you're from the UK please take no offense; it's just the way it is. It's like being in a city that's riddled with Meth addicts and you have to gather up a small group of people in order to make a complete and full set of teeth. I just found it odd that Susan's father was a "dentist."

Regardless of their teeth, sometime during his practice, he acquired this *thing* that was built around the turn of the century; the last century. The twentieth century. Around 1900. It is apparently known in the dental world as something used to house instruments and dental materials of all sorts. It had about 300 drawers and hidden shelves and who knows what else. This "thing" probably weighed 450 pounds.

The most dominating feature of this monstrosity was, oddly enough, a complete paradox in the fact all the weight was supported by four VERY thin legs that measured maybe 1¼" squared at the base and traveled up at a slight radius to maybe 2" at the base of the cabinet itself. To make matters worse this thing was finished with tiny and dainty, little steel wheels that I'd be surprised if they saw 1" in diameter. Worse still, was the fact that one of the legs was broken with the fracture traveling up the middle of the leg from where the wheel was inserted. Some genius decided he would "fix this good as new" and had two smallish screws inserted into the middle of the fracture, where it caused another small fracture that grew larger over time. Just the thought that someone actually designed *these* legs for *this* cabinet is a complete absurdity, but that one broken leg and one tiny little wheel were the banes of my existence for what seemed like an eternity. And that was only because I had Susan frothing at the mouth and spitting as she spoke to warn that I had better not break her Dad's dental bureau, "or else."

Of course, she offered no help of any kind; I was her Filipino houseboy for a few days. I did manage to get that miserable hunk of kindling from Irvine, CA to Chandler, AZ with little further damage. I did, however, break the back out of one of the drawers. If she reads this she won't even finish the sentence; she'll be checking drawers immediately. I kind of fantasize every now and then that on my way out to Arizona that back of the U-Haul opened up and Susan's bureau slid out and onto the freeway, splintering into a million pieces with a few of the larger pieces smashing through the windshield of Susan's Lexus and impaling her heart.

I believe that this particular cabinet was made of oak so it would have been apropos that a dagger of oak pierced her heart. That's the only thing that can kill these people. Besides it would have been nice to know that my wearing a garlic necklace, in her presence, was no longer a necessity. It's still a pleasant thought in my mind from time to time.

The other thing that sticks in my mind was the summer heat. Of course, Arizona is the closest place to hell, but with the temperature in Irvine pushing 100 I drank a gang load of water. Even so, I had a severe headache from being super dehydrated and as is usual with dehydration, I vomited several times in those five hours of loading the truck . . . by myself. In the interim and predictably, Susan showed up a few times wondering why it was taking me so long to load the truck, which elicited thoughts of her tripping, falling, hitting her head, and drowning in **my** vomit. I don't believe I would have helped her at that point.

The U-Haul door was finally closed and locked and I was ready for bed before I made the 365-mile trek to the east end of the Phoenix Valley the following morning.

Susan's directions to her new house, in Chandler, were so bad I'd have been better off getting them from an individual in Bangladesh, India, speaking Mandarin Chinese with a Russian accent. Truly Brutal. Once exiting the 10 Fwy at Chandler Blvd., in Chandler, I drove around for what seemed like hours. Susan could not be reached and I was lost. I shoved the gear into "park" and waited.

I was about to turn the truck off to conserve gas, but after putting the back of my hand on the window and melting away the skin on my knuckles, I left the truck running with the A/C on. I knew it was hot, but didn't know just *how* hot. Other than that, up to this point in the trip, and finding that these U-Haul trucks get about four miles to a gallon of gas, the trip was uneventful.

I dozed off and fell asleep and sometime later I was awakened by the ringing of my cell phone. It was Susan. She admitted her directions were off a bit. Once I had true directions I was finally able to start closing the gap between where I was and Susan's house. On the way, I passed a bank that had one of those monument signs that flashed the time and then immediately after, the outside temperature. It read in triple digits. 115 degrees.

"Are you kidding me?" I thought to myself, "that has got to be a mistake."

I pulled up in front of 2442 Rock Rose Way, Chandler, Arizona and when I opened my door I was hammered by a wall of what seemed like superheated gasses from the blast of a nuclear test.

I checked my face for more peeling flesh and thankfully everything was still intact.

"Jesus Christ! It's hot!" I had a sneaky suspicion this was not going to be a good day. I walked into the empty house and toured it for furniture location.

Of course, Susan was there to direct me with each and every piece of furniture, but I had a request before I started.

"What are the chances of getting the AC turned on, Susan?" I asked. "It's like a hundred and eighty degrees in this joint."

Her response was that of Satan, "Well if the door's going to be open we'll lose a lot of cool air and I don't want to waste the energy."

I looked at her in disbelief and (this is tongue-in-cheek) could only fantasize about pouring lighter fluid on her and setting her ablaze; to make her more comfortable in her hellish element. Thankfully, for both of us, I had my doubts there was no one around. Even though it was the middle of the day, and I don't *think* anyone saw me drive up, I couldn't take any chances. Someone with truly bad intentions may have grabbed it, but I wasn't that *someone* and it would have only disrupted the peacefulness of my existence. I thought about it, though.

I returned to the truck and opened the back roll-up door and began the arduous task of unloading it; in 115-degree heat.

Susan darted around on her coarsely furred hooves and when I came in with a piece of furniture, she grunted and nodded to where I was to place it. When she bent down to get a level view of the furniture, I could see the knobby, horn-like, protrusions at the top of her skull that seemed to be in a constant state of sloughing off. I believe at some point, she pulled out of a trunk a goat's skull on a rope and put it around her neck. It matched perfectly with her ensemble as she continued, throughout the day, to morph into a spindly little four-legged beast that gnashed its teeth when a piece of furniture was misplaced; a beast who could only glare and grunt her displeasure, or direction. I dared not turn my back on something so hostile and revolting for fear of this dreadful animal pouncing on my back, biting down, and having the vertebrae in my neck being ripped away from its comfortable location, thus rendering me dead, or a quadriplegic. I backed away at every juncture.

I'm not sure if I was hallucinating from the heat or seeing what was beneath her skin. At the time, I thought I was hallucinating, but now I'm not so sure. I think God was trying to tell me something and I was just too damned tired and delirious to realize it.

The intent of "Susatan" was to have each piece of furniture placed in an exact location (I swear this is the absolute truth!), and if I was a half-inch off from where she directed, she demanded it be moved to the correct location. About midway through the move, I stood up and advised her that I would not be moving anything once it was in the general vicinity of where she directed. I told her it was too damned hot, I was doing this alone, and I was in no mood for exactness of her furniture locations, that she had better give me a location to place each item and be done with it. I wasn't placing anything anywhere, so she could "see what it looked like." Thankfully, her outwardly bitching and complaining stopped shortly, thereafter; however, she continued to mumble her dissatisfaction under her breath, but it was better than listening to her nasally, nails-down-a-chalkboard, voice screeching at me.

After about seven hours the truck was unloaded, the house was filled, the insides of my thighs were chaffed, and I was spent. Truly spent. I needed some sleep; about fifteen hours worth I figured. I don't have much memory after that other than I was back in Orange County the following day. I think.

A week later, Tiffany and I began talking about making a move to Arizona and starting over in a new place; one which would be conducive to raising our two young daughters and away from the B.S. in Southern California with rising home prices, mediocre economy and the crime that seemed to be getting worse. The Phoenix area was a safer place to be and to raise a family.

We talked about me finding a job with a construction firm and continuing our comfortable life until the girls were grown, moved away to college and we grew old together. The thought was a pleasant one, and it was something I was completely in favor of because all I could think about was my daughters and my wife— the love of my life. Tiffany, however, had other plans.

I started browsing the jobs in the Phoenix, Arizona area on the web.

A few months passed and on July 13, 2004, my little Megan turned four years old. Tiffany decided to plan a birthday party at our home on Springbrook North, in Irvine, California. That birthday party was held on Saturday, July 31st. That weekend and the following week would also be the last time I would spend any quality time with my children for nearly a year and a half.

As our plans were only tentative to that point, my quest in finding a job was not a diligent one. Besides, I had a great job working for a construction firm in Anaheim, California, where I started and ran the tenant improvement division. Seriously looking for work could wait. After all, a move was tentative, right?

"HEY, FLY SHIT!"

"People may forget what you said, or what you did, but people will never forget how you made them feel."
– Unknown

Date Unknown; like it matters.
UDC Corporation, Inc. is owned and operated by the Schafer family and they run a family-tight ship. I was one of their employees. Out of some 140 employees, every single one of us was a member of the Schafer's immediate family. The Schafer's loved us and, for the most part, we deeply loved them. George Schafer started UDC some thirty years prior to my arrival, and I can tell you this; there isn't a single man alive that has a better work ethic than this man, or a deeper love for his employees, and a deeper love for this country.

George, oddly enough, was never short for a nasty quip when he entered a room and it was normally aimed at the one he least recognized. I believe to this day, it is his way of testing the Moxie of the new guy. I was one of those new guys and I quickly witnessed the "wrath."

Prior to meeting George for the first time, I had heard horror stories about his comments and the looks he shot at people as he passed them. I had heard stories that chilled me to the bone and I can assure you I was terrified to work for such a "tyrant."

One of the stories I had heard (and there were many of them) took place many years before. George had just purchased a new pump action shotgun, which he brought to the UDC office to show someone. As he usually does, he got a wild hair up his ass and decided to show his employees the same gun, but it was the manner in which he showed the shotgun that got everyone's attention.

Once the lunch break was over George grabbed his gun, went downstairs, jumped up on one of the lunch tables, slammed the pump on the underside of his new shotgun back and forth, and screamed, "All right, you mother fuckers, lunch is over! Get your asses back to fucking work!"

Now, there's a test of someone's Moxie! This is one of those times you can look at all the faces around and know who's worked for George and know him. There were a couple of people that smiled and shook their heads, but more than anything there were wide-eyed laughs that reeked of caution.

One of the old salts said to him, "George, get off the goddamned table. You're gonna scare the new guys." Nearly everyone eventually left the lunch area and went back to work.

As the story goes, George had two people quit that day; the new guys. For one of them, it was his first day and I hear he never returned for his check. I could never completely verify the whole story, but there were enough people who witnessed the jumping on the table with the shotgun.

But that was just George. Of course, this was long before this country turned into such a litigious one where people sue for being slightly sprayed by the sneeze of a coworker, saying they'd contracted some debilitating malady. Had that incident taken place in today's world, George would have been arrested and we'd have been working for a wimp with soiled shorts.

I asked George about that incident one day and all he could muster was a very boyish little smile, an ever-so-slight chuckle and then, "Ah, hell, don't listen to those sons-of-bitches. They're all lying bastards." He never admitted it, but by his own reaction, I know the story was true.

When I first met George, I had been working for UDC for a week, or so. A few of us were talking about trivial crap when he walked into the room.

We all turned and everyone greeted him with the usual, "Hi, George," but he said nothing to acknowledge us. I stepped aside to introduce myself and as I started to raise my hand to offer my introduction, he said, "Who the fuck are you?"

I was stunned. Even after hearing the stories, I was stunned. I stammered out the words, "I'm Eric Di Conti, sir, I just started here and I wanted to introduce myself."

He looked me dead in the eyes, "Humph! You won't last long," and walked away; my untouched hand was still out in front of me.

As he left the room everyone burst out laughing at me. I nearly soiled myself and these idiots were bellowing at the spectacle. I believe to this day, that George, too, was chuckling to himself after he left the room.

That was the beginning of my employment at UDC, Corp. in Anaheim, California, one that would last several years. However, it took a couple of years before I was able to get into George's good graces. I stayed unsure of him for a long time and used his daughter, Debi, as my liaison when I needed something, or wanted to understand what George was thinking. I didn't dare go to his son and my immediate boss, Shawn, as he had just as dry a sense of humor as his father and even though Shawn would laugh as he was giving me the game plan, I would rarely get a straight answer out of him.

Many people thought of Shawn as a hard ass without a heart, but those who truly knew him know that the tough exterior was just the business side of him, albeit seemingly ruthless sometimes, but nonetheless business. I thought Shawn truly is a good man with a good heart; nearly as big as his Dad's and I liked Shawn a lot. He, too, would prove me wrong several years later, when he was sentenced to a prison term of 86 years.

Shawn was looking out for what his father had built for his family's future and wanted to preserve it. Don't get me wrong, I had my share of outrage toward him and used a great many expletives in front (and after) of his name. I have also sent my share of e-mails letting him know my personal feelings on certain matters where I think he was wrong, but my respect for Shawn never ceased. I also believe he respected me for my candor and honesty when I addressed those matters.

Shawn, like his father, was never short for a joking shot at someone and for the most part, always said what was on his mind no matter who was around, but he is also extremely sensitive and is hurt when people think of him in a negative manner. Maybe because he is so much like me, in that respect, that I sympathized with him on so many levels. One thing I can say with absolute certainty, when I compare Shawn to myself, if there's a chink in your armor, Shawn will find it. And, just as I do, he LOVES pushing one's buttons when there is a joke to be played on a person.

George, however, had the instincts of a dog. When he knew you were afraid he would keep barking. And each time I would back away thinking he hated me, those who knew him best would tell me what a loving man he was and how big his heart was. I was also informed that when George stops barking at you is the time you need to worry. That was just George. Thankfully, during the years I worked there, George never stopped barking at me and I grew to love him. He also never lost his constant smirk.

Eventually, George would let me into his inner circle of trust and would actually be the first to address me in the morning. As he would have pet names for everyone I would finally be awarded mine. As I had gained a few pounds since the time I started working there, I became "Double X" to George. I lost weight. He would dump on me for smoking and be so ruthless in explaining that my girls would become fatherless if I had kept it up, I eventually quit smoking and have not picked up a cigarette since; the date was June 17, 2002. There were a number of pet names, or loving insults, if you will, and I fail to remember each; however, one does stick in my mind;

When business was slow and work was tough to come by, in my "insignificance" to George's company, I became the name he calls me to this day.

"Hey, Fly Shit! You find us any work yet?" He yelled one day.

"What the hell?" I thought to myself. Then I asked, "What the fuck is that supposed to mean George?"

"Hell, you can't find us any work. What good are you? You're just a little pile of fly shit," he said.

I just shook my head and smiled. "Yeah, George, you're right. Just a little pile of fly shit that you're paying a shitload of money to, for doing nothing."

I then added, "Thank you so much, George. I love you for who you are."

He walked out and headed to his office with his usual departing, "Fuck you!"

As he disappeared around the corner I thought to myself, "I love that guy."

Fly Shit would become my pet name for the remainder of my tenure at UDC, Corp.

I also found out early on, the one to **truly** fear was George's wife, Teresa; the matriarch of the family. Teresa had just as much love emanating from her, but she ruled the roost and the longer one worked there they would eventually come to this realization. Teresa was the iron hand when she needed to be, but was also the calming factor of the family. She is one of the kindest human beings on the face of the planet and if one of her employees had a problem, she and George would fix it. If an employee needed money, for whatever reason, the Schafer's would write a check, no questions asked, and rarely expect it back. If they didn't get it back, Teresa would remember it, but I don't think George really cared. He was just thankful he was in a position where he could help someone. That's just the way the Schafers are, but if you outright screw someone in the Schafer clan, Teresa's fiery Italian background would surface and you have an enemy for life.

As Teresa was the family's, and more importantly, George's, calming factor, Debi was the calming factor of her brother. My office was just outside of Debi's and as was our ritual, every morning when she arrived at work, we would chat about nothing and about everything. Debi would become my confidant who knew just about every facet of my life. She was involved in my initial employment interview with Curt Schendel and with me on my last day of work at UDC.

Debi had met Tiffany a few times and would later tell me that there was something about Tiffany that really bothered her, but she just couldn't put her finger on it. She had always had an uneasy feeling about Tiffany when she was around, or when I spoke of her. I would hear these very words from several people in the years to come and as I asked these people why they, as my friends, hadn't told me their feelings, their responses were all the same; "Would you have listened to me?" Point taken. No, I wouldn't have.

In my darkest hours, Debi would be the only person that kept me focused on the important things. When my brother and personal hero was in The Gulf on the USS Princeton (CG-59 class) and later on the ground in Baghdad and Ar-Ramadi, Iraq, in the most dangerous part of the world during the second Iraqi conflict, Debi was my calming factor. My brother, Marc, a Naval Chaplain and at the time, a Lieutenant Commander was assigned to the 2nd Battalion, 5th Marine Division out of Camp Pendleton, California, who did several "tours of duty" in Iraq. In harm's way on a daily basis he was my constant worry. Debi was just as worried for him as me, but I never knew it.

My brother, Chaplain Marc Di Conti aboard the USS Princeton

In the months he was away Debi and I would put together care packages and send them to my brother; many of them would contain UDC paraphernalia that the Marines would use in the Humvees they drove. Marc would send photos of non-slip dashboard pads that, instead of the usual coins and the like, held bullets and rifle clips. Bumper stickers emblazoned with the UDC logo on the back of vehicles, which put UDC on the map in Iraq. I would begin to call, UDC, "UDC International."

UDC T-shirts, compliments of George Shafer, would be worn in photographs by some of the Marines and were a beautiful sight on a foreign shit-hole of a land mass, as UDC's logo is nothing but Stars and Stripes. There is nothing better than receiving an e-mail and seeing a photo of these brave men wearing our colors. George's colors.

George was also, along with my maternal grandfather, the most patriotic man I've ever met. There was another story that was shared with me; however, it, too, is still unconfirmed, but a great story just the same. Again, long before I arrived, there was an employee who was in charge of raising the American flag each morning and taking it down each evening. A couple of times, this person raised the flag prior to sun up, which is absolute sacrilege.

One can NEVER raise our country's flag unless there is a light illuminating her. It is desecration of our flag and is not tolerated, especially by George. The story goes that this person didn't take this very important task seriously and after several warnings, was subsequently relieved of his duties at UDC and given his final check. He was a good worker, but he disrespected the most important thing we have.

I swear that if George's building was on fire and in danger of burning to the ground, he would be spraying water on the flag and let the building burn.

"Screw the building," he would say, "it's insured, but our flag? Well, she is irreplaceable." That's how much this man, a blessed veteran of our military, loves our country. I have an immense respect and, as I said prior, a deep love for him.

I need to add that also in those many care packages was Don Francisco Coffee, compliments of the Gavina Family who were the roasters of this coffee. My oldest daughter, Analiese, went to school at Sacred Heart Academy in La Canada-Flintridge, California. Another student at Sacred Heart, and friend of Analiese, was the daughter of Jose Gavina, whom I'd met at several school functions. Because of the friendship between our daughters, Jose and I normally sat at the same table in these functions and became friendly, usually catching up with each other since our previous meeting. The Gavinas are a family of good people with good hearts and always willing to help someone.

I had originally sent, in these care packages, Starbucks Coffee. But my brother told me of a story that stopped those Starbucks purchases and shipments of the same. Prior to being deployed the $2^{nd}/5^{th}$ was treated to a huge breakfast for family and friends of those leaving our great country to fight on foreign soil; some would not be coming back alive. Many of the local businesses donated their time and food for this breakfast, but when Starbucks was asked by my brother to participate, he was summarily turned down, saying they "do not support political organizations."

Of course, Marc explained to them that they were NOT a political organization, but rather worked for whoever happened to be Commander in Chief, Democrat, or Republican. Starbucks was unrelenting and suggested that Marc looks to their website for clarification of their donating policies. When he did, he found that the recipients of Starbucks support are organizations such as Greenpeace, PETA, NOW, Rainbow Coalition, etc. And they don't support "political organizations"?

Starbucks was contacted by me, as well, to possibly help with getting coffee to the troops; however, people in the corporate offices in Seattle were somewhat of an adversarial roadblock. They weren't about to send anything to our troops. Yes, this is true and the "BS" e-mail that surfaced a few years back about Starbucks being supportive of the war is just that; plain old bullshit. Though they do admit that because their employees get a pound of coffee a month, they are free to send it overseas, if they wish. That, I believe, is what they consider their support.

After my personal experience with the attitude of Starbucks corporate people, I called the Gavina's corporate offices and spoke to Jose's sister, Leonor Gavina. I told her about Starbucks' stance on the matter, as well as asked about the possibility of sending coffee to our troops.

Leonor agreed to help before I even finished what I wanted to say, "I would be proud to send coffee to our troops, Eric."

From that day forward my brother had a shipment of coffee sent to him every month. I supplied the Gavina Coffee Makers and the transformers for use in 208v plugs used overseas and the Gavina Family supplied the coffee. I requested a Don Francisco Coffee banner from Leonor which she sent to me without hesitation and I, in turn, shipped it to Marc.

Several weeks later, I received an e-mail with an attached photo of some forty troops piled on top of, and around, a military vehicle. With their armament in the hands of each of these wonderful men, their smiles as wide as the Euphrates River, a picture was taken. Atop the vehicle were two men holding the banner Leonor provided me. With the banner came a clear understanding that the Gavina Family was supportive of our troops and our troops were very thankful for the Gavina Family. I had the photo framed and presented it to Leonor several months later with more thanks to her for her family's selfless generosity. To this day the photo still hangs in the lobby of their corporate office in Vernon, California.

Marc with the Marines of the 2nd/5th and the UDC and Don Francisco's Coffee banners. Marc is in front wearing the white ball cap.

My brother, Marc – UDC at Hurricane Point, Ramadi, Iraq

Debi Huerta and I became very close in the years I worked at UDC. She helped me through some of the most difficult times, which was just after Tiffany's clandestine exit from California and secret entry into Arizona with my two daughters; Debi was in the next room and heard the very conversation I had with Tiffany when she informed me she had left California with the girls.

From that point, she would make it a point to find me each morning and ask me into her office for our morning talk. Debi Huerta, her caring for what was happening in my life, knowing I needed to talk to someone in order to help me focus at work, her motherly tactic (even though she is only 3 years older than I) in broaching sensitive subject matters and getting to me speak about it and the instinct to see it, I will be forever grateful to her. We remain close friends to this day.

I left the safe confines of UDC, Inc. on October 7, 2005. On that day I received notes of good luck from a few employees and a "Good Luck" card with the signature of nearly every employee on it. I received a beautiful heartfelt card from Debi that I still read from time to time. From Curt Schendel and Shawn Schafer, with the blessing of the family, I received my company truck for pennies on the dollar. And my most prized gift and possession came from George Schafer. I was humbled by how much I was appreciated by this family and company and was choked up several times prior to my leaving, but the gift I received from George Schafer made me cry real tears. He handed me a crumpled-up gift bag that had obviously been used several times prior, or knowing him, it may have been pulled out of the trash. In that gift bag, wrapped in paper towels he'd procured from the restroom, was a lone pepper shaker.

Confused, I looked up at him and shrugged.

He said, "It's to put some flavor on that fly shit you'll be eating in Arizona. Good luck, Eric and don't be a stranger." He turned and walked away. That's when I realized I had truly made it into George's circle; at the end of my employment with his company. I knew he liked me, but that gift was my rite of passage and I was both happy I had made it, but deeply saddened I was now leaving. The pepper shaker sits on a shelf in my living room to this day.

As Tiffany was so intent in the initial stages of her interest in moving to Arizona, I checked the job market there periodically. By her spiriting away the girls that early morning in August 2004, I started looking with some seriousness and nearly a year and a half later I would find a job in Tempe.

Through it all and in light of how I was treated by Curt Schendel and the Schafer Family, I was in no hurry to leave the beautiful weather of Orange County, California for the Africa-hot Phoenix Valley, but I knew where I needed to be and that was with my "family." Unfortunately, the reconnection and reuniting with my "family" would be short-lived.

Only a short five months later, on March 2, 2006, Tiffany would walk into the office of an attorney named Donna Farar-Jewett, located at 8121 E. Indian Bend Road, Suite 126, Scottsdale, AZ 85250 and would tell this woman a story, who directed her to clean out our "marital bank account" of over $68,000.00. She then told her to go to the McDowell Mountain Justice Court in northeast Phoenix Valley where Tiffany told her story again, requested and received an Order of Protection against me. As cliché as it may sound, my life was about to change in ways I never imagined.

"I'M THE LUCKIEST WOMAN IN THE WORLD"

(Yeah, whatever.)

"Beware of bad people with bad hearts – They slither through the bushes like an evil beast." – Unknown

JULY 31, 2004

This was the day we celebrated Megan's fourth birthday. We invited several friends and family (Tiffany's) and I promised myself I would take the day off. So I did. It was Saturday, so I wasn't actually *working*, of course. I took the day off from one of my addictions; Gambling. Yeah, Yeah, Yeah. I know. A gambler. You're thinking, "His wife left him cuz he's a *gambler*." That wasn't the reason.

The party started early in the afternoon. Katie's Godfather, Uncle Geno, as we called him, came down from Los Angeles. So did a few others, but most lived on the south side of *The Orange Curtain*. Many in LA, when traveling to Orange County, call their entry into the OC, "Passing The Orange Curtain." Reason being is the belief that only the affluent live in the OC. Not true. A fallacy of huge proportions, but I can say that the police agencies in Orange County tend to accost those with a darker complexion. I'll stop there for fear of retribution.

NOT THE LOVE OF MY LIFE

Others included Orange County friends Annette and Jason who would be married a few years later. Tiffany and I actually stole Annette from a Jewish pre-school the girls were in, in Orange, California. Annette worked there and we had forged a close friendship with her and after a year of the school not wanting to deal with me, we pulled the girls out and offered Annette a full-time job watching the girls at our home. She accepted with little hesitation. The school was getting on my nerves anyway. They had a few bomb threats that forced the school to be closed for a day and completely inconvenienced everybody, but the last straw was when I told the school administration that if another bomb threat came in, I was going to make T-shirts for my girls that they would wear to school each day. They would say, "Don't hurt me, I'm Catholic." That was the beginning of the end, but Annette and Jason would remain friends long after our departure from Temple Beth Shalom, on Tustin Ave in Orange, California.

During that party, Tiffany was telling everyone, "I'm the luckiest woman in the world to be married to a man like him." I only tell of this day, not because anything life-altering happened, or that this day was of any significance beyond the fact it was Megan's birthday. I only tell of this day because of the statement that was made.

As I heard her say these words I thought to myself that *I'm* the luckiest *guy* in the world. That thought would change exponentially in the days to come. A few days later, I would think that it may have been the alcohol talking that day. However, in the months to follow I would reflect back to those subtle little red flags and recall many times during our marriage when alcohol was a part of many arguments, but I just never saw it then, or maybe just never wanted to.

I do believe alcohol played a large role in Tiffany's demeanor that day, as well. It had to, because seven days later, Monday, August 9, 2004, shortly after I left for work, *The Love of My Life* grabbed a few things, loaded my daughters into our car, and moved to Arizona. And, much like that old joke about a kid who goes away to summer camp and upon his return he finds that his parents have moved, but have left no forwarding address, she didn't tell me. I was that kid, I guess.

THE WRETCHED LIFE OF A PARASITE

"Midway along the journey of our life, I woke to find myself in a dark wood, for I had wandered off from the straight path." – Dante's The Inferno

AUGUST 8, 2004

The night prior to Tiffany's departure, the girls were in bed, as were Tiffany and I. She became a little amorous, my hormones put their party hats on and before you know it we're a tangled knot of sweaty flesh. It was, as it often was, pretty incredible, but looking back on that interlude it's difficult not to get nauseated at the thought. One of the most beautiful women I had ever laid eyes upon would eventually turn into pure and wretched hideousness.

The key element here is how I describe that she was "the most beautiful woman I had ever laid eyes upon," and she was, but there is something missing in that statement. When one reads these words the thought is that with the beauty comes the whole package of beauty inside and out. Keep in mind I speak nothing of her heart, or her character, but rather the superficial exterior that makes up one's features. The exterior hides everything from the world unless there lives an ugliness underneath, which surfaces from time to time, for the world to see.

We all have some of that ugliness which many people call their "demons," or "skeletons" for whatever reason, but some have far more than others and fewer individuals, allow these to surface. When they do surface, the ride could quite possibly be a wild one. The outward beauty of an individual hides a lot and I always thought that Tiffany's outward beauty went to the core of her being. Somewhere along the line, she changed, a metamorphosis of sorts. However, this wasn't an ugly caterpillar that morphed into a beautiful Butterfly. This was something far more ominous.

The actual "change" didn't happen in the blink of an eye, but I believe it was always there, lurking in the darkness of a vile and miserable heart, waiting for the moment to destroy anything that came close. Like a leech that latches onto a person; it starts out a very small worm-like creature, but as it sucks blood from its host, it becomes a massive spectacle, growing many times its original size.

Only when it has gorged itself to the point its hooks cannot sustain the weight of its own body does it release itself and fall away, but not before its host has given up a great deal of himself, or has died. Either way, the host loses, but the leech is fat and happy. Though the leech looks like a helpless victim of circumstance, floundering under its own weight, it is actually metabolizing what it has stolen and waiting for the next miserable soul to pass by.

As it is a cyclical life for leeches, happy with its host, it is for a woman who claims to the world to have found true happiness but is only looking for the opportunity to appear helpless with the expectation of looking like a victim, floundering in misery.

I hope I don't sound bitter. I guess I am bitter, to some degree, but then I probably should be. Shouldn't I? At least, *to some degree*? Understand that I have forgiven Tiffany, but my "bitterness" isn't why I've written this book. I've written this so people know what one woman can do if she is either sick enough, or angry enough for whatever reason, and I am living proof (and there are many others to be sure) that one's life can be altered drastically by one little comment, or statement, or accusation by one lost soul who doesn't *think* about the repercussions of their actions, or simply does not care. To be honest, a woman doesn't even have to be angry; just be malicious enough and then possess the contentment, satisfaction, and enjoyment to do what Tiffany did.

This book is only three things to me: a catharsis for my own well-being, my chance to tell my side of the story, and possibly a warning to anyone who is seeing the slightest hint of red flags in their relationships that need to be looked at more closely. If they see them, as I did, and do nothing about it, as I did not, they could very well end up without any money, a place to live, shunned by people in schools, churches and communities, or even dead by a self-inflicted gunshot wound. Thankfully I'm not as weak as Tiffany had hoped I would be. I did the one thing she never expected; I stayed and fought back. And I'm still standing.

Countless times, prior to going through what I went through, I read in the paper about men who had shot and killed their estranged wife, mother-in-law, and anyone else who happened to be in the immediate vicinity and then often times, turned the gun on themselves. So many times I wondered how they could be driven to harbor such intense anger that they could lash out in such a vicious manner. Or, felt so much loss, despondency, and hopelessness to carry out such an evil act. Though it could never happen that I would be driven to this crescendo, as I am far stronger than those weak souls who were pushed to the edge, I understand completely the anger and seeming hopelessness before them which, in turn, was their driving force to end everything and take the culprit/s of their misery with them.

To be sure, I have a better understanding of who I am and in my faith, know that God has a special place for Tiffany and her mother, Susan. What they didn't consider is the one thing that will heal them; reparation. You reap what you sow.

In light of that, I have nothing to worry about, however, in my sometimes childlike mind, it would be nice to hear something bad has happened to her; she caught on fire when her black gown got too close to the caldron she was stirring, or that she was intoxicated, lost her balance, fell from her broom and crashed to the earth in a heap. You know, normal stuff that most people think, but rarely verbalize.

NOT THE LOVE OF MY LIFE

Note: You will find I drift off into different tangents at any given time. I have to believe it's from the lack of Ritalin in my system. Bear with me because I always come back around to whatever it was that I was talking about . . . most of the time.

"LET ME TELL YOU GUYS SOMETHING"

"I never give anyone hell. I just speak the truth and they think it's hell." – Harry S. Truman

Sometime in the mid-1980s

I am reminded of a story I tell often; mostly to men when they tell me of their own woes of a failed, or failing relationship. It's a true story about when I was working on a 77-story building known then as the First Interstate Tower, in downtown LA. It is now the US Bank building. I'm not sure of the year, but the one and only statement that belched from the mouth of a man with whom I worked has haunted me since the very day it was made. I refer to it often.

Every day at lunch a bunch of us guys in our early twenties, would hang our feet over the edge of the second level and watch the most beautiful women in LA pass below us. It's a story that often garners smiles and fantasies of wishing they could have physically been where I was, so many years before, seeing the wonderful beauty that I had seen, and in telling the story, wishing in their hearts that I could be more descriptive than I already was when describing just how beautiful these women were. Don't get me wrong; to be certain, not all of them were beautiful and if I attempted to pass on such an impossibility, a blatantly and wholly irresponsible lie, this writing would be an ineffectual travesty. Of course, there were some unattractive women that passed below, but I prefer to tell you about the beautiful ones, as they are the subject of the haunting statement that was made. Besides, why would anyone want to read about the few women that could make a freight train take a dirt road, or scare dogs off the back of a meat truck? They have no bearing on the crux of this story; the *hot* ones do.

Like the pigs that we were in those early and dumb youth years, we'd hoot at a few of the ones who dressed with low-cut tops, or really short skirts; these are the ones who we believed, in our immature little minds, dressed for just the type of behavior we elicited. Mostly we just remained quiet, in awe of many of the incredibly stunning women who were sauntering below our feet.

There was one other guy in our group, a much older guy who preferred to work through lunch and away from the edge, but within earshot of us. He'd listen to our dialog and laugh to himself at our naïve youth.

One day, as God is my witness, an absolute "12" passed by. I don't need to describe her, because no one would believe it. You can conjure up in your own minds what a "12" is to you and THAT is what I was looking at. What *we* were looking at. She was an angel sent from heaven that I'd never seen the likes of before, nor have I seen anything close to her since. A true goddess. We all had our mouths open until I came to and called out to the old man of our group; he HAD to see this gal! Reluctantly, he laid his tools down and walked to the ledge. I pointed the woman out and we just watched in silence as she passed beneath us.

I looked at him and said, "See? Isn't that the most beautiful thing you've ever seen in your life?"

He scanned the faces of the guys still seated at the ledge who were waiting for a positive response from the man who never indulged in our lunchtime activity and rarely spoke unless he had something important to say. After looking at all of our faces he smirked and then turned to look at me. He looked me right in the eye and said, "Yeah, Eric. She is pretty damned beautiful. Real pretty. But let me tell you guys something; somewhere on this earth, not sure where, but somewhere, I know there's a guy tired of fucking her."

We all looked at him in stunned silence, not believing what we'd just heard cross his lips, nor did I understand what the true meaning of his words was until more than twenty years later. Only then was I able to make that very same statement about the only other woman who came closest to matching the beauty of that "12," who passed beneath my feet so many years before. Only then was I able to understand what he meant by explaining that no matter who it is in this world that you are lusting after, or even in love with, there's another individual who has tired of that person in a way that, in many cases, the thought of them is nauseating. Stomach turning to the point that one could, in the blink of an eye, sell his/her soul to the devil to never see the other again.

I can assure those of you who've never felt this passion have never been in a relationship with a person as immoral, depraved, wicked, corrupt, iniquitous, nefarious, and evil as I have.

I do have to "thank a merciful God" (that's a favorite line of Tiffany's, but it rings so true here) that this marriage only lasted the eight years it did and I didn't find that, after over 20 years of marriage (I'm speaking hypothetically), that I was completely disemboweled by this vicious animal in the clothing of a beautiful woman. She was, *"the love of my life,"* but, oh, the evil things this woman did . . . But I'll get to those things in due time.

"WE'RE IN ARIZONA"

"The further away you run from your sins the more exhausted you are when they catch up to you; and they will." – Unknown

August 9, 2004

This was the day I *thought* had changed my life forever, however it was just the tip of the iceberg.

On the morning of August 9, 2004, I awoke at my normal time of about four in the morning, took a shower, got dressed, kissed my sleeping daughters, then went in and kissed Tiffany goodbye. She smiled and sleepily said, "Have a nice day, baby. I love you," before she turned over and went back to sleep. I went downstairs, walked out the front door, and headed for my truck. I arrived at my office in Anaheim a little after 5am, took my bag from my shoulder, and laid it at my feet; leaning it against my file cabinet. I reached for the "ON" button on my computer.

I pressed the green button on the front of the hard drive, the little lights flashed, the motor began to hum and my computer screen flashed to life. As I did every Monday morning, my first task was to check for any e-mail that came over the wire after I left the past Friday. I read and responded to those I was able to. I shuffled through paperwork that needed to be dealt with and made notes for a meeting I had later that morning. At about 8am, as I normally did each morning, I made a call home. No answer. Hmmm. Odd.

"Maybe they're still sleeping," I thought.

I continued what I was doing in my office and called periodically throughout the morning. Still no answer. Weird. Really weird.

Each attempt to reach her was met with Tiffany's voice mail. I was confused by the radio silence and began getting worried that something was really wrong. I would find out something *was* wrong and *I* was it.

I had stopped calling the house phone by 11am and continued calling Tiffany's cell. I tried calling again at about 2:30 that afternoon. As the phone rang I wondered, "What the hell could she be doing all morning and early afternoon that she couldn't have the decency to call me to say 'Hi'?" This had been our practice for many years. On about the seventh and final ring, before it put me into voice mail, my call was answered.

"Hello?"

"Hey, honey! Where've you been? I've been trying to reach you all day. You got me worried, for Christ sakes!"

No response. All I could hear was slight breathing on the other end. She was trying to think of something to say.

I spoke again, "Is everything alright? Are the girls OK? What the hell is going on?"

Finally, she spoke, "I found something." The line was filled with intermittent static.

"Huh?"

"I found something," she repeated. More static.

She found something? Jesus! Are you kidding me? "That's great, honey! I'm so happy for you! Are you going to let me in on what it was you '*found*', when it was you started your scavenger hunt and why you didn't tell me earlier?" I told her again I was worried about her and the girls.

More breathing. "So where are you?"

"We're in Arizona," she mumbled.

"Arizona? What the hell are you doing in Arizona?"

"I told you that I found something."

"Oh yeah, that. So what was it that you '*found*' that would make you take the girls on a road trip?"

"I found your *other* birth certificate," She said.

My 'other birth certificate'? Okay, I'll bite. Before I could get out my next sentence, she continued, "Yeah. I don't even know who you are!"

"What the hell are you talking about?"

"I found the birth certificate that says you were born in California," she snapped.

I'm thinking to myself, "Yeah? And? You were the one who picked the goddamned thing up at the Federal Building in Westwood (California)! I **asked** you to pick it up for me, so I could get my lost Passport replaced and that was five years before!" She's just now having this epiphany that she's "found something" that has caused her to go to Arizona?

Here's another little hint of a problem: **RED FLAG!** Did I see it? No. Completely missed it, but here's how that came about, or shall I say, what she used as her ***first*** excuse to get out of a marriage;

Many years before, my wonderful paternal grandfather, Nonno, gave me some insight into my family and my life. As was always the case, when I was with him, I hung on every word. My grandfather was my mentor and my guide through life. He was my hero and my savior. He was my disciplinarian and my comforter. I would have done anything for that man. If anyone ever harmed him I could probably even have killed that person. I loved no man more than I loved my grandfather. He died in 2002, and I miss him so deeply and ever since his death, think of him often.

I was in my early twenties and one early afternoon, as I did so often, I dropped by my grandfather's house to say "hi." My grandmother was alive then, and as I entered the house I gave her a kiss. Her kisses were always so sloppy and wet, I gag even today when I reflect back on them, but those nasty old things were always filled with so much love, I never complained.

Nonno was where he always was; in the kitchen. And as I rounded the corner to give him a hug and a kiss, he blurted out the very same question he has always asked when I came over for a visit, "You wanna couple of eggs?"

"Jesus, Nonno, it's like one in the afternoon! What the hell are you cooking breakfast for? You should be cooking lunch food or something."

"Hey! This is my goddamned house!" he snapped. "I gonna cook whatever I wanna cook. Sit down. I gonna make you some eggs, so sit down."

"Nonno, I don't want . . ."

I looked over at my grandmother who was now sitting on the couch, thumbing through a magazine. She just smiled and continued reading her magazine. She wasn't about to help out in any way, as when I walked into their home, I was at mercy of its occupants. I smiled back at her and, just as I was instructed to do, sat down at the table and waited for my eggs to be cooked.

He brought two plates from the kitchen and sat them on the table. He'd thrown some Spam on the plates, as well, and once he sat down, he remembered he forgot his milk.

"You want some milk?"

I didn't argue, "Sure, Nonno." He brought two glasses.

My grandfather didn't like anyone telling him what to do, let alone suggesting a better way of doing things, and he never liked anyone helping him. He was proud that way. I think I got that trait from him. I don't like asking anyone for help either; it evokes a sense of weakness.

I reflect back to a few years before when I pulled up in front of his house to find him standing up on the roof. A rope was tied around the waist of his skeletal, seventy-eight-year-old body.

"Nonno! What the hell are you doing up there? Get off the goddamned roof before you kill yourself," I screamed at him.

"You shut your goddamned mouth! I do whatever I wanna do, ya hear? This is my goddamn house, and it needs a new roof!" He screamed back.

"What the hell is the rope around your waist for?"

"So I don't fall off the goddamned roof!" He used the word 'goddamned' like a comma when he got worked up.

We were still yelling back and forth. "What's it tied off to?"

"The goddamn vent line!" he yelled back.

"Jesus Christ, Nonno, that's not good enough to tie off to. Let me come up there and help you . . . Please?" I begged.

"I don't need your goddamned help. I'm fine. If I needed someone to tell me how to re-roof a goddamned house then I'd a hired someone to do it and I don't need you up here either!" He was pissed.

I stood and stared at him for about an hour, not saying a word, waiting for him to ask me to hand him something. He never did.

I finally broke the silence, "Nonno! Are you sure. . . . ."

"Yes, I'm sure!" He interrupted. "Goddamnit! Can't cha see I'm busy?"

"Ok, Nonno. I'm gonna go now. Be careful up there. I'll be back tomorrow. OK?"

His mumbling trailed off as he descended the sloped roof on the opposite side of the house.

When he wasn't doing major overhauls on the house, we sat and talked for hours as we always did when I visited. He always fed me a few tidbits of family information each time I visited. I think now that it may have been his way of getting me to come back for another visit. He'd whet my appetite for the family history that no one really knew, but yearned for. He'd give me just enough to keep me wondering about what followed.

He had a million stories, like the time his brother lied about his age and joined the Italian Army at sixteen, or seventeen years old, without permission. His mother grabbed his hand and dragged him out of the house, saying, "C'mon! We're going to find your brother."

I would inevitably return, but not for the information he was giving up; I returned because I didn't like being away from him. The family information he provided me was merely gravy.

During this visit, he told me that he'd "made special some things, in case anything happened," and that what he had made was "for the grandchildren." He produced a small book with a bunch of loose papers inside all bearing the names of my brother, sisters, and cousins; the whole lot. We were all there in the book.

"Just so ya know," he says to me.

I made several shooting glances in my grandmother's direction, who was well within earshot and I know she heard every word, but never looked up from the magazine she had on her lap. Men talk and women say nothing. It's a cultural thing I guess, however, that "culture" died in the sixties. In that respect, I was not so lucky in my relationships. I would find women who spoke their minds whenever they had the hankering to do so.

I never uttered another word to him about that conversation, or the content of the book. Ever. That is until I reacquainted with Tiffany and married her.

"So when you coming home?" I asked Tiffany, still confused.

"I don't know yet. I'm going to help Natalie (her brother's wife) do some things and then I'll let you know."

That doesn't sound too good, I thought to myself. This was just too weird to comprehend.

The following Friday, I received an e-mail stating the girls "have found peace" in Arizona and that Tiffany would be "enrolling the girls in school out here."

At this time I was really confused. Just four days earlier she was going to help her sister-in-law "with some things" and then come home and now she and the girls have found "peace" in Arizona. This was getting way too weird.

I knew she missed her mother and I knew she was close to her philandering brother who could do no wrong in the eyes of the Nelson clan but to decide to start a new life in Arizona without the common courtesy of telling your husband was beyond words or comprehension.

After thinking about all of this I wondered what she told the trust fund baby, Mr. Christopher Ball, to get out of *that* relationship. Or what she told her friends when they found out she was getting back together with an old boyfriend who hasn't a pot to piss in. Hmmmmm.

Probably this; "Well (sobbing then regains her composure), he smokes pot all the time and he get really violent when he's high and I just can't live like that." Then she'd start crying again and everyone would feel sorry for her. Job well done.

Now her brother, Tim, is a piece of work all by himself. This guy is idolized by his family, another **red flag** that went unheeded but certainly not unnoticed. Here's a guy who, early on in his relationship with his current wife (I was "dating" Tiffany at the time, in the very early 1990 s), quipped to me that he'd met a "rich girl," his "meal ticket." Her family owned the Champion Sprinkler company and she would be one of the heirs to this small fortune. If you're not familiar with Champion Sprinklers walk outside and look at the sprinkler heads in your yard, if you have one. If not, take a walk and look for some grass. You'll see those little round heads with the little notches on opposite sides, for easy replacement. Around the perimeter will be the word "Champion." You can't miss it.

Anyway, the relationship flourishes, and as fate (probably forced fate) would have it, they decide to get married. The usual crap that goes into weddings is followed by the matriarch of Nelson clan leading the way, making all the decisions. The wedding was drawing nearer and as is usually the case everyone is excited, but a little, infinitesimal wrench is tossed into the works; Tim had decided to take a small trip right before the wedding. Of course, I don't know each and every detail, but the trip was only a few short miles; to see the friend of his soon-to-be-wife. I'm not sure how it was that he was outed, but his sexual encounter, with a co-worker/friend of Natalie, was discovered and the wedding was off.

A few months later, after much consideration by Natalie, and a huge amount of objections and strong adverse reactions from her mother and father, the wedding was back on. The sick part of this was that sometime before the wedding Tim confided in me, "That was close." He said smiling, "I nearly lost my meal ticket."

I just looked at him in disbelief and muttered, as patronizingly as I could, "Yeah, you sure did." I shook my head and walked away.

I never said a word about the comment that he made. As Tim is the clan's patron saint of piety, it would have fallen on deaf ears.

Tim and Natalie would be married soon after, but not before Tiffany decided that the relationship with me needed to end and we went our separate ways. The good part is that they saved a few bucks on the wedding reception, as two names were left off the guest list: mine and the girl who decided it was OK to bed the future husband of her friend.

Tiffany and I would reunite several years later and rekindle our relationship. Note to self: If you break up, stay the hell away.

Rekindling any relationships could very well be a death sentence. It's a **RED FLAG**! Run towards the light!

Note: Sometime in 1998, the saintly Tim would, once again, bed another close friend of Natalie's and once again have his hopes of gaining his wife's family fortune dashed. Tim's father, Brad, inadvertently found them out one afternoon, when he dropped by to visit, and once again, the family was in turmoil over the fact that Saint Timothy had done it again; putting the future of the family's earnings in jeopardy. Natalie found out that Tim moved out for a month or two, and then he was able to weasel his way back in with the promise of never doing it again. During the short time they were married, Tim and Natalie had a daughter, Sydney. Tim wasn't amused. He said to me, "How tough is it to just have a son? They knock the dicks off of the dumb ones, so I got fucked with a daughter."

Tim claimed that the reason he strayed was that Natalie first had a daughter, instead of the son Tim desperately wanted and it was Natalie's fault this happened. Of course, his family sided with Tim.

I know what I would like to write about the mental capacity of one who, when they are told so, believes a two-foot pile of kangaroo excrement smells like roses and tastes like chicken, but it wouldn't be very nice. I happen to like Natalie very much. She is a woman who, like me believes in the family unit. Like me, loves deeply. Like me, has a genuine, if not naïve, trust in people. Natalie is a woman who is beautiful, inside and out. I will always have fond memories of her and have a warm place in my heart for her. To be sure, I don't want anyone to think she's an idiot; Natalie just happens to love a guy who happens to be part of this Nelson clan. Everyone else, in the eyes of "The Nelson Clan," is a second-class citizen, and sadly, whether she wants to believe it or not, so is Natalie. We all are.

"I HATE FLYING"

"Our own interpretive truths are worth about as much as buried treasure." – Unknown

September 2004

After a month of listening to Tiffany tell me she didn't know who I was and therefore felt that we would be better off parting ways, that she would stay in Arizona to be close to her mother, she felt enough time had passed that I could come to Arizona to see my daughters. At the time I was deeply involved in a project at work and needed to do some scheduling, so as to find time to make the trip. Actually, by me giving Tiffany nearly every penny I had for her and the girls to live on (Tiffany didn't work) I had no financial means by which to travel to Arizona. Considering the fact that Tiffany likes being in control, this *invitation* was her way of taking charge and giving me permission to visit, though I half expected she knew I didn't have the money to get out there and was just extending the invitation to say she tried to reach out to me. I didn't bother commenting; it wasn't worth it at that point.

Fortunately, I did end up finding a way to scrounge up the money. I rented and packed a car for the five-and-a-half-hour drive to the Phoenix Valley. I left not knowing exactly where I was going, or what I would find once I got there. All I can remember is that I missed my daughters so desperately; I couldn't get there fast enough.

I checked into a hotel next to Chandler Fashion Square, in Chandler, Arizona. I saw both Katie and Megan for the first time in a month and all I could do is cry. I missed them so much and all I could think of is to ask myself why their mother, whom they loved deeply, would put them through so much. I would be in that hotel for two days before checking out and heading back to California for work on Monday morning.

Ironically enough, it would be over a year later when I'd have moved to Arizona, and a few months after that, I would be apart from my daughters for another month, but that separation would be under the direst of circumstances.

I would drive to Arizona for visits a couple more times before I realized that the time I spent driving was taking away from my time seeing my daughters and my daughters seeing *me*. I called Southwest Airlines and purchased a ticket, which, after doing the math, was actually cheaper than driving.

Every week over the next year, I would leave John Wayne Airport in Newport Beach, California on Flight 1256 at 11:55 AM bound for Sky Harbor Airport in Phoenix, Arizona. I would land at 12:05 PM.

I have never been a good flyer. In fact, I detest flying. It scares me. The thought of being thirty thousand feet in the air and having something go wrong with an engine, or two. Or maybe a wing falls off. Maybe the pilot falls asleep or has a heart attack, or God forbid, the pilot is a woman. I know. I know. I'm a pig for feeling that way, but I promised this would be the complete truth . . . to some degree. If I didn't say that I was afraid of female pilots, I wouldn't be truthful.

It actually plays into why I fear flying and why I have been known to get off airplanes and take the next flight if I find there is a woman captain behind the controls, or in the cockpit for that matter.

Allow me to explain; several years ago I was traveling in Mexico on an Aero Mexico Flight and when we landed the nose gear collapsed which caused the plane to go skidding down the runway, leaning forward, at about a twenty-five-degree angle. What was really scary was the fact that during the "landing" I could barely see the airstrip because the sparks from the underbelly of the cockpit, which was being ground down to dust, were flying past the window. The sparks were so dense I actually thought we had caught fire.

When a plane lands at speeds in excess of 150 mph, after the initial bump of landing, the wheels normally make the rest of the landing pretty smooth. Okay, you got that picture? Now take away the nose gear and when you hit the ground at that speed, reversing the engines and applying the brakes is pretty much moot. Everything slows down so rapidly, I liken to being at a stop light and thinking the light is about to turn green, so you take your foot off the brake and ever so slightly, press on the gas, but an instant later, when the light does not change, slam on the brake. The nose of the car dips down quite deeply and somewhat violently. In a plane and in this situation, you can extend that violent movement to about twenty full and continuous seconds, and let me assure you, it makes for a pretty undisciplined ride. I hope you're visualizing this scenario. Let me take it a step further to reinforce my detestation, and fear, of flying.

On this particular flight, seated directly behind me, was a woman the size of a Volkswagen Beetle in a black car cover. Upon touch down, all I could hear was "Aye! Aye! Oh mi Hey-su Chreeeees-toh! Aye! Aye! Aye! Mi Hey-su Chreeeees-toh!"

She finally stopped when, being that she was following the flight attendant's instructions by using her seat belt, the bolts holding her seat in place gave way and she came flying forward. The problem was that it crashed into the back of ***my*** seat, dislodging ***it*** from its home as well. I was slammed into the seat in front of me and found myself stuck underneath a now very quiet German-engineered vehicle.

By this time the plane had finally stopped and all I could think of was getting the hell out of the plane before it exploded, but I had more than three hundred pounds of a wooly mammoth on top of me and I couldn't move. I also had a problem releasing my seatbelt from across my waist. I was upside down and my weight was straining against the latch within the buckle. I was screwed.

"Aye, mi madre," she started up again. "Esta bien, esta bien."

Thank God she wasn't dead! She started to crawl off of me, crushing me more as she pushed away on the back of my seat with those sausage-like fingers, increasing the weight on top of me. My seatbelt finally gave way and was unlatched. I caught a glimpse of her through the space in the seats and saw all of her gold chains with religious icons hanging from them. She was, as many Mexicans are, very religious and her prayers stated as such.

Once she realized she was all right, her whole persona changed as if night had fallen and a full moon had suddenly risen out of the east. Her Spanish was now laced with English so the fellow passengers, who were her neighbors to the north, understood her displeasure with such a harsh landing.

"Aye, pinche cabrone!" She was absolutely incensed and continued her tirade, "Madre fooker! Pandejo, cabrone! A la verga, cabrone! No sabe nada Fooker!"

It was kind of humorous to hear, but all I wanted to do was get the hell off the plane because I could now smell smoke. I couldn't see it, but I could sure smell it. I wriggled free from under the seats and headed for the doors that were now open; the inflated slides belched out to the side like a tired dog that hasn't the strength to pull his tongue back into its mouth.

As I passed the cockpit from inside I could hear the hysterical wails of a woman. She was screaming as if she was being stabbed over and over again. She was in complete and total inconsolable hysteria and I realized at that very moment I would never get on another plane with a woman in the cockpit. To date and to my personal knowledge, I never have.

I jumped out the door and slid to the tarmac, away from the plane. Before I could get up, I was hit again by someone behind me, knocked to the ground, and everything went black; however, I was still conscious. As confusing as it was and due to the darkness, I momentarily thought I had been knocked unconscious, but I wasn't.

I had a big hairy leg wrapped around my neck and I immediately realized that the wooly mammoth was on top of me again and her dress had fallen over my head. I panicked. I kicked and probably screamed like a girl, as I writhed to get out from under that car cover. When I finally did, I remember doing a crab-crawl and then flipping over on my backside and continuing to crawl away holding my butt above the ground as I scurried away; all the while shooting menacing looks at the animal who had accosted me. I was free, and I was alive.

NOT THE LOVE OF MY LIFE

Every time I get on an airplane I am reminded of that flight; it is the first thing I think of upon entering the cabin and upon landing it's the last thing I think of, as I walk off the plane.

As I settled into my seat, on Southwest Flight 1256, I immediately took out the small crucifix I carry with me when I fly. I was deep into the recall of my "near-death" experience under the weight of Trixie Tons-o-Fun and as I usually do, I began to pray.

I was shaken loose from my personal thoughts and prayers when I heard a voice next to me. "Sir, are you okay?"

"Yeah, I'm fine. I hate flying," I responded. And I have every right to, I thought to myself. I wondered if I looked that distraught sitting in my seat. I must have, for a person to inquire to that extent.

As I also do on every flight that I take, I held the cross, tight in my hand until we touched down.

THE RADIO EXPERIENCE

"Come follow me," Jesus said, "and I will make you fishers of men." – Mark 1:17

November 15, 2004

Tiffany and the girls had driven out from Arizona to see some friends and instead of staying with me in the small apartment I was living in, next to the University of California, Irvine campus, Tiffany opted to stay in a hotel nearer to her friends. Yet another Red Flag I should have seen, but did not. There was a slight drizzle falling that night, and as I drove up to the hotel, I was feeling sorry for myself for being away from my wife and children, living alone in a small studio apartment, and having done poorly on my football bets that day. I was down for several reasons; most of them selfish.

Tiffany had designated a time for me to arrive and as I pulled into the parking lot of the hotel I realized I was early. I was tired of listening to my usual radio station and started looking for something else to listen to as I waited. What I found on the radio that night would change my life dramatically. I would ultimately write my brother about these events as I did so many times before for prayer, direction, and his opinion of my world and many other things that brothers confide in each other for. He was in the middle of a war zone, in a very dangerous war and he still found time to counsel his pathetic little brother. I love him for what he gave me then and continues to give me now.

NOT THE LOVE OF MY LIFE

The following is the actual e-mail I sent to my brother, who was on tour in Iraq, in a live war zone of the Sunni Triangle.

-----Original Message-----
From: Eric Diconti [mailto:ediconti@udccorporation.com]
Sent: Monday, November 15, 2004 2:14 PM
To: 'Diconti LT Marc G'
Subject: Interesting happenings

Marc,

OK I told you that while I was listening to the radio something strange happened? Here it is:

It was about 2100. Tiffany and the girls were on their way back to their hotel from the party and I had one more birthday gift to give to Tiffany since I was not going to see her today (her actual birthday) as they were driving back to Arizona. I started flipping around the radio stations (I didn't want to listen to the football game) and came across a station with some guy preaching, which I passed over. I kept flipping. I thought 5 seconds of listening to him and his crap was enough. In those 5 seconds, the only conclusion I was able to come to, about what I had just heard was, I thought to myself, "What a great speaking voice."

Normally, I do pass by these stations, as it is usually some evangelical psycho screaming about how we're all going to hell if we don't call in and pledge a hundred dollars, right away. And $100.00 will only keep us, as individuals, out of hell. If we want the whole family to be saved we need to pledge $100.00 each. A family of six can get away with a $500.00 pledge. Nice discount. Tithe? I got your Tithe right here!

As I said, I passed over this station and continued on. But something kept me thinking about this guy's calming voice and how in five seconds, I could ascertain that he indeed did have a calming voice. Weird, I thought. I kept flipping. There was absolutely nothing else on the radio and I thought, "What the hell? Let's hear what this idiot has to say. If nothing else, I'll get a good laugh." I turned the dial back, looking for the station I'd heard a few minutes ago. Actually, I was listening for the guy's voice, because I had *no* idea where it was on the dial. I also thought it would be a good time to reflect back on the day. Truly, I am thinking this at the time. Bang! There's the voice! I stop and start listening. The guy is encouraging listeners to say a prayer for a loved one who is away from us. I'm thinking, "Wow!" That's weird. I hadn't said my evening prayer for you, Tiffany, and the girls. What great timing and thanks for the reminder, dude! So I turn the radio down and start to pray.

    I asked the Lord to keep you safe and make sure he stays with you while you spread His word and watch over your flock (sic). I didn't need to tell Him where you are, He already knows. I asked Him to watch over Jim so that he can do his job as your "bodyguard" and asked Him to watch over both your families. I haven't heard back from Him yet, big brother, but IF He contacts me, I'll let you know.

    I also asked Him to give me direction and point me down the right path so that my family could be whole again. I asked Him to give Tiffany some guidance so that she too, could find her way back to me. I relayed how damned depressed I was and how I have never experienced depression this deep before. I also said to Him, that (although I would *never* do it) I understand how truly weak people kill themselves when they are despondent. When they are faced with extreme depression, like I feel that I have right now. I said to Him, "Is THIS what it feels like? Because, if it IS, then I understand and I pity them." I then thanked Him for making me stronger than the others. I told Him that I was so miserable I couldn't stand it and needed some help in quelling this misery. I again asked that He help me and guide me to put my family back together and make this feeling of misery go away. Amen.

    I'm thinking, "That was painless but I don't feel any better. Oh well, turn the radio back up so I can at least hear a soothing voice." The voice actually made me feel good to listen to it. I turned the radio back up and hear the voice talking about how people complain, "How could you do this to me, God?"

and "How can you get me out of this God?" When we should be asking God, "What are you trying to tell me or teach me?" "What are you trying to show me?" Because there is always an underlying message that He is trying to convey and it is our job to understand His message. Fair enough. I concur.

After hearing this and while I'm still trying to digest it, I immediately hear the voice say, "Pain is inevitable, but misery is a choice." This guy is *killing me*! I actually said out loud, "What?" I'll be damned if the voice didn't say again, "Pain is inevitable, but misery is a choice." I just asked God to stop me from feeling miserable, and this voice says that I have a "choice." OK, that's freaky. The voice is now talking about Psalm 84 and more specifically Verse 6. This guy is like a freaking garage sale, there's crap all over the place, and it's flying. I'm trying to field all of it, too!

Now, this is where I got confused. I have a hard time with thee's and thou's of the King James era and the best I could get out of it was that it was talking about finding the Lord . . . I think. It said something about, "rather entering His door one time, than a thousand other doors" and then something about a bird in a nest . . . Hell, I don't know. All I know is that after asking Jesus for guidance, I feel like I'm getting this crazy message over the radio, from this soothing voice, telling me to (and I'm paraphrasing) "Find the Lord and be safe." If I'm even hearing the dude right. It didn't matter, Marc, I started crying. Not like you see middle easterners do, when a loved one dies; screaming and rolling around on the ground and throwing themselves in front of trains and stuff, not *that* kind of crying. Just crying. Just tears rolling (not streaming) down my face because, all of the sudden, I understood again. *This* is what I need to do (again, IF I'm understanding the voice correctly). It's *my* choice to do something about my misery and stop feeling sorry for myself. I have to do whatever it takes to make my family whole again and the *only* thing I've got to do is to trust God.

I do trust God, Marc. Little by little I am coming together with him. It's taken all of my life to get to this point, but last night was a huge juncture in my life. I finally felt good. Better than I've felt in a long, long time. It was OK, Marc.

That voice turned out to be some guy from the Calvary Chapel in Costa Mesa that does a Sunday night service over the radio. I don't know his name and it really doesn't matter, because last night, I felt good for the first time in a long time. I don't know if it was listening to the soothing voice or finally *knowing* what I needed to do. Whatever it was, is irrelevant, I finally slept through the night. It was the first time in about six months.

I love you big brother. Keep your head down and Psalm 91 close by.

E

I always closed my e-mail to my brother with "Keep your head down and Psalm 91 close by."

Marc told me the story of a general who commanded several thousand troops to commit to memory Psalm 91 and to believe in that Psalm.

Psalm 91 tells us that if we believe in the Lord, follow Him and trust Him as our Savior, no harm will come to us and even though others around us will fall, we will not be touched. He will be our Protector. In getting his men to truly believe this and live it while fighting on the front lines for something like three years and while troops from other companies were decimated, he did not lose one man. Not one. This general would come to be known as "The Psalm 91 General."

"I'M SO GLAD WE'RE BACK TOGETHER"

"Society is built upon trust and trust built upon the confidence in one another's integrity." Carved over the entryway of a bank in Brooklyn Heights, New York.

October 2005

It was a long and lonely drive away from UDC, the family I had acquired there, the beaches and waves of the Southern California coast, the smell of the ocean that wafted in and piqued my olfactory, and the everyday occurrence of the sounds of shrieking seagulls. There were so many memories I was driving away from and smells I would miss, but wouldn't soon forget, as the California coast was at this time, etched into my soul and will never leave.

It was hard leaving a place I called home and had known for so many years, I just kept thinking how truly sad it was to have to come to this, that I would be forced to leave one of the truly wonderful places in the United States because one woman decided she wanted to be elsewhere; and that she felt it necessary to take our children with her without ever consulting me. But the important part was that my girls needed me. Kathryn and Megan needed their father and not just on the weekends; they needed me in Arizona full time.

I found a job with a commercial contractor in Tempe and stayed there for about ten months. It wasn't a good fit and I didn't like the way they did business or treated their employees. They claimed to be an "employee first" company, but I pretty much found that to be a joke.

I met a man at the church Tiffany had found for us and began going to. She raved about this guy and told of his exploits in construction and the fact that he was planning to build a school for the church that was growing. The name of the church was Risen Savior Lutheran Church on Alma School, just south of Ocotillo Rd., in Chandler. Risen Savior would be my spiritual home for the next year, but the finest hour came when, in church one Sunday, Tiffany leaned over and whispered in my ear, "I'm so glad we're back together."

I smiled and gently squeezed her hand. "So am I."

On a side note; my brother, Marc, upon his return from one of his tours of duty in Iraq, would deliver a sermon here. Through me, an associate pastor at Risen Savior and several months of planning, we were able to coordinate the sermon of a Naval Chaplain recently back from Iraq. Marc spoke of what it was like to be in a war zone and know that the men there are closer to God than anyone else in the world. One errant bullet or fragment from an exploded mine and they would meet their maker, so the importance of true salvation was paramount. He received rave reviews from those in attendance.

Each Sunday, prior to relocating from California, I would make small talk with the "construction guy" Tiffany had met and raved about for so many months. Our girls were, at this time, attending the school there and she would see Paxton Anderson on a daily basis and oftentimes would speak of my construction background to build me up and groom me for a possible position with Paxton's company, Dynamite Custom Homes, LLC.

We became friendly after a time and when my employ with the commercial firm in Tempe was nearing a parting of the ways, Paxton and I spoke of the possibility of me coming aboard and building some custom homes.

This was a new venture since my expertise was in commercial construction and I knew little about residential construction, but what the hell, I thought, how tough could it be?

In June 2006 I would get a call from Paxton Anderson to say he could use my services, that he was building more homes and needed a guy who knew the business. Less restrictive hours and better pay are always good incentive. I was interested.

That relationship would turn out to be a test of wills, as nearly a year later I would find out that good ol' mister Anderson was neck deep in mortgage fraud and would eventually cause a loss exposure to M & I Bank in excess of $40 million to satisfy an addiction to horses. The plan Paxton Anderson devised was nearly foolproof, too, but he didn't count on my honesty and it would be my honesty that would come back to haunt him, but not before my life had fallen apart by the accusations Tiffany would soon make.

"DO YOU WANT TO MEET ME FOR DINNER?"

". . . . In a world that seems to be God abandoned." –
Robert Penn Warren

March 2, 2006

A few days prior, on February 27th, or 28th, I was speaking to some friends who needed some electrical work and minor repairs done on their home and had decided to use Tiffany's brother, Tim, for that work. They asked my opinion of their choice and I spoke very candidly about my view of how I felt he conducted business. I told them, that if it were me I would look elsewhere, that I felt he wasn't the most honest of the people I knew in the business, but if they did use his services, to be wary. That night he confronted me on those statements, which I didn't deny making. He walked away mad and Tiffany was even more livid that I would make disparaging comments about her brother. I told her that they asked my opinion and I had no problem giving it to them.

I reminded her of something she already knew which was, "I couldn't give two shits about that punk" brother of hers and that he was "a crook and I don't trust anything he does."

I went to bed, woke up the next morning, and went to work.

About 2PM Tiffany called and wanted to meet at an Albertson's parking lot to talk. When I got there she told me she wanted me to move out of the house, that she was still mad about what I said about her brother.

I was speechless. After a moment I asked, "Are you kidding me?"

"No, I'm *not* kidding you" she replied, "You made my brother cry and no one makes my brother cry."

I actually laughed in her face, thinking it was a joke. What she was saying just didn't seem to add up to the horrific devastation she was making it out to be. I shrugged, got back into my truck, and drove back to work. I figured she would cool off in a while however, when I got home she informed me that it was her brother's house we were renting and he didn't want me there anymore, so I had to move out and that she was staying there with the girls. This was just too weird for words. **RED FLAG!**

I got a hotel room for what I believed to be the time it would take Tiffany to come to her senses. On March 2nd, 2006, I would realize that day was not to come. I have to laugh about all the red flags that were there the whole time, right in front of my face, and I refused to see them.

At about 3:30PM my phone rang. I looked down to see the words "il Capo," (the boss) on the screen of my phone.

"Ah yes, how sweet it is!" I thought to myself, "Tiffany is calling to tell me to come home."

"Hi!"

"Hi, Eric. Do you want to meet me for dinner?" She asked. "We need to talk."

"Sure. Where?" I asked.

"Nothing But Noodles," she said. "I've got some things to do, but I can be there by 7:30PM." This was the favorite place to eat for my daughters. It's at the corner of Germann and Alma School in Chandler, AZ.

"I'll be there at 7:30." Weird, I thought. I would have thought it would have been better to meet somewhere quiet if she wanted to talk. Eh, whatever.

At 7:27PM my phone was ringing again. It was Tiffany asking where I was and that she was running a little late and would be there shortly. I said I was actually about 200 yards away and was pulling into the parking lot momentarily, but would wait for her.

I pulled my truck into a parking space and put the truck in park. It was still running when a young kid with curly hair who looked to be about 30 years old approached my truck. I thought he was going to ask for money.

He said something that sounded very familiar to me, but it didn't register until he repeated it. "Ericco Di Conti?"

I was a little taken aback, "Yeah? What can I help you with?'

"I'm an officer of the Court and before you do anything you should read this." He handed me some folded papers and continued, "You are being served with an Order of Protection and you are forbidden to contact your wife, or children for any reason."

I was still in shock, "OK, but what does this mean?"

"You should probably get an attorney." He turned away, walked to his motorcycle, and drove off.

What I was about to read would change me forever. It would also change the way I viewed our society for the rest of my life.

ORDER OF PROTECTION COURT CASE NO. CC2006023696

PETITION for Order of Protection
NCIC # 0711
Ct. # AZ007053J

"It takes only a moment for fear to find its way, to seep through the carefully constructed armor. Once it does, it finds a permanent place. It is as true for a hardened criminal as it is for a young boy." - From the book "Sleepers" by Lorenzo Carcaterra

March 2, 2006

I know this is a very cliché statement, but if you've never before been "hit in the stomach," and lost the ability to breathe, then you wouldn't understand my first few moments after reading the Order of Protection. It's almost like the surprise of hearing that a close friend or relative has died in a car accident, or maybe that you or a loved one has just been told you, or they, have an inoperable form of cancer and death is imminent. Whatever the case may be, ***that*** is what it felt like, because after reading the Order of Protection I may well have died myself. Never has anyone said anything about me, like the things I read, in my life. Ever. Sure, I've been called an asshole and a plethora of other things relating to my skills at being in a relationship, but never have I been accused of abusing women and children. Certainly not *molesting* children.

The person I was reading about was NOT me; it couldn't be, but sure as hell, my name was at the top of the page and throughout the document. What made it worse was the fact I was now considered a "defendant" by the State of Arizona.

I thought to myself, "Whatever happened to 'innocent until proven guilty'?" Not when it comes to an Order of Protection. I guess the liability is too great and if by some horrible stroke of bad luck a person comes back (I know it's happened before) and injures (or kills) the other, the Courts have their asses in a sling and everyone gets sued, loses their job, etc. They cannot take chances in this area and I know that. I had to wait until the Court saw I wasn't a bad guy, that Tiffany was lying, and gave me permission to hold my little girls in my arms again. I thought I would just go to the courthouse in the morning, explain my situation, and everything would be alright again. As I read the document I realized there was "No hearing set" and I would have to wait.

As I re-read the four pages that were handed to me I felt a nauseating feeling wash over me again. One of the three items in this Order was one that makes people end their lives by the mere fact that an accusation was made; true, or not. It was the most vicious of atrocities that one could accuse another of and quite frankly, about as agonizing and painful as one could ever experience.

The document read as if this was a person who, did not deserve to live among us and should be locked up forever. The first item told of how Tiffany had left for the store but upon her return, she heard screams coming from inside the house and could see, through the window, that I was forcing a "red liquid" down the throat of my older daughter, Kathryn. This was an outright lie and was only written to sway the judge to grant her an Order of Protection. The third item on the document reeked of the most cruelty, read:

12/16/2005

My two young daughters were playing on a sofa and the defendant became angry. He grabbed the 5-year-old under

> *the arm, forcibly pulled her over the back of the sofa, and slammed her feet on the ground. While still holding tight under her arm, out of fear, she urinated on herself and the floor. As the defendant screamed at her and pulled her to the bathroom to clean her, the 5-year-old reached out clung to her godmother (SIC) and begged her not to leave her alone with her father. She was then bathed by her godmother at which point she pointed out the "rubs" and "rashes" on the inside of her thighs.*

The underhanded comment, as it was written, was that I had sexually abused my daughter was so horrific, after the initial reading of it I have read it only once since that night. I have glanced at it, but have never read each and every word in it and never read that document in its entirety again, that is, until the writing of it above. It is written exactly as it appears on the actual document.

I will put it away again and hopefully the next time I read it again will be years from now, when the day comes that I sit my daughters down and explain everything to them. Explain exactly what their mother did to me and *try* to explain the reason why. I had been trying to figure that out myself but I have only come to one viable explanation. That explanation would come to me in the months that followed that miserable night and after so much more information surfaced about Tiffany, *"the love of my life."*

Actual Order of Protection as it was filed on March 2, 2006

ERIC L. DI CONTI

COPY

JUDICIAL BRANCH OF ARIZONA IN MARICOPA COUNTY McDowell Mountain Justice Court: 18380 N. 40th Street Phoenix, AZ 85032-

Tiffany Nelson	Ericco Di Conti	Court Case No. CC2006023696
Plaintiff	Defendant	
11/15/1964	unknown	**PETITION for**
Date of Birth	Address	**Order of Protection**
	AZ	NCIC #0711
	City, State, Zip Code, Phone	Ct. #AZ007063J

DIRECTIONS: Please read Guide Sheet before filling out this form.

1. Defendant relationship: [X] Spouse [ ] Ex-spouse [ ] Lived together (now or before) [X] Child in common [ ] Dating (never lived together) [ ] One of us pregnant by the other [ ] Parent [ ] Other:

2. [ ] If checked, there is a pending action involving maternity, paternity, annulment, legal separation, dissolution, custody, parenting time or support in .

3. Have you or the Defendant been charged or arrested for domestic violence OR requested a Protective Order?
[ ] Yes [X] No [ ] Not sure
if yes or not sure, explain:

4. I need a Court Order because:

Date(s)	Describe what happened, or may happen:
2/27/2006	Defendant was left alone with our 7 year old daughter while I went to the market. Upon my return, I heard her screaming from the inside of the house and saw her standing in the window, screaming for my help. Defendant had tried to administer cough syrup, our daughter gagged and spit it up, at which point he grabbed her under her arm, dragged her to the sink, berated her and contiued trying to force the liquid down her throat. He then forcibly moved her out of the way so that he could begin removing the stain from his clothes. My daughter was visibly shaken and aboslutely terrified of him at the time.
2/28/2006	Defendant was confronted by my brother as to false allegations defendant made against my brother. They spoke together outside and upon returning back inside the house, defendant positioned himself such that I was unable to use the computer or phone thereby isolating me from communicating with my brother and family members.
12/16/2005	My two younger daughters were playing on a sofa and defendant became angry. He grabbed the 5 year old under the arm, forcibly pulled her over the back of the sofa and slammed her feet on the ground. While still holding tight to her underarm, out of fear, she urinated on herself and the floor. As defendant screamed at her and pulled her to the bathroom to clean her, the 5year old reached out clung to her god mother and begged her not to leaver her alone with her father. She was then bathed by her godmother at whcih point she pointed out the "rubs" and "rashes" on the inside of her thighs.

03-02-2006 17:02   JACK COX 623 847 4800   PAGE:5

Order of Protection Pg.1

NOT THE LOVE OF MY LIFE

5. The following persons should also be on this Order. As stated in number 4, the Defendant is a danger to them:
Kathryn Di Conti (11/13/1998)
Megan Di Conti (7/13/2000)

6. Defendant should be ordered to stay away from these locations, at all times, even when I am not present:
[X] Home: 13917 E. Galveston Street, Gilbert, AZ 85296;
[X] Work: 30 E. Oakwood Hills Drive, Chandler, AZ 85248;
[X] School/Others: mother's home: 2442 W. Rockrose Way, Chandler, , AZ 85248; Our Lady of Mt. Carmel: 2121 South Rural Road, Tempe, AZ 85284; brother's home: 13732 E. Galveston, Gilbert, AZ 85296;

7. [X] If checked, because of the risk of harm, order the defendant NOT to possess firearms or ammunition.

8. [ ] If checked, request an order for the Defendant to participate in domestic violence counseling or other counseling.

9. Other:

Under penalty of perjury, I swear or affirm the above statements are true to the best of my knowledge, and I request an Order/Injunction granting relief as allowed by law.

Order of Protection Pg. 2

ERIC L. DI CONTI

3/3 Chandler P.D.
Phil Besse #252

TRIAL COURTS OF ARIZONA IN MARICOPA COUNTY
McDowell Mountain Justice Court: 18380 N 40th St, Phoenix, AZ 85032

Tiffany Nelson Plaintiff	CC2006023696000 Court Case No.	
11/15/1964 Date of Birth	AZ007053J Court No., NCIC	**ORDER OF PROTECTION**
Ericco Di Conti Defendant	0711 Court No., DPS	☐ MODIFIED

WARNING TO DEFENDANT
This is an official Court Order. If you disobey this Order, you may also be arrested and prosecuted for the crime of interfering with judicial proceedings and any other crime you may have committed in disobeying this Order.

NOTICE: Only the Court can change this Order. Nothing the Plaintiff does can stop, change, or undo this Order without the Court's approval. You must return to the Court to modify (change) or quash (stop) this Order. If you disagree with this Order, you may ask for a hearing by filing a written request for hearing with the Court named above. This Order is effective for one year after the original service on you and is valid nationwide.

NOTICE TO PARTIES
This is not a custody or visitation Order. You can only file for custody or visitation as a Title 25 action in Superior Court. All violations of this Order should be reported to a law enforcement agency, not the Court. Either party should notify this Court if an action for dissolution (divorce), separation, annulment or paternity/maternity is filed.

The Court finds reasonable cause to believe that the Defendant may commit an act of domestic violence or has committed an act of domestic violence within the past year (or good cause exists to consider a longer period).

1. IT IS THEREFORE ORDERED that the Defendant not: commit a dangerous crime against children defined in A.R.S. 13-604.01 or custodial interference, or engage in conduct that would place the Plaintiff in reasonable fear of bodily injury; or threaten, intimidate, endanger, assault, unlawfully imprison, kidnap, harass, stalk, trespass upon or damage the property of, or commit any other disorderly conduct upon the Plaintiff and:
   Kathryn Di Conti   11/13/1998
   Megan Di Conti   7/13/2000

2. The Defendant shall not contact Plaintiff: in person; by phone; in writing; electronically; The Defendant may contact the Plaintiff through legal counsel, legal process or with permission of the Court.

3. ☑ The Defendant shall not contact persons listed above:
   Kathryn Di Conti: in person; by phone; in writing;
   Megan Di Conti: in person; by phone; in writing;

Order of Protection Pg. 3

NOT THE LOVE OF MY LIFE

You can file an action for custody or visitation separately in Superior Court.

4. ☒ The Court finds that physical harm may otherwise result and, therefore, the Plaintiff is granted the exclusive use and possession of the residence at: 13917 E. Galveston Street, Gilbert, AZ 85296
The Defendant may return once with a law enforcement officer to obtain belongings.

5. ☒ Defendant shall not go on or near where Plaintiff and/or parties listed above:

   Reside(s):
   13917 E. Galveston Street, Gilbert, AZ 85296
   Place of employment:
   Queen Anne Designs: 30 E. Oakwood Hills Drive, Chandler, AZ 85248
   School:
   Our Lady of Mt. Carmel: 2121 South Rural Road, Tempe, AZ 85284

6. The Court finds that the Defendant represents a credible threat to the physical safety of the Plaintiff or other protected person and/or may inflict bodily injury or death on the Plaintiff. Upon service of this Order: **not ordered.**

7. The Defendant has not received actual notice of this hearing and has not had an opportunity to participate.

8. Other Orders necessary for the protection of the Plaintiff and other designated persons: **None.**

9. The Defendant shall appear for a hearing: **No Hearing Set.**

   WARNING: IF YOU FAIL TO APPEAR, AN ORDER MAY BE ISSUED WITHOUT YOUR INPUT.

10. The Defendant has not received actual notice of this hearing and has not had an opportunity to participate.

    BRADY does not apply.

The Honorable Michael Reagan   3/2/2006

CERTIFICATION
I hereby certify that this is a true copy of the Order on file in this Court.

Judicial Officer or Clerk of the Court By: _____

DESCRIPTION OF THE DEFENDANT

SEX	RACE	DATE OF BIRTH	HEIGHT	WEIGHT	EYES	HAIR	SOC. SEC. NO
Male	White	5/18/1959	6' 0"	220	Brown	Black	Unknown

ALIAS (if known): N/A   Defendant is: NOT Military   NOT Law Enforcement

salt & pepper

03-02-2006 17:02 JACK COX 623 847 4800   PAGE: 4

Order of Protection Pg. 4

When the whole scenario finally sunk in, I called Tiffany's cell phone to ask why she was doing this; it went to voicemail. I called the house phone and there, too, I was met with the outgoing message, "Hello, you have reached. . . ."

The message I left was to the girls, "Hi girls, this is Daddy. I don't know what's going on right now, or why your mommy is doing this, but I'm gonna fix this. I promise. If it's the last thing I do, I will fix this. I love you both very much and I'll see you soon. I promise. I love you so much. I'll fix this, Katie and Megan." I hung up the phone and at that very moment, I realized how alone I was. I didn't know where I was going to go or who to call.

I had only one friend who had moved to Arizona from California, ironically, on the same weekend I had moved Susan Nelson here. He lived in Gilbert, Arizona, a town that bordered Chandler. I dialed the number of Ryan Quinn; no answer. The anxiety started to set in. I called one of my closest friends in California, if for no other reason than to tell someone what was happening. Not that anything could be done by calling Laura Verdi, or that she could make the Order of Protection go away, but just to hear a friendly voice.

I met Laura through mutual friends and from the day we met I knew we would be friends for many years. When she answered the phone I could hear a lot of noise in the background. She was at her sister's house in El Segundo, California, having dinner, drinking good wine, and having a generally good time. I wasn't going to ruin it. I told her to have fun and I would call her later. I wouldn't talk to her again until Monday, March 6th and in those three days, I would learn a great deal about the judicial system in the State of Arizona.

That night I drove to a hotel and on the way came to the realization I had no clothes, toothbrush, razor, or anything but the clothes on my back and I had to work the following day. I pulled into a hotel somewhere in Gilbert and walked into the lobby. I told the gal at the desk that I wanted a room, gave her my ID and debit card, and while I filled out the information card, she ran my card through the system.

"Uh, I'm sorry, sir, but this card isn't going through," she said. "Have you got another one?"

I said, "It's a debit card. There's plenty of money in the account. It's good I can assure you." I encouraged her, "Please run it again." She rolled her eyes and slid the card through the bank machine again.

"No, I'm sorry. It isn't giving me an approval." She had that "I told-ya-so" look in her eyes. "Have you got a credit card you can use?"

I had five credit cards that I kept for emergencies and they were at the house I was longer able to enter without violating the Court Order and winding up on the business end of a jail cell.

I shook my head, "No I don't. That's all I have."

"I'm sorry, sir," she said.

"Listen, I'll just run to the bank, pull out some cash, and be back. Where's the closest Wells Fargo?" She directed me to a branch, I walked out and headed to the bank.

It was relatively close and as I pulled in I had a terrible thought come to me. I sat in the cab of my truck and stared at the ATM. I shook my head from side to side.

"Naw. She wouldn't do that," I thought and got out of my truck.

I walked up to the machine, slipped my card into the slot, and punched in my PIN. On the screen popped up a screen with several monetary amounts to choose from. I punched the button adjacent to the $200.00 amount.

"We're sorry but this transaction cannot be completed at this time."

I punched the button next to $140.00.

"We're sorry but this transaction cannot be completed at this time."

I hit the button next to *$100.00*. Same thing. *$60.00*. Same thing. I leaned forward and rested my forehead on the machine. I couldn't believe what was happening. I punched the button next to the *$20.00* amount. The machine started making some noise and finally spit out a crisp new twenty-dollar bill. The receipt that followed showed a balance of only a few dollars and change.

Sardonically I said aloud, "Well at least I can eat for a couple of days."

A few short days earlier that Wells Fargo account held in excess of $60,000.00 and now it was empty. My worst fears, as I was staring at the ATM from my truck, came true. I had no money, I had no place to sleep, and I had nowhere to go. I was beaten.

I drove out of the bank parking lot and started looking for a quiet street to park on. I needed some sleep. I drove to my office, pulled into a parking space, and fell asleep. The next morning, I straightened up my crumpled shirt, drove to the Quick Trip up the street, and bought some coffee and a small tube of toothpaste; there were no toothbrushes on the shelf. I did the old finger brushing routine and drove back to my office.

That day, instead of working, I spent a great deal of time on the phone with the Court trying to find out what I could do to get my little problem fixed. It was no use. In that respect, I was screwed and worse yet, I still had no money and had nowhere to go.

I would spend the next two nights sleeping in my truck until I could get a hold of someone to help me.

Monday couldn't come soon enough and I finally spoke to Laura. I told her the whole story from start to finish and although I knew I left some key elements out due to my trying to get it all out in one breath, Laura suggested the one thing I didn't believe I needed.

"Eric, you need to get an attorney."

"An attorney? What the hell for?" I asked. "I don't need an attorney. I'll just go in there and tell them the truth."

She responded, "You're being stupid. If you think you're going to walk into court and tell them 'the truth' and everything is gonna be OK, you're an idiot." She over-emphasized her point, "You **need** an attorney, Eric."

I then explained that I hadn't the money for an attorney, so getting one was out of the question. I tried to steer her away from the whole lawyer thing and went onto another subject, but she wasn't playing ball.

"I'll get one for you," she said and then asked, "How much are they?"

"Hell, I don't know Laura and besides, if you put up the money for an attorney I have no idea when I would be able to pay you back."

I told her that every penny was gone. All the money that Tiffany and I had in the bank, some $68,000, was no longer there and I was pretty much hosed.

She countered, "Tiffany probably has an attorney and if you walk into court by yourself you'll never see those girls again. That's what she's banking on, Eric." She continued, "You need to rethink this. Please. Let me help you. Whoever she has, no matter how inept he, or she is you're gonna be fucked in more ways than one."

She was right. I'd have been better off strolling through the Serengeti, in the middle of the night, with fresh meat draped over my shoulders expecting not to encounter any hyenas, but I was still unrelenting.

"Laura, I can handle it," I said. The pride my grandfather passed down to me was far too great to give in and accept someone's help, especially when I had no way of ever paying it back.

We ended our call and I believe she was pretty pissed at my stubbornness.

"HELLO, IS THIS ERIC DI CONTI?"

"There are more tears shed for prayers that have been answered, than those that went unanswered."
– Truman Capote

Monday, March 6, 2006

Monday was another day of learning. I was sitting inside my trailer at a job site and started making calls. The trailer was situated at the west end of a parking lot in a shopping center called Lakeview Village, located in southeast Phoenix, at the corner of Elliot and Higley. I made calls to the Courts and calls to attorney's offices to see what kind of money I'd be shelling out, as if I **had** any money to shell out in the first place. Five thousand here, seven thousand dollars there; another group wanted ten thousand before they would even look at the facts of my quandary. They all wanted far more money than I could ever come up with.

At about 9:30AM, I heard a couple of cars pull up in front of my trailer, so I got up, went to the door, and opened it out to the fresh spring morning air of Gilbert, Arizona.

"HOLD IT, RIGHT FUCKING THERE!" a very menacing voice shouted at me. I had my left hand on the doorknob and my right hand holding onto the jam above my head.

"LEMME SEE YOUR FUCKING HANDS, ASSHOLE!"

NOT THE LOVE OF MY LIFE

I was frozen with fear as I was standing there, in the doorway of my construction trailer, face-to-face with a couple of Chandler cops, out of their jurisdiction, with their hands on their guns; one of them pointing his finger at me.

"LEMME SEE YOUR FUCKING HANDS!" He screamed again. Some of the workers saw what was going on and started walking toward the trailer.

I thought to myself, "Jesus Christ! Just stay where you guys are. Don't come down here. I don't need this right now." Moving away from the jam, with my right hand, I waved them off. As I did one of the cops quickly glanced over his shoulder to see who I waving off. The few guys walking toward the trailer headed back to their respective jobs, looking over their shoulders as they walked back. They never stopped watching what was going on at the trailer.

"DON'T MOVE!" Came the voice again. I really couldn't tell which one of these guys was firing the orders, but I knew one thing with absolute certainty, I didn't want to get lead poisoning; I stood very still after that.

As they approached the trailer they told me to step away from the door. I did so without argument and allowed them inside to scope it out. Once they found the trailer empty they hustled me inside to have a talk.

When they offered me a seat, I thought how nice it was of them to be so polite. Their guns now had the strap over the back of them and snapped securely into their holsters.

"Are you Eric Di Conti?" One of them asked.

Are you kidding me? **Now** you ask who I am? They were lucky I didn't have a bad heart, because if I was someone else, there may have been a different outcome and they may have been looking down at a guy, pale blue in color, with pupils fixed and dilated.

"Yes, I am," I answered. "What the hell was all that about?"

"Your wife came into the station this morning and said you violated a Court Order," one of them said. He had a copy of the Order and reached over to hand it to me. I declined saying I knew what it said.

"Did you call her after you were served an Order of Protection?" Another one asked.

"Hell yes I did! But I called her before I even read the goddamned order." I continued, "I had no idea what was going on. I have never raised my hand to a woman before in my life and I would never harm my children. I was confused and didn't know why she would say these things, so I called her."

"By the way," I asked. "What the hell was up with your hands on your guns? Was that necessary?"

"Your wife said you had a bad temper and we shouldn't take any chances. We didn't know if you were going to get violent. Sorry about that," the cop said. He explained that the most dangerous situation for them to be in is a domestic dispute and they need to proceed with a great deal of caution. I had no problem understanding their concerns.

After going back and forth, speaking in a calm manner and telling them my side of the story, one of the cops said, "I don't know what you did to piss your wife off, but you've got a problem. She's got it out for you."

"No shit!" I thought.

They explained that I cannot contact her again until I go to court and only if I get the Order thrown out. They also said that Tiffany demanded that I be arrested for violating the Order, but one of them thought she may have been a little overzealous in her quest to have me arrested. He told her he would look into it.

I explained I was looking into finding an attorney when they showed up and promised I would not call her again. That I would just wait for the Courts to make the call; after all, I had done nothing wrong. When the boys left, I think I was still shaking.

"Jesus, I need an attorney," I said to no one at all.

About 3:00PM, my phone rang again. I looked down to see who it was and though I didn't recognize the number I answered it anyway.

"Hello? Is this Eric Di Conti?" A woman's voice asked.

Jesus Christ! Is the District Attorney in on the torment Eric Di Conti game?

"Yes. Who is this?"

"My name is Michelle Kunzman. I have been retained by Laura Verdi to represent you," she said.

Once again, I was stunned beyond words. It had dawned on me that Laura had done what I told her not to do. I couldn't pay her back and if I could, I didn't know when. Besides that, my pride was at stake. A bad feeling was creeping back into my gut, an ice ball was growing there and I felt sick.

Deep down I knew I needed help, but refused to accept it. What I wanted to do was to prove that even though I could be beaten down, I couldn't be completely destroyed. The problem, given my predicament, was that it would have taken an act of God to do it without an attorney. To be honest I think it was an act of God that brought a guardian angel named Laura Verdi into my life and now that angel was making sure I didn't get disemboweled.

After some small talk and other BS that goes along with meeting someone on the phone and trying to gather information, Michelle asked, "When would be a good time for you to come into our office so we can talk?"

I thought for a moment before I spoke and asked myself if I *really* wanted to do this alone. If I *really* thought I could muscle my way through this. If I *really* felt that I would be believed once I walked into court and told my story. If accepting Laura's help was *really* the right thing to do. If I *really* wanted to have that debt on my hands. I then asked myself if I *really* wanted to take the chance of never seeing my daughters again. I didn't have to think much further than that.

What an idiot I had been; putting my pride in front of what was most important. I was about to reach out and grab the hand that was extended to me, as I was hanging over the face of a cliff and losing my grip. It would be the first time in my life I had ever accepted the fact that something was bigger than me and that I needed help.

Hypothetically speaking; what had happened is that Tiffany had stepped between me and the girls and basically said, "You can't see them ever again, because I said you can't. I made up these stories and told everybody who counts and because I'm a great actress and can cry on queue and you're pretty much fucked. Everyone believes me, so why don't you just run along, little man."

That very moment is when I got pissed. FINALLY! I saw what was in front of me. I saw the "forest through the trees." This woman has labeled me a pedophile and expects me to roll over and give up? I don't think so. Not now. I've been something that resembles a decent father, a fairly decent one anyway, up until Tiffany and I had Kathryn and Megan. For the first time in my life I want to be a great Dad and someone is telling me I can't. I can't because I'm a "pedophile"?

It took Laura Verdi, my guardian angel sent from heaven, to tell me I'm an idiot for being so prideful. I should have been humbled by her offer and just accept the same. I saw the light and now I felt I was empowered like I have never felt before. I wanted to be a Daddy to these young girls and someone was telling me that I wasn't good enough to be a Daddy? At that moment, I didn't care how long it took. I believed I could outlast Methuselah if it took that long.

I let out a deep sigh. I expended every molecule of air from my lungs and took another deep breath.

"What did you say your name was?" I asked.

"Michelle Kunzman, I'm with the law firm, Gillespie and Associates."

I had wondered if she thought I had hung up on her. I was silent for a long time while all the above thoughts flashed through my mind.

"You know Michelle, I told Laura not to do this. I told her I could hand. . ."

She cut me off, "I know. Miss Verdi told me you were stubborn and would be angry, but if you ever want to see your kids again, I suggest you accept her help. The story I was told, if it's true, puts you in a pretty bad situation and I can assure you, if you walk into that courtroom alone; if you think you have problems now? You have no idea the problems you're gonna have before you walk out."

She didn't have to convince me further. "Miss Kunzman, I've been thinking long and hard about this and know that I have a problem and I don't think I have much of a choice, but to accept Laura's help. When do you want me to come in?"

"Good. I'm glad we understand each other," she said. "When *can* you come in?"

"Anytime that's good for you," I responded. "Just tell me what time and I'll be there." I probably sounded defeated as I gave in.

"How about 4 o'clock this afternoon?"

"I'll be there." She gave me the address and directions to get to her office and we hung up.

The Gillespie office is tucked away behind some buildings and cleaners, just north of Glendale Avenue, on 16th Street in Phoenix. It's a modest building and inside, just as modest. I checked in with the receptionist and sat down, holding the only thing that stood between me and my girls; the Order of Protection.

After a few moments, I was ushered into a small conference room that looked as if it doubled as an office for someone. My hands were sweaty, so I cupped and blew into them. I wanted to keep them dry before Michelle came in. I didn't want her to shake a clammy hand, although I imagine she has done just that more times than I could imagine, or that she cares to remember.

Sometime later and well past 4 o'clock Michelle walked into the room. She carried with her a yellow legal pad and a pen. She introduced herself and sat down. She was blonde, very attractive with these beautiful, unbelievably kind, blue eyes and she appeared quite young. I was surprised by her youthful looks, though I would find out later that those looks were deceiving; she was actually just five years my junior.

A few months later I would be told that the moment Tiffany saw Michelle Kunzman, she immediately believed I was sleeping with her. Tiffany had a way of believing I was sleeping with every single attractive, blonde I ever came in contact with. Yes, I have a penchant for blondes, but for a few months I had my testicles hooked to a barbed wire fence and the last thing on my mind was banging my legal counsel. Even if she *was/is* my type and she truly is very attractive, I wouldn't be comfortable in a relationship with her. I would be a little worried every day that if, God forbid, the relationship went south. . . I mean, she *is* an attorney and could probably put a pretty big hurting on me, regardless of her petite stature. The only other woman, small in stature, I was ever afraid of was my mother and she frightened me beyond belief.

Later on in this meeting, Michelle would leave to ask DeeAn Gillespie, the namesake of the law firm, to join us. DeeAn was a no-nonsense woman and it was quite apparent when she entered the room. She was a large woman close to my 6'1" height with short-cropped hair and she was all business. Although I'm sure she is a very compassionate woman with deep feelings for her clients, she never showed them. It was either black, or it was white.

Don't get me wrong. She wasn't the type to be unmoved if you had fallen into a pit of pongee sticks and were impaled in several locations. She would certainly help you off of the bamboo spears and out of the pit. Hell, I bet she'd even tell you how bad the injuries look, that it really must hurt, and suggest you get a dressing on the entry and exit wounds.

But she would also inform you that it was damned lucky it happened to you instead of her because if **she** had fallen in the pit and been impaled, you would **really** be fucked, because at that point she couldn't represent you. DeeAn wanted the facts and nothing more and I liked that in her. Michelle had recently come out of "employment law" and "family law" was a new arena for her, so her mentor was DeeAn. I liked that too. As I retold my story, Michelle would take more notes of the things she either missed or tiny little things that I may have left out.

In telling DeeAn my story she had this way of letting you know she was filing away, in the scratch-pad of her brain, everything you said by this little rapid fire, "Yeah. Yeah. Yeah."

"I was approached by a guy who'd just gotten off a motorcycle and asked if I was Eric Di Conti. I said, 'Yeah, can I help you?' and he said 'I'm an officer of the Court and I'm serving you with. . . . .'"

"Yeah-Yeah-Yeah," she would interrupt. She knew the rest of the scenario. It went on like this for an hour, or more. As I told the story, she would inject her "yeah-yeah-yeah." Several times during this meeting, as I was speaking, she would look over to Michelle and call out a statute that the part of my story applied to.

She would say something like, "That falls under 5863," to Michelle who would hurriedly write it down, trying to keep up. She turned back to me to listen.

There were a few times, as I continued, she wouldn't even bother looking over at Michelle; she would just call out numbers, "Forty-one nineteen" and never take her eyes off of me. Michelle would write.

I continued my story.

"That's a 1241. Make sure we file that right away," she would say.

It was like being in the shadows of a war room and listening to military personnel call out coordinates, on a faraway place, for an impending air strike against the enemy. Inside I was laughing to myself, but it was so cool sitting there and listening to her fire off these statutes, if that's what they ever were, as if they were as commonplace as breathing. I was impressed at how efficient she was. Michelle wrote.

One thing was for sure; this woman knew her shit and I was one happy sonofabitch to be sitting there. I was suddenly so grateful to Laura Verdi for her generosity and that she basically told me to shove my pride right up my ass and retained this firm herself, to represent me.

When I was finished with my story, up to the point I walked into their office, I was spent. It was a long story with a lot of facets and moving parts and not one of them made any sense to me. One thing that both Michelle and DeeAn said to me was the one thing I was most afraid of; that, by this accusation, I could quite possibly never see my two daughters again. But they also revealed how they felt about what I was being accused of.

"This is all bullshit and the courts will see it," one of them said. "One thing you can't do in this state is make these accusations and get away with it. She could lose those kids by making an accusation like that . . . if it isn't true."

I was shocked to hear that, but also relieved, "Really?"

"If you want to go that far, we can. It's up to you, but it'll cost you some money."

Money, I didn't have. I just wanted to hold my daughters in my arms and tell them I love them. That's all I wanted and needed right then and I couldn't do a damned thing to quell that need. I let DeeAn and Michelle know what I felt was most important right then, too.

"I do need to advise you, though," DeeAn said. "Don't be stupid. You follow that Order of Protection and stay away from your wife until we can get in front of a judge. If you violate that Order, there is nothing we can do to help you. You'll be in jail and your kids will be gone. Do you understand me?" She was very direct and there wasn't the slightest hint of a smile on her face when she delivered that warning. Quite frankly, she scared the shit of me.

"I have no intention of doing anything stupid. I promise you," I said. "I'm not going to jeopardize anything and especially my chance to see my girls again." I think I was shaking.

DeeAn got up, shook my hand, and disappeared down the hallway.

I looked over at Michelle wide-eyed and said, "Jesus Christ! Is she part fucking pit bull?"

Michelle laughed and told me that DeeAn Gillespie has been around for years and knows most of the judges and attorneys in every court. She told me DeeAn has a reputation as a hard-ass, of sorts, and will fight for those she truly believes have been screwed. That she doesn't just take on clients for the sake of a check and she hires only those with the same ideals. That was relieving to hear since most attorneys are cockroaches with no real sense of pride, ethics, or morals.

The best part of this is that she knew Donna Jewett very well and that if she took on a family law case it was normally one that involved well-to-do Scottsdale residents with a lot of money and normally those divorces were decided outside the confines of a courthouse. I had the impression that Ms. Jewett was not a litigator.

In a few short weeks, I would find that the impression I had of Jewett, through the description of her background, was correct. She would fumble through the hearing like a barefoot blind man, in a dog park where no one cleaned up after their animals.

In a few short weeks, I would be amused at how many times she stepped in a pile of her own, self-produced, excrement; the feces squishing through her toes. And you know, if this has ever happened to you, when you try to get it off, it seems to spread to the furthest reaches of whatever body part it happens to be on. Unless you can get to a water hose, the fight is useless. Let me just say, Donna Jewett would be a mess that day and her inexperience, painfully clear.

NOT THE LOVE OF MY LIFE

Me and Laura Verdi

"WELCOME TO IN-TOWN SUITES"

"There are not many who seek me here....." - Dante

March 6, 2006

The previous day I had finally contacted Ryan Quinn and borrowed enough money to secure a room in a place near the corner of Guadalupe and Country Club Dr. in Mesa, Arizona. It was called In-Town Suites and they were an establishment that took on long-term boarders at *by-the-week* rates. I signed up for a week. There are several of these types of hotels around the valley and I find most were always at capacity.

These types of hotels are in fairly decent neighborhoods and as opposed to their counterparts in the seedier parts of town, which were rented by the hour, seemed out of place. The only reason I can come up with, that would allow for these oddly placed hotels, is a minuscule phenomenon; the housing boom several years prior.

Someone had a brilliant idea to build these hotels to accommodate workers and it took off. Low-cost housing for the workforce would inevitably increase the profit margin for the construction companies doing the work. The majority of the clientele in this place was of construction workers and those who had purchased homes and were waiting for them to be completed, so they could move in, a vast majority of their belongings in storage. Phoenix, Arizona, for the past fifteen-plus years, was among the most transient of all cities in the United States.

I pulled into the parking lot and found a space near the office. I walked in and saw that the gal behind the counter was helping another guest.

She glanced up at me and then back to the form she was filling out, "I'll be right with you," she said to the paper.

"Take your time, I'm in no hurry," I responded.

"That's a first!" She told the paper.

When she was finally done and the guest exited, she looked up at me.

"Welcome to In-Town Suites."

I explained that I would need a room for a while, but wasn't sure how long at that point. I filled out the little registration card she handed me and after looking it over, I signed the rental agreement for the room and paid the weekly fee.

For a little over two hundred bucks, the room would be mine for a week and at the end of that week, I would be required to start the process of renting the same room all over again; back down to the office, stand in line, and sign another rental agreement, pay my two hundred bucks and change, get my pass key reprogrammed, and go back to my room.

A few moments later another, rather plump, girl came out from the back to offer some help to the girl checking me in. It was obvious she had just come in from the outside and had just smoked a cigarette; the stench she brought with her, that of a spent cigarette, was appalling. It was the smell of a heavy smoker that rarely bathed, the stink emanating from her pores. Being in construction I know this smell; I endure it on a daily basis and I can assure you, it is the perfect workout for one's epiglottis.

She smiled at me as she approached the desk and flashed a set of beautiful teeth; about six of them. I could easily see the rotting black stubs of some others that had been eaten away. Probably from a few short years of methamphetamine use, or should I say *abuse*.

She looked to be in her early forties, but I have to guess that she was much younger. She had a wedding ring on and I noticed she had some pretty severe stretch marks across her stomach from one or more pregnancies; her shirt didn't quite cover her entire midsection. I didn't figure she'd bathed that morning as her hair was disheveled as if she'd just crawled out of bed, her clothes undoubtedly the garments she'd slept in.

Looking at her slovenly appearance I thought to myself, "Good Lord, how did this young lady get to this point in her life? What brought her to this very juncture where our lives intersect and we are face-to-face in the lobby of a by-the-week hotel? Where did she come from and what is her story."

I felt a deep sorrow for her at that moment. I'm not sure why, because my own life was about to capsize and, in fact, was listing dangerously to the starboard side. Maybe I just didn't understand the enormity of my predicament and was able to feel for this young lady; wanting to help her for some unknown reason. Or maybe it's just the innate sense of caring for other human beings; a natural instinct we all possess to some degree.

I stopped myself for a moment and processed the absurdity of my caring. I wanted to *help* her and I could barely *help* myself; no home, very little *borrowed* money, very few articles of clothing, no toothbrush or deodorant, no shampoo, no comb, marked as a pedophile and wife beater. I chuckled to myself; "I'm a pillar of excellence aren't I?" Nonetheless, based only on her appearance, I continued to ponder her existence on a purely speculative level.

"Here's this young lady who has a husband (hard to say where *he* is), her children (the number unknown to me) somewhere out there, possibly the ward/s of the state if I'm correct that she is/was a drug addict that had her children removed from her home. She could very well be a victim of spousal abuse, as well. . . ."

My thoughts were interrupted by this young lady. I was looking, not at her, but through her and she probably sensed it. Her smile waned. Maybe from embarrassment of sensing I was assessing her and she felt vulnerable, or maybe it was just time for the niceties to end and time for business.

In her deep southern drawl, she gave me the ground rules, "We open ate levem AM and we close ate sevem PM; there's no-un hee-err ayefter sevem PM. If'n yall gonna need inabody ayefter thayt you gonna hayfta call this hee-err numba own this hee-err card. If'n yall call the numba, yall gonna hayfta wait awall far-im ta get ta ya. The mayne'll be sleepin' but heel get taya soon-nuf. Everthang heer is fer yalls comfert and enjoyment. Glad ta hayv-ya."

I gathered up the papers I had just signed. "Thank you," I said.

She flashed her six teeth at me again and just as quickly as they appeared, her upper lip dropped down while still trying to hold the smile. Her teeth were tucked neatly out of sight and from my view. Thankfully. My last thought was that if someone shaved her head and gave her a banjo, she'd look just like that kid in "Deliverance." Anybody who has seen the movie, "Deliverance" starring Burt Reynolds and Ned Beatty, knows exactly what I'm talking about.

As I exited the office, the first gal behind the desk called out, "Oh! The sheets are changed once a week!"

"Awesome," I thought to myself.

I found my room and slid my electronic pass key into the slot. The green light flickered, letting me know I was granted entry. I swung the door open to a little queen size bed, a small table with two chairs, and what looked to be a pediatric fold-out sofa bed. The kitchen area had a three-burner electric stove and a microwave with two cabinets for whatever. Next to that was a small refrigerator. The bathroom was like any other in a cheap hotel; a toilet and a shower with a tub. There were two tiny bars of soap left at the sink and in the tub. No shampoo or conditioner. A single roll of toilet paper was supplied and would not be replaced. As soon as the door closed behind me, I could use what was supplied by the hotel, but when it was gone, I was on my own. These digs offered exactly what the transient border needs; the barest of essentials. A roof, a bed, something to warm, or cook food on, something to preserve the perishables, a shower, and a toilet. Pure heaven, if you're on the run for whatever reason. The place reeked of anonymity.

"I gotta do some shopping," I said to myself.

As a cathartic measure, each and every night, I would write a letter to my daughters after returning to the hotel from work. For years, each time I have written anything, to anyone, I am reminded of the wisdom and acumen of my old friend Fernando Vargas. My passion has always been for writing, each time I had an urge to fire off a letter, e-mail, fax, or whatever else to allow someone in on my feelings at that moment, Fernando would chastise me for doing so. His "as an attorney I would advise against it" lectures were epic and numerous. Early on, and well before I was diagnosed with ADHD, my written attacks on whomever, would be brutal and unrelenting. If I wanted to tell someone I hoped their family died in a fiery plane crash, I would do just that. If I felt a certain individual should have the unfortunate pleasure of contracting some random malady, I would write a letter telling them I hoped they would contract anal herpes. And always the good friend, I provide a copy to Fernando for his (after-the-fact) review.

His response was usually the same. "Did you *actually* send this, Count? What the fuck is the matter with you? If you write something make sure you don't mind having it public record the next day." I usually just shrugged and looked as dejected as I could.

With the help of Ritalin and growing up a little, his lectures finally got through to me. I began writing with thoughts of "what if" and "will it" scenarios. What if this pisses someone off and, if so, will it come back to haunt me? In this respect, I owe a great deal of thanks to Fernando Vargas.

I would not send my daughters the letters as it would be a violation of the Court Order, but I filed them away on my laptop for the future. I decided I would eventually let them read the letters when they were older and could understand what happened way back in March of 2006. I wrote a letter a day. In them, I explained what I was doing, what I was feeling, what was going on with the lawyers, and how much I loved them and missed them. The letters were the only thing I looked forward to every day and probably the only thing that kept me going. I would eventually write 37 of these letters. After writing the first letter to my daughters I closed my laptop and went to bed.

That first night was a cruel one.

Even though it was in a fairly decent area it was after all a by-the-week hotel that was filled with transients. There were people trampling the concrete walkway outside my door all night long. People banging on doors demanding to be let in. People were yelling that they were going to the little all-night gas station for more beer and would be right back. Yelling to someone not to forget the fucking cigarettes. Others yelling that they needed sixty-three more cents for a forty ouncer and that somebody better come up with it or there would be an ass kicking. Still others, screaming that someone in their respective room had taken their money and they wanted it back. There was the sound of a periodic siren and the echo of a police radio below. It sounded like a mini warzone without the guns. I didn't sleep worth a damn that night.

In the morning I would open the door to a walkway littered with trash and empty beer bottles. The parking lot was strewn with debris, broken bottles, fast food bags, and wrappers. The path to my truck was one of weaving and stepping over everything one could imagine. As I got to my truck I stepped over a discarded condom, thrown from the balcony. Thank God it didn't land *on* my truck. That would be the last time I parked next to the building.

The following nights were the same. Same voices, same demands from those voices, same mess in the morning, but each afternoon I returned from work the parking lot had returned to the pristine condition I had seen it in when I pulled into the parking lot for the very first time. Good cleaning crew.

Except for the mistaken or transposed unit number in the head of a prostitute I didn't associate with many people other than the basic "hello" as we passed each other.

The two times that someone did bang on my door I opened it to a skanky-looking street urchin who wanted to "party." I assured her that I was not the guy who called for her services and sent her on her way. She would walk away confused and trying to remember the unit number she was supposed to call on.

I couldn't wait to get out of there.

"ARE YOU READY?"

"Stay out of courtrooms, but if you must go in, be well armed and don't compromise" – Hunter S. Thompson

March 27, 2006

IN RE THE MATTER OF
TIFFANY NELSON AND ERICCO DI CONTI
CASE #FC 2006-050978
ORDER OF PROTECTION HEARING
COMMISSIONER SUSAN BRNOVICH PRESIDING

I met both Michelle Kunzman and DeeAn Gillespie at their office that afternoon to discuss what would happen at the hearing. Michelle was calm and spoke softly, giving me the reassuring smile that everything would be alright. DeeAn came in as confident as anyone would be if they were taking a gun to a knife fight. She knew what the outcome of this hearing would be and in looking back she had her whole script memorized. They gave me the usual "stay calm," "don't get excited," "don't get angry and lose your temper on the stand," etc., speech. It was the usual bullshit one would be told who isn't a regular visitor to a witness stand and I can assure you, I am not. I absorbed and heeded every word.

DeeAn and Michelle rode together in DeeAn's car and I followed in my truck. My stomach was in knots and I felt as if I was going to throw up. But for the brief time, I saw Tiffany get some of my belongings that she'd strewn into the garage (clothes, personal items, etc.), under the watchful eye of a Pinal County Sheriff Deputy. This would be the first time I would see her in nearly a month. We pulled into the parking lot at the McDowell Mountain Justice Court-Northeast Division and stopped.

As we walked toward the main entry DeAnn asked, "Are you ready?"

"I don't have any choice; I have to be ready."

Michelle put her hand on my shoulder, "You'll do fine."

As we walked in and went through the metal detectors I felt sicker and sicker. Nauseated beyond words. We walked through the large lobby. My head was down as we walked and made a left and headed down the long hallway leading to the courtroom the hearing was to be held. I looked up for a moment and saw Tiffany sitting with her attorney, Jewett, and with them, the whole Nelson clan. Watching us as we walked, the whole group sitting straight-backed in their pseudo-aristocracy, was Tiffany's special needs mother, Susan and her red-faced stepfather, Greg, who was sporting raised spider-veins on his nose and cheeks and who has the look of a very hard drinker. Tiffany's brother, Tim, and sister Whitney were seated next to them. Other than my attorneys I was alone but for a single acquaintance I worked with; Joel Halfhill. He was there as a character witness for me.

Tiffany had an evil look on her face that, as I got closer, seemed to meld into a gargoyle-like form with increasing hideousness; her eyes grew beadier through the slits she was peering. All this, of course, would stand to reason since I now believed she was Satan's spawn. As we continued down the hall, we passed by the glares of the rest of the clan, mimicking the feelings of their "poor abused family member who had fallen victim to a monster." The whole pathetic group made me sick just looking at them.

As I passed by I found myself feeling, not nauseated any longer, but stronger; invigorated by their demeanor. I decided at that very moment they were nothing more than cockroaches that needed to be exterminated in the courtroom. My walk now had meaning to it. My daughters were at stake here; not my pride. That would come later, but first, I had to beat back the six miserable piles of dog shit standing between me and my two young daughters. Passing by those people was like a rite of passage from that fantasy world I lived in, thinking my marriage could be salvaged by picking up and moving to Arizona, to the real world and the epiphany that everything in the past year and a half had been carefully planned and executed with extreme precision. I would learn later the planning started far earlier than I had thought.

I was on the verge of being completely fucked by my estranged wife and the judicial system that is supposed to weed out the lies and protect law-abiding citizens. If I laid down I would be doing exactly what Tiffany wanted me to do. That wasn't going to happen. She started a small fire and it was about to become a forest fire that she couldn't control.

A few months later I would find out her "plan" which I thought began only a year and a half before, was actually hatched several *years* prior, but I was too blinded by "the love of my life" and I think she knew it. That's probably why it was so easy for her.

We sat in the hallway just down from the Nelson clan and discussed further what DeeAn's plan of attack was. A while later the door swung open into the hallway and from inside the bailiff stepped out and called us in. The Nelson clan entered first and took their seats; Tiffany and Jewett were at the table to the right of the bench. DeeAn, Michelle, and I followed and were seated to the left; the "defendant's table," as it were.

I remember looking at Donna Jewett and thinking how odd her appearance was. She was dressed in a top made out of T-shirt material with some kind of stain on the front of it; I thought maybe it could be coffee. Her ensemble also included a pair of white Capri s and sandals. Her toenails were filthy and hair was unkempt. She hardly looked as if she belonged in a courtroom, let alone representing clients. In fact, she would have been better suited strolling down Van Buren Avenue, pushing a discarded shopping cart.

The other very odd thing about her appearance was that she wore, what looked to be, very thick glasses and they made her eyes seem small and squinty. She had the facial appearance of a person afflicted with mild Down Syndrome. Later, I would get another look at her; a much closer look. After the hearing, we would be face to face in the hallway outside the courtroom. That close-up would reaffirm my opinion that she *looked* like she could indeed, be afflicted.

The time when one is waiting for the judge, or in this case, the Commissioner, to enter there is a sense of uneasiness and discomfort. The feeling of the unknown washes over you and once again that ice ball remerges in the pit of your stomach. I ignored it. I had a job to do and that would just complicate things if I looked nervous and even though I had done nothing wrong I certainly did not want to appear untruthful to the Commissioner. I sat calmly and waited.

NOTE: *The following is the actual excerpt from the Order of Protection hearing and can be verified through public records in Maricopa County, Arizona. A "Digital Copy of Proceedings" of the same can be purchased from the courts for about $20 and although I am **NOT** advertising for the court, I want it to be known that the following **is** verifiable. It pains me to know that the courts actually make money on things like this, but conversely it calms me to know that for a mere twenty bucks the following information can be had......and my story validated;*

Superior Court of Arizona
Maricopa County
Case # FC2006-050978
Nelson v. Di Conti
March 27, 2006
Commissioner Susan Brnovich

At 2:43PM Commissioner Susan Brnovich entered the courtroom. We all stood and waited for her to excuse us to be seated, which she did before we were fully upright. We all sat back down

She looked to be in her early forties, blonde and somewhat attractive. She apologized for bringing a cup of tea with her as she said she was suffering from a sore throat and maybe sipping from it during the proceeding.

She addressed us and advised that the hearing was recorded both by audio and video and after we were all sworn in the hearing began.

Commissioner Brnovich looked to Donna Jewett, "Call your first witness."

TIFFANY NELSON

> *"Common in most narcissists, and those who thrive on hysteria, runs a strain of stupidity in which they entirely misjudge the odium that their performance generated." – Unknown*

Jewett fumbled over some papers as if she had lost something. "We call Tiffany Nelson."

Tiffany approached the stand as stoic as ever. Every step she took seemed as if it were choreographed. As if she had previously studied the floor for future placement of her feet when she was called to the stand. There is a very explicit reason for everything she does and everything she does is normally part of a well-thought-out plan that is beneficial to her or her family.

I'm sure she wanted her gait to be perfect when she moved and the only way to do this was to visualize every step before she made it. She wanted the commissioner to see this very determined woman, plowing toward the stand, was there for all women who are "victims of abuse" and her testimony was to be the benchmark. As she always did when she wanted to appear sophisticated, Tiffany wore her "uniform": a pair of black pants, loafers, white T-shirt, and a pale yellow cardigan sweater (her favorite); her hair was pulled back so as not to conceal her external beauty. She made sure her look was sullen; it had to be for this act. I noticed immediately she carried with her a small handful of tissue.

I leaned over to Michelle, "She'll be crying soon. Just wait."

NOT THE LOVE OF MY LIFE

Jewett began her questioning by asking Tiffany to recount all of the events she put into the Order of Protection. Tiffany did as she was asked and as painful as it was to listen to her actually say these words out loud, in my heart I was hoping she would say it was all a mistake and that she wanted to retract the Order of Protection. I just could not imagine that she would follow through with such a vicious and vile story, knowing, full well, that it was a horrific lie.

Tiffany sat there and repeated, almost verbatim, what was written in the Complaint. I was even more devastated when the verbalization made it a reality. This really *was* happening and it was happening to me! As she spoke I became angrier at what she had become. I was angry because I never saw it coming, but worse still was the fact that I didn't know why.

"Un-fucking-believable!" I said to myself.

Jewett then asked about the contents of our computer and was told by Tiffany that she hired an expert to do a forensic analysis on it to retrieve data.

"There is a beheading. There are horrible, horrible images that he has put on there," Tiffany said, referring to me.

Jewett continued, "And have you seen another video that is disturbing to you?"

There was a pause and then Jewett asked, "Uh, Your Honor, may I have a word with my client?"

Commissioner Brnovich allowed Jewett a visit with Tiffany and explained to Jewett how to turn off the microphone where Tiffany sat. They whispered for a few moments and then turned the microphone back on.

Jewett repeated the question and in her mock sophistication, Tiffany replied, "Girls of questionable age."

Smugly Tiffany added, "I had a forensics expert pull the hard drive and read it." She wanted to spar with DeeAn. She was arrogant enough to think she could bullshit her way through DeeAn's questioning, but lucky for her, Jewett wasn't smarter than the way she dressed.

"And what did the expert find on the hard drive?" Jewett asked.

DeeAn was surprised. She leaned over and whispered, "Do you have pornography on your computer?"

"Yeah," I answered in a tone that would suggest it was a very stupid question. She realized that it may have been a dumb question and should have been asked in a different manner. I think I may have chuckled a bit, as well.

She pressed, "Child pornography?"

"Jesus Christ! Hell no! What the hell are you thinking, DeeAn?"

"OK," she was satisfied. But for the initial shock and immediate inquiry, I think she realized that children weren't my style, though she was thrown for a split second.

Jewett asked Tiffany, "Have you seen on your children, in the past year, marks or injuries as a result of the behavior that you've described to the court?"

Tiffany's answer was that she had seen rubs and rashes on their legs and groin area. Jewett wanted her to describe each child individually and Tiffany started with Katie saying that she "has had a very chaffed, raw vaginal area while we were in California," and out here Tiffany explained that Megan, "says all the time that it hurts to get into the bath and that her thighs are sore, up where her legs met her groin area. They are just red and raw."

Jewett then asked a question that didn't make much sense to me, "Okay, uh, are those the result of the grabbing you've seen, or something separate?"

Huh? "The result of grabbing?" I wondered what the hell that meant. I mean, I was being accused of grabbing the girls by their arms, and in perusing the geography of one's body, coupled with my limited mathematical capabilities, I would venture to guess they were about two feet off the target; maybe eighteen inches on a child. With Tiffany's answer, the "light" went on.

"They have to be something separate."

Sonofabitch! That was a dagger right in my heart and I felt like I wanted to vomit right there. My stomach was back in knots and I felt the blood drain from my face. I was cold all of a sudden and afraid that Tiffany would continue to tell these vicious lies on the stand, but that line of questioning ended as quickly as it had started.

Once again, I think Jewett realized if she continued down this line of questioning she would invariably back herself into a corner and expose herself to some more serious legal issues she was not equipped to handle. I saw it immediately; she wanted off the subject of molestation, but not before inferring, on record, there "may be" an issue.

Jewett stammered for a moment and then said, "We talked about the grabbing. Have you seen any bruises, rashes, rubs, or anything like that on your children as a result of grabbing their arms or legs?"

"Their arms have been red from him grabbing."

"When was the last time that you saw your children's . . . name the child and give me the approximate time . . ."

Tiffany cut her off, "Katie over the medication incident, her arm was red from being grabbed and Megan, there was a, uh, redness to her when he put her over, and of course, mine too! He's a strong man!" She continued, "We've all had marks on us from him grabbing us and moving us away."

"And are those from the incidents that you've described?"

"Yes, Ma'am."

Wow! She decided to throw herself into the pit of victims of abuse. This woman knows no boundaries and probably thought to herself, "what the hell, I'm doing pretty good up here, I'll say he banged me up too!" She knew I had NEVER laid a hand on her, but she said I did anyway. What a miserable human being she was to sit up there and say these things, I thought, but I was also surprised that the subject of molestation ended so abruptly and moved to the physical abuse of the children . . . and her.

I can only surmise that Jewett's visit to the stand to speak with Tiffany was to tell her that if they started down that road of molestation she had better be damned certain that she can ***prove*** what she is alleging because if she failed to do so she would experience a misery she has never before known.

While Jewett and Tiffany were conferring with the microphone turned off, DeeAn whispered to me that it would be very unwise for Jewett to entertain a line of questioning that went down the road of molestation. She said that Commissioner Brnovich would be less than accommodating to any objections that Jewett made on cross-examination if she decided to broach that subject or travel too far into it. Jewett knew she would be given very little latitude by the commissioner and could very well open up a can of worms she couldn't close, once DeeAn started her cross-examination. The funny thing is that Tiffany almost drew Jewett into it, but the odd-looking counselor caught herself before stepping into that pit of fire.

Tiffany continued on about how I would push her around and push the girls to the ground, get angry and become physical with her and the girls, sometimes leaving bruises. She testified that each of them was terrified of my mood swings and that she never knew when I would explode into a rage.

Of course, the story turned very sad, and her fear was so immense that she was lost. Her voice quivered, and she wadded up her face as if she was crying, but no tears were visible. The harder she tried, the drier her face stayed. Her performance was pathetic, but eventually, the tears did begin to flow. She actually had a look of relief on her face, probably because she had succeeded in causing the tears to appear.

"What a good actress," I thought.

"Nothing further," Jewett said as she slithered back to taking notes. She wasn't looking like she felt very good. My guess was that her confidence level had dropped.

DeeAn jotted down a few things and then without looking up from her pad of paper she asked her first question. I believe it was DeeAn's way of letting Tiffany know that she wasn't going to give Tiffany the common courtesy of making eye contact because she had no respect for her. It was a brilliant move if that's what she was attempting to show because I know it bothered the hell out of Tiffany.

"Ms. Nelson, you filled out an Order of Protection on March 2nd, is that correct?"

Tiffany was now whispering, "Yes, I did."

"On March 2nd, you didn't put anything about pornography, did you? Yes, or no?"

"No," she said. "At the suggestion of my attorney."

DeeAn was surprised. "Your attorney suggested that you not put the pornography in there?"

"Nothing was confirmed yet."

"But have you seen it with your own eyes?"

"Yes, I had." Tiffany just contradicted herself. She testified to seeing pornography on the computer. Now she said nothing had been confirmed, but she has seen it with her own eyes, which doesn't make a lot of sense.

DeeAn went on to point out that when Tiffany filled out this Order, she didn't allege that I had been physical with her, but she is now alleging this in court.

Tiffany's only response was to whisper, "Perhaps it was omitted mistakenly."

Tiffany has a habit of whispering when she becomes very angry, or when she wants to make a precise point. I can read this part of her personality like a book and know every word she uses in her catalog of "buzz words."

"Have you ever called CPS at any time?"

"No."

"Have you ever called the police, at any time, on your husband?"

"No."

"Have you ever reported these alleged 'red marks' on your children, at any time, before filing the Order of Protection?"

"Yes. My family is very well aware of them," Tiffany said smugly.

"Well, anybody other than your family? Have you ever made any allegation to an independent third party?"

Barely audible Tiffany said, "Yes. My friends."

"None of them are here today, are they?" DeeAn asked.

"No," she said. "I didn't think it was necessary at the time," still whispering but visibly annoyed that she had been expertly backed into a corner. Fittingly, it would be the same corner her mother would soon be in.

DeeAn continued her questioning on various things that were so boring I'm not going to bore you with it. It was nothing more than a dog and pony show.

"Nothing further."

When DeeAn Gillespie was finished with her questioning, Jewett jumped back in. Since it didn't seem like they were getting anywhere with the stories they brought to court that day, she apparently wanted to take another route which was to say I was neglecting my children. She asked Tiffany to tell the court about the time that she had taken Katie (the older of our two girls) to a "doctor" for therapy and how I had "refused to allow Katie treatment."

The fact of the matter is, as it turned out, the person Tiffany was taking Katie to see was not even a doctor as she had said that she was. It turned out this "doctor" was a "life coach." This is a joke of all jokes when it comes to counseling individuals. They are the least qualified of all professionals, but many claims to be miracle workers, as this particular woman did. I put a stop to that immediately. What further bolstered my decision was the fact that this woman kept having heart attacks and had to cancel several meetings; one of these heart episodes occurred after I had made a special trip and flown in for this meeting. No one called to tell anyone that this woman was in the hospital.

She was a joke and I let Tiffany know it, but oddly enough she continued to refer to this woman as a "doctor" throughout her testimony, and in response to Jewett's questioning. I wasn't impressed and I don't think anyone else was either.

Jewett concluded her re-direct at which point Commissioner Brnovich asked DeeAn if she had anything further. DeeAn respectfully looked at Commissioner Brnovich and advised her she had nothing further.

"You may step down," she instructed Tiffany.

SUSAN NELSON-STEPHANSON

"Learning is a gift, even if pain is your teacher."
– Unknown

Susan Nelson-Stephanson came up and seated herself on the stand. She strolled toward the bench, stepped up onto the platform of the stand, and sat down; her back so rigid and straight it looked as if she had a brace of some sort under her sweater. Jewett began her direct examination by asking pointed questions about what she had witnessed me do that could be, in her opinion, considered "violent behavior."

Susan explained that I have a very loud and booming voice, which I do. She said that I use my voice as a tool of intimidation. She said I use it to scare people and get their attention. Okay, yeah, sometimes I do use it to get one's attention, like, say, when my girls are running through a parking lot. A big booming voice is really helpful in these instances. Then Susan said that I make myself "big."

"He puffs himself up and makes himself big," Susan said.

I leaned over to Michelle and whispered, "Does she mean like a peacock?"

Michelle chuckled aloud which drew a glance from Commissioner Brnovich.

Then Susan told a story that one day I had become angry with Katie because she had interrupted me. Her testimony was that I grabbed her under her armpit and yanked away the small child so violently her arm almost came out of the socket. Her voice quivered for a moment as if she were trying to show the Court how upset she was

"Katie's little feet barely touched the ground as he yanked her and dragged her to her room," she stopped and swallowed hard.

"What do you mean?" Jewett asked her to clarify.

Susan gave Court a visual of what Katie looked like being whisked away by holding the palm of one hand up and open. With the other hand she, ever so lightly, brushed the fingertips across her open palm.

"Like this," Susan said as she dropped her head so as not to have to look at what her hands were doing. As if the mere movement of her fingers brushing against the open palm of her hand was so disturbing it brought back too grisly a memory to look at.

"Jesus Christ," I thought. "What a pile of bat guano this dirt-bag is dishing out." I leaned over to Michelle and told her it was complete bullshit. She had taken two stories and made them one. Taken things that were said over the course of a two-week period and did a word search in her head to make some pretty interesting dialog.

Never in my life have I been that violent toward a child. Have I taken my daughter/s by the arm and escorted them to their room? Of course; when they don't go after I've asked them to go there twice and told them two more times after that. Sometimes kids need to be ushered to where they're going, but I have never dragged a child as Susan described the manner in which Katie went to her room.

"No more questions, Your Honor," Jewett belched out and smirked like she had just sealed the fate of a scorpion crawling across her kitchen floor; its death imminent.

Commissioner Brnovich turned to us and said, "Counselor, your witness."

DeeAn Gillespie never got out of her seat. She didn't need to. "Mrs. Nelson? Mrs. Stephan . . .?"

"Stephanson," Susan interrupted.

DeeAn smiled and said, "Stephanson, then." She realized that Susan had little, or no, respect for her at that moment, and that was just fine with DeeAn.

Susan was fearless and wanted DeeAn to know it. In all the years that I had known the Nelson's, Susan was one that felt far superior to anyone she ever came in contact with. She was of better pedigree, had better social graces, had better friends, had better clothes, shopped in better places, and when it came down to it, she was in better financial shape. If you don't believe any of the above, you can find her and ask her yourself; she'll make you aware of where you stand in the food chain. It'll be subtle, but eventually, you'll find out. She obviously passed on these traits to her daughters, one of whom I eventually married.

That smile from DeeAn would be the only bit of nicety emerging from her during the hearing. But then the smile was deceiving. DeeAn's smile seemed like she was saying, "Okay, ya wanna play? Let's play."

"Mrs. Stephanson," DeeAn started. "You indicate that Katie's father had asked her a number of times for her not to interrupt?"

"Not asked her, *told* her. To 'be quiet, ' 'Shut up,'" Susan said.

"And she continued to interrupt, is that correct?"

"Yeah."

"And you disapproved of the discipline her father implemented."

Susan waited for a moment and then for effect attempted to drive it home when she said, "I was **appalled**."

"And that was in 2004 sometime?"

Susan then stammered and said she didn't remember, but she finally came up with, "Katie had to be about five or six at that time; in order to be cooking in an oven."

"And Katie is eight now?" DeeAn asked.

"Uh, seven."

"That was in California before your daughter moved here in August of '04, is that correct?"

"In California, yes."

"And you live in California, is that correct?"

"I *lived* in California. Correct."

DeeAn then asked, "Now that's the incident that stands out most in your mind, is that correct?"

"That's correct."

"And you indicated that you had seen Katie's father do this a lot of times, correct?"

"Yes."

"How many times in the last year can you *specifically* recall Katie's father picking her up by the arm? How many times?"

Susan interrupted, "This is the normal discipline . . ."

DeeAn shot back, "Ma'am, please listen to my question. How many *times in the last year have you personally* observed Katie's father pick her up by the arm?"

"I can't give you a number," Susan responded.

"Any?"

Susan, still trying to make a point, said, "It's the normal discipline he administers."

"Ma'am?" DeeAn knew she had Susan in a corner, "please describe an incident, within the last year, where you have seen this occur. Please describe the details."

DeeAn was now leaning forward over the table, her hands clasped with her palms to the tabletop. She was on a roll. "Where were you? Where was Katie? And I **will** remind you, you **are** under oath." DeeAn smirked ever so slightly, and I have to believe that Susan saw it, as well.

Susan's whole expression changed in that instant. It was at that very moment, Susan knew she was hosed.

She glared back at that big beautiful woman to my right and defiantly snapped, "I understand," Susan then paused for a moment and continued. She was shaking.

"I can't give you a specific number of times that I've witnessed this."

DeeAn countered, "Ma'am, I'm not asking for the specific number, I'm asking for the details surrounding an incident. Certainly, if it's a profound incident, you would remember some details."

Susan just sat there and continued to glare at DeeAn and then realized she had better say something, "When you see this behavior repeatedly, profound is not the word."

"Ma'am, can you give me . . ." DeeAn stopped. "You are Tiffany's mother, correct?"

"Yeah."

"Can you give me the details of **one** incident that you claim you've seen in the year of Katie's father picking her up by the arm?"

Susan was beaten, "No."

DeeAn continued, "Can you give me the details of **one** incident within the last year where you claim Katie's father has said things like, 'we're going to put you out with the garbage'?"

"Uh, that particular phrase, no."

"Can you give me the details of **one** incident within the last year where you have heard Katie's father say other things to her that you claim are abusive?"

"Let me think." Susan was desperately trying to save herself from becoming what she already was; a completely worthless witness. She sat there for a full fourteen seconds (yes, fourteen seconds-it's on the video) staring at nothing, trying to conjure up a rationale statement that would sound believable, but she knew she had long since soiled herself and there was no way to wipe it away.

Finally, she spoke, "Could you repeat the question?"

"Yes. Can you give me the details surrounding one incident in the last year where you claim you've seen Katie's father be verbally abusive to her?"

Another twelve seconds passed (this is true, I swear) without a word from Susan before she spoke. "I would describe the incident as a man towering over a girl. . ."

"I'm not asking for your impression, I'm asking for the specific incident. Where were you? Where was Katie? Where was her father? What was going on?"

"I cannot give you specific incidents," she said. "It was repetitive behavior."

DeeAn asked again why she couldn't remember and Susan cut her off, repeating that it was repetitive behavior. She wouldn't let that one go; she was hanging over the side of a cliff and she thought she had seen something that resembled a branch. She grabbed onto it to break her slide, so she didn't fall off the side of the cliff.

"I cannot give specific incidents. It was repetitive behavior. I cannot give you a date, a time, a scene." Susan tried to drive home what she believed to be her trump card and emphasized, "It was *repetitive* behavior."

DeeAn let her speak. It was obvious that Susan was not going to answer the questions as they were asked and I realized at that point DeeAn had given her just enough rope to hang herself. For the past several minutes DeeAn had been trying to get Susan to describe to the court a specific incident and she could not. All she could do is indicate that I am a big man and my favorite hobby was the intimidation of children.

There was a two-second pause in DeeAn's cantor and in those two seconds, I finally got it! I was on the same page. DeeAn was the teacher and Susan, the student. I leaned back in my chair and glanced over at Jewett. She had a very desperate look on her face. A look I imagine a mother would have if they were watching their small child walk out into the street and into the path of an oncoming car, traveling at about the speed of sound. Not much you can do at that point except to hope the death is instantaneous. Susan had just been set up and I was now smirking.

During this pause, Susan just sat there looking through DeeAn with a glazed stare. The back brace I imagined she was wearing early on had melted away and Susan was now hunched over in her chair, melding into the still-life setting of the stand on which she sat. Her body, arms, and face drooping as if she was becoming a part of a surrealistic canvas created by Salvatore Dali.

She looked beaten, a sense of hopelessness that you may see on the face of an animal with one of its legs caught in a trap, after a long night alone in the wilderness. The final sense of fear and hopelessness come after a series of transitions in time which starts with surprise and, initially, a great deal of pain. The tenacity of the animal is tested in the first few hours and when it realizes fighting the trap is no use and the pain too great, the animal will rest. With a primitive little mind, it will try to rationalize its predicament, lick its wounded leg and sit for a while. After a time, it will begin to tug its leg to see if it really is stuck and hope it's just a dream, only to find the situation it is in, is very real.

Maybe this animal was out in the late afternoon foraging for food for its young when it stepped into the trap and now the sun is setting. Maybe this animal is rarely out at night and must be back in its burrow and a new sense of panic sets in. Maybe it will be eaten by another animal above it in the food chain and another sense of fear sets in. Or maybe the fear is that it cannot protect its hungry young who are waiting for its return.

The animal knows it must get free and its fight to get out of the trap is renewed, but very quickly the animal becomes reminded of the excruciating pain that is associated with this *thing*, this *"messenger"* that has interrupted its life. The fight stops as quickly as it started. The sun goes down and darkness envelopes everything around the animal; it is alone, tired, maybe hungry and thirsty. It lays its head across its front legs and tries to sleep, maybe it whimpers a bit. It sits there all night with no hope of getting free. The animal has given up.

As the sun rises in the morning the animal cannot feel its leg any longer. The blood supply has long before been cut off and everything below the teeth of the trap is useless bone and flesh, but the area just above the teeth of the trap is vibrant and alive with nerve endings sending impulses to its brain; synapse firing away, reminding it of its unbearably painful existence. By now, with every little movement, the pain is magnified. The animal is spent. Suddenly, it hears the rustle of nearby brush being disturbed or leaves being trampled, and it may raise its head out of curiosity, but the animal knows there is no hope. The sound gets closer and then, from behind a tree, a figure never before seen by this animal appears. Another *"messenger"* has entered the animal's life.

The figure is walking upright and carries with it a long thin object. The hunter stops short of where the trap is, squats down on his haunches, and looks at his quarry. The animal now realizes that the trap belongs to the hunter and feels the urge to fight but cannot do more than instinctively growl and bare its teeth at this intruder, but knows in its heart the growl is useless. The hunter stands and raises the long thin object; one end tucked into his shoulder. All the animal sees now is the round end of the object; it has a hole in it. The animal knows all is lost and closes its eyes just before a bullet tears through its brain and ends its life.

DeeAn finally looked up from her deep thought and note-taking and stared at Susan for a few seconds. She spoke very softly at first.

"Miss Jewett asked you about the last time you believe you saw what you considered to be violent and abusive." She briefly looked down at the notes she had been taking and after another slight pause DeeAn continued, the volume of her voice had increased slightly and she was now looking directly at Susan. "Please describe the details of the last incident you were *testifying* to, in response to Miss Jewett's *question* that you say *happened* at the latter part of '05!"

Susan then meekly told of a birthday party at a place called Bounce U in Gilbert. She testified that the birthday party was for Katie. When DeeAn asked what it was that I did, which Susan found to be objectionable, Susan conceded that she could not give her any specifics, nor could she remember what words I used. DeeAn asked her if she called the authorities, or called the police.

Her response to the question was that she did not, but then as DeeAn was asking if she had intervened Susan interrupted and asked, "Can you call the authorities for verbal abuse?"

DeeAn smiled and Susan confirmed again that she could not remember what the specifics of the verbal abuse were and again stated she could not remember the words.

DeeAn was done with her.

Susan was that trapped "animal," the stand on which she sat and could not leave, was the "trap." The "time" she spent on it was like spending a night in the wilderness, frightened and thirsty. The "young" she was trying to protect, and could not, was Tiffany. The myriad of transitional "emotions" Susan felt up there came from each and every question that the "hunter," in DeeAn fired at her, each one more painful than the one before. In the end, there truly was a final sense of hopelessness that had washed over Susan as she sat there, unable to answer the hunter's questions. But the "bullet" was yet to come.

DeeAn ended her verbal beating of Susan Stephanson and lowered her voice to a point that was just audible to the Court and everyone in it; just above a whisper. Her final comment was the "bullet" putting an end to Susan's life on the stand.

DeeAn had her head cocked ever so slightly and the grin she flashed earlier had returned. The recipient of that condescending smirk was Susan Stephanson. DeeAn looked at Commissioner Brnovich, then to Jewett and said, "I have no further questions."

Jewett had another question. She asked Susan if I frightened the children when I yelled and Susan's response was only when I grabbed them. Jewett was done, as well.

Commissioner Brnovich spoke. "Alright, you may step down."

All I could do was stare at DeeAn Gillespie. Watching what she did to Tiffany's mother, Susan Stephanson, is what I would compare to watching a Mako shark in a pond of small children.

The forty, or fifty, feet Susan had to walk to get back to her seat must have been one hellava long one.

Looking at it from a very humorous angle, the ever "brilliant" (as she likes to think of herself), ex-paralegal, Susan Stephanson was teased with a lure, dangled in front of her. A little voice in Susan's malfunctioning brain said, "DeeAn is your friend. You can trust her. She is on your side. She believes Eric is a monster, too."

Susan nibbled on that lure and as she did, she regurgitated a story she had rehearsed over and over. After all, DeeAn was her *friend*. As DeeAn asked the questions, Susan would nibble. It wasn't until Susan decided to grab that lure with the whole set of her capped teeth and bit down, that she realized DeeAn had just yanked the pole back toward her and set the hook. She had asked a question Susan couldn't answer; "When did all this happen?"

Oo ops! Only then did she make a very painful discovery. She must have been saying to herself, "Damn! That feels kinda pointy. Does the hook embedded in, and protruding from, my cheek make me look stupid?"

DeeAn Gillespie used an old trick of making the witness feel intelligent; their self-worth increased by their "knowledge" of facts and events. And by this knowledge, their testimony seemed damning to the defendant, only to be led right into the path of that oncoming car. By the time they realize what has happened, it's too late. Susan Stephanson had just gotten her ass handed to her and I was chuckling inside. I wanted to lay a big old fat kiss on DeeAn, but figured I'd be tossed out of court.

Next up was Tiffany's sister. I won't even go into the details of this one, because she didn't remember anything about anything. Her testimony was about as worthless as leaving a voicemail for a deaf man.

Commissioner Brnovich asked Jewett, "Does the plaintiff have any other witnesses?"

Jewett spoke up, "No, your honor."

"Ms. Gillespie?"

"Yes, Your Honor, I'd like to call Eric Di Conti to the stand."

ERIC DI CONTI

"A secure home does not have bars and locks and alarms everywhere, yet a burglar cannot get in." – From the book Tao of Leadership by John Heider

As I stood up I thought to myself, "Here we go."

I walked to the stand and as I stepped up to the swivel chair behind the short podium, Commissioner Brnovich informed me I was still under oath. I acknowledged that fact, cleared my throat, and sat down. I felt myself start to shake, but realized it was psychosomatic when I looked down at my hands, spread my fingers apart, and held them away from me; they looked as if they were a part of a statue. Not even the slightest movement could be detected. Conversely, my mouth felt like I had shoved half a sleeve of saltine crackers into it and attempted to swallow them with no water. My tongue was sticking to the roof of my mouth and as I spoke, it seemed my tongue had doubled in size. It felt massive in my mouth. I rationalized to myself that this is what happens when the sympathetic receptors in the brain tell the body to send its fluids elsewhere.

The control center in the brain says to the body, "Body, I need 150cc of saline in the small intestine. Titrate to effect then let it trickle into the large intestine and finally to the lower colon. This guy's gonna be one constipated sonofabitch when he gets off the stand. I can't have his bowels inflamed to the point we're overworking ourselves later on. Let's go! On the double!"

I'm sitting up there sounding like I'm in the throes of a mental breakdown and have regressed back to the age of three. My mouth was undoubtedly screaming back to my brain, "Like I don't need to swallow? I need to talk up here and can't do that if you don't give up a little moisture! You wanna see it bound up? Just wait 'til the judge hears him speak; an x-ray will show rocks in there! We don't need to sound like we have a severe speech impediment, do we? Now give it up!"

I looked down and noticed there was a small pitcher of water and a glass sitting in front of me. I filled the glass and gulped it down. I was ready.

DeeAn asked me to recount an incident in which Tiffany tried to say I had shoved medicine down Katie's throat. It was a bullshit story and because it was so ridiculous, it bothered me just having to discuss it. It was so petty and the accusation was so off-the-wall, I couldn't believe the Court didn't see right through the bullshit Tiffany was flinging. They obviously didn't and it became a part of the Order of Protection. I got through my side of the story, but not before I was asked if I had ever "grabbed" my wife. I responded quite strongly that I had never grabbed my children, as I was accused of doing, I had never grabbed my wife, as I was accused of doing, nor had I ever raised my hand to my wife, and in fact, I told the court quite adamantly, "I have never raised my hand to a woman in my life." And anyone who has known me in the past, or knows me now, knows this to be the absolute truth. Tiffany knew this as well.

I was asked about the prospect of my computer containing a beheading and pornography, to which I responded positively to both. The beheading was that of one of the first guys in the Middle East who was kidnapped and then with the camera rolling, was beheaded with a large knife. Yeah, I know! It's a sick-ass thing to keep on a computer, but I was quite amazed at the callousness of these pricks that would do something like that to another human being. I didn't watch it more than twice but saved it for some reason. Whatever. Tiffany of course knew it was there because I showed her the beginning, but she thought better of watching the thing through and left the room. She was smart because it was pretty horrific. She claimed that I was obsessed with the video, which wasn't even remotely close to the truth.

She also tried to use the video to show the court I had some serious mental issues. Maybe I do, but if I had to choose who had more severe mental issues, my money would be on the sick fucks, would hack the guy's melon off of his shoulders, and then Al Jezeera TV for airing it. And *I'm* sick? Some people have their priorities jacked up.

With regard to the pornography, again, I conceded that there was and is, in fact, pornography on my computers. Child pornography? Not a chance in hell. Now enjoying shit like *that* is a sickness beyond comprehension. Those people should have a bullet put into their heads and I would love to be the one to pull the trigger.

Just the thought of knowing that by pulling a trigger and allowing a lead projectile to come screaming out of the barrel of a gun, and in doing so, I had caused a great deal of gray matter to be scrambled in someone's head and ending their life, is a soothing thought. These people do not deserve to live for any reason. Those who knowingly accuse another of the unconscionable act of abusing a child, especially in a sexual manner, are the life forms just above pedophiles themselves.

Tiffany had used my past history of abuse and used that very private information to bolster her claims of abuse against my two daughters. That, in and of itself, is an unconscionable act. My wife accused me of molesting my two beautiful little girls and expected me to cave in and run away. What she didn't expect was that I would fight. For the most part, I'm pretty easy-going and can take just about anything. If someone hurts a child of mine, I will hunt them down and kill them. If someone does what Tiffany did, then that *someone* has one hell of a fight on their hands. I had come to the courthouse that day because I wanted to fight. The possibility of losing my girls to this vicious lie was very real and I wasn't about to let that happen without a fight. Tiffany didn't expect it and she wasn't ready for it.

On cross-examination, Jewett sounded like a first-year law student questioning me. She didn't appear to have any idea what she was even doing. Asking questions like, "Do you yell at your kids if they run in the street?" She asked if I'd yell at them if "they run through a parking lot without looking," if "I discipline them." With every question she asked, there would be a slight wince as if to say, "Shit! Did anyone hear that?" The problem was that we all heard it; so did the commissioner. I think a chimpanzee dressed in a suit could have put on a better showing than the woman who resembled an individual slightly afflicted and dressed like she resided in a double-wide.

In the end, Tiffany's story had the aerodynamics of a floor safe and it was apparent in Commissioner Brnovich's ruling. She gave her ruling after I was excused from the stand and before I even reached the defendant's table.

"Based on the testimony that's been presented I don't find proof by a preponderance of the evidence that domestic violence has occurred." She continued, "This appears to me, to be issues that are appropriate for a divorce and custody, but certainly not appropriate in this arena, so I'm going to dismiss the Order of Protection."

A huge weight was lifted off my shoulders that very moment. I had not seen, or spoken to, my girls in a month and now no one could stop me. I desperately needed to hold them and let them know that I love them. Hold them in my arms and kiss their beautiful faces. Feel the soft skin of their cheeks against my face. I nearly cried I was so overwhelmed, but something interrupted my joyous inner thoughts.

A hideous screech bellowed throughout the courtroom, so hideous I imagined it to be a baboon in labor. I whipped my head around and saw it was Tiffany, wailing and thrashing around so violently she resembled a Middle Eastern woman throwing herself over the coffin of a loved one while screaming to Allah. I may have ducked, as well. It was pretty pathetic and pretty humorous all at the same time. I guess it was her last-ditch effort to get the Commissioner to re-examine her ruling and change it. Too late! Check please! I chuckled out loud as I passed.

In the hallway, as I was speaking to DeeAn and Michelle, we were approached by the waddling, impish-looking thing with thick glasses; it was Jewett.

"Do you want to see your children?" She spoke as if she were the one who had the power to make this happen. It was as if she and *only* she was the driving force to allow me access to my children.

I shot back, "What the **hell** do you think, lady? Like you can fucking stop me?" I leaned in and was about three inches from her face. I could see each and every blemish on her skin. Every crease on her face was clearly visible.

I could see that her expertise in applying make-up was lacking to the point I mused her use of such may have been an experimental phase; heavy on one side, light on the other. Some on one side of her forehead and not on the other. Whatever it was she used was brushed across her hairline, so the hair, too, was flecked with make-up. Her eyeliner looked as if it were from the day before and she just never removed it but slept on one side of her head because one eyeliner was smudged on one eye. Close up, she looked like she had been at an all-night party and just never bothered to clean up before the hearing.

I could see very clearly she didn't pluck, or wax, her eyebrows, or trim her nose hairs, for that matter; she had two very long strands protruding from one nostril. The most nauseating part of all of this was that it didn't appear that she knew what toothpaste was. Her teeth were caked with plaque and her breath could have killed a small village. I finally realized I didn't want to be this close to the woman and backed away. As I did, DeeAn admonished me for showing Jewett disrespect. The Nelson clan overhearing the commotion began to laugh. They had hoped I would have lashed out like that in the courtroom, but in the courtroom, I didn't have a miserable little hobbit in my face. Thankfully. In the end, it turned out that DeeAn was an Eskimo with a club and Jewett, a baby harp seal who'd just been beaten to death.

DeeAn said that she and Jewett would speak and set up a time for me to see my children. We walked away from the place I will remember for the rest of my life and headed for the exit.

As I walked out of the courthouse and into the beautiful sunlight, I felt completely vindicated. Feeling the sun warm my face was one of the best sensations I could feel at that moment. The only thing better was to feel the faces of my daughters against mine. What a great day to be alive. This is what many of those, who ended their lives, would undoubtedly have felt had they not been so weak.

What a beautiful feeling, however, I would find that this feeling of euphoria would be short-lived. The real fight was about to begin and the start of it was several days away at a location just a short twenty, some odd, miles southeast of where I stood. What I wanted now was to see my beautiful Kathryn and Megan. Right now, little else mattered.

"ARE YOU IN CALIFORNIA?"

"The voices of children may first be detected by the ear, but their pure sounds of innocence go straight to the heart." – Jimmy Buffett

March 28, 2006

A time was decided upon that I could call and speak to Katie and Megan the day following the hearing. In anticipation of this call, I couldn't sleep the night before. I didn't know what to say to them, or tell them what had happened, or that I had been writing them a letter a day, or that I needed to hold them so badly and I loved them so deeply. I didn't want to show any emotion and possibly cry; I didn't want them to know I was hurting inside and their mother was the cause of this pain. I wanted them to believe that I was stronger than I felt I was.

I drove to St. Anne's Catholic Church in Gilbert, pulled into the parking lot, found a place way back in the corner, and stopped. I just sat there staring at my watch; it was nearing the six o'clock hour which was the time that Tiffany said would be a good time to call. I took turns looking at my watch and then at my cell phone. I said a prayer that the phone call would be answered and I would actually be able to speak to the girls. I'm not sure why I pulled into the St. Anne's parking lot, I guess I felt safe near the church for some reason. It's not a bad thing. Maybe I subconsciously felt the angels that cruised around there would park on the hood of my truck and keep me calm during the call. Maybe I pulled in because I felt sorry for myself and thought that if the conversation went south, the closer I was to a church I could run into it, throw myself on the alter, curse God for putting me through this and demand to be told why I am still paying for my ill deeds of the past. Or maybe, I just happened to be near St. Anne's as the designated time to call was approaching and I didn't want to be late. Whatever the reason, I sat in the parking lot of a Catholic Church and waited until the precise time I was scheduled to call.

The second hand on my watch swept past the twelve and as I dialed the number from my cell phone, I was awash with so many emotions I had forgotten what I wanted to say to my girls. On the second ring, Katie answered.

"Katie?" I asked.

The beautiful little voice responded excitedly, "Hi, Daddy!" At that very moment I was overwhelmed with so much emotion I felt I was going insane. A huge lump in my throat appeared and I felt I was suffocating, and for a moment, I could not speak.

"Daddy?" Katie asked again, "Are you okay?"

I croaked out, "Yeah, baby. I'm great!" I tried to sound upbeat. I was holding back over a month of anguish and the fear of losing Katie and Megan forever. "How are *you* doing?" I couldn't help it; the tears started to flow, my voice cracking.

When Katie said, "I'm fine, Daddy. We miss you," I lost it.

"I'm so sorry this is happening sweetheart, but I'm gonna fix everything. I promise. I'm not sure how yet, but I'm gonna fix it, okay? I love you and Megan so much that I ached every day that we're apart. I'm gonna see you guys real soon, okay? The judge said I can see you now and I'm gonna set it up so we can see each other. I love you so much!" I was rambling and I didn't care. There was so much I wanted to say, but what do you say to a five and a seven-year-old that they can understand?

Then came the heartbreaker. A question asked by Katie thoroughly destroyed even the slightest bit of respect I had left for Tiffany, if any were possible at this point in time.

Katie asked me, "Are you in California?"

I was in a vacuum again. Speechless. That question took me completely by surprise and although I never, in a million years, imagined there would be any cause for this question to be asked, my mind was scrambled and my thought process firing in every direction. There were a few certainties, as was obvious by now; I knew that Tiffany was sick enough to tell vicious lies about me and I also figured she would *have* to tell the girls something, but I never really thought about *what* she could possibly tell them. To be honest, I may have thought about it for a split second, and then as selfish as I was, I turned to the problems *I* had. Stupidly I never thought about what Tiffany would say to the girls and because of this indiscretion, I wasn't even remotely ready for that question when it came.

When I was finally able to speak I asked, "Why would you ask me that, Katie?"

Her answer was as devastating as it could ever be. "Mommy said that you didn't want to be our Daddy anymore so you moved back to California. It made us sad."

I was suffocating again. Back in a vacuum devoid of air and I struggled to both understand what was happening in this little child's mind and keep myself calm; wanting to make Tiffany suffer unimaginable pain and anguish for bringing the girls into her cruel little game.

"You know what? I have never left Arizona, sweetheart. I could never leave here, if you and Megan weren't with me. I've been in Arizona this whole time. I've been staying in a hotel until I can find a house to live in."

She was satisfied that I hadn't left the state, but still worried that I didn't want to be her daddy any longer.

"Do you still love us?" She asked.

"Oh my beautiful little angel, of course, I love you. I always will. You and Megan are all I've got in this state and I will never want to do anything else, but be your Daddy. You two are my world and everything in it."

Megan was the next to come on the phone and asked the same question. "Are you in California?" I promised her, too, I was not in California and had never left. I told Megan that as long as she and Katie were in Arizona I wasn't going anywhere. I explained that things were kind of crazy right now, but that I was going to get everything fixed as soon as I was able to.

"When are you going to come and see us?" Megan asked.

"You know what, baby? I'm gonna see you very soon. We're just working out a few details and in a day or so we can be together. I promise."

"Okay, Daddy. Hurry, cuz, we miss you," she said.

I fell apart again. With my voice cracking and tears streaming down my face, I told her I missed her, as well, but everything would be OK in a very short time and we would be together again. I explained, the best way I could to a five-year-old, that I had an attorney and we were working out the details of a visit so that the three of us could see each other. After a short twenty-minute conversation we hung up the phone.

I just sat there and as I stared out the windshield of my truck I realized I was alone again. I was back where I was the day before, a week ago, two weeks ago, a month ago. I hated being alone with nowhere to go and no one to speak to. The tears began to flow once again. A few minutes later I had had enough of my self-pity. I wiped my face, got out of my truck, and walked toward the entryway of the church. I walked in, dipped my fingers into the Holy water, made the Sign Of The Cross, walked to one of the aisles, genuflected, plopped myself down in a pew at the back of the church, and just sat.

I recounted the past month, the months since I arrived in Arizona on October 7, 2005, the first fifteen months I was away from the girls after Tiffany spirited them away from California and the bullshit excuse she used to be nearer her mother. I recounted the past seventeen years since I had met Tiffany, fallen in love with her, and realized early on she was *the love of my life*. I asked myself where it all went wrong and could only come up with the answer I had always known to be the truth; I was running from myself and in doing so wasn't true to anyone else. I had been living a lie for my entire life because I was ashamed of who I was and where I had come from, but one thing was for certain; I was no pedophile, I was no abuser of children and I was no abuser of women.

I'm not sure how long I sat there, but when I walked out of St. Anne's the sun had long since tucked itself behind the western horizon of the Arizona desert and I was surrounded by the night. A harvest moon was rising out of the east and I stood there by the fountain in the courtyard and admired the beautiful orb before me. It's brownish orange hue and massive appearance was mesmerizing to me. I wondered how it was that our atmosphere was able to magnify this little object, so far away, to the point that one may think he could throw a rock and hit it. A few moments later the moon had risen high enough above the horizon and passed through the area of physical magnification, that it returned to its normal size.

I said to myself, "See? Not everything is as it seems." I contemplated the notion for a moment and smiled at the fact of how true it really is. Nothing really *is* as it seems. I'm not a pedophile or an abuser. I'm a good man with a good heart. And Tiffany is not the abused and beautiful princess held captive in a tower, but rather a wretched human being, running from her own demons.

I walked back to my truck, got in, and drove back to the peaceful confines of In-Town Suites. I wrote another letter to my daughters and went to bed. In the few seconds, or so, just before one falls into a state of unconsciousness and the sounds you hear are as if you are in an echo chamber. As in anywhere in the world, once night falls the cockroaches come alive and active. They scurry everywhere, but nowhere in particular. They are in search of something, but nothing in particular. This night was no different than any other I had spent to this point and the vermin were once again voraciously active. There seemed to be a million voices all calling out at once;

"Don't forget the fucking cigarettes,"

"I ain't getting' nothing for you if you don't gimme any money, mother fucker,"

"Where are my keys, bitch? You best be givin' me my fucking keys!"

"We need milk for the kids. Don't forget the milk!"

"I know, you fucking bitch! Whatayathink, I'm stupid?"

The voices became more and more distant and as I slipped into unconsciousness they disappeared.

A week or so later, I would finally move out of In-Town Suites in Mesa and into the home of Marcus Kuno. I worked with Marcus, building custom homes for his long-time friend, Paxton Anderson. Paxton had put us together, knowing I needed a viable residence where my daughters could stay with me and Marcus needed a renter for his vacant house, as he lived with his girlfriend. It was a perfect setup for both of us. At the time I was building a home for Mark Acre in the Mirabel area of north Scottsdale. Mark had pitched in the Major Leagues for the Oakland A's and had retired a few years prior. He and his wife Dominique were building this home to live in and start a family, however that plan would change several months later.

Arriving home from work, a couple of days after moving in, I pulled into the driveway of 14843 So. 8th Street, in the Ahwatukee area of Phoenix and walked into the house. I put down my things and visited the bathroom, to relieve myself after a long drive from North Scottsdale. As I exited I heard a tapping. At first, I couldn't tell where it was coming from, but the second series of taps drew my attention to the front door.

"What the hell. . . . .?" I thought. "Why the hell would anyone be knocking on my door?"

I didn't know a single neighbor and no one even knew where I lived; except for the courts. Immediately, my heart began to pound. When anyone knocks on *my* door, it's normally bad news. I cautiously walked toward the door and peered through the peephole. I could see a figure there, but the sight was extremely cloudy and could not even make out facial features, let alone gender. My heart was reverberating in my ears. I stepped back, reached for the knob, turned it, and pulled the door toward me.

As I opened the door I immediately recognized this person. She was beautiful; stunningly so. Wearing a terry cloth tube-top with no bra, nipples obvious in their perfect location as they were forcing the cloth outward to give the appearance this woman was smuggling raisins. Her terry cloth pants matched the top and were tight around her hips, which flowed down to almost her ankles. The sun was overhead and just behind her and shown through her pants affording me a silhouetted view of her long thin legs. The pants were slightly see-through and I could make out a floral design on the front of her panties. As I gazed at this woman a small breeze kicked up and it gave her wavy blonde hair a push. I was frozen in time. Back in a vacuum and fantasizing over this beautiful woman before me. She tilted her head, ever so slightly, to one side and smiled seductively; her green eyes blazing with kindness. Her beauty was nothing like I had seen in a long time. I was smitten and for an instant, thought of nothing but my torrid desires. My thoughts of fantasy were interrupted when Tiffany spoke.

"Hi. I just wanted to drop by to see where you lived," she said. "Do you mind if I see the girls' rooms?" The Court asked if I had a separate bedroom, apart from mine, for the girls. I promised that I did, so I guess that was the reason for the visit.

"Uh, sure," I responded without thinking and pulled the door open for her to enter and as quickly as I had agreed to let her in, I came to my senses. Her right foot had just crossed my threshold and was on the tile in the entryway.

"No. You can't come in," I said.

I pulled the door back to the position it was a few moments before and she pulled her foot back so as not to get her toes caught under the sweep.

"Why?" she asked, her smile had recoiled and disappeared back into its shell like a disturbed hermit crab.

"Because I'm the only one here and I don't trust you. Now get the fuck off of my stoop!"

Tiffany stood there stunned and amazed that her persuasive tactic had failed. She did an about-face and stomped back down the walkway on which she came. I watched as she left and noticed the terry cloth pants she wore were pulled so tightly across her backside they boasted another floral design, albeit smaller, on the back of her thong undergarment. She sure did look good, but I thank God every day for my fortitude and strength that afternoon.

Had I let her in, there is no telling what evil could have come my way. Her ploy to have me arrested for child molestation didn't work and I knew if she did that, she had the will to pull something else. Like say, seduce me into having sex with her, then pinching and hitting her groin area to cause bruising, and then go to the police with the story that she came to my house to see the girls' bedrooms and as soon as she entered, I brutally raped her. The presence of my semen and the bruising around her groin area would land me in prison for 25 years. Fuck THAT! I'm grateful I sent her on her way.

Marcus would eventually sell his home and I would be forced to return to Inn Town Suites until I found another place to live.

PAMELA CHAMBERS

"Life does not come without risks. You either take them or you watch life on TV." – Possibly Dale Carnegie and although I'm not certain, I like the quote.

March 29, 2006

In the conference room of Gillespie and Associates I sat with Michelle Kunzman, going over a list of people on a court roster. As DeeAn and Michelle didn't want to take any chances, we would pick someone from this roster to accompany me when I was finally reunited with my girls. It would be necessary for a third party to witness our interaction and note that the girls were not afraid of me as Tiffany and her family had claimed they were. We settled on Pam Chambers. She was known to DeeAn and Michelle and they worked well together.

I just hoped when the girls did finally see me, Tiffany didn't have them brainwashed to the point they actually were afraid. I was taking a slight risk here but knew that if the girls weren't afraid, at least I would have a witness other than Tiffany who would say otherwise. If they *were* afraid, well, I didn't have a plan for that just yet. I'm sure that DeeAn wanted to see a report of that meeting, as well, just to appease her own doubts, however minuscule they may have been.

There was always something new to me in this arena. This time it came in the form of "legal wrangling." I didn't realize just how difficult and involved that first meeting would be until we had set up a time and a place where I could be reunited with my girls. Tiffany and her lawyer didn't like it. They balked and it was back to the drawing board. We picked another place and they balked.

It would have been very easy for me to just bull my way through, drive over to where they were staying and see the girls, but my main concern was not frightening the girls. The other concern was that the Nelson clan would have undoubtedly conjured up yet another story of me being violent during the visit, or provoking me into an altercation. I had to do this the right way and do it with a third party, and as much as I yearned to be with them, I had to wait.

On March 30, 2006 came a letter from Jewett saying they have rejected our offer and made the decision to have one Jodi Lightfoot be the third party witness. This was completely out of the question, as I didn't really need this witness, but rather wanted one to dispel any notion there was abuse, and the girls were frightened of me. The third party was my call and my call only. Though I spoke to the girls every day now, I still hadn't seen them and as long as Jewett continued her evasive bullshit, I was growing restless. The back-and-forth letter writing went on for several days and after a week I had had enough.

On April 4th, 2006, Michelle Kunzman filed with the court an **"Accelerated Motion For Expedited Order To Compel Mother To Permit Father Access."** It was as if Moses himself were standing by me because almost immediately the seas parted, Jewett and Tiffany became very accommodating to our requests and all I had to do was pick a time and place to see my girls. I thought, "Damn! That was easy. And we didn't do this earlier? Why?"

After over a month of being away from Katie and Megan, I would finally see the girls at Peter Piper Pizza, in Scottsdale, on the evening of April 5th. Pam Chambers would be there as well. As individuals on the court roster of psychiatrists, psychologists, and counselors, they are used as they are needed by the court and paid by the requesting party and a vast majority do not come cheaply. Pam Chambers was no different, but I will say this; she was worth every penny she was paid. Her only concern was that of the children and how they interacted with me.

NOT THE LOVE OF MY LIFE

    I arrived early, pulled into a parking space a few doors to the south of the main entrance, turned off the engine, and waited. I was so nervous I could hear my heart pounding in my chest and feel the blood surging through my veins, feeling the pressure of the carotid artery pulsating in my neck with every beat. I never even had to use my fingertips to feel my pulse. I looked down at the second hand of my watch and counted them; twenty-two beats in a fifteen-second span. "That's eighty-eight beats in a minute," I computed.

    Though my standing pulse has never been higher than sixty-six beats a minute, I became concerned that I would "tach-out" by the time the *miserable soul* and my beautiful angels arrived. As the meeting time grew nearer I felt my heart rate increase and as I was afraid to count the beats of my heart again, I envisioned myself grabbing my chest and keeling over in the cab of my truck; a victim of a massive heart attack. That would have sucked out loud. I tried to calm myself while I sat there and waited in misery for my heart to slow down. Pam and I had agreed to arrive a few minutes earlier than the meeting time, so we could discuss our game plan and I could pay her for her presence; however, it would turn out that rush hour traffic would force her to be late.

    The white Toyota Four-Runner pulled into the lot a few minutes past six o'clock and my heart almost stopped. Tiffany and the girls had arrived before Pam! Through my side view mirror, I watched as she pulled her car into a space, the brake lights glowing brightly when she came to a stop. The taillights continued to glow brightly as she didn't take her foot off the brake even after the engine was turned off. She must have been giving the girls last-minute instructions, I thought. The taillights went dark and a moment later, the driver's door swung open, and stepping out from the car was my adversary. Looking like some secret service agent, she glanced around and then opened the rear door for Katie and Megan to get out. They hopped out and the three of them walked toward the front door of Peter Piper Pizza, Tiffany's head turning from side to side as if to be the first to spy my truck before the girls did.

    The girls had changed so much in that month and I was once again saddened by that. Tiffany initiated and the court imposed sabbatical that I was forced to take. The sun was fairly low on the horizon and the girls' blonde hair glowed under it. I remember the smoothness of their perfect skin as their hair brushed and bounced against it while they walked. And even though the battle with ADHD rages and rankles my brain, playing its own little game with my memory and attention span, that very moment will be etched in my memory forever and I can think back to that very second in time and replay it over and over again; it is in slow motion.

As I sat there, I again thought back to the newspaper articles I had read about estranged men, in a similar situation, murdering their spouses, and whoever happened to be near, for the mere fact of wanting a divorce. I mused that this was far worse than just wanting a divorce; this would have been a perfect opportunity for some crazed freak, after bullshitting his way through a court hearing and being granted a visit with his children, to jump from his vehicle, walk up to his estranged wife and put a bullet in her head. Luckily for Tiffany, I am a very stable man with no real propensity to violence and my only real concern was to be with my children. Other than the upcoming divorce, Tiffany was a non-entity in my life at that point. She was nothing more than vermin. A sewer rat, foraging for scraps of someone's pocketbook. Even a sewer rat has a right to live and a right to scrounge around for its meager existence. If it comes close, I would just kick it away and send it in another direction. If it returned I would kick it a bit further away and if it continued to accost me, it would grow wings.

The only way I could see myself becoming that enraged, of course, is if someone was to harm my children or someone I love. Only then could one rest assured I would hunt them down and inflict the worst kind of pain imaginable. So unimaginable, they wouldn't believe it even while it was happening.

I watched and sat without moving, hoping they wouldn't see me before Pam Chambers arrived. As desperately as I wanted to hold them and kiss them, I didn't want to make the mistake of ruining what we had accomplished to that point. I wanted a safe environment for myself and the only way to accomplish that was to wait for Pam to show up.

I thought again about how dramatically my life had changed from a little over a month ago, but what I didn't yet know is that my life had been altered beyond belief. I would find out just how drastic the change would be, later that month. That messenger would be one of Tiffany's closest friends and confidants.

Tiffany and the girls reached the door and before they entered she scanned the lot one more time. To this day, I don't know if she saw me, nor do I particularly care. I was more worried about the girls seeing me which, depending upon their own frame of mind, could cause them to cry and I did not want that to happen; I wanted to walk in with Pam. A few moments had passed and Pam still hadn't arrived and I was getting nervous that she wouldn't make it.

My phone rang. I looked down and saw the name *Pam Chambers* on the screen. I hurriedly answered it and was told that she was just a few minutes away, that there was a lot of traffic and she was very sorry. I looked over at the front door and saw my little Megan with her palms flat on the window of the front door and she was looking right at me. She just stood there. We stared at each other and after a few seconds, she turned and told her mother and Katie of her discovery.

Katie appeared at the door as well and as she pushed the door open, I rolled down my window and said, "I'll be right in, sweetheart, I just have to wait for someone. When they get here, I'll come right in, I promise. I miss you so much, I can't wait to hold you. Now go back inside, honey, I'll be right in."

She meekly said, "Okay," and retreated inside. Tiffany took them both by the hand, looked at me, and glared. They then disappeared from the door.

How Megan was able to find me, I'll never know. It was so strange how she just appeared and knew which direction to look to find her Daddy. I guess the connection between a child and parent doesn't diminish, but rather both send energy through the air and it somehow finds the other. I liken it to, among many other species of animals, the Emperor Penguin who after many weeks, or months away from its young can still pick out the "peep" of their offspring through the din of tens of thousands of other peeps. Somehow they just know where to look and somehow, through the energy that emanates from our souls, Megan knew where to look also.

My phone rang again jerking me out of my deep thoughts. It was Pam and she called to inform me she was finally pulling into the lot and because we had never met, she gave me the description of her car and what she was wearing so I could recognize her. She pulled into a stall a few spaces down from me and exited her car. I got out and walked toward her, my hand extended in front of me. She took it and as we were shaking hands I formally introduced myself, thanking her for coming.

Pam Chambers is a very attractive little thing, maybe 5'3", if that. She had wavy brown hair that bobbed as she walked toward me; her gait of short steps was a quick one. As she approached her lips parted revealing a beautifully warm smile and stark white teeth; her hand was outstretched to shake mine, ten feet before we were actually face-to-face. It seemed she was excited to meet me and under the circumstances, I wondered why. Though this was to be an emotional meeting, of sorts, she had this way about her, a demeanor that gave me the impression she was about to walk into a long-anticipated party and she couldn't wait to get inside. In retrospect, I believe she is just a person who loved her job and was excited about reuniting a father and his two children. As I reflect back and replay our initial meeting, that night in Scottsdale, my thoughts of Pam are fond ones and I smile.

I gave her a brief recap of what she had heard from DeeAn and Michelle, I paid her and we walked through the doors of Peter Piper Pizza.

The girls rushed toward me and just as I kneeled down they both jumped into my arms. They squeezed my neck so tight I was amazed that little children had that much strength. As I fought back the tears all I could think of was I never wanted them to let me go. I wanted to just sit down where I was, tuck them into the bend of my arms, and hold them forever, not caring that I was in the middle of a pizza joint on a filthy floor.

They finally released their grip and I stood up. Tiffany was in front of me; Pam was to my left. Tiffany went into an act of incredible niceties, by which I was stunned. All the horrible things she had said about me, all the crying on the witness stand about how horrified she was of me, all the evil glares she shot at me and my attorney, it was gone . . . all of it.

She was now my "wife" again; smiling, giggling, reaching over to touch my arm (which I leaned away from, so as not to be touched by her), telling me how nice it was to see me and the girls together. I stared at her in disbelief, my forehead and nose wadded up like my olfactory had just registered the stench of rotting flesh.

I stepped back and tried to get a grasp on what was happening I thought to myself, "Are you fucking kidding me? You fucking whack job! Who the fuck *are* you?"

It then dawned on me that she was back on stage. She and her clan got their asses handed to them in court and since she failed to deliver an Academy Award winning performance there, she had to switch gears and appear to Pam Chambers she was a sweet and loving mother and estranged wife that just wanted to be friends with her soon-to-be ex-husband. I sure as hell didn't buy it and I had hoped that Pam didn't buy it either. Histrionic Personality Disorder is a scary thing. And how I never saw this sick trait in Tiffany is beyond me. Was I too blinded by her beauty to see this all those year before? God knows I must have been.

Tiffany wanted to have a word with Pam alone and as she started to walk toward the front door, I nudged her and whispered, "Good luck." Pam smiled and walked out with Tiffany to chat. Their conversation was brief and as Pam came back inside, Tiffany went to her car and drove off. I was half hoping she would be killed in a car accident, but quickly abandoned the thought as too harsh at that point in time, although I would rekindle my passion for her demise as more information about Tiffany's past activities surfaced. That would be a few weeks down the road.

When Pam returned I introduced her to the girls and we sat down at a table. I went to the counter and ordered the cardboard and gummy grease. They pass off pizza, and four drinks. Pam was talking to the girls, so I took my time getting back to the table. I wanted her to have as much time to talk with them as possible. I needed her report. I needed her to see there was nothing to worry about, as the Nelson clan had attempted to persuade the court.

Other than the fact we were finally reunited there is little else to tell of this night. With the exception of our initial few minutes back together, the girls treated me as if nothing had happened and acted as if we were never apart. Tiffany came back an hour and a half later and scurried the girls away, packing them back into her car and disappearing into the night. After they left, Pam looked at me and said she had no doubt in her mind that these girls were ever abused, or more importantly, afraid of me. The one thing Pam told me that night was that it was obvious there never was a problem between me and the girls, and if there had been, she would see it right away; the girls weren't afraid.

We set up another meeting and this time we would have dinner together at Red Robin a few days from then. There would be a total of three meetings with the girls and Pam Chambers, as the acting eyes and ears of the court. She would issue her report to DeeAn Gillespie and it would be filed away for future reference. The accusation that I had molested the girls and abused them had been dispelled and I was thankful for that. Although that battle had been won I would contact Pam a few times over the next several months for various reasons, or just to say, "hello." I remain indebted to her for her part in making that time in my life easier to endure however, I am most thankful that she was able to weed through the lies that were being thrown my way and see that I was, and am, a good person and a good father to my girls. I will never forget Pam Chambers.

"THERE'S SOMETHING YOU NEED TO KNOW"

"Terrible thing, to live in fear. All I wanted is to be where things made sense; where I don't have to be afraid all the time." - From the movie Shawshank Redemption

It was a Saturday morning and I was sitting in my third-floor *penthouse* of the In-Town Suites looking around the room, admiring all I had accomplished. I had five hanging shirts, two pairs of jeans, one pair of slacks, two pairs of shoes, a half a loaf of bread, some bologna, three bananas, and a half gallon of milk; all of it mine. And as I had turned my focus to all the amenities the two-star hotel afforded me that morning, a phone call I had never expected came in.

I looked down and was terrified to see the name "Ryanne Ritter" on the screen of my phone. I just stared at it and allowed the phone to ring, the whole time contemplating if I should answer it and wondering why she would be calling me. She and her husband, Charlie, were very close friends of Tiffany's and not on "my team." They had one child, a boy named Brody, who was a playmate of my daughters. They were friends of Tiffany and classified as "the enemy." In fact, she was Tiffany's business partner in, as it turned out, a short-lived venture to produce pajamas.

I stared at the phone and listened to the ring which seemed to get louder and louder and I wanted it to stop. I didn't want to answer the phone for fear of the unknown. Why were they calling? What did they want? The ring was magnified in my head and I could not quiet the noise. I looked at the phone as if it were a bill collector calling; you know there's nothing but bad news on the other end of the phone and they want something, but because you don't have what they want, you choose not to speak to them and give *them* that bad news.

I tried to quit the ringer, fearful that my neighbors would hear it through the walls and become agitated by the menacing disorder while they slept off their cheap beer drunkenness and the impending hangover. Before I was able to get the ringer turned down it fell silent; the little light in the upper right-hand corner of the phone flashing red. The screen shows the call back number and under it, the words *"Missed Calls – 1."* I stood and put my hands on my hips, still staring at the phone and the blinking light . . . wondering. The backlight on the face of the phone went black; its ninety-second time limit had expired. Still, I stood and stared at the phone. A few seconds later I was startled and jumped when the phone rang again. The backlight of the phone came back to life and illuminated the name "Ryanne Ritter" once again.

I thought to myself, "What the hell is going on?" and then leaned toward the phone and asked it, "Why are you people calling me? What do you want?" The phone went silent once again and still, all I could do was stand and stare.

After about five minutes I decided to return the call. I needed to know what they wanted. I thought maybe it was a set-up for Tiffany, or a fishing expedition, or something to get me angry. I wasn't sure what I was getting into when I called the number back, but one thing was for certain, I would be more cautious than I had ever been up to that point.

After only two rings it was answered, "Hello?" It was Charlie.

"Hey, it's Eric. I was in the shower and didn't hear the phone," I lied. "I saw you called. What's up?"

"It's Charlie," he said.

"Yeah, I know." I was very short with him. "Whatdaya need?"

He could sense my discomfort and annoyance with him, as well as hear the tone of an untrusting voice.

"Well, uh, Ryanne wanted me to call you . . ." his voice began trailing off.

I could hear Ryanne in the background giving her husband instructions as to what to tell me. I was very wary of what was happening, trying to strain my ears to hear what Ryanne was telling Charlie. Finally, Ryanne became frustrated with her husband and took the phone from him.

"Hi, Eric? There's something you need to know," She started off. "I just can't sit by and do nothing anymore. You're getting screwed by Tiffany."

I know my mouth was hanging open and my chin resting on my chest. "Holy shit! Are you KIDDING me," I thought? "Thank God, you called because I had no fucking idea I was getting screwed by Tiffany. What a lifesaver you are! Thank you so much for calling me and enlightening me. I don't know what I would have done had it not been for you calling me." All I could do was shake my head and wonder where this was going.

Actually, I thought it very odd that we were even speaking after all that had transpired and still wondered if this call was a setup. A million thoughts were surging through my brain, trying to compute every aspect of the past and present to conclude a viable answer for a reason this conversation would be taking place. I could not. I was back in a vacuum. The air had been sucked away from my immediate location. But for the muffled "whaw, whaw, whaw" and "blah, blah, blah," no sound was coming to my ears. I strained to hear but the harder I tried, the less I heard. I heard myself say, "Wait! What? Say that again? Fuck! Slow down, Ryanne. What the hell did you just say?"

I stopped the conversation so I could collect myself. "OK, Ryanne, you're talking way too fast and my brain cannot process what you are telling me," I said. "Please! You gotta start over for me. Now what the hell are you trying to tell me?"

"Okay," she started again. "Tiffany is screwing you."

I interrupted, "I know. I got that part. *How* is she screwing me?"

"Eric, I was with her when she went to the attorney's office and I was with her when she went to the police station."

"Whoa!" I interrupted again. "Whatdaya mean '*the police station*'? *What* police station?"

She quieted herself, "The Chandler Police Station."

"Why did she go to the Chandler Police Station, Ryanne?"

"She told them that you molested the girls. She filed a police report and wanted them to arrest you."

Now my chin really *was* on my chest. "Are you fucking kidding me?" was all I could get out of my mouth. I started to shake.

"Ryanne, I'm being investigated by the police? Please tell me this is a fucking joke. Please tell me you're kidding." I stopped myself.

"Okay, Ryanne, I need you to tell me everything."

I could feel the tears streaming down my face and even as I write this, my eyes instinctively well with tears. I cannot help it.

Hearing the words of Ryanne Ritter and engaging in the dialog I did that day, happened a million years ago and it happened just a moment ago. Just a mere moment ago. It was one of the most pain-filled days of my life and I do not want to relive it, but in order to tell my story, I must.

I must let others know what kind of damage, and untold misery to one's psyche that one short sentence can bring to another human being. This is exactly the type of thing that results in the suicide of a weak individual. Those who are not guilty of these accusations, but cannot bear the burden of the same, or face their accusers, will take their own lives and leave little doubt in the minds of the survivors of what the truth may be. What the survivors believe to be the truth will stand only because the weak soul didn't stand up and fight. They will die with a blemish upon their soul and a mark against their name because they didn't have the courage to stand up to their accuser. Those who ***are*** guilty should be thrown into a pit of vipers; cast down with the sodomites for all eternity.

I thought very seriously of the words Ryanne spoke, the profound impact this could make, and the very few options I had. Telling the court I molested the girls was bad enough and I made it through that, but now I was being told the police are involved and these greasy pricks are always on a witch-hunt.

My mind was racing through every TV show I had seen that included a dirty cop. Every episode of "20/20." Every segment of

"Inside Edition." Every broadcast of "Investigative Reports." Every segment of "60 Minutes" and a plethora of other reality shows where some disfavored, scanty bastard is wrongfully accused of horrible acts and ultimately gets tossed in the hoosegow for the better part of his life. The good ol' boys who put him there get slaps on the back and hugs all around. When the miserable vermin in cheap suits finger someone, even though there is no proof, they'll make themselves *believe* the person they're investigating is a fucking criminal and treat him as such.

In our society, when we are dealing with the abuse of children, you are **guilty** until proven innocent. They'll come to your home, tell your neighbors why they're there, come to your work, and talk to your friends. They will expel every semblance of normalcy and destroy a man's dignity because they need that sense of self-worth. They need to feel that the presence of the well-placed shield was done rightfully so. That their existence in their personal and respective bubbles is justified by how many people they can arrest, or confessions they get.

In the end, it boils down to percentages, because if an arrest is made, there are a bunch of *happy* people and only one *unhappy* person. Conversely, if an arrest is *not* made, the opposite happens. So here is the detective's caveat; do I want one person happy and incur the wrath of ten unhappy people, or do I want to have ten people happy and only one poor slob, pissed off? I think we all know the answer to that. Like the hyenas that roam the plains of Africa looking for the sick and slow of foot, the detective is going after the lone miserable soul that has no way to protect himself. I thought to myself, "They're coming after me."

"Ryanne, this is not a good thing and I'm sick to my stomach right now," I said. "What are the police doing with whatever Tiffany told them?"

"I don't know what they're doing, but I know she's lying because she said that you molested Brody, too, and I know it didn't happen, Eric." Brody is Ryanne and Charlie's son and the same age as Katie.

"Oh my God!" I was staggered. "She *said* that?" I tried to continue, "Ryanne, I would nev—"

She cut me off, "I know it's not true," Ryanne said. "Charlie and I knew it wasn't true, but we had to ask Brody just to be sure. No offense, really. I swear we know you wouldn't do anything to hurt your girls, or Brody, but we talked to Brody and asked him about it." I was actually glad that they did.

Ryanne continued, "Brody said that if anyone ever touched him he 'would kick them in the balls and run'." We both laughed at his response and I believed in my heart, Brody would do just that.

Brody is one of the brightest young boys I have ever encountered in my life. A precocious little guy, well beyond his eight years of existence. He had the vocabulary of a fifteen-year-old and could out with the sharpest twenty-year-olds. He even gave me a run for my money a few times. He is more well-read and well-versed in more subjects than I can count and has educated **me** several times on things like; the interaction of the dung beetle and horsefly and how they help the environment, or the bio-physical properties of bat guano and how rich in nutrients it is, or explain in great detail how whales communicate through sonar. Brody never ceased to amaze me with his remarkable intelligence. He will go far in his life and I truly believe this young man will be a well-respected individual one day, with a great many people looking up to him. I look forward to that day.

"When did all this take place? I mean, how long ago did this happen? How did she decide to do this?" I asked. I was still unsure of what had and was taking place.

"She and the girls were over at my Mom and Dad's house and we were all talking about what she was going to do. So she starts telling us that you molested the girls and she said she took them to a doctor to find out for sure. So, my Dad says something like, 'That's a pretty serious accusation you're making, but I don't believe Eric could do such a thing.' But Tiffany didn't even seem to be fazed by what my Dad said and she just kept on talking. Then she says, 'you better take Brody to the doctor too, because I think he molested him, too!' I started crying because I had never heard anything like that before and I was scared. Then she says that you may have molested my brother's two kids, too. It was too much to listen to and I was really scared, Eric, but I don't think she thought we all believed her, so she pulled out this letter and gave it to us. She said that you were hiding it and she found it after you left the house."

"What letter?" I asked.

"It was a letter you wrote to your father and she said there was a bunch of stuff about how your father abused you and that abuse always gets passed down the line, so you would have to be an abuser, too and the letter was proof."

"Oh my God!" I thought to myself. She had taken that private letter, I had written to my father some twelve, or thirteen, years earlier and passed it on to the Ritter's? That was a vicious act in and of itself.

I asked, "Did you read it?"

"Well, yeah. She gave it to me. She had a bunch of copies and said she showed a bunch of people."

I was so elated to hear that all of our mutual acquaintances now believed I was an abuser with many facets to offer the community. Conversely, the dirt bag of a soon-to-be ex-wife knows no boundaries and is completely lacking any moralistic character whatsoever. A judge would later tell her that her possession of these letters is unlawful and was to return any and all copies to me. I'm sure she kept a copy, like a serial killer keeps trophies, but if she ever makes it public, she'll be back in court and on the business end of a lawsuit.

"Who else read it?"

"Me and Charlie . . . and my Mom."

"Your Dad didn't read it?" I asked.

"No. He said that he didn't want to read it because it was a private letter to your father and it wouldn't be right."

I thought, "No s hit, it wouldn't be right! I wish he had passed on that trait to you, Charlie, and your mother, for Christ sakes. What a miserable bitch Tiffany is."

I looked at my watch. We had been on the phone for 20 minutes. I finally asked, "Ryanne, why are you telling me this now?"

"Because I found out that she's a bad person and can't be trusted."

Okay, I was at least a step ahead of the Ritter's. I already knew she couldn't be trusted.

She continued, "We had some fabric, for pajamas, in order that I paid for and when Tiffany realized that we didn't believe her story she started backing away from my family, but before she did, she took the fabric and refused to give it to us."

It was all becoming clearer to me. Tiffany and Ryanne started up a business making pajamas for kids and moms. With the purchase of these pajamas, was an option to have them embroidered by Ryanne and Tiffany, as they had an embroidery machine as well. Tiffany eventually feels her story is falling on deaf ears and decides her welcome has been overstated. Besides, she doesn't want to surround herself with those who are not on her side to bolster her story of abuse.

Anytime she seems to be headed for turbulent waters Tiffany will remove herself and pretend it never happened, but before her exit from this particular episode, she took a little memento, another trophy, worth a few thousand dollars. Ryanne was the ever-present and loyal friend to Tiffany until she got screwed herself and thus emerged the revengeful business partner wanting her "pound of flesh." She would get it, too.

In the nearly sixty minutes we were on the phone that morning, Ryanne would recount, in detail, each and every wretched little deed that Tiffany had committed to carrying out her exit plan. Ryanne was with Tiffany the day they had the initial meeting with Jewett. She was there when Jewett had called her husband, a detective in the sex crimes division of the Phoenix Police Department, and asked him to do a little checking on Eric Di Conti and get back to her. She was there when the act of malfeasance was carried out and he reported back to his loyal wife, Donna Jewett. Ryanne was there when, while on speaker-phone, Jewett's husband told Tiffany not to file a police report because there was nothing on my record and the investigation would be linked to me forever. Ryanne was in Jewett's office when she, as her attorney, demanded Tiffany not file a police report.

Jewett warned, "If you do and it's not true and Eric finds out about it and he makes a stink, you'll lose those kids. If you do this you better hope he never finds out."

Ryanne was with Tiffany when she went to the police station the following morning and was present throughout the whole interview process while the initial report was being filed. Ryanne was present when Tiffany boasted of skimming money "for years" from our marital account and offered to teach others this skill.

Ryanne also received a phone call from a woman who invited her to an "intervention for Tiffany at Paradise Bakery," which was designed to get Tiffany to leave me and check into a shelter for battered women. This was due to the extreme "abuse" of which she and the girls were "victims." Ryanne was told there were several other women, who considered themselves friends of Tiffany's, who had secured a room at this shelter. Ryanne declined, saying she didn't think Tiffany was being truthful about anything. These "friends" of Tiffany's ended up having this intervention anyway, telling her a room was secured for her and the girls. Apparently, Tiffany made every excuse in the book as to why she couldn't go to this shelter but thanked them for their concern. In the end, she and the girls never went to this shelter.

My *untrained* opinion would suggest that if she was to walk into this "shelter for battered women" the professionals who ran the same, would know immediately that Tiffany, nor the girls, had ever been abused in any way. Tiffany had enough smarts in her maladjusted brain not to make a mistake of that magnitude. Just as she was smart enough not to take the girls to be interviewed by Wendy Dutton of Child Protective Services, as she was advised to do by Officer Besse of the Chandler Police Department. This little snap of advice is plainly visible in the police report, which you will see further on in this book.

Wendy Dutton is a specialist in cases like this and is used often by agencies to sniff out the truth and once again, had Tiffany made the mistake of having the girls interviewed by this woman, her tall tale of abuse and molestation would be found out. There wasn't a chance in hell she would put herself, and certainly not the girls, in front of Wendy Dutton for any reason.

The individuals that work in these shelters, or for the CPS, are trained to detect whether, or not, something is amiss. The slightest iniquity of those accused, and of whom they interview, must be determined and many of these individuals are very good at what they do. And although many are just as overzealous, as some in law enforcement, and can be gullible enough to believe they are doing the right thing, by taking the word of a very good liar, it is my profound belief that Tiffany just couldn't take that chance. She needed the loyalty of those she could sway. Those she could draw into her world of feeling sorry for the battered wife and physically and sexually abused children; the world of the victimized.

I think back and realize had it not been for Ryanne Ritter, her husband Charlie and her mother and father, I would still be vacillating in the misery that nearly every divorce brings when so many things are left uncovered. What I would go through in the coming months would be more confusion than some people may have been able to take. Especially when a person doesn't know the reasons why certain aspects of his, or her, life played out the way they did. It is said "everything happens for a reason," but when things happen and you don't know why, there is a great deal of anguish that accompanies the confusion. And that anguish can cause great harm to one's psyche and make him, or her, do stupid things.

The fact that Ryanne Ritter was Tiffany's business partner, friend and confidant and in being so, was present during so many meetings, lunches, interviews, and conversations with Tiffany, which were backed up by others present during those conversations, she became a beacon of hope. I needed this kind of messenger. Her knowledge was a wealth of information and would ultimately help me more than I ever imagined. I am thankful that Tiffany trusted her, but I am more thankful Ryanne was able to figure out who Tiffany was and then came forward to inform me of everything she knew.

Incidentally, another little tidbit of information that made me smile was the fact that after Tiffany's incessant vouching for her brother, Tim Nelson, Ryanne's mother and father decided to give him a try, doing work around the house. As it turned out, Tim used unlicensed and incompetent contractors who did more damage than good and in addition, clipped them for, what I was told was, several thousand dollars in the process. I cannot confirm the amount of money lost, as it is merely what I was told. It was money they never saw again. Further, at the time of doing the work, Tim Nelson wasn't even licensed as he had claimed. What a clan the Nelson's hail from!

The following is the actual statement of Ryanne Ritter as it was submitted to the Maricopa County Superior Court in a defamation suit I would file against Tiffany, several months later. The document below is Public Record and can be pulled from the archives, along with my entire civil suit, under the case number CV 2007-003198.

RYANNE RITTER STATEMENT

IN THE SUPERIOR COURT OF THE STATE OF ARIZONA
IN AND FOR THE COUNTY OF MARICOPA

ERIC DI CONTI,	) **Case No.: CV 2007-003198**
	) STATEMENT FROM
V.	) RYANNE RITTER
TIFFANY NELSON	) REGARDING
SUSAN NELSON-STEPHANSON	) TIFFANY NELSON
	)
	)
	)
	)
	) *(Honorable A. Craig Blakey II)*

STATEMENT OF RYANNE RITTER

REGARDING TIFFANY NELSON

Written on this day, 30 September, 2006

NOTE: *Included in this statement is information regarding the false police report filed by Tiffany with the Chandler Police Department and Officer Philip Besse (#00252) on 3 March, 2006. Police Report # 06-02-5810*

On, or about, March 2nd, 2006, I accompanied my friend, Tiffany Nelson-Di Conti, to a meeting with an attorney that I had found for Tiffany (at her request), through a friend of mine. Her name is Donna Jewett and practices in Scottsdale, AZ.

I went with Tiffany, at her request, because she said that she didn't feel well and could quite possibly throw up while explaining her situation to Ms. Jewett. At this time she was seeking dissolution of her marriage to

Eric Di Conti, but prior to starting the divorce, she wanted protection from him through the courts in the way of an "Order of Protection."

Prior to us leaving my house in Chandler, Tiffany removed, without anyone's permission, two (2) .5 mg Zanax she got out of a prescription bottle that was at my house. The prescription was not in her name and I advised her against taking them, since they were not hers. She said she had to take them, because her mother (Susan Nelson-Stevenson) had stopped giving them to her, from her prescription bottle. I told her that two (2) Zanax at .5 mg's was way too much to take anyway and that she should put them back where she found them, but she insisted that she needed to calm down. Before I could do anything, she put them in her mouth and swallowed both of them. I was very disappointed by what she'd done since we were on our way to see an attorney and for her to be out of sorts during this meeting, was inappropriate. Under the circumstances and understandably, I drove to this meeting.

Upon arrival, we were ushered into Ms. Jewett's office and sat down. Tiffany began her story of abuse and the claim of the need of protection from Eric. Tiffany seemed to be slurring her words to some degree. After a few minutes, she said she didn't feel well and acted as if she was going to throw up. Tiffany then asked me if I would finish the story because she was "just too upset." I finished telling Ms. Jewett what Tiffany had told my whole family, and many of her friends, about Eric's minor physical abuse and molestation of their two girls, Katie and Megan (at the time, 7 and 5 respectively). The whole time, Tiffany seemed to be "crying" (but there weren't any tears) and gagging while I spoke. It was as if she was sickened by what she was hearing (which is exactly what she had told me later on) in the relay of information to Ms. Jewett, Tiffany reiterated that she wanted an order of protection from Eric, that she was afraid of him, that he was "unstable" and would stop at nothing to get to her and harm her and the girls.

Ms. Jewett directed Tiffany to the courthouse in Scottsdale, off of the 51 Fwy, saying that she knows the court and its employees at that location. She also informed us that there is a judge there that ALWAYS grants orders of protection in his court. She said it was because the one time he denied a request to a woman, she was later killed by her husband. She told us we were guaranteed to get one approved up there.

We left Ms. Jewett's office and we went directly to the courthouse Ms. Jewett described where Tiffany filled out the form for the request. When we went into the courtroom, Tiffany went back into her act as an abused woman for the judge and also told of Eric's molestation of the girls. Just as Ms. Jewett promised, Tiffany was granted an Order of Protection almost immediately. Upon leaving the courtroom and filing the paperwork with the clerk, she asked that a process server be used to serve the order to Eric.

She called Eric and asked him to have dinner with her that night. She suggested that they meet at 7:30pm at a restaurant called "Nothing But Noodles," at Germann and Alma School, in Chandler. Later that evening we met with a process server and after a short discussion and payment of $150 for his services, he left to wait for Eric.

She laughed about choosing this location, because "it was the girls' favorite place to eat" and she would really stick to Eric by having him served there. She was very amused by her choice and joked about it as we left the courthouse. She said it would add, "insult to injury." She joked about how creative she was, to think of this location. She even laughed out loud about it. For several days afterward, she told me several times that she wished she "had a camera so she could see the look on his face when he realized he'd just been screwed." **Side Note: When the Order of Protection was served on Eric, Tiffany and my husband, Charlie, were sitting across the street in our car watching Eric as he drove into the parking lot of "Nothing But Noodles." They left shortly thereafter and I'm not certain if they actually witnessed him being served, or not. (They were not present at Nothing But Noodles while Eric was served) After the Order was served, Eric attempted to call Tiffany on her cell. She used this excuse to call the police and asked to have him arrested for disobeying the Order. Chandler P. D. declined to make an arrest, citing the timing between the Order being served and the calls that were made.**

The drive home from the court was pretty uncomfortable. She never stopped talking about all that had transpired that day and that she would be rid of Eric for good. She laughed and joked about everything the whole time. It was very uncomfortable for me to hear her say these things after what I had witnessed earlier, but I guess I still had my doubts about what the truth was, seeing as how convincing Tiffany was telling her story.

I believe it was later that day; I accompanied Tiffany back to Ms. Jewett's office, as she needed copies of the Order of Protection for her files. I agreed to go back with her, due to Tiffany's anxious state of mind. She asked me if I had any Zanax with me and if I did, she wanted me to give it to her. I told her I did not have any and I declined to discuss this with her any further.

Donna Jewett spent a few minutes with Tiffany and me at this meeting. It was during this meeting, Tiffany informed Ms. Jewett that she was planning to file a police report with Chandler Police Department and was going to tell them that Eric was molesting the girls and needed to be arrested. She was asked by Ms. Jewett if she knew "for a fact that this was happening" and Tiffany's response was that she didn't "need" to know. She said all she had to do was tell them Eric was doing this and they would arrest him. She added that because she was a woman, "they would believe her."

She urged Tiffany to hold off on filling any kind of police report for possible molestation. She made if perfectly clear to Tiffany that she did not have hard evidence that the girls were molested. Jewett also said the behavior Katie and Megan were displaying could be a result of the initial separation from their father after she left California with the girls, the year prior and are continuing this behavior now. **Side Note: Tiffany never told me the reason she left California with the girls was because of Eric's "abuse." On the contrary, she stated that there was "never any abuse" and that "Eric would NEVER hurt me or the girls." But I could not understand why that, while Eric was at work one day, she loaded up a few belongings and along with the girls, put them into her car and left for Arizona to be with her mother. She said that Eric had no idea this was coming and he didn't find out until later that afternoon, while she was already at her mother's house. She was pretty amused by his lack of knowledge. She stated to me that, "Abuse was NEVER an issue."** *Ms. Jewett told Tiffany that she "could ultimately lose her children" for filing an 'erroneous' police report with these allegations. She stated that the Order of Protection would be sufficient protection for the time being.*

Ms. Jewett then added that Tiffany was making a huge mistake if she did this. She told Tiffany, "do not file that report," because there is no proof of any abuse, of any kind. She said that if she did go ahead and file the report, nothing will come of it. Worse yet, she said, Eric will have this report, with his name attached to it, on his record forever.

Ms. Jewett then said something very interesting; she said that "if Eric finds out that this report exists," before the final divorce documents are signed and he makes an issue of it, Tiffany would "lose custody of the kids." She told us that the courts don't take too kindly to women who make these allegations about fathers where there is no proof, or the allegations are untrue. In addition to this she said, there wouldn't be a single court around that will take Tiffany seriously; that she "would be a marked woman in the court system." Donna Jewett told her that this is serious business that she was dealing with. She told her NOT to file this report and advised her to let it go. Tiffany sat there with a slight smirk on her face. She said she would "think about it" and we left Ms. Jewett's office. Prior to Tiffany and I leaving Donna Jewett asked about any money in any bank accounts that Eric might access. When Tiffany told her that she did, in fact, have a large sum of money in one of her accounts that Eric has access to, Donna told her to clean it out before Eric could; that eventually she'd have to split it with him, but it's better if she has the money in her control. Tiffany did just that and laughed about Eric not having a "pot to piss in" because she had all the money.

My family thought her story was fishy within the first week of this whole episode beginning. My family began doubting Tiffany after a visit to my parents' home, where she first began telling us her stories of her and the girls being victims of physical and sexual abuse, by Eric.

Interestingly, and completely out of the blue, one day she also told me and my husband that I should get our 7-year-old son, Brody, "to a psychiatrist, because Eric may have molested him, as well." In addition to my son, she hinted that my niece and nephew may also be victims of Eric's sickness. She never made any mention of being abused before, nor did we ever see any indication that there was anything more than a loving relationship between Eric, Tiffany, and their two daughters, Katie and Megan. In fact, the week before Eric was asked to leave the house on Galveston St., in Gilbert, Tiffany sat in the TV room of my parent's house and raved about what a "wonderful man, husband, and father,"

Eric was. She told me and my mother that her "marriage would last forever" and she "would do whatever it took to make it work," because of how much love and devotion there was in her relationship with Eric.

Side Note: The reason she asked Eric to leave the house was that she felt that he lied about her brother's business practices. My parents asked Eric what he thought about hiring Tim Nelson for some remodel work on their house. Eric said he didn't trust Tim and would not hire him for anything, that he felt Tim may try to pad the costs of certain things, thus making my parents pay inflated prices. We hired Tim anyway, at Tiffany's urging. We spoke to him personally and make light of Eric's comments about him. He was very upset and confronted Eric on them. I understand that Eric did not deny his comments. Tiffany called me at my parent's house right after the confrontation and we laughed about how upset Tim was.

The following day, in complete contrast to our conversation the night before, Tiffany called and said that Eric lied and that she is "kicking him out of the house for making her brother cry over his comments." Shortly thereafter, she began her stories of abuse and molestation as the reason she wanted Eric out of the house, protection against him, and ultimately, a divorce. One day, while we were sifting through Eric's things and putting them aside from hers, she confided to me, that during the time she was apart from Eric, she communicated via E-mail with him. She stated, "He must have kept all of the E-mail," because she said she came upon a small black binder with ALL the correspondence between the two, during that time. She said that while the Order of Protection was in place, Eric came to get some of his belongings (with a Sheriff's Deputy). He'd asked where the binder was and she said she told him she didn't know what he was talking about. She said that the E-mail in the binder could really hurt her in court, so she stowed them away in a trunk somewhere and because she doesn't "technically know <u>which</u> trunk it's in, [she's] not really lying to anyone." She found humor in this comment. The subject of the binder and her comments about it were later repeated in the presence of Donna Jewett and me.

My family continued to disbelieve her stories, but Tiffany was so convincing in her demeanor Tiffany had me truly worried about the possibility that Eric had molested my son, Brody. Even though I knew, deep down in my heart, that Eric was not capable of doing such things, Tiffany had me doubting myself and ignoring my gut feeling. My family knew Eric from spending many, many hours together at my parent's house and just couldn't bring themselves to believe her outlandish stories of abuse and molestation. My father and husband pointed out that Brody and Eric were never alone together for anything to happen and IF something did happen, our very outspoken son would have said something to that effect.

During another visit to my parent's house, Tiffany was telling everyone there that we needed to lock our "doors and change the alarm system codes," as well as the entry code for the front gate because Eric will come in here and kill everyone in the house. Tiffany said Eric was a "monster that needed to be stopped."

The following morning, March 3rd, 2006, I was contacted, via phone, by Tiffany again. She informed me she'd made up her mind and was going to file the report anyway; regardless of what she was advised by her attorney. She asked if I would accompany her. After the previous day's meeting in Ms. Jewett's office, I didn't feel the least bit comfortable going with her.

*I said to her, "Tiffany, you should have someone from your family go with you, not me." I said to her, "have your sister, mother or brother go with you because I just don't feel right about going," when someone from her family should be there instead. She said that each one had declined to go with her, but she wouldn't say **why** each one of them refused to go when I inquired. She said she just needed some support from a friend and added I was her "friend" and she needed me. She sounded as if she was crying. She begged me to go. I resisted and told her that her family should be giving her support first, but she said again that they all refused to go with her and that I was the only one she had left to go to for support. After much begging, I felt sorry for her and against the wishes of my husband and family, I went.*

I continued to urge her not to file the report and that it was not right to do this because there was no proof of her claims. I reminded her of what Ms. Jewett's acquaintance said that she "could ruin Eric's life by filing" the report. She said that she didn't care what anyone said and she was filing it anyway. I believe she knew that she would be filing a report that was baseless and that she lacked any proof to bolster her claims of what she said was true. I was very disturbed by her intense disposition and inclination to follow through with filing a police report. I questioned again about her desire to file this report and all she would say was that she "had to do it."

At 10:30am on the morning of March 3rd, 2006, we walked into the Chandler Police Department on Chicago Ave. *After speaking to the woman behind the windowed counter and telling her that she needed to speak to a detective, Tiffany turned around and motioned to me to sit down with her by the front doors. At about 10:50am, we were greeted by Officer Philip Besse who asked us to join him in the interview room. We sat down, at which time Tiffany introduced herself and me to Officer Besse. He said the interview would need to be recorded. Tiffany began telling her story of physical abuse, verbal abuse, and molestation, by Eric. She spoke of Katie being obsessed with touching men's genitals and excessive masturbating and although I had spent countless hours with both girls, I have NEVER witnessed this behavior.*

Tiffany spoke of a very private letter that Eric wrote to his father where he expressed what it was like growing up with him as Eric's father and how horrible the abuse he endured was. He wrote about some very private moments in his childhood that Tiffany thought would bolster her case of abuse against the girls. Tiffany boasted of having "made several copies of it" and allowed others to have a copy to read. She gave me and my husband a copy of this letter. She also said she has copies of a letter from a woman stating that Eric told her he had dreams of molesting children.

She continued telling her story and there were several times that I felt very uncomfortable with her mannerisms. At one point, she was demonstrating how Katie masturbated and Officer Besse asked Tiffany to stop, that he got her point. I was getting disgusted at how Tiffany was acting, so I was grateful that Officer Besse insisted she stop.

During the interview and Tiffany's descriptions, there were many times that Tiffany had to stop because she was acting as if she was gagging. She also seemed to be crying several times during the interview, but again, I never saw any tears. At that point, I had some very serious doubts that what she was saying was true. Her antics during this interview appeared to me contrived and well rehearsed. Officer Besse said he would turn the case over to a detective in the Sex Crimes Division and they would do a more thorough investigation.

When we left I was very worried that what I had just witnessed was a complete act and that Tiffany knew what she had told the police was a lie. Conversely, I am very glad that I was there to witness this interview between Tiffany and Officer Besse.

Less than two weeks later, Tiffany was contacted by a detective at the Chandler Police Department. His name was John Beekman. During this conversation, she was told that she would need to take the girls to a forensic analyst and medical examiner for further evaluation. He said that if these individuals came back with a report for positive findings, an arrest would be made and Eric would be charged with a "sex crime against a child." To my knowledge, Tiffany never made these appointments and never took the girls to anyone other than their pediatrician, Diane Matsumoto, who said she refused to see the girls unless they were evaluated by a medical examiner to rule out sexual abuse. I asked her many times if the girls had admitted that anything had happened and she passed off the question and changed the subject. In the weeks following, each time I asked her if she'd made these appointments, she responded that she hadn't, but "I still need to do it."

I do not know the outcome of these evaluations, or if they ever happened. I do not believe Tiffany ever followed through with any examinations. **Side Note: I found it VERY strange that Tiffany told this detective (John Beekman) that Eric was "never physically abusive to her or the girls," as she had claimed in her interview with Officer Besse.** *I don't believe she ever had* **any** *intention of making those appointments, due to her demeanor when the subject was broached. It was like she knew it was a complete lie and had no reason to follow up and if she did, the "medical examiners" would prove her story false and she would be found to be a liar.*

Several days after the police report was filed, there were several things that bothered me and I confronted Tiffany about them. I asked her why she allowed Eric to move to Arizona and in with her and the girls. I asked her if Eric was a "child molester," as she claimed, then why she would allow him back into her home. Her only comment was that when she divorced Eric, she didn't "want to put the girls on a plane to California, for visitation, after she divorced him."

Side Note: At the beginning of April, right after the Order of Protection was thrown out, Tiffany commented to me that she was thinking about getting back together with Eric. I was stunned by this statement. I asked her why she would even consider this if he was a pedophile. She said that the girls "needed a father." I think she sensed that I knew her story of abuse and molestation was a lie. She changed the subject and stated that Eric would get back to her in a heartbeat. She said that all she'd have to do is say the word and he'll come back. She said he loves her too much to stay away. She also said that he loves her more than she loves him. I then asked her, "Well what about your ring?" Tiffany had pried the center stone out of her wedding ring and sold it to a Phoenix Fireman. This man was a mutual friend of Scott Woodford (also a Firefighter with the Phoenix Fire Department), who is the husband of an acquaintance (Erin Woodford-R.N. Banner Medical Center) of Tiffany's. He wanted a stone that was over 1 ct. for his fiancé. This was done that first week that Eric was out of the house; sometime between March 1st and March 5th. The stone itself had an estimated value of over $5000. She sold it for $1500. Her response to me was, "Well, if we're going to get back together, I'd want a new one anyway." I dropped the subject.

Within a few weeks of the interview with Officer Besse, I realized that nearly everything Tiffany had told my family and me was a lie. Everything she said about Eric was a complete lie and I felt terrible that I was drawn into Tiffany's act and had become a party to Eric's fall from grace within the community. Had I not been there to hear her lies, Eric would never have known the horrible things that she said about him.

Another incident that I believe is notable took place at a luncheon with me and a friend of mine (Amanda), Tiffany offered to help her "skim money out of the household bank account." My friend was having marital problems and she offered to show her how to report inflated household expenses to her husband, thereby having him give her more money from his income. She would then make up two spreadsheets (a secret one with actual data and the other with the inflated data, for her husband to see), with all the expenses. Tiffany said that she has "been *doing it for years and Eric is so stupid, he has no idea how much money I have."* She said that she has enough money to do what she wants once the divorce is final. She told Amanda, in my presence, *"If the marriage doesn't work out, you have a nice little nest egg at the end."* She detailed this plan with unbelievable enthusiasm and was smiling much of the time.

Tiffany also boasted of *"a while back"* taking some $80,000 out of her account and placing $40,000 each in the account of her mother, Susan Nelson-Stephanson, and her brother, Timothy Nelson. The only details she would give is that, if it came down to it, she was going to tell the court it was a business loan that she was repaying to her mother and brother.

On another occasion, I received a call from a mutual acquaintance of Tiffany and mine, by the name of Susan Blessing. She said that she and several other women (Melissa Nordquist and Tamara Gerbich are two names I remember) were meeting at Paradise Bakery for an intervention with Tiffany. When I asked what the intervention was for, Susan said it was to get Tiffany away from Eric and into a shelter for battered women. I could not believe what I was hearing from Susan. I declined to go, as I had already started having my doubts about Tiffany's veracity and the abuse I was hearing about (grabbing the arms and verbal abuse) did not warrant a *"shelter for battered women."* **Side Note: A neighbor and her husband (Mary and Dave Houseman) were seated at a booth just behind their table and they overheard much of the conversation between these women. After hearing Tiffany bad mouth me, Mary turned to say "Hi" to Tiffany and let her know that she was listening the whole time.** A short time after this meeting took place, Tiffany showed up at my house crying. She said that she didn't know why her friends would have an intervention and wanted her to go to a shelter. She said to me, *"Eric would never lay a hand on me."* This was a complete contradiction to what she had told others and me, about Eric. I'm not clear where this conversation went from this point, as I was growing weary of her stories and was never clear what was truth and what was fiction. I pretty much let it go in one ear and out the other. I do remember that Tiffany said she was confronted by Melissa Nordquist, who told her that, due to the abuse Eric was inflicting, she was unwilling to continue a friendship with her if she stayed with him.

Tiffany told me that she couldn't lose Melissa as a friend. Eric was out of the house a couple of weeks later.

In closing:

The horrible stories that Tiffany told about Eric being "unstable," with a "crazed temper" and "violent, unpredictable outbursts," turned out to be completely false. In all the time I have known Eric, I have never known him to be violent or unstable. Eric is the epitome of what I feel a father should be and the girls, who he has with him every other week, have been a joy to be around ever since he was reunited with them after the Order of Protection was lifted. They love their father very much and don't like venturing too far from him. He seems to be their rock that they rely on continually and Katie and Megan, who he is very protective of, are the foundation and nucleus of Eric's life that he shows an incredible amount of love and devotion.

In these last few months, what I have seen through the interaction between Katie, Megan, and Eric, I cannot imagine that ANYONE would accuse this man of the horrible things that Tiffany said he did. They just didn't happen and I believe that Tiffany knowingly and maliciously, disparaged Eric for no reason other than to get out of a marriage that she was no longer interested in being in.

The above is true and correct to the best of my recollection.

Respectfully submitted,

Ryanne Ritter

I need to add a postscript regarding the language in Ms. Ritter's statement regarding the appointment with the girls' pediatrician, Diane Matsumoto. I cannot confirm the medical evaluation, of both Katie and Megan, to rule out sexual abuse by me. I was told, according to those working for, and in, Dr. Diane Matsumoto's office, even though I am the father of the 'patients', non-disclosure in relation to doctor/patient confidentiality is in effect. Nor can I confirm that when Dr. Matsumoto refused to see the girls, Tiffany took them to two different pediatricians for examination. Unfortunately, the names of those doctors were unknown then and remain so today.

All I have to go on is the sworn statement of Ryanne Ritter and considering how much has surfaced, and the amount of information Ryanne was privy to, I believe every word she has said. It was Tiffany's hope, according to Ryanne, that one of the doctors would bolster Tiffany's claim that I sexually assaulted the girls. Obviously, there was no one siding with Tiffany and no medical report as sexual abuse ever occurred. It sickens me to think, if this is true, that a parent would put two small girls (ages six and nearly eight at the time) through this type of examination, not once, but several times. I pray to God these examinations never took place, but the fear in my heart is overwhelming that they did.

On Monday morning I went to the Chandler Police Station and filed a request to obtain a copy of the police report Ryanne Ritter had just informed me existed. The following is that report and I was just as stunned, at reading its contents, as I was when I received the order of protection; maybe more so.

The *false* Police Report was filed with the Chandler Police Department on March 3, 2006, and in it, there are many contradictions. I'm surprised the Chandler Police didn't pick up on any of them. Anyone would think they have a keen eye for such inconsistencies, but then again, they had the beautiful and statuesque 6'1" Tiffany in front of them, claiming to be a victim and they probably fell all over themselves to help her.

This is exactly as it was filed and anyone can obtain a copy of the same to verify its content.

ERIC L. DI CONTI

Chandler Police Department
Incident Report

Report Date: 03/03/2006 10:58
Report No.: 06-02-5810

INCIDENT					
Report No. 06-02-5810	**Report Date** 03/03/2006 10:58	**Occurred From**	**Occurred To**	**Report Type** Original	
Incident Type Sex Offense - Child Victim		**Case Status** Pending - Sex Crimes	**Case Status Date** 03/07/2006	**Cleared**	
Location Information 1010 E REDWOOD DR Chandler, AZ (Maricopa County)					
CAD Dispo: 05 **Grid**: O18 **Beat Assignment**: 14			Total Damaged Property Value: $0.00 Total Stolen Property Value: $0.00 Total Recovered Property Value: $0.00		

OFFENSE 1
- **Main Charge/Offense:** 13-1405 SEXUAL CONDUCT WITH MINOR
- **City Violation:**
- **Location Type:**
- **(NSU) Action Taken:**
- **(NSU) Reinsp Date:**

PERSON 1
Person Type Reporting Person	**Business/Person Name** Tiffany Nelson		**Business Phone**
Home Phone (480) 385-9827	**Person Address** 2442 W ROCKROSE WY Chandler, AZ 85248		**Grid**
Other Phone	**Employer Address**		**Job Title**
Race White	**Sex** Female	**SSN**	**DL Exp. Date**	**DL Number**
Birth Date 1964	**Birth Location**		

Age: 041
Min. Height: 6'01"
Min. Weight: 140 lbs
Adult/Juvenile: Adult
Hair Color: Blonde/Strawberry
Eye Color: Green

PERSON 2
Person Type Investigative Lead	**Business/Person Name** Eric Diconti		**Business Phone** (602) 541-0847
Home Phone (480) 332-9656	**Person Address**		**Grid**
Other Phone	**Employer Address** 2330 W University DR Apt. 8 Tempe, AZ 85281		**Job Title** Superintendent
Race White	**Sex** Male	**SSN**	**DL Exp. Date**	**DL Number**
Birth Date 1959	**Birth Location**		

Age: 046
Min. Height: 6'01"
Min. Weight: 225 lbs
Adult/Juvenile: Adult
Employer: Nitti Bros Construction
Hair Color: Brown
Eye Color: Brown

Reporting Officer/Employee Offcr PHILIP Besse (00252)	**Department**	**Report Status:** Approved
Copies To		**Date/Time**
Final Review Supv ID# Sgt Bryan Cox (00564)	**Department** Chandler Police Dept	**Date / Time** 03/08/2006 09:19

Initial Police Report Pg. 1

Chandler Police Department
Incident Report

Report Date: 03/03/2006 10:58
Report No.: 06-02-5810

PERSON 3
- **Person Type**: Victim
- **Business/Person Name**: Kathryn Diconti
- **Home Phone**: (480) 385-9827
- **Person Address**: 2442 W ROCKROSE WY Chandler, AZ 85248
- **Race**: White
- **Sex**: Female
- **Birth Date**: 1998
- **Age**: 007
- Adult/Juvenile: Juvenile

PERSON 4
- **Person Type**: Victim
- **Business/Person Name**: Megan Diconti
- **Home Phone**: (480) 385-9827
- **Person Address**: 2442 W ROCKROSE WY Chandler, AZ 85248
- **Race**: White
- **Sex**: Female
- **Birth Date**: 2000
- **Age**: 005
- Adult/Juvenile: Juvenile

Reporting Officer/Employee: Offcr PHILIP Besse (00252)
Report Status: Approved
Final Review Supv ID#: Sgt Bryan Cox (00S64)
Department: Chandler Police Dept
Date/Time: 03/08/2006 09:19

Initial Police Report Pg. 2

ERIC L. DI CONTI

Chandler Police Department
Incident Report

Report Date 03/03/2006 10:58
Report No. 06-02-5810

Topic ORIGINAL REPORT

On 03-03-06 at 1058, Tiffany Nelson came to the CPD lobby to report that she suspected her estranged husband, Eric DiConti of sexually abusing or molesting their 2 young daughters. I spoke with her in the CPD lobby and obtained the following information.

Tiffany explained that she is currently married to Eric DiConti and has been for about 7 years. She said they have 2 daughters, 7 year old Kathryn and 5 year old Megan. Both attend Mt Carmel school in Tempe (Kathryn is in 1st grade and Megan, kindergarten). Originally they lived in Calif but in 8-2004, due to physical abuse, she took the children and moved to her mother's house (on Rockrose Wy) in Chandler. She then purchased the house on 1010 E Redwood Dr in Chandler. She said in 10-2005, Eric moved to Az to live, with the rest of the family. Then they moved to a house in Gilbert at 13917 E Galveston St. She said he there were no problems between Eric and herself for about 3 weeks and then she said he became physically abusive toward her again. She said in 2-2006 Eric moved out again. She does not know where he is currently residing. She said she will be vacating the Gilbert house this afternoon and moving back in to her mother's home on Rockrose Wy in Chandler.

Tiffany then told me that she suspects that some bad things have occurred between Eric and their 2 daughters. I asked her specifically to tell me what she was talking about. She said she has both physical and behavioral concerns. She said both daughters act like they're terrified of Eric. She said when he lived with them, he slept in a separate bedroom from her. She said during that time (and continuing today) the girls refuse to sleep in their own beds, insisting on sleeping with her in her bed. She said Megan used to be a "chronic bed wetter" and this stopped when Eric left. She said she has seen raw places on Megan's leg and genital area that she thought were chafed or abraded injuries. She said Katy has dramatic behavioral issues specifically with sexuality. She said Katy has a big problem with aggressively touching males genitals and self-rubbing her own vaginal area.

Tiffany said Eric behaves very angry and loudly and used to think that was why the girls were scared of him. She said Eric has told her that he has had dreams about molesting a 5 year old daughter he has with another woman. She also said she has copies of letters that Eric wrote to his father confronting him about molesting him (which she doesn't believe happened) and has letters written to her by the mother of another daughter Eric has, "warning her" of Eric's dreams of molesting his daughters.

Tiffany explained that she is planning on filing for divorce and has contacted an attorney about this. She said last night she had Eric served with an order of protection and already he has violated it. She said he was served at 1930 last night (03-02-06) and immediately afterward, he called her on her cell phone then called her house and left messages. She requested that I speak to him about not violating the order any further. I told her that I would do that, but I should not speak to him about this case at this point. She said she understood and agreed.

I called Eric on his cellphone at his work number. He said he did get served with an order last night and did try to call Tiffany, then called the house. He said he was blindsided by this, didn't understand what was happening and wanted to ask her about it. He said he read the petition for the order and said "I am not the person she describes" in the petition. He also said he understands he is not to contact her or the children as specified in the order and he said he will abide by it.

Tiffany feels strongly that Eric has done something bad, sexually, with one or both of her children and

Reporting Officer/Employee Offcr PHILIP Besse (00252)
Department
Report Status: Approved
Copies To
Date/Time
Final Review Supv ID# Sgt Bryan Cox (00S64)
Department Chandler Police Dept
Date / Time 03/08/2006 09:19

Initial Police Report Pg. 3

NOT THE LOVE OF MY LIFE

Chandler Police Department
Incident Report

Report Date 03/03/2006 10:58
Report No. 06-02-5810

requested that an investigation be conducted. I told her that I would forward this case to the supervisor of the sex crimes detective section for investigation as appropriate. I explained to her this could include forensic interview and possibly medical examination. I told her she should not speak to the girls about this problem or enroll them in any therapy until they hear back from CPD. She said she understood.

STATUS: This case is Pending - forwarded to CIS sex crimes, Sgt Boggs, for follow-up as appropriate.

Reporting Officer/Employee	**Department**	Report Status:
Offcr PHILIP Besse (00252)		Approved
Copies To		Date/Time
Final Review Supv ID#	Department	Date / Time
Sgt Bryan Cox (00S64)	Chandler Police Dept	03/08/2006 09:19

Initial Police Report Pg. 4

Below is the follow-up to the original Police Report, this Supplemental Report that states there is no evidence to file an arrest warrant, as Tiffany had basically contradicted everything she had claimed in the original report she had filed.

Further, there was never any disclosure by either Katie or Megan and as such, the case would be closed as "Unfounded." Two months after the initial complaint was filed on May 3, 2006, the investigating officer writes he has had no contact with Tiffany, nor had she sent him the documents she promised she would send.

This would be another huge miscalculation by Tiffany; she figured all she had to do was make her claims and the Chandler Police Department would just go find me, arrest me, and put me in jail. She never anticipated an investigation and she certainly didn't expect Wendy Dutton, a forensic *expert* in her field, would get involved. As intelligent as I sometimes give her credit for, she's really not that sharp.

NOT THE LOVE OF MY LIFE

#2

Chandler Police Department
Incident Report

Report Date 03/14/2006 14:33
Report No. 06-02-5810

	Report No. 06-02-5810	**Report Date** 03/14/2006 14:33	Occurred From	Occurred To	**Report Type** Supplemental
I N C I D E N T	**Incident Type** Sex Offense - Child Victim		**Case Status** Pending - Investigation	Case Status Date 05/03/2006	Cleared
	Location Information Chandler, AZ				
	CAD Dispo : 05 Total Damaged Property Value : $0.00			Total Stolen Property Value : $0.00 Total Recovered Property Value : $0.00	

Reporting Officer/Employee DET JOHN Beekman (00288)	**Department**	Report Status: Approved
Copies To		Date/Time
Final Review Supv ID# SGT JESUS BOGGS (00S22)	Department	Date / Time 05/03/2006 12:47

Page 1 of 3

Supplemental Police Report Pg. 1

ERIC L. DI CONTI

Chandler Police Department
Incident Report

Report Date 03/14/2006 14:33
Report No. 06-02-5810

NARRATIVE 1

Topic: SUPPLEMENTAL REPORT

This is a supplement to case #06-25810.

On 03-10-2006, I was assigned to investigate a possible sexual offense involving two girls (ages 5 and 7) and their biological father. This was reported by the mother of the children, Tiffany Nelson. Note - no disclosure was made by any child. Tiffany's concern is based solely on behavior she feels is caused by molestation. See original report for details.

On 03-14-2006 at about 1000 hrs, I contacted Tiffany by phone at her parents home (Tiffany told me she is currently staying there with her kids while the divorce proceedings between her and Eric go on). I informed her that I was assigned to investigate her complaint and asked her about her and Eric's relationship. Tiffany told me she and Eric got married and lived in California. In August of 2004, she said they separated and she moved to Chandler. Tiffany said this was due to Eric's abusive behavior and her and the kids fear of him. Tiffany said Eric was never physically abusive to her or the girls, but was constantly yelling and using obscene language when he yelled or spoke to her. She said he would stand in front of her not letting her walk around him, but never touching her either. Tiffany stated he used to yell at the kids and would grab them roughly by the arm or shoulder when disciplining them for things like spilling juice at the table.

Tiffany said they stayed separated until October of 2005. She told me Eric moved to Chandler and they lived in the same house on Redwood Drive. She said she only reconciled with Eric after he agreed to stop his behavior and abide by some rules she established, such as no more lying to her. Tiffany also said she was thinking of Kathryn and Megan and did not want to share custody due to being separated. Tiffany told me it was about two weeks before Eric went back to using profane language, intimidation, and an aggressive attitude to her and the girls. She said she caught him lying to her again and kicked him out of the house on 02-28-2006.

Tiffany told me her children have told her they are happy Eric is out of the house and tell her not to let him come back. She said they were afraid of him the whole time he had moved into the home and that was when they began to sleep with her. Tiffany said she and Eric slept in separate bedrooms and their's was not a sexual relationship - "He is not able to perform." She said Megan stopped wetting the bed and they are different children with Eric gone.

I informed Tiffany that I spoke to Wendy Dutton at Child Help USA. I said Wendy (expert forensic interviewer of children) and agreed that with no disclosure from the children it would be inappropriate and baseless to conduct an interview. I told her we also agreed that it is more plausible that the behavior of the children is more directly linked to the environmental changes Eric brings into the home and the divorce they went through. Tiffany said this was possible and I gave her information about a book that Wendy suggested she read to her kids. I also told Tiffany that if she had a counselor speak to the children and disclosure was made, to call me. Shes aid she understood.

On 03-28-2006 at about 1000 hrs, I called Tiffany for an update on her children. I also asked her about the dreams she said Eric had talked about. Tiffany said the kids have been doing well. She said Eric told her about these dreams about ten years ago and was referring to dreams he had about his then 17 yr old daughter from his second wife. Tiffany told me she is Eric's third wife and Kathryn and Megan are their biological children. She said she had spoken to this second wife about the dreams, but was told

Reporting Officer/Employee: DET JOHN Beekman (00288)
Department:
Report Status: Approved
Date/Time:
Copies To:
Final Review Supv ID#: SGT JESUS BOGGS (00S22)
Department:
Date / Time: 05/03/2006 12:47

Supoplemental Police Report Pg. 2

Chandler Police Department
Incident Report

Report Date 03/14/2006 14:33
Report No. 06-02-5810

the woman had no concerns about it then or now. Tiffany noted that Eric has not said anything like this about their own kids.

Tiffany said that Eric had written the letter many years ago detailing sexual abuse by an unknown older man when Eric was very young. She said she does not know whatever came of this alleged incident, other than no law enforcement contact was made. Tiffany told me Eric has also accused his former girlfriend's step-father and her own step-father back in November 2005 of being convicted child molesters. Tiffany said this is all false.

I asked Tiffany about her concerns on the computer she and Eric have in the home. She told me she has hired an "independent computer forensics technician" to examine it for child porn. She said she would call me if anything was found on it.

Tiffany also informed me that the order of protection she filed against Eric had been quashed. She said this was on 03-27-2006 when Eric disputed it. She said she would send me a copy. She also said the divorce is still on. I told Tiffany to call me if there was any disclosure from the children or child found on the computer. In the meantime, if I do not hear from her, I will be closing out the case as unfounded. She said she understood.

As of this date (05-03-2006), I have not heard nor received messages from Tiffany regarding this case.

No further - case unfounded.

Reporting Officer/Employee: DET JOHN Beekman (00288)
Final Review Supv ID#: SGT JESUS BOGGS (00S22)
Report Status: Approved
Date / Time: 05/03/2006 12:47

Supplemental Police Report Pg. 3

"YOU ARE NEVER GOING TO BELIEVE WHO I TALKED TO."

"Luck is a very thin wire between survival and disaster and not many people can keep their balance on it."
– Hunter S. Thompson

I couldn't wait for Monday morning to come and when it did, the first call I made was to Gillespie and Associates. I asked for Michelle Kunzman and was informed she had not yet arrived at the office. I told the receptionist that I needed to speak with Michelle and that it was of some importance that she return my call at her earliest convenience. I hung up the phone and sat there, recounting over and over the conversation I had with Ryanne two days before.

I was in a state of euphoria knowing that Tiffany had fouled her surroundings by the little act of thievery, she committed upon her business partner. By Tiffany's miscalculation of Ryanne's loyalty, I was in an excellent position to vindicate myself. All along I knew I needed some luck and now that I had it, I felt like I was the luckiest man alive. And I truly was. Or, so I thought for a while. In the coming months, I would discover how devastating it is to have a police report filed on you. Not just any police report, but rather, one that portrays you as a pedophile, regardless of the fact you were never charged, let alone arrested.

Sometime later that morning my phone rang; it was Michelle. I excitedly told her everything that had been conveyed by Ryanne and I'm sure that I was rambling with the consciousness of a six-year-old trying to tell the story of a captured lizard. Michelle told me to slow down several times so she could put her pen to paper as I spoke. When I was finished there was silence on the other end of the phone. I asked if Michelle was still there. She was still reeling from what I had just told her, amazed that Ryanne had broken ranks and defected to the other side. Michelle told me that I had better get to the police station and request a copy of the police report. She said that we would need it for the case.

She also asked if Ryanne would be willing to testify against her former friend, to which I responded by explaining that if I were an attorney and all I thought about was to get people on the stand to bolster my case, I may have asked, but I'm not. All I was interested in was getting as much information from her as I could at that point in time. Besides, I explained that Ryanne could be skittish at times and to jump on her and ask her to testify against her former friend could quite possibly cause her to clam up. That was not a chance I wanted to take, especially when she had so much information to offer. I suggested that we move through this one as slowly as possible.

Though Michelle agreed to tread gingerly, it would come to be realized the services of Ryanne Ritter would not be needed in the arena of Family Court. We would save her for the civil suit I would file several months later. The next step was to go before Honorable Eddward P. Ballinger. I thought they misspelled his name, too, but there really **are** three Ds in his first name. I mused that one of his parents had a stammer and the other, not wanting to embarrass their spouse, just spelled it phonetically; Ed-dward.

Later that morning I would meet Michelle and DeeAn for a dissolution conference at the office of a Judge Pro Tempor. I figured we'd speak further at that time.

ERIC L. DI CONTI

JUDGE CUCCURULLO

> "You shall do no injustice in court. You shall not be partial to the poor or defer to the great, but in righteousness shall you judge your neighbor" – Leviticus 19:15

April 24, 2006

The Honorable Judge Ballinger is what I would imagine "Joe Judge in Scottsdale" to look like. He was a tall, handsome man with salt and pepper hair, his voice was subtle and calming and when he spoke his words were deliberate, well thought out, and direct. He was a I-follow-the-law-by-the-book-and-to-a-tee judge and it appeared he did not deviate from the law. The following year I would find this assumption to be horrifyingly true when a stupid blunder, on his part, would cost me a few hours of freedom. However, all that happened at this stage was Ballinger figured out the temporary child support payments that I was to pay and then told us we would have to attend a Dissolution Conference in front of a judge pro tempor. When he was done speaking, Judge Ballinger summarily sent us on our way.

The judge pro tempor, we were slated to appear in front of, went by the name of Cuccurullo, or something like that; the conference would be held in the offices of her law firm. I don't really care what the name was, or the spelling of the same is, as she was as useless as reading glasses for a blind guy. She was a scarecrow-looking woman with a whiney little voice that gave me a rash when she spoke. I remember her hair being pretty big as if it was teased up like you would see on *any-woman-any-town* in the 1960s. The only thing she was missing was horn-rimmed sunglasses, peddle pusher, or Capri's, Keds, and a scarf.

A judge pro tempor is a person who *wants* to be a judge and does this shit as practice. I would have thought this woman would take charge of the conference between Tiffany and Jewett and me and my attorneys, but all she did was bitch that it was taking too long and she had other things to do. I thought to myself, "Well if you had other shit to do, ya shoulda stayed home today, lady."

I believe some lawyers want to be judges so they can wield an immense power that no one else possesses, or is able to possess in *their* world.

When in the courtroom, all attention is upon the lawyers and it is their clients who most often look up to them. They even have judges listening to them! It's almost as if many of them were destined to be a person of authority because they were the ones getting pushed around in the schoolyard, or unable to compete in most sports due to lack of ability. Or maybe they were unable to land the hot chick, or guy, in school, etc., so the only "I'll show them" recourse, they had was to become an attorney. They made people take notice when they were speaking in open court. But then to take it a huge step further they could become a judge and *really* have some power!

I have personal knowledge of two women who became attorneys after an ugly divorce; they practice family law and for the most part, only represent women. Go figure. Make that three attorneys; Cuccurullo claimed she went through an ugly divorce, too, though I'm not certain if she only represents women. It kind of surprised me that she would confide in us her inadequacies as a spouse.

In the conference room of this scarecrow's office, we argued over what both sides felt important to their respective sides and some trivial BS that was as insignificant as a mouse breaking wind, but we plugged along. In the end, it was determined that among the other truly insignificant things;

1) Tiffany, after working for 15 years as a paralegal-ish person making nearly $80,000 a year in Los Angeles, was unable to make any more than a mere $2,800 per month in the Arizona workforce, more specifically as a "real estate expediter," which would factor in the figuring of child support.

2) Tiffany's "salary" coupled and figured into my $75,000 annual salary, I was to pay some $400 and change each month in child support.

3) The girls would stay at Our Lady of Mount Carmel Catholic School in Tempe as long as I paid the full tuition and did not fall more than 30 days behind. In the event that I **did** fall behind, Tiffany could unilaterally pull the girls from the school and place them in a school of her choice.

4) We would both be responsible for whatever credit cards were in our respective names, which would include the five credit cards in my name that were left behind when I made my unceremonious departure from the home I lived in. One of which boasted the purchase of a ring from a jewelry store I had never been in. Another went to the purchase of lingerie in some rat-hole I had never heard of, and so on. After I was excused from my duties as a husband and separated from them, these cards were never seen again, so I'm sure you get the picture. It would be several months later I would get bills from these credit companies saying the cards were maxed out and the balance owed them was due, in full, immediately. Of course, even though the purchases were not made by me, Tiffany was my loyal wife, and since Arizona was a community property state I was responsible for paying these debts no matter who made the purchases.

5) From the $68,677.38, which Tiffany removed from the bank account the day before the Order of Protection was served and before I went to the ATM that fateful night, I would receive a paltry $7,593.01 and of that amount, I would pay to Gillespie and Associates $7,593.01, so I basically walked with a big fat goose egg.

6) The biggest and most precious of everything decided in the "conference" was custody. Tiffany wanted nothing more than to have my custody broken off completely and did her damnedest to undermine the court's decision at every turn, including trying to get Dr. David McPhee, who you will read about a little later, to write a letter to Judge Ballinger saying he thought custody should be "every other weekend and one day a week with no overnight stays." She would tell Dr. McPhee, in my presence, the

court wanted a letter from him stating as such. Thankfully, Dr. McPhee, along with the people representing me, would quash her plans before they started. She was informed that the only body that could change custody was the court itself. The final decision on custody would be to remain as it was; 50-50 custody, alternating weeks. Being that I was living in fear of losing my girls, due to her actions in carrying out her long, thought-out plan, maintaining 50-50 custody was my biggest victory. Little else mattered to me, but it was also Tiffany's biggest loss. Of course, for Tiffany, losing the chance of having more custody also meant losing a great deal more money in child support than the girls would have been entitled to, and to her, by virtue of what Tiffany is made of, money to her was of great importance; little else mattered.

In the end, we walked out of the law offices of Cuccurullo less than satisfied as the judge pro tempor, by her own admission, had complained that going through a divorce herself, she felt she was "jacked" by the system and by her former husband.

It was all too apparent what side of the fence she was standing on, by her biased demeanor and her underhanded comments in trying to persuade me to want less than 50-50 custody, that the girls would be better served with their mother the majority of the time. Her insistence that Tiffany really couldn't make very much money in Arizona. Her feeling that the missing funds were a mere technicality and I shouldn't fuss over it; that I should be overwhelmed with happiness that $7,593.01 was a very generous gift. I could go on and on, but it would be useless to bore you with my woes of that "conference."

Another thing, all too apparent, was that I'm certain this "conference" had to be the very first one that Cuccurullo ever did. If she very gets on the bench as a REAL judge I pray for the well-being of any man before her and I pray to God Almighty, it is never me.

Upon leaving, I was handed a questionnaire/survey that asked my opinion on her performance during the "conference." It was an anonymous and confidential survey and by each person filling it out, the courts could see how their pro tempor did by the answers given and armed with these surveys could determine if these individuals were ready for a seating on the bench. What I did was put my name on the top of the page along with the Family Court Case number, made a copy of it, and sent one to the courts and the other to Cuccurullo. I had no problem with her knowing what I thought of her "expertise" in a setting such as the one we were in. In fact, I *wanted* her to know what I thought of her. In my opinion, a first-year law student would have faired equally as well, if not better than this completely misplaced malefactor. Next stop; the courtroom of Eddward P. Ballinger for his final blessing of the divorce decree.

"DADDY, JIM IS BOTHERING US."

"Though one can be overpowered, two can defend themselves, but a strand of three cords is not easily broken." - Ecclesiastes 4:12

July 2006

Both of the girls were in their room speaking very quietly one day and when they came out, they were holding hands and looking worried.

"Daddy, can we talk to you?" Katie asked.

"Sure sweetheart. What about?" I was floored that two little girls, who were barely six and not quite eight years old, would have the courage to approach me in this manner. They were obviously in their room discussing how to address a problem they had and when it was decided how they wanted to approach me, as a show of unity they did so together, holding hands. It was a beautiful sight.

"OK," Katie said. "You promise you won't get mad?"

I laughed. "No, I won't *promise* I 'won't get mad'." I saw that both of my daughters were now very serious, so I too, became serious.

"What's wrong? Come over here and tell me." I urged as lovingly as I could. "Remember our 'rope?' That's gonna keep us safe. You know that right?"

Our "rope" refers to the quote at the beginning of this chapter. At the beginning of our journey through hell, dealing with lawyers, the court system, police, and everything else that haunted us, I used that Bible Verse to show them that as long as we stuck together, as a family, we would become that "rope." As Ecclesiastes speaks of "a strand of three cords" we, too, were three and if we stayed together and became that "rope" we could not be broken either. It was the easiest way for me to explain to these beautiful little faces the importance of staying close as a family and even as young as they were, they understood immediately. We became that "rope" and have been ever since. I refer to the "rope" often and even made a few little replicas of a piece of twine, separating the three strands and putting knots at the end of each.

They both agreed that the "rope" was an important factor in our lives.

"Well if we have the 'rope' then what do you have to worry about? Come over here and sit down with me, so we can talk."

I told them how proud I was that they were in their room discussing how to approach me with their problem. I told them that not every kid their age would have the understanding of addressing a problem the way they did and then have the courage to come to their father with it.

"Especially two little girls coming to their *father*!" I said.

They both smiled at me, which told me they had eased up a bit, and then, as I listened intently, they told me what was bothering them.

They said that their mother's boyfriend, Jim, had been hugging them, patting their behinds, kissing them, and calling them, "babe." I sat there and listened to my girls as calmly as I could, all the while, knowing my blood pressure was increasing as it surged into and back out of my heart for another cycle through my body. I hoped to get through their story with as little emotion as possible, but when they got to the part where their mother forced them to "kiss Jim back" and tell him they loved him, as well, my agitation became more apparent.

I nearly lost it when Katie said, "The part that bothers us the most is when Jim comes in at night and lays down in our beds with us."

"What?" I demanded.

"Are you mad, Daddy?" I realized my emotions were now clearly displayed.

I stopped myself. "No sweetheart. I'm not mad at you guys, at all. I promise. But I need you to tell me exactly what you mean by what you just said. I mean, I want to understand exactly what Jim is doing before we can make a decision on what we're going to do about it."

"Are you going to talk to him?" Megan asked.

The girls became a little worried. And well they should have been, knowing how protective I am of them, but I assured them that I would not approach Jim on this. I said I would tell their mother that they were not comfortable with Jim doing this and that she needed to tell him to stop immediately. What I *wanted* to do was find him and beat him so severely, he'd be eating his meals out of a straw.

I wrote a pretty scathing e-mail to Tiffany, giving her my opinion on the matter, and felt that she was not being a very good parent to allow such a thing to happen, especially when she had claimed that her children had been molested. There isn't a mother on the planet who would allow another new man in her life to lay in bed with her children if she truly believed that her daughters had been molested by anyone. Her actions did not represent those of a parent whose children had been violated in such a manner.

When I received a response back that basically told me to mind my own business, I filed a motion and asked that the court to intervene and issue a Order of Protection against Tiffany's boyfriend. I pled my case as vehemently as I could and brought to the forefront that I had been accused of molesting my daughters and that the girls were already uncomfortable with this man. Unfortunately, the judge didn't feel my concerns were strong enough to warrant an Order of Protection and also said that the "minor children's mother needs to file a complaint, as well." Much to my surprise and desolation, my motion and request were denied.

I cannot believe that, the way the courts see it, as a father of "minor children" I am not capable of addressing the court and offering my concerns, that the mother must confirm my concerns. I was disappointed that the court is so biased as to disregard a father but defer to the mother instead for *her* concerns. I wondered if this judge wasn't the original judge that presided over Tiffany's request, for an Order of Protection, and dismissed me so as not to cause a conflict within his division, or maybe I was just being overly sensitive to the situation. Or maybe, since Jim Norton was, in fact, living with Tiffany it would be impossible for the courts to force him to move. There could have been a number of reasons for the denial, including his belief that what was going on was OK, but even though I asked, the good jurist would explain none of them to me. Regardless of what the judge believed, one thing is certain; for the girls to come to me in the manner that they did, something was definitely amiss.

I told both Kate and Megan that I would go through the courts for help and not cause any trouble for anyone. As sad as it is, their main concern was being retaliated against by their mother and her boyfriend. I again related our strength through staying together as a family and being like the rope in Ecclesiastes 4:12.

"No one can touch us, or break us apart, if we stay strong like a rope," I would tell them.

NOTE: The following document is the Request for Order of Protection I filed on July 28, 2006 and is public record. It was filed under the **Case #FC 2006-05098**. I must warn you, as I had just started writing these motions, it is not written very well, but as time went by I became quite adept as a composer of these documents. I would receive future compliments, from the Court, on my ability to formulate them. Please also note that the name of the boyfriend, Tiffany was seeing, was referred to as Jim **Newton** and not **Norton**, as is his correct name. My girls weren't certain of his name, which made this episode even less palatable. It appears in its entirety, and exactly as it was filed with the Court. Nothing has been changed.

REQUEST FOR ORDER OF PROTECTION

Eric Di Conti
14843 S. 8*th* Street
Phoenix, AZ 85048

In Pro Per

IN THE SUPERIOR COURT OF THE STATE OF ARIZONA
IN AND FOR THE COUNTY OF MARICOPA

In Re the Marriage of:	) Case No.: FC 2006-050978
TIFFANY NELSON,	)
Petitioner,	) REQUEST FOR ORDER
	) OF PROTECTION
ERIC DI CONTI,	) AGAINST JIM NORTON
Respondent.	)
	)
	)
	) DATED JULY 28, 2006
	)

(Judge Eddward Ballinger, Jr.)

_____

7/28/06

<u>Request for Order of Protection against Jim Newton</u>

I am requesting an Order of Protection on the behalf of my two young daughters, Kathryn (Katie) Di Conti and Megan Di Conti, ages 7 and 6 respectively. My estranged wife (Tiffany Nelson-Di Conti) and I are in the midst of wrapping up a divorce after more than 8 years of marriage. Both girls are a product of that marriage. Our custody/visitation is 50% (one week on and one week off with both parents) with drop off and pick up on alternating Fridays.

In the Resolution phase of this disillusionment, it was ordered by the Honorable Eddward Ballinger, that the girls see Dr.

David McPhee for counseling so as to enable them to "weather the storm" of a divorce as well as, help them to understand and adapt to the new lifestyles they are going to be living. Dr. McPhee is on the court's roster of approved psychological professionals.

Tiffany Nelson-Di Conti is currently involved with another partner whose name, according to my daughters, is Jim Newton. He is a fireman employed by The Town of Gilbert. The current location of fire station from which he responds is unknown.

On the week of 7/7/06 through 7/14/06 the girls were in my care. On July 10th, 2006 my daughters mistakenly met this man while their mother was on a lunch date with him. I had a work meeting in the same restaurant (and unfortunately at the same time) they met at. My work meetings are on the same days at the same time at this restaurant. It was a very uncomfortable meeting of the girls and the rest of our week together was filled with questions as to "why [their] Mommy was with this man." The girls were returned back to Tiffany on Friday, 7/14/06. The following day, Megan's Birthday Party was the first time the girls spent any length of time with him. He spent extended periods of time with them, on the days he did not work, over that week. The girls then came back to me the following Friday 7/24/06. He has only been in my daughter's lives, or spent any time with them, for one week.

Although I don't have a problem with the girl's mother being involved with another man, I do take issue with the manner in which he is involved. The reason for this request of an Order for Protection is that I have been informed by both my daughters of the following: 1) Mr. Newton continually refers to both Katie and Megan as "Babe;" 2) Mr. Newton has been, after encouragement from my wife to, "Give Jim a hug goodnight," they begrudgingly do so, at which time he kisses them goodnight; 3) Mr. Newton has laid in the same bed with them at night; 4) Mr. Newton has rubbed their backs on several occasions, while they were in bed; 5) Megan stated "We think Jim is having sleepovers with Mommy, but she doesn't want us to know; and on a lesser note 6) both have stated that "Jim kisses mommy in front of us."

Both Katie and Megan have expressed discomfort with <u>all</u> of his actions and expressed vehemently that, they "don't like *it when he does that." They don't understand why "Mommy is kissing someone else, when she is still married to [me]."*

It is my opinion and I hope the court agrees that this is irresponsible behavior on the part of Mr. Newton and certainly my wife, to allow this man to engage our children, in such an inappropriate manner, at such an early stage of our divorce as well as, such an early stage of their relationship. The girls are still trying to come to terms with what has happened in their young lives with respect to our divorce and to have this man behaving in this manner, after less than a week of being around them is, unconscionable. I would ask the court to grant this Order of Protection to ensure the girls are faced with as little emotional strain as possible. They've suffered enough without having their mother throwing another man at them in the hope that they'll accept Mr. Newton into their lives.

I would ask the court to order Mr. Jim Newton to stay away from Katie and Megan and have no contact with them, as long as they are in the care of their mother.

At the very least, allow Dr. McPhee the opportunity to assess them further and possibly give my wife some direction as to how she may introduce this man into their lives, in a healthy manner, without inappropriate touching. All that is happening is that the girls are becoming more and more confused by the actions of Mr. Newton and the allowance of his actions by my wife, Tiffany Nelson-Di Conti.

Respectfully submitted,

Eric Di Conti

There would be several other letters and motions filed on this matter, including a letter pleading with Judge Eddward Ballinger to have the girls assessed by a third party, court-appointed counselor, but that request went ignored completely. The early part of this divorce was the most frustrating, in that my attempts to bring some normalcy and a sense of safety into the lives of my daughters were dashed, seemingly at every turn and I just could not figure out why.

HEARING FOR FINAL DISSOLUTION OF MARRIAGE

"The boundary between instinct and reason is of a very shadowy nature." – Edgar Allen Poe

September 19, 2006

We were back in Judge Ballinger's Courtroom and this time, Tiffany didn't have her entourage with her; it was just her and Jewett. I was once again with DeeAn Gillespie and Michelle Kunzman. We were in front of Ballinger for maybe twenty minutes where he congratulated us for being so agreeable in what was to be divided. I'm not sure where he arrived at that determination, because I didn't get much more than a few shirts, couple of pairs of pants, shoes and a couple of boxes of stuff Tiffany *didn't* throw away and 50-50 joint custody of my girls.

After perusing the file, he asked both Tiffany and I if what was contained in the file and decree is what we decided amicably in the Dissolution Conference. Once we responded positively he added his signature to the bottom of the Decree and Parenting Plan. I wanted to let him know how I really felt about the whole process and as I sat up in my chair and cleared my throat it was obvious I was about to say something, but Michelle put her hand on my wrist. I looked over at her and she ever-so-slightly shook her head from side to side, as if to say, "Don't fuck this up now."

I glanced at Michelle and then down at the table in front of me and finally slumped back into my chair. Judge Ballinger was giving his final ruling on the matter and as he did so, I faded into my own private thoughts. His words began to fade from my hearing as if he were walking away from me as he spoke until everything he was saying was completely undetectable to my ears. Although he was speaking and my eyes were able to send impulses to my brain telling it so, my auditory senses had ceased to respond.

As I lapsed back into my very familiar vacuum, I thought to myself, "How much more fucked up could this get? I've had everything taken from me. Every penny that Tiffany and I had, disappeared from our bank and was hidden away in some other phantom bank account. I have been accused of molesting my own children and had a police investigation conducted due to that accusation.

Tiffany, I was told by parents at the school, even passed out small fliers, at the girls' school, identifying me as a pedophile. I lost over a month of my girls' lives due to this detestable and repugnant hideousness of a human being by the lies she spread throughout the community. I spent thousands of dollars of Laura Verdi's money and $7,593.01 of my own money; which was "awarded" to me, out of the $68,677.38 she clipped from our account on March 1, 2006. The amount awarded to me was basically thirty-nine dollars, over eleven percent of what was stolen from that particular account. If I was to figure eleven percent of the amount actually skimmed and stolen out of our accounts over the years, the figure would be much greater, but not nearly the amount I should have received. And I still had outstanding attorney's fees totaling nearly $15,000 left to pay. How much more 'fucked up' could this get?"

In the end, the most important factors of this divorce were that the court saw through Tiffany's lies and I had equal custody of my children; far more custody than many men get – or even want sometimes. I was very thankful for that and in the grand scheme of things it outweighed the negative aspects of the divorce.

With child support and custody set, Ballinger wish us luck and we were excused from his courtroom; however, it wouldn't be the last time we would be before him.

Upon exiting the courthouse, as Michelle, DeeAn and I, walked to our cars, Tiffany approached us. Jewett was not by Tiffany's side. She had already slithered to her own car and crawled onto the highway in search of more sick and diseased urchins to devour. To this day, but for one statement Tiffany made, I don't know what it was that Tiffany said, or asked of me.

After tilting her head to one side and allowing her hair to flow to her shoulder, she reached out and touched my hand and said, "Eric, it's me, Tiffany. We had so much together."

"Holy shit!" I thought, "Are you kidding me? After all the bullshit you pulled, you sick and twisted bitch, you're pulling this?"

Recoiling, I pulled my arm away and said, "Don't touch me."

This was a woman, though she gained a great deal monetarily, knew she was beaten on all other fields of battle, figured that the last ditch effort to draw me back into her sick and twisted little world was in order. The fact that she attempted to do it in the presence of my attorneys was amazing in and of itself, but all she ended up doing was prove she was nothing more than an oozing eyesore, milling about our society.

She shrugged and said, "Huh! Well I tried to be nice." She then turned and walked away.

"That woman has some nerve," Michelle said, as we watched her stroll across the parking lot as if she hadn't a care in the world.

"Yeah, no shit!"

As Michelle, DeeAn and I parted ways, I thanked them for everything they did for me and my girls. Their job was done. They got me through the dismissal of the Order of Protection and negotiated a divorce settlement with 50-50 custody. Had I had more money the battle would have raged on, well past September 19, 2006. I would have been able to prove that each move Tiffany made had been carefully planned and orchestrated to fit into the final act of her self-directed play.

She would have been exposed on so many levels, she may have been the one who disappeared from society and not me, as she had hoped and planned. Ultimately, I believe I would have gotten far more in a settlement. Everything happens for a reason and this was one of those times that I was called by a higher power to hang it up for the time being. There would be another time to fight in another battle, but for now, it was time to focus on being a Dad and enjoy my girls.

ON A SIDE NOTE: Each time we enter, or exit, a courtroom we are reminded of how the judicial system in this country works.

Each and every law in this country is made up, and written, by lawyers. Each and every law is interpreted by lawyers. Judges are lawyers. You can't go into a courtroom without a lawyer and if you do, be prepared to have your ass handed to you. Courts, which are run by lawyers, make it impossible to win at anything, within the confines of the courthouse, if you don't have a lawyer by your side. The courts are a place where lawyers help other lawyers make money; a lot of it. If you don't have any money to pay a lawyer, you will lose a larger percentage of what you win, so ultimately, without a lawyer, it is a losing battle. Conversely, it's a losing battle *with* a lawyer, as well. The laws in our country see to it that other lawyers keep the lawyers who write and interpret the law monetarily safe. Judges make certain of it.

Providing you can afford one, there is no alternative **but** to hire a lawyer, thus perpetuating the disease of our addiction to needing a lawyer. By the need for a lawyer, there is no in-between and no gray area; either you have the means, or you don't have the means. And in the judicial "caste system" of social order it is the difference between the "elite" and the "untouchables." The winners and the losers. If you do not have the means by which to hire a lawyer to protect yourself, the lawyers make sure you are punished for not having the means to keep them fed. The "Goog ol' Boys Club." It boils down to being able to legally extort money from whoever isn't a lawyer, or one of *them*.

Lawyers and judges are a strange breed of predatory animals who don't allow anyone into their circle and those who aren't in that circle are nothing more than the sick and feeble stragglers in a migrating herd of wildebeests. They can offer nothing more than a good meal to those higher up in the food chain. Don't get me wrong; DeeAn Gillespie and Michelle Kunzman did wonderfully for me, I am forever grateful to them and I do not see them in this light. It's the lawyer-born concept of *needing* or the *must-have* in a lawyer, that is so wrong and really pisses me off.

"ARE YOU WITH THESE GUYS?"

"Though they bear a droll resemblance to humans, they carry their brains and souls in their pockets."
- Unknown

October 2006

A month had passed since the final Hearing For Dissolution and I had gotten myself back to focusing on work, as well. I was, and had been, building in the residential market for Dynamite Custom Homes for several months. Dynamite Custom Homes was "operated" by Paxton Anderson who was the man Tiffany had met at Risen Savior Lutheran Church. He had the outward appearance of the wonderful, wealthy, family man and custom homebuilder who was looking for an addition to his "team." And shortly after meeting him in January of 2006, he did just that. With my Contractor's License, I would eventually become the Qualifying Party for Dynamite Custom Homes.

Shortly after coming aboard, I would learn he also had an insatiable appetite and proclivity for thoroughbred horses. His obsession for these animals didn't stop at gambling on them at the satellite wagering and watering hole of Skip and Jan's, located at Priest Road and Elliot Road in Chandler, Arizona. Each time I walked into the place, early on, I would be asked by one of the cocktail waitresses, "Are you with these guys?" Thinking back, and not to pat myself on the back, I wonder if it wasn't a question of surprise as opposed to one of general inquiry; placing the emphasis on the "with" as opposed to the "these" in the question. Of course after several visits and getting to know each waitress they stopped asking, which may have been a curse. By then, I *was* associated with "these guys."

Skip and Jan would ultimately lose their gaming license for a year, due, in part, to their allowing a small bookmaking operation to be conducted inside their establishment by a patron we all knew and utilized equally. This off-track betting site would be an almost daily meeting place for Paxton himself and several acquaintances. Most of them would have a hand in Dynamite Custom Homes in one manner or another.

One of those characters was a salesman who called himself, "The Godfather." His name was **Michael Auditore** (pronounced "ah-da-tory"), but when he introduced himself he would say, "Call me Audi, like the car," which didn't make much sense to me; the car is pronounced "ow-dee" and he called himself "ah-dee."

Audi dabbled in brokering insurance from medical, to vehicle, to marine, to liability, to workers compensation, to you-name-it. If it could be sold, he would sell it. He worked from his home in Ahwatukee, where he lived with his wife and twin girls. When he ventured away from it, which was daily, he would normally be in one of two places, Skip and Jan's, or Rocky Point, Mexico where he had a small fishing boat, which he claimed he chartered from time to time. Unless he had just arrived at Skip and Jan's, I rarely saw him sober.

Another of his flaws was shown brightly when a girl of any size or proportion and any varying degree of beauty, or lack thereof, sat at our table. The only criteria were that she was female.

He always made it a point to pull out "the little blue pill," he carried with him, to let the girls know he was "equipped" if they were interested. It was pretty comical the way he held the Viagra next to his face, between his forefinger and thumb, then made his eyebrows dart up several times, as he held it for the girl to see. I don't believe he ever had any takers, but I chuckle when I think back to his antics. Audi had a thick New York accent and boasted of having connections in organized crime and just about every dim-witted hillbilly in the place believed his claims. His only problem was that he talked about it incessantly and never forgot to use the term "Mafia," in his dialog.

First of all, those who truly *are* "connected" don't ever talk about it and if they *were*, they would NEVER use the term "Mafia." The word "Mafia" is an insulting and foul connotation, made up many years ago by some scumbag journalist, which, in the minds of the milk-toast public, elicits unsavory thoughts toward Italians. Secondly, if there was a guy who truly was *connected* and was running his mouth as openly as Audi, his ability to speak would be interrupted on several different levels. It's people like Michael Auditore that give Italians a bad name; it is also people like Michael Auditore that wind up dying of lead poisoning, in the world he claimed to be a part of.

Michael Auditore was Paxton's *go-to guy* and when he needed it, Audi would lend a hand in getting "insurance" for various things, most of which was handled in back office meetings. When documents needed to be prepared and shown to city officials and banks, proof that insurance was "*in place.*" If a document needed to have a certain date on it, regardless if that date had already passed, Audi made sure Paxton was in *compliance*. And Audi was compensated nicely for his efforts.

Another character and close acquaintance of Paxton Anderson was a guy named **Michael Furois** (Fur-wah). Though he lived in an upscale neighborhood of Ahwatukee, I never knew him to have a real job, or even know what he did for work, though he claimed to be a financial advisor who had a pretty keen understanding of the tax laws. He claimed he was married, however on the several trips to his home, I never saw his wife. On the horses, in Skip and Jan's, he always made small wagers and hoped for the "big hit," which came in for him from time to time. Mike was jumpy and startled easily, but also an affable guy whom I liked very much. I never quite understood why he was associated with this group of whack-jobs because he just didn't quite fit the psychological characteristics of the rest of them. He may have wondered the same thing about me; I hope he did anyway.

Pat Reesman made the Greek God, Bacchus, look small and outweighed most sumo wrestlers. He was at least *two* of me and at the time, I weighed 230 lbs. Standing around 6'3", I estimated his weight easily in excess of 450 pounds and possibly eclipsed one quarter of a ton. I believe he was at a maximum human density before one would normally be confined to a wheelchair, or bedridden. Rotund would not even be a word one could safely use to describe this behemoth, nor would the term, grotesquely obese. The work van he drove listed heavily, to port, when he was behind the wheel. He had a small alarm company that he and his sons ran and the way he gambled, I'm surprised they were able to stay in business. He would throw down some heavy green at the windows and when he lost, he would pout and complain to anyone within earshot that he meant to bet on the winner. When he hit, the payoff was normally substantial.

His drinking habits were epic, as I had personally witnessed him (the absolute truth) down over thirty (30) Long Island Ice Teas in one afternoon; and Skip and Jan's does not "short-pour" anything. He topped it off by drinking another ten (10) Corona's before he walked out. When the bill came I grabbed it just to count the total number of drinks that were tallied on it; *31 Lng Il, 10 Cor*. Truly amazing.

Pat invited me to his house one night and, for some reason, I went. He was very proud of his home and wanted to give me a tour of it. His house was also in the Ahwatukee area of Phoenix and is backed up to the transition lane where Ray Road meets Chandler Boulevard; a basketball hoop in his backyard was visible from the street, as you passed.

Upon entering the house it was obvious that a party was going on and when I got to the center of the action I knew that I no longer wanted to be there. One of Pat's sons was on the couch in the family room with a very young girl on his lap. She may have been fourteen, or fifteen and had a beer in her hand. All around the room and outside in the pool were young kids; most under the age of eighteen. I told Pat to give me his tour and then I had to leave, that I just remembered I had somewhere else to be. I was nervous.

He walked me through what I would describe as a very blah house with little character; a cookie cutter floor plan that is seen in nearly every house in the area. I couldn't understand why Pat was so impressed with his home. In a couple of rooms, we walked into and had some activity happening under the sheets of the bed and we exited as quickly as we entered. Pat never wanted to know who was in the beds. Nothing much beyond losing a bet on a horse race really bothered Pat . . . which bothered me. I had to get out of there and get out quick, but before I could he wanted to show me the master bedroom.

This room was as big as any I had ever seen and the one imposing feature in it was a standard king-size bed that had the appearance of a caricature one would see in a cartoon. The mattress was bowl-shaped with the corners angling upward and the bottom of it could be seen protruding below the sideboards of the wood bed frame. The mattress was clearly under a great deal of continuous downward pressure; it nearly touched the floor. The bedposts were leaning at a very drastic approach toward the center of the bed. If the posts were to continue in a straight incline they would have probably intersected each other about ten feet above the bed. It was painfully clear that this was the resting place of Pat Reesman when he assumed a dormant state. I'm certain that the bed hated him.

I thanked Pat for the tour and headed for the door. He urged me to stick around and grab myself a beer, but after being accused of child molestation and all the bullshit I went through in court, Pat's house was the last place I wanted to be when the police showed up to quiet the party. Or worse yet, the visit of a worried parent, looking for their daughter and upon seeing what was going on, calling the police. I was as nervous as a whore in church and couldn't get out of there fast enough. I was in my truck and back on Ray Road, heading home, within a few minutes.

Steve the Bookman was another one of those characters that was a nice enough guy as long as he was sober. Once the alcohol hit him, but for the word "obnoxious," there wasn't a much better way to describe him. He was loud, wanted to be friends with everyone and he never shut up. He was also the reason that Skip and Jan lost their gaming license. He would take on new players in his two-bit operation without ever checking the guy out. As long as another guy vouched for the new player, he was in, no matter how well the person *vouching* knew the new player. It was crazy in my eyes.

"You wanna play?" He would ask. "I'll get you a number." And within a few minutes, the guy had his own ID number with which he could call in to place his bets.

Being, or becoming too complacent, in any setting, can bring a great deal of trouble, as would be the case for Steve. As luck eventually runs out for garrulous people, Steve signed up a "player" who also happened to be an undercover detective for the Phoenix Police Department and in the interim, got himself caught on a hidden camera in the detective's shirt. He was arrested at Skip and Jan's and made the evening news that night. The newspaper said that his operation was connected to the Genovese crime family in New York, but knowing how most journalists whore themselves and stretch the truth to sell a story, I wasn't accepting this as truth. If the Genovese family had a guy like Steve working for them, he wouldn't be working for them, or standing upright, too horribly long, if you catch my drift.

Joey Plany was Paxton's money-man in the office. He cooked all of the books for Dynamite Custom Homes and sent out draw requests to banks when a task had been completed on one of the custom homes we were building. At Skip and Jan's he was just another cockroach gambler who loved the exacta. He hit many of them and to the best of my recollection, he boasted a pretty good win percentage.

Joey, due to the premature loss of hair and not wanting to look like he was balding, kept his head shaved and supported several tattoos. He had a couple of characters from the Chinese alphabet on the back of each tricep, but couldn't remember what the characters meant, or signified. Or so he claimed. It just struck me as odd that a person would put a tattoo on his, or her, body and then forget why it was there, or what it meant.

In fact, I remember a guy I worked with at UDC Corporation, a 3rd generation Italian, whose son tattooed the word "WIAO" down one of his forearms. I asked my co-worker what it meant and he said it was some kind of slang for the word "Friend" in Italian.

I looked at him in complete disbelief, thinking "It sure as hell *better* be a slang, because there is no fucking 'W' in the Italian alphabet." I walked away shaking my head at the thought of this moron; thinking something is so cool that he had to have ink injected into his skin and then misspelling it, or not even having the sense to at least do a perfunctory background on what he wanted attached to his body. People are so stupid sometimes.

Joey, with the presence of his tattoos, had the menacing appearance of a gym rat, as he visited the gym on a regular basis and was built pretty well; however, he was also one of the biggest pussies I have ever encountered in my life. This guy would back down from any altercation no matter how minor. A few years prior, he received some jail time for a drunk-driving charge, which he did on several consecutive weekends for a time. From the time he got up on Friday morning, he refused to eat anything solid; he would only drink water. The rationale he used was that if he ate anything solid, at some point he would have to defecate and he didn't want to go to the bathroom for fear of getting raped. He concluded that if he was seated on a toilet he was more vulnerable to an attack. I always laugh when I think about it.

If Joey Plany was *one of the biggest pussies* I ever met, then **Jason Rongstad** ranked up there with the biggest, *all-world, pussy*. Jason was a nice enough kid and possessed the proverbial "boyish good looks" which included a demure way about him that many girls were attracted to. The problem was that he possessed few social skills and couldn't wipe his own ass without someone telling him to do so.

The story I got from a few of his close friends was that he was a prodigy at golf and won a gang load of amateur tournaments throughout high school and received a scholarship to play at a major Division I College. His only drawback was that he didn't know he had to actually *go to class* in order to continue to play golf. With his scholarship retracted, he wound up back at home in Montevideo, Minnesota and sleeping until noon every day. That is, until he got hooked up with Paxton Anderson and was mesmerized by the lure of quick money, through the construction industry.

Jason was an infrequent visitor to Skip and Jan's, but he used our boy Steve the Bookman on a regular basis. Jason would ultimately get his contractor's license and after Dynamite had their license revoked, would carry the business through his own; JR Custom Homes.

Paxton Anderson made the largest wagers of anyone in Skip and Jan's, at any given time. He liked it that way. He always had to be the biggest and the best and carried a grotesquely large amount of money anytime he ventured into the place. It was not uncommon for Paxton to drop several thousand dollars on any given race, or combination exacta, or combination trifecta, or Pick Three, or Pick Six wager. Paxton threw a lot of money down on the horses and didn't care if he won, or lost, as long as he was betting on them. I would find out later the reason he didn't care was that the money he was throwing down wasn't even his, so why *would* he care?

His drinking habits were unknown only to him, as on many occasions after a few cocktails he would have episodes of blackout and never remember what he said, did, or where he went. To hear Paxton tell it, he drinks only a few when he goes out. Probably because his memory fails him after the third, or fourth drink.

His mouth is one that, to this day, I am astonished that he hasn't been beaten to death over how he speaks to people and openly uses the word, "nigger" in any setting he may be in. This short little man who resembles Barney Rubble, of The Flintstone's fame (with a beard), will use the "N" word to a black man and thinks nothing of it. It's commonplace in his world. When he started his tirades about anyone non-white, I usually put some distance between us. Working with the guy is one thing, but I am not one that anyone could even remotely call a racist and I won't associate myself, away from work, with anyone who is. I had always thought it would have been nice to hear that Paxton said the wrong thing to the wrong person and was relegated to eating his meals through a tube. Unfortunately, it never happened; at least as of this writing, it hasn't happened.

"WE'RE WAITIN' ON SOME LOOT"

"He, who has the gold, makes the rules." – A bastardized version of The Golden Rule

November 2006

For some reason money had become scarce and many of the sub-contractors were having to wait to get paid, even after the bank wires had been distributed. A few were never paid due to, according to Paxton, shoddy work, which disturbed me because Paxton rarely showed up on the job sites. I would let him know that his assumption of shoddy work was incorrect and that payment should be issued to each respective sub-contractor. Most often he would refuse, saying "the guy was an asshole" and that I "should find another subcontractor," which I did.

It was around this time I started questioning his business tactics. Each house I was building seemed to have, not one sub-contractor, but two and sometimes three for a single task. The grading would be done by one guy, usually Chris Trout of CST Enterprises, as would the concrete work, which was done by Payne Custom Concrete. Doug Payne and I would have many conversations about Paxton's payment practices and he would ultimately be the only subcontractor that Paxton would pay with any regularity. In the end, even Christ Trout would be owed several thousand dollars; a debt Paxton ignored. His normal cry to any subcontractor that complained he wasn't getting paid was, "Sue me and if you ever do see any money from me, you won't see a dime for at least two years."

One contractor, who would then be fired for "shoddy work," did underground plumbing and a second would do rough-in. That plumber was subsequently fired for "shoddy work," and a third would come in for finish work. The first half of the framing was done by one contractor and then fired for "shoddy work," at which time a second framer was hired to do the second half of the framing and then fired for "shoddy work." The third framer was then put into place to build the roof structure and summarily fired for "shoddy work." It went on like this for the entire project.

The worst part of this practice was that after each phase of construction, Paxton would keep the money from the progress payment the bank had wired and very little of the money went to the sub-contractors. If any money was paid out, it was to placate the noisy ones and keep them quiet, so they didn't start making waves.

Paxton's ace-in-the-hole was the fact that at the time, under Arizona Law in residential building, a sub-contractor cannot place a mechanic's lien on a property unless he, or she, is in contract with the owner of the property. To circumvent any issues of this nature, Paxton saw to it that ALL subcontractors were in contract with Dynamite Custom Homes, or JR Custom Homes and anyone who attempted to lien a property was sent a nasty letter citing the statute under which the person filing the lien is subject to a $5,000.00 fine, payable to the contractor, unless they removed said lien. The liens were normally removed within twenty-four hours. With the latitude of that beautiful little loophole in Arizona law, it was a great racket and Paxton utilized it at every turn and every chance the opportunity presented itself.

What finally drove me to actively look into what was going on was when an invoice came in from a stucco contractor that had been doing work on Mark Acre's house located on Lot 28, in the Mirabel community of North Scottsdale. Mark Acre, who remains a friend of mine, had played professional baseball and was a pitcher with the Oakland A's. Now retired he wanted nothing more than to build a house in which he could live in with his wife, Dominique, and start a family.

The invoice I reviewed was for around $42,000. I initiated it, giving my approval and handing it off to Joey Plany. He said a check would be sent out that afternoon for the full amount and I, in turn, called the sub-contractor to inform him of the impending payment. That was it; I heard nothing more about this until I saw the stucco contractor, some two weeks later.

"Hey, what happened to the check you said you were sending?" he asked.

I was surprised, "What do you mean? The check was sent that night. You didn't get it?"

"Nope. Nothing." He responded.

"I wish you had said something sooner. If I say the money is coming in the mail, it shouldn't take more than a day, or two. Why didn't you call me?"

He just shrugged.

"Okay, let me go to my office and find out what happened. Maybe it was returned for a bad address, or something." I knew that wasn't the case.

I hoped I was wrong, but I feared the check was never even sent. When I walked into the office I asked Joey what had happened to the check. He very coyly looked up at me and said, "Me and Packy had to get a horse nutted."

"Huh? What the hell are you talking about? What the fuck is 'getting a horse nutted' mean?"

Joey handed me an application for stud service. "Don't tell Packy I showed you that, bro."

I looked down at the fees and I felt a huge lump in my throat when the amount of $47,500.00 registered in my brain.

"Remember The Golden Rule, Luigi," Joey said smiling. "He, who has the gold, makes the rules."

"You mother fuckers got a horse laid instead of paying our sub-contractor? Are you fucking kidding me? Why?" I was pissed. "When is he going to get his fucking money, Joey?"

Joey tried to placate me. "Jeeze, Luigi. We're waitin' on some loot. He'll get paid as soon as this next draw comes in. Take it easy."

"Fuck that, Joey." I yelled, "I'm NOT going to take it easy! You owe this poor bastard money for the work he did and you pissed it away on a fucking horse, blowing his load into a mare you and Paxton own? Fuck you! Fuck both of you!"

I turned to walk away but decided I wasn't finished yet and walked back into Joey's office.

"You had better fucking hope that money comes in and you better fucking pay my guy as soon as you get it, or you're gonna be horse-fucked yourself. I hope the fuck you understand what I'm fucking tellin' ya."

"It will, Luigi. He'll get paid as soon as some more loot comes in." Joey loved using the term "loot" when it pertained to money and in a very short time, I would realize just how prophetic the term would turn out to be.

I turned and stormed out of the office. Joey may have soiled himself during my tirade, but I didn't really care, nor did I care if he called and told Paxton what I had just said to him. I was burning up inside and was ready to beat the shit out of something. I brought these stucco guys into this deal and they did the work because they trusted me and now they're getting screwed by Paxton because a horse needed to get laid? I wasn't going to let this go.

The following day, after calming down, I went back into the office and asked Joey what the hell was going on. I wanted to know why the subs weren't getting paid and why the horses were taking a front seat to them.

Joey looked at me and said, "Okay. It's like this, but don't ever tell PA I told you all this."

Joey proceeded to tell me the most amazing tale of deception, diversion, swindling, and fraud through document alterations. As he spoke and told me how one thing was done, he would pull a document from the file cabinet to prove what he was saying. There were countless documents.

In all my years in the construction industry, I had never heard a story quite like this. From start to finish it was as if he was telling me of a newfound leisurely activity that I should be jealous of and would want to join. And when he was done, I simultaneously felt like I had been run over a few times by the same bus and exhilarated at what a genius plan Paxton Anderson had hatched. I cannot tell you just how many light bulbs began to glow and then blaze, with white light, over my head.

Numerous times, during his story, I found myself thinking, "No wonder . . ." this, "No wonder . . ." that and "Well, that explains why . . ." It went on and on and on and on until he had sighed heavily and said, "We're trying to get everybody paid, Luigi." I looked at him, and all I could do was shake my head and walk out of the office. I'm sure he watched me walk away wondering what, if anything, I would do next.

As I drove away, I ran all the information I had just received through my head, over and over and over. Much of what he told me I had feared they were doing, but at the same time refused to believe this "God-fearing" man in Paxton Anderson would do such things to unsuspecting, hardworking people, as well as the people for whom we were building these homes.

CHRISTMAS IN MAUI 2006

Katie and Megan, Maui 12/26/06

"Every time a bell rings, an angel gets his wings."
– Clarence from It's a Wonderful Life.

December 25, 2006

In August, the girls' mother had failed to be with the girls and I, on their first day of school at Our Lady Of Mount Carmel. She had decided to take a short vacation with her boyfriend to Rocky Point,

Mexico. This was a well-traveled destination for Phoenicians, as it was only a few hours' drive to the Mexican coast. Tiffany and Jim Norton decided to take their trip over the weekend and through the following Wednesday, which meant she would miss the girls' first day of school and their weekly-scheduled Tuesday evening dinner. The girls were devastated that their own mother would have rather spent the time with her boyfriend than be with them when they walked into their new classrooms.

I was more than disappointed and quite frankly, I was pissed that she would prioritize her needs in this manner, but we held our heads high as we walked through the corridors. I kissed both of them on the lips, told them I loved them and that I knew they would be awesome students and that I would be there at their classroom doors when school let out. Tiffany didn't even bother calling the girls to, if nothing more, wish them luck, claiming later there was no cell service, pay phones, or even hotel phones with which to call them. The girls knew in their hearts this was a lie and they told me so.

The girls were so saddened and distraught that their mother wasn't there for them. On their first day of school, I made them a promise. I promised both of them, "I will never lie to you, I will never break a promise to you and I will never take a vacation, or travel anywhere, without you two being with me. Ever." It is a promise I have never broken.

I had been saving a few bucks each month and after nine months of dragging the girls through our divorce, I decided we needed a break; a fun break. I decide to surprise Kate and Megan with a trip to Hawaii, but my main concern was being able to keep it a secret. I was required to inform the girls' mother of any trips I wanted to take but had to do so by way of thirty-day advance notice and therein lay the problem. I knew better than anyone, that if I laid out the whole plan to Tiffany it would never be kept a secret.

My "plan" was to wake up on Christmas morning at around 4AM and for each of them, concealed in Christmas wrapping, a fully packed suitcase. They would then find out we were traveling to the tropical paradise they had only heard people speak of before. It would also be their first time on a plane. It was a wonderful plan and I couldn't wait to execute it.

What I did was send Tiffany an e-mail that I had planned to take the girls to California to see my brother, who had just returned from another tour of duty in Iraq. It was the only way I could have given notice of an impending trip and still stay within the court's guidelines of the decree.

My next problem was that I needed to get Tiffany to accept the girls on Christmas Eve, as her part in celebrating that holiday with the girls. I would offer her Christmas Eve and I would take Christmas Day and the following year, we would switch, me on Christmas Eve and she would take the girls all day Christmas. It was a very fair offer and one that is practiced often among divorced couples.

When I told her the "trip to California" was a surprise, she balked, saying she didn't care if it was surprise, or not, she was spending time with the girls on Christmas morning. We went back and forth, via e-mail, over the next week, or so and I finally begged that I had already purchased airline tickets for this trip (which was true) and it would cost me more money to change the itinerary at this late stage. She was unrelenting, so I played the only card I had. I told her that since the girls were with me for that week, I would not yield and if she didn't return the girls back to me on Christmas Eve, I would be forced to call the police to retrieve them.

As it turned out she had far more trump cards than I did, especially since she worked in a law firm. She requested and was granted an "Emergency Hearing" on the matter. Even though the Decree stated that we had to work through a "Parenting Coordinator" in Barry Brody, another money-seeking cockroach in the law business, if any problems arose. She sidestepped that little order and went right to the top; to Judge Ballinger. As *bad* luck would have it, Judge Ballinger was presiding over another case that was settled rather quickly and had time to hear our argument.

While I was driving in Fountain Hills one morning my phone rang. It showed "Private Number" on my screen and for some stupid reason, I answered it. It turned out it was from Ballinger's division and I pulled over to the side of the road. I never even saw this coming and was shocked that he would conduct a hearing telephonically between the three of us. Tiffany pleaded that she and her family have a long-standing family tradition to wake up Christmas morning, open presents, and have a family breakfast, which I knew was total bullshit, but who was I at this point? I was still reeling from the fact that I was testifying via cell phone about who the girls were going to be with on Christmas.

When it was all over, Tiffany was granted visitation for four hours on Christmas morning, but she would have to pay five hundred dollars toward the cost of changing the tickets to a different flight. I was disappointed that the judge had sided with her, but more importantly, I had to figure out how the hell I was going to finagle paying for the cost to change the tickets for a trip to *Hawaii* and not California. I decided to tell Tiffany the truth and that I didn't want the surprise ruined. I admitted our true destination was not California, but that I had actually planned to take the girls to Hawaii.

Tiffany pounced on the opportunity to bash me and began a motion-writing campaign to the court saying that I was untrustworthy and I should be disallowed to go anywhere. And just as I had feared, she also informed the girls of my Christmas *surprise* within hours of our conversation. Once again, the cards played in her favor. I was still able to go, and Tiffany was also still made to pay the five hundred dollars toward the fight change, **but** she would still get the girls until 12 noon on Christmas Day. I was screwed.

With the girls now aware of where I had intended to take them on our trip and Tiffany knowing I had made the promise of never lying to them, or breaking a promise to them, she had her own little plan. She thought that if she could somehow destroy our trip, it would be her way of showing the girls that I break promises, too, thus restoring the girls' faith in her. I knew exactly what she was doing and further reinforced my promise of a trip to Hawaii.

Instead of trying to hurt me and allowing the trip to proceed, as planned, Tiffany decided it was in **her** best interest to hang onto the court ruling of keeping the girls until 12 noon, on Christmas Day. As it turned out, it only hurt the girls.

I called Hawaiian Airlines to change the fight from a non-stop from Sky Harbor to Maui and found that there were no other flights past the time we had originally scheduled. My only choice was to get my ass to a travel agency and have them do the work on their computers, where the resources were greater, or I wasn't going anywhere. It took about three hours with a representative of Travel At The Foothills, in Ahwatukee, to figure out how to get the three of us to Maui, but it was finally done.

The end result, and possible itinerary, was a 10:51 PM flight out of Sky Harbor and arriving at LAX, in Los Angeles, at 11:12 PM. The flight to Maui was scheduled to leave at 7 AM the following morning, December 26, and arrive in Kahului, Maui at 10:33 AM. This meant that the girls and I would have to sleep in a terminal at LAX until the morning. I had to make a decision of whether, or not, I would accept these accommodations quickly, as they could have been purchased by another wayward traveler. I called and pleaded, once again, with Tiffany to allow us to leave as already scheduled, that the girls shouldn't have to sleep in a terminal at LAX.

All I heard on the other end of the phone was a maniacal laugh and Tiffany, in as condescending a manner as she could, saying to me, "Are you having trouble keeping your promise to the girls? Go fuck yourself." Her laugh trailed off as she hung up on me.

"I'll take the tickets to LAX and then on to Maui," I said to the travel agent. The added cost of the tickets was $1,750, which I had to borrow from a friend; I was NOT going to let my girls down and I was NOT going to break the promise I had made.

As I walked out of the travel agency, I looked down at the receipt and thought to myself, that the money was insignificant and I could make it up somehow, as long as my girls had something to be excited about. They hadn't much to be excited about all year and this was for *them*, not me.

I started thinking about the itinerary and about how a woman could knowingly let her two young daughters sleep in an airport terminal, without so much as a sniff about their safety. Especially being that the terminal was LAX; the biggest shithole of all west coast airports. She just didn't care, as long as there was a possibility of the trip being dashed, and I believe she expected me to cancel it, she wasn't budging. Whatever her desires were, she had to know there was a slight chance of me following through and I just couldn't believe she would allow the girls to be placed in this position; but she did.

On Christmas morning the girls were back at 12 noon, as scheduled, and the first thing the girls did was apologize to their mother and how she "was being mean," to me. I told them to forget about that, that we are only going to look forward to the trip and the people who are waiting for us in Hawaii. Already "in-island" was Bill Sheppard, his wife Micey, who helped me with the expense of the tickets, Ryanne and Charlie Ritter and their grandson, Brody. Another friend, Shawnna Gutierrez and her two kids, Summer and Jack were also part of the group.

We went home, opened the few presents I had for them and busied ourselves until it was time to go to the airport. At least we would still get to travel on Christmas Day. At least that wasn't ruined.

Sky Harbor Airport, in Phoenix, is a fairly small airport, considering it's categorized as international and it is also one of the cleanest. The girls were shaking with excitement from the time we left the house until the plane left the ground, but by then, though this would be their first time in an airplane, the girls were too tired to care about being up in the air. They fell asleep within minutes. As they slept, I leaned my head against the small window and while I attempted to make out the shapes of the landscape below, I thought about the events that brought us here. The dark landscape below and the lights that twinkled back at me silently passed below. Another thing occurred to me; for the first time in years, I wasn't afraid of flying. I wasn't afraid because the only two things that I truly cared about in this world were with me and if the plane went down, it would be OK. I wouldn't be leaving anything behind.

We landed, on time, at LAX and as we walked through a terminal, completely abandoned by humans, I scanned the horizon for a bench to lay claim to for the night. There was none in sight. I was carrying several bags myself and the girls, who were pulling theirs behind them on wheels, complained the bags were heavy and hard to pull. I commandeered a luggage cart that someone had left behind and loaded it up with all of our things. Megan was falling asleep as she walked, so I perched her up on top of the luggage, while I pushed it along; Katie walked sluggishly beside me. The terminal we were in was obviously closed for the night, so I decided to look elsewhere for a place to settle in for the night.

I decided that we would head over to Thomas Bradley International Terminal, where I knew there would be benches on which to sit and for the girls to lay down. We found one in a quiet area, on the second level, away from everyone so the girls could sleep. I wasn't about to close my eyes for one second. Not in this town and not for any reason; I was going to make sure my girls were safe. Megan was out as soon as she went horizontal, but Katie, the beautiful little trooper that she was, didn't want me to be lonely, so she stayed awake with me for most of the night. She finally succumbed to her body's need for rest about thirty minutes before the sun came up.

As the girls slept, I looked at the precious little faces of Katie and Megan, my eyes welled up with tears. I, once again, pondered the path we had taken over the past nine months and where that path had brought us. Due to the actions of their mother, these two beautiful little girls had endured so much pain, I asked myself why a parent would allow two innocent children to endure this. I couldn't, for the life of me, figure out what the catalyst for Tiffany's actions was, but I knew one thing for sure, the girls felt safe with me. They felt safe and they were sleeping peacefully, hopefully having dreams of coconuts, pineapple, grass skirts, beautiful flowers, white sand beaches, and the warm waters of Hawaii.

As the sun peaked over the eastern horizon, on December 26, I woke the girls up and told them that we had to get over to the other terminal so we could catch our plane. They were groggy, but as soon as it registered the plane was really, and finally, taking us to Maui, they were suddenly very much awake . . . and hungry. We grabbed a quick bite at the scummy little MacDonald's they had there and then headed back to the terminal from which we were due to depart. After checking in our luggage we sat in the waiting area for our flight to be called.

A voice came over the loudspeaker, "Now boarding Flight 4761. Non-stop service to Kahului, Maui."

The girls looked at each other and then at me. Their smiles were so big they looked almost like a couple of caricatures in a comic strip. I smiled back at them and once again, my eyes welled up; Tiffany hadn't won. She didn't break me and most importantly, I was keeping my promise to two little girls.

We spent a week at the Maui Coast Hotel in the town of Kihei, about 12 miles from the famous whaling town of Lahaina. The time we spent with our friends and the fun that Katie and Megan had, will forever be etched in my mind. For all the trouble, pain, and suffering they had to endure through the divorce of their mother, I thanked God this trip happened. They needed it. For years, they spoke about our trip to whoever brought up the subject of Hawaii.

"Our Daddy took us there for Christmas!" They would say to that person. It always makes me so happy that I was able to do that for them.

We came home, on New Yea'rs Day, 2007, the same way we left; via Maui to LAX and then to Sky Harbor, in Phoenix. Of all the places I have been in this world, because I was with my girls, our Christmas in Maui 2006 remains the best trip I have ever taken.

Caught in the Rain - Hawaii

Molokini Sunset - Hawaii

"THE KEENLAND YEARLING SALE?"

"Stay away from greed. The skinny pigs always stay alive; it's the fat ones that go to slaughter." – Chinese proverb

February 2007

After Joey told me of the activities that he and Paxton had been engaging in I knew I had to make a serious decision about my future. This was fraud and the situation was a grave one. These two assholes conducting business and committing fraud was one thing, but the fact that they were using **me**, the qualifying party on the contractor's license, to stay in business was not a good thing. This was a federal beef and I wanted no part of it. I was a single Dad with two young girls to care for and the information to which I was now privy, told me this was no place that would ensure any kind of a future pension plan, but rather would actually insure something along the lines of penance; behind a series of electric iron gates. After doing the Alcatraz tour many years ago I never again had any inclination to see the inside of a prison cell, but if they got caught I would be dragged down with them, which meant I would be seeing one firsthand.... and it would be Federal.

A sudden flashback came into full view; the document that Joey had received from a place called Baccari Bloodstock, regarding the stud service provided that Paxton decided to pay in lieu of paying the stucco contractor, was in his hand. He turned and placed it in a short filing cabinet behind him in his office. He placed the piece of paper on top of a stack of others. I was so pissed off when I confronted Joey about not paying our sub-contractor, I never noticed what Joey actually did with that document, but after calming down I had time to reflect on every detail in the office during that conversation.

I needed to look at that stack of papers in the filing cabinet and I needed to do it soon in the event that Joey spoke to Paxton about our conversation and the papers were removed. A day later I would make up my mind to enter the office at night and go through the cabinet.

I had my own key but was still nervous and anxious about what I might find. I half expected to find many more documents that reflected much of the same information on the Baccari Bloodstock document. I began to think about all the sub-contractors who were demanding payment from Dynamite Custom Homes; sub-contractors that Paxton had claimed were incompetent and did not deserve payment and there were many. I wondered if they, too, were the victims of stud fees, overpayment for work completed on the homes we were building.

I entered the building around eight o'clock in the evening. All, but a few hallway lights were off which created a dimly lit corridor for me to walk. As I reached the door to our office space itself I slipped the key into the lock and turned it. A barely audible click coming from the knob and the slightest of vibrations I felt between my thumb and forefinger told me the key had done its job. I pushed the door open and as I stepped into the foyer of the office an eerie feeling washed over me. I started to panic. What if Paxton was driving back from the bar and saw my truck in the parking lot? What if he came in and surprised me while I was going through the cabinet? What if the Feds were already aware of their operation and *I* was being watched? I didn't have much time at all and the only way to get the needed information was to get in there, grab the papers, get out and go to a FedEx Kinko's, make the copies there and then get back to the office and replace them where I had found them.

I rushed into Joey's office opened the file cabinet and grabbed a stack of papers about an inch thick. As I thumbed through them I saw several names of horses I recognized from conversations at Skip and Jan's, as well as by placing wagers on some. I made one last check of the cabinet drawer, for anything else that may be associated with the documents I now held, slid it closed, and headed for the door. I couldn't have been in the office for more than sixty seconds, but when I got back into my truck my heart was pounding uncontrollably and I was sweating like a Tijuana hooker sitting in the sun. I started my truck, rolled out onto Ray Road, and headed to FedEx Kinko's which was about a mile down the road.

No one was inside the store except for two employees working on whatever it was they had in front of them. One young kid looked up from his work and nodded to me in acknowledgment of my presence. I nodded back and stepped up to one of the copiers.

As I started making copies I carefully removed any staples that attached some of the papers. I was careful to replace the staples, trying to use the exact staple holes that were made originally. It was a tedious process, but one that had to be conducted for fear of being found out if anyone looked closely at the papers after I returned them to their home inside the cabinet. It took me about two hours to make all the copies and once I was done, I rushed back to the office and replaced the documents where I had found them.

As I was making the copies, I quickly read over the information that each page contained as it exited the copier. I was shocked to see the huge totals, printed on several invoices, which Paxton had paid.

One such invoice dated October 24, 2006. It had a list of horses on it and at the bottom, a total of $194,225.00. The heading of this invoice read "Keenland – Consignor Statement"

"Sonofabitch!" I said under my breath. "The Keenland Yearling Sale?"

Another invoice listing horses, dated three days later on the 27th of October, showed a total of $146,795.79 which included commissions for the Baccari Bloodstock firm from each sale. Three days after that was yet another bill for $47,250.00. Just those three invoices, over the course of six days, totaled $388,270.79 and there were so many more invoices, copies of cashier's checks which paid many of these invoices, numerous e-mail with instructions to transfer funds from the Dynamite Custom Homes account at Chase Bank into other accounts in Lexington, Kentucky. There were complete bank account numbers with the names of those holding the account, which were to receive these funds.

There were invoices with names of veterinarians that were owed money for their services, invoices from transportation companies that tricked the horses from track to track, invoices from stables housing the horses Paxton owned. It was amazing the number of horses, good horses, which this degenerate had acquired through relieving innocent people of their life savings and relieving the banks of far more money. The names of horses included, but were certainly not limited to; Cap and Gown, Darlin, Gold Hearted, House of Soviets, Magic Alphabet, Miracle Worker, Rah Rah Bertie, Shin Fein, Brave Boco, Quiet Celebrity, Water Walker, and Sweet Melody. I was astonished by the sheer number of horses Paxton Anderson owned.

I finished copying the documents and with all the staples replaced in their original position, I rushed back up Ray Road to our office and carefully laid the stack of papers back where I had found them and left.

When I got home I walked into the living room and plopped myself down onto a well-worn couch and sunk deeply into it. With a bright moon shining through the blinds, I hadn't bothered to turn on any lights and for some reason, I felt safe in the darkness, as if no one would know I was home; not that I ever had any visitors anyway. I just sat there and contemplated everything I had been told by Joey, discovered in that file cabinet, and what I knew to be true of the money woes of Dynamite Custom Homes.

The money that Paxton spent at the Keenland Yearling Sale that October was at a time when Dynamite Custom Homes was under financial strain. While we were having a difficult time making payroll, let alone paying our sub-contractors, I was having a difficult time understanding how we could be having money problems with all the money coming in, and all the while, little "Barney Rubble" was pissing away hundreds of thousands of dollars on the things that mattered most to him; horses.

I finally knew why no one was being paid and that there was never any intention of paying these people. I had enough knowledge about Paxton's business practices to make his life miserable if people started asking questions, but one thing I didn't previously have was hard evidence to prove what I would be claiming.

With what I had just copied there was enough information in my hands to bury Paxton Anderson and Joey Plany. What I now had was proof that what Joey had told me, paying for stud fees instead of paying our sub-contractors, was true; and it was also illegal. As far as I was concerned I had them by the short hairs and the best part of it all, they had no idea I had these very damning documents.

Another flashback flared into full view. It was Joey Plany saying he was "waitin' on some loot." As I sat there, I digested the word "loot."

I thought about what I had discovered, the conversations I had with Joey, and how he so eagerly allowed me into the sanctum of his and Paxton's world of deceit and thievery, which were troubling. The whole plan that Paxton devised and executed, though horribly wrong and illegal, truly was genius in my estimation.

I continued to be troubled that the term "loot" kept creeping back into my brain and I didn't know why, but it finally hit me; every penny that was wired into our account *was* "loot!" Each one of those four-legged animals was purchased with the "loot," or stolen money, from the bank loans acquired by people who just wanted to build a home. Dynamite Custom Homes had started out as a legitimate company, but the lure of easy money and Paxton Anderson's obsession with horses and his deep desire of wanting a Kentucky Derby winner changed all of that. It had become his own personal financial institution that gave him the latitude of slipping into the world of horsemen to make his purchases and then slip back out, virtually undetected; it was also a front for bank fraud. Paxton had the gold and he was making the rules.

I laid my head back, closed my eyes, and wondered how the hell I had gotten where I had found myself; in the middle of an illegal operation that could very easily land me in prison by the mere fact that I was the qualifying party on the contractor's license and by the untrained eye, I was deeply involved. Those were my last thoughts as I drifted off to sleep.

The following morning I woke up where I had sat down the previous night and being a very fitful sleeper I was surprised to find that I hadn't moved a bit; the stack of papers I had copied still lay in my lap with my right hand holding it. I must have been extremely tired when I got home. I got up and made some coffee to get me going again. As I sat and read the papers more closely I could see the extent of Paxton's small, but substantial, empire he had amassed in a few short years. It looked as if he was, in one way or another, tied to just about everyone, who was anyone in Lexington, Kentucky. If they were tied to the heavy hitters in the horse world, Paxton either had them in his crosshairs or had used the veterinarian, or stud service, or trucking company, or anything else that *they* had used. It seemed this was his only way of feeling important in this world and by the expedient way he was acquiring a decent stable of horses, he was well on his way to becoming one of them. He was a part of "The Sport of Kings."

"STEVEN EVERTS, COUNSEL FOR TIFFANY NELSON"

"Unless you can get past the circus, there is little justice in a courtroom." – Jim Murray, renowned syndicated columnist and sports writer for The Los Angeles Times

March 2007

With a job that was now paying me less than what I was previously making, I decided to have my child support modified to accommodate the change in my declined financial status. I went downtown to the Superior Court Building on Jefferson Ave. and into the section of the courthouse where all motions, pleadings, complaints, lawsuits, etc. are filed. It is also where individuals convicted of traffic violations can pay their fines, pay enrollment fees for DUI classes, and make restitution payments. Way in the back of this room which is usually filled with disconcerted and generally pissed-off people, not wanting to part with their money, is a little window with no telltale signs that this is a working section of the courthouse.

This little *stepchild*, of office space, I discovered, is where people can go for help in filing for child support and modifying child support. In the times I have been here I have only ever seen a few people being helped at any given time. Normally it's an individual questioning the validity of wage garnishments, or a woman who hadn't received her support payment and demanded to know where it was. Another woman was desperately trying to find the father of her children, as he had quit his job and skipped town, and she couldn't feed her seven children on public assistance.

Still another was a woman who claimed her employer mistakenly paid the Clearinghouse, the branch of court that distributes funds from support payments, too much and wanted an immediate refund. It's amazing what private information some people openly discuss with perfect strangers; she was pleading with the gal behind the window that she had lost her children due to her continued use of methamphetamine and didn't know why the courts would take them from her.

This viable candidate for the *Mother of the Year Award* said she "got screwed by the court" because she, "didn't do it as often as they said and only two of my fucking kids were there; not *all* of them." What an excellent point she was making! I could see exactly where this poor woman was coming from, now if only it was legal to club this wretch to death with a nearby chair for general stupidity. . . . .

When it was my turn at the window I made a joke about the class of some people that come to this particular window. This woman must have played poker because she never even smiled and her expression never changed. She was stone-faced and asked what it was that I needed. I decided I had just better stick to business because no one was handing out warm smiles and hugs. I asked the gal what I needed to do to modify my support payments.

With perfect clarity and elevated volume, she said, "Ya wanna modify your child support payments?"

I dropped my eyes and said very softly, "Uh, yes, ma'am."

"Higher, or lower?" The volume of her voice was still up there.

I could feel the weight of a great many eyes on the back of my head when she asked that question. I didn't turn around, but I would bet a bunch of money there were at least twenty people who had to rub their own necks after the speed at which they conducted their head whips toward me. I'm certain it caused them some discomfort.

I knew that the audience within earshot of this woman's question, which I would guess encompassed an area the size of Delaware, was waiting for my answer. Before I answered, I turned my head slightly to one side to get a peripheral view of the people in the back of me. Shit! As I suspected, most of them were women.

"Uh, could you repeat the question?" I asked as softly as I could.

"Higher, or lower? Do you want to pay more for your child support payments, or make your payments less, sir?" She was still speaking very loudly. Her and the people seated behind me were all waiting for me to answer.

In almost a whisper I said, "Um, lower."

"Lower?" She boomed. "Okay, just fill this out and bring it back. Someone will call you in a while."

"Mother fucker!" I heard a woman behind me mutter.

"Yeah, No shit!" Another woman said, "This bitch don't wanna pay no fuckin' money for no kids? What a bitch this mother fucker is!"

Still another said, "If my mother fuckin' old man did that, I would cut his mother fuckin' dick right, the fuck, off! Know what I'm sayin'?" Trust me when I say, I didn't have a lot of supporters.

I could hear all of the snarling from the beasts that surrounded me. Their respiration increased and I could hear a few of them in close proximity drawing air deeply into their lungs and then exhaling. I imagined that steam was probably rising from it, as well, but I kept my head down and didn't look their way, for fear of being mauled to death.

When a man walks into a place like this, he is walking into a den of pissed-off, hungry, animals who most often feel that the former "man in their life" is the bad guy. They would just as soon see him hit by a train, traveling at a high rate of speed than have their support payments decreased in any way. I happened to be in their world at this moment and in attempting to *legally* have my support payments lowered to reflect the proper percentage, "as described in the statute of the Great State of Arizona." Because I doing this, I was doing one of *their own* wrongs.

The only reason I was there was because I was making less money and my former "bride" had claimed that she was unemployable in the

State of Arizona, as a paralegal-secretary-legal assistant. She claimed, in court, the only job she could find was a "real estate expediter" making a couple of hundred bucks a week, but a month, or so later, she was employed with a law firm in Scottsdale making about fifty thousand a year. Normally, there can be no change to support for two years, *unless* "there is a substantial change in the income of one or both custodial parents." It's in the Statute. The magic number is a twenty-five percent change, either way, and with Tiffany's pay increasing by over fifty percent and mine having decreased by about ten percent, I was well within the guidelines of the law.

None of these women cared in the least and I'm sure they wanted to rip my heart out and eat it right there on the floor. I kept my head down and finished filling out the form. The beasts continued to talk among themselves and every so often, glanced my way, if for no other reason than to pull their lips back, with their facial muscles, to show me their incisors.

Before I got there, no one was speaking to each other and stayed to themselves, but when I stepped up to the window an immediate sisterhood was formed and it appeared a fairly lethal one. Even though I'm a fairly big man at 6'1", weigh in at 230 lbs., and in pretty good shape for my age, nearly all of these beauties outweighed me and a few could grow a better beard, so it would stand to reason I was a little nervous. When I was finished filling out my form, I handed it to the loud lady and I sat back down. I pulled the collar of my shirt up over my neck; I didn't want to give these psychos a target on which to pounce and start gnawing.

I was finally called and a woman helped me by inputting all the necessary figures into the correct boxes using her computer. I answered all her questions and in about fifteen minutes, she made a copy of the modification request. She explained I would need three copies and pointed me to the window to file the request, which I did and quickly left the building. That was an educational experience, but I was relieved to get out of that lair.

Once I filed the "simplified" request for modification I had to wait for the court to set a date, which came a month, or so later. I was to appear back in Commissioner Brnovich's courtroom. She was the same woman who threw out the Order of Protection nearly a year

NOT THE LOVE OF MY LIFE

before. This was welcomed news as I felt she would learn my way in her decision to modify.

I was sitting in the courthouse when The Love of My Life walked in. I was surprised to see her with some skinny little guy who didn't appear to be much bigger than a twelve-year-old boy might be; however, his gray hair showed he was either much older than twelve or that he possessed a complete inability to deal with stress.

As I was giving him the once-over and sizing him up, which, considering his size, didn't take long, I remember thinking, "What the fuck. . . . .?"

He was wearing a suit that hung on him as if he were a child and the suit belonged to his father. He walked fairly straight, but he seemed to tuck his butt under his body as he walked. He was propelled by a bony set of legs (I could see the knot of each knee, through his pants, as he walked) that were positioned slightly out in front of him and he took very short steps. In addition to the odd manner in which he walked; his arms did not swing in unison with his gait, but were held straight at his side. The jacket he wore made me laugh. It had shoulder pads that looked grossly out of place and even considering how frail this little guy was, it was, after all, 2007. I mean, c'mon! Shoulder pads are one thing, even though they went out in the 1980s, but the mere size of the ones Tiffany's attorney was sporting, screamed of a troubled man. It was a fashion faux pas that would agitate a Quaker and send him into a frenzied killing spree.

All I could do was stare and wonder what he was thinking, or more importantly, who the *hell* let him out of the house? As a fellow man, I felt a sympathetic sorrow for him, but as the opposition, I hoped a whole civilization of people witnessed what I was seeing and sentenced him to a stoning, for general purposes. Had the great philosopher, Socrates, laid his eyes upon him, he would have been forced into an aggressive and lengthy therapy. The padded shoulders of the jacket this little guy was wearing were just wrong; plain and simple.

When we walked into the courtroom, we took our seats at the counsel tables, just beyond the swinging gate separating the spectators from the playing field. Commissioner Brnovich was once again on the bench and asked that everyone identify themselves.

The little guy stood up and squeaked out, "Steven H. Everts, Counsel for Tiffany Nelson." My head whipped around toward him.

"Jesus Christ," I asked myself. "What the hell was *that*? Did that weasely little noise just come out of *him*?"

He sounded like the great jockey, Billy Shoemaker, and come to think of it, wasn't a hellava lot taller. At that very moment, I realized that I had a new name for Mr. Everts; The Jockey. It fit well and it would stick in my mind.

After looking over her file, Commissioner Brnovich asked if anyone had any comments and I started off by explaining that the income of both of us had changed by a large percentage and in being so, I felt the support should be lowered to the correct amount. I also wanted it on record that Tiffany had lied in court, about being "unemployable in her field" and then a month later was employed *in her field* with a law firm, that she had planned to do exactly what she had done, once child support was set in her favor.

The Jockey argued that I had added information onto the modification form that wasn't valid and therefore should be tossed out. School tuition was the big one. The woman asked if I paid any tuition; I said I did and she added it to the form that figured into the final support obligation. How was I to know?

In the end, Brnovich ignored my testimony, saying not enough time had passed to request a modification. I responded that regardless of the time frame involved, the law allows latitude for a "substantial change in income," which I had proven exceeded the mandatory 25%, but she was hearing nothing of it. Brnovich ordered that the support remains in place for a time "longer than it has."

What a pile of bullshit I was listening to! Was it because I didn't have an attorney and she did? There is always preferential treatment to fellow a *jurist*, I thought. This is a "simplified modification" and the histrionic Tiffany felt the need for an attorney? This was a travesty, but one I had no control over. I had just been beaten by a little man with a Napoleonic complex. Unfortunately, he would be a tormentor of mine for the next eighteen months, as he would represent Tiffany over that time and amass a small fortune from her, of over forty thousand dollars. During the time that The Jockey represented her, Tiffany was awarded about six thousand dollars in attorney's fees, which, as I addressed earlier on; I'm not sure how that whole misdirected pile of ostrich shit works.

If I could afford an attorney why, in God's name, would I walk into court *without* one? And if I can't afford one, why the hell should I be made to *pay* for one? Especially when it's the attorney of an opponent and he is attempting to *legally* sodomize me. It just doesn't make the least bit of sense to me and to date, judges have refused to address my questions about it and no one had been able to explain it. It's rulings like this that enable the "system" to stay in business and all for the simple reason that no judge can be held accountable for *legally* sodomizing the community in which he, or she, serves. It's a business and it cannot be made to lose. And as long as there are jurists, *on their knees* in front of other jurists, the business of ratfucking the public will reign.

Let's see; a whole bunch of money is wasted on some selfrighteous prick with an, "Esq." attached to his name. It's OK, or it is encouraged, to petition the Court to have some, or all, of that money paid by someone else, but that, "someone else" is some poor slob who is just this side of qualifying for public assistance. If that "someone else" doesn't have an attorney, nine out of ten times, he/she (mostly "he" I would bet) will join in the experience of lining the pockets of a cockroach. In a socialistic world, the big boys would gather up all the money made by everyone and disperse it evenly among all the people and everyone would be on the same social level. The rich giveth to the poor, so the poor can live a more lavish life without really working. As warped and perverse as this may sound, it was a pure and unadulterated form of reverse socialism at its worst; *I* was giving to the "rich."

I think England's Former Prime Minister, Margaret Thatcher, summed it up perfectly when she said, "The problem with Socialism is that you eventually run out of someone else's money." The irony of this was that I started running out of money when *The Love of My Life* began skimming our marital account and finally "ran out" on March 2, 2006.

The Jockey and another little guy named John Zarzynski would eventually lose a pretty big fight with me. It was a motion filed, in which these two fucking morons, teamed together and tried to get visitation for Tiffany's mother, who, in my "unprofessional," but extremely educated opinion, is an idiot. Apparently, She is held in extremely high regard within the community. If you don't believe it, just ask her yourself.

This woman has claimed openly that she feels she is royalty among the lower class of people around her; the "lower class," being anyone outside her clan of maladjusted criminals. She has an incredibly convoluted view of life and what she feels it owes her, is beyond words. Her sense of entitlement is completely off-the-chart and for all intent and purpose, she is in a dream world that rivals Alice's, as she was lurching through Wonderland. And we all know what Lewis Carroll was on when he wrote *that* freakish novel.

What this team of midget wrestlers wanted was to further separate me from my girls by getting the court to rule that Susan Nelson should have the rights of a grandmother who rarely saw her grandchildren. Susan wanted to take the girls for something like a month, out of each year, and have that month of visitation during *my* custodial time. It was a nice try, but the court felt that since the girls already saw this . . . person . . . on a regular basis (like three to four times a week) she was denied access to *my* custodial time. If she wanted time with the girls, she would have to use the custodial time of her daughter. Judge Ballinger sent the circus sideshow packing and I walked out feeling pretty good about myself.

One time, I was even attacked by Susan Nelson in a crowded hallway outside Commissioner Brnovich's courtroom. The incident happened on March 23, 2007 as the group of us exited the courtroom of Commissioner Brnovich and headed into the next hearing before Judge Ballinger. Upon exiting, I made a comment, complementing The Jockey, Susan yelled for me to "shut up." When I turned around Susan slammed me in the ribs with a file she was holding. It didn't really hurt, but it was nice to see her lose control of herself, in full view of video cameras. All these months they had been trying to get me to snap and I never did and *she* was the one to lose it. On March 26, 2007, I wrote a letter to Judge Ballinger recounting the incident to get it on record. I could have very easily had Susan Nelson arrested for assault, but it wasn't worth it. At the time, it was pretty comical.

Another missed opportunity for the Nelson clan to get me to "snap" was at Our Lady of Mount Carmel School. Early on, school always seemed to be a problem for Tiffany. The whole thing with the first day of school was a big one. It still breaks my heart to think about the girls being so disappointed that their own mother wasn't there, while the mothers of all their friends made it.

At the time of the "missed opportunity," I was going to school every day, whether it was my week, or not. The reason for this practice was due to a time when Tiffany brought her boyfriend to school with her. While Tiffany waited outside Megan's classroom, Little Jimmy waited outside Kate's room. Once the bell rang, to end the school session that day, kids started to file out of their respective classrooms where their parents normally stood. Once Kate saw that, instead of her mother being there, the boyfriend was there to collect her she became frightened and ran to find her mother. When I was told of this, I explained to my daughters that from now on there will always be a parent waiting for them when school ended; no matter what. I would keep that promise until shortly after Susan's husband attempted to goad me into a physical altercation in the schoolyard in full view of two hundred children and parents.

I guess this brainless goofball was trying to impress someone, or test himself, to check the size of his *kiwis*. On this particular day, he must have assumed them to be quite large, but lucky for him I wouldn't buy into it and engage him in a tussle. This imprudent and dim-witted man hadn't the sense to assess his physical attributes, or lack thereof, before his mouth wrote a check bigger than his body was able to cash. Greg Stephanson had, and still does, have the look of a life-long drinker; his face is always flush and pink and his eyes are constantly bloodshot. He has a gut on him, into which I am sure he has had a great deal of money invested. I doubt he can see his toes if he was standing upright and tilting his head down. His arms look more like something that would be hanging from the shoulders of a starving Ethiopian. But regardless of the above, he threw his elbow into my path, as I walked past him, with the hope I would snap and beat the piss out of him in front of two hundred witnesses.

I stepped out of the way and told him very calmly that he would be making a grave error if he touched me; that he would end up unconscious and in an ambulance. All he could do was stare at me through his glazed-over and bloodshot eyes. He didn't say a word. He doesn't say much unless Susan tells him he can. On more than one occasion, I have witnessed Susan berate him in public and he just takes it, like some scrawny little kid on a playground being harassed by a bully. Sometimes those being harassed turn on their tormentors, with a fatal vengeance, and even at that point, the bully is confused as to why he, or she, is being sought out for retaliation. As the saying goes, "you just can't fix stupid."

The following letter was written to The Jockey explaining my concern over the behavior of the Nelson clan and the people close to them. I asked that he help me in bringing this under control before it became out of control and people started making special trips to the local hospitals; because that's where this was heading. I told him that I would not hesitate to protect myself and if I had to, I inferred, there would be great pain associated with the same. I assured him that he did not want that to happen. I reiterated that this was the third such request for help from him, as Tiffany's attorney, and I had hoped he would actually do something with this new information. He, too, must have been convinced I would lose control, because the letter which was written on April 22, 2007, went completely ignored. Again, before I ever started writing the haunting of Fernando Vargas came back, however this time I ignored the vivid memory of my old friend chastising me with his sharp tongue. I wrote the letter as if I didn't care if it became public.

LETTER TO STEVEN EVERTS

ERIC L. DI CONTI
14843 South 8th Street
Phoenix, Arizona 85048
Cell (480) -###-####

April 22, 2007

Law Offices
Udall, Shumway & Lyons, P.L.C.
30 West First Street
Mesa, Arizona 85201-6695

Attn: Steven H. Everts #004831
Attorney for Tiffany Nelson
FC2006-050978

Re: Private phone conversations with daughters

Mr. Everts,

My intention is to have as little contact with you as possible, as it may incur unnecessary costs to your client, but I am forced to do so because of your client's continual adversarial behavior. She apparently is having some trouble with the concept of "doing what is best for our children."

Let me start off by saying that shortly after the hearing(s) at the Northeast Judicial District on March 23, 2007, I began having pointed questions being asked by Katie and Megan about court proceedings that had happened and will happen in the future. I was asked point blank by Katie, "Why do you keep taking Mommy to court?" I was stunned by this question, but not surprised, as Tiffany has a propensity to inform the girls of what goes on in court, from time to time. I do not engage them in this type of conversation. If I remember correctly, and please correct me if I am wrong, Judge Ballinger specifically stated that conversation about Court, and what goes on in it, is "completely inappropriate," as the girls are "too little."

My answer was, "I don't 'keep taking Mommy to Court' it's just that there are some things that need to be worked out between us." I then asked her why she would ask that question and who told her I was doing such a thing. Her response was this: "Mommy says that she has to keep going to court because you keep making her go talk to the judge." I assured Katie that was not the case and I told her that I can't talk to her about it because she is not old enough to understand. I added that one day, when she's a lot older, "we can sit down and talk about everything, but not for a long time." The conversations that your client is having with our daughters are out of line and are in direct defiance of Judge Ballinger's orders on March 23rd.

In addition, Dr. McPhee, who was appointed by Judge Ballinger and acted as the Therapeutic Interventionist, also expressed great concern for, and warned against, conversations such as this with the girls. Your client has refused to comply to that end either. She refuses to comply with anything the Court advises on and it is hurting our children. The children do NOT need to be informed of any Court proceedings at any time, nor should I be put into a position to explain why we are in court. Both Dr. McPhee and Judge Ballinger were quite succinct in their advisement and your client needs to be reminded of such.

Point two: I am still getting reports from my daughters that Susan Nelson and her husband are continually telling the girls that they do not like me and if I am to pick them up they will not have it done at their house "because they don't want [me] near there." That's a pretty harsh thing for a child to hear about someone they love, don't you agree? These words are also something they should NOT be saying to these two small children, again per Judge Ballinger's orders.

Point three: As you are well aware from my letter to Judge Ballinger, after you and Mr. Zarzynski testified in Judge Ballinger's Courtroom (which, oddly enough, was after I was assaulted by Susan Nelson in the corridor outside Commissioner Brnovich's Courtroom), I am "confrontational when around

Susan Nelson," there was a "confrontation" of sorts, at the girls' school that following Monday, March 26th. At this time, once school let out, Susan Nelson's husband twice attempted to provoke me into a physical altercation with him, the latter attempt by throwing his elbow out towards me as he was walking by. Let me remind you this was in full view of my two daughters and about 200 other children and parents, several of whom witnessed his actions and are willing to testify to the same. This was an attempt to get me to lose control and lash out against them so they can show the Court how "unstable" I am. Sir, I assure you, this will NOT happen, but the continued attempts by the Nelson Clan, to achieve this goal are becoming tiresome. When one person can't get it done, they throw another person into the mix; a new face, if you will, to continue their quest. This brings me to the next subject.

Point 4: Your client has recruited another individual with the hope of enraging me. I called to speak to my girls at the usual time of [around] 8AM on Saturday. The first call was made at 8:22AM. In usual fashion, there was no answer, so I left a message. I sent a text message a minute later saying I was trying to contact the girls. I called back at 8:52AM and Tiffany answered the phone saying the "girls are playing out back" and then hung up the phone. I called back and asked when I could speak to them, to which Tiffany replied, "When they come in they will call you," and hung up the phone again. I called back again to find out when she thought they might be available to speak to me, as I have been trying to reach them. Only this time the phone was answered by a man I can only assume was Jimmy Norton. Although he's been hanging around for a time, this is a new voice and a new person on the Nelson bandwagon. He, too, was adversarial in his demeanor. He refused to give me his name when asked, saying only, "It doesn't matter who I am." I said that I would like to speak to my children and, other than that, I told him I had nothing to say to him since he has nothing to do with my children. He poked fun at a stutter in my speech and then made a feeble attempt to frighten me with some verbal heroics *that he may have read in a comic book somewhere. He, too, hung up on me.*

At 9:00AM my phone rang and I picked it up to hear Katie's voice on the other end. With the phone call came high-pitched screeches and extreme static when either of us spoke. These noises are ear-piercing, painful, and make having a conversation of any kind terribly difficult. I have asked that Tiffany not use a device causing these problems and to refrain from recording our conversations, as the girls and I have a "Right to Privacy" when we speak to each other. Tiffany has refused to comply with these wishes. Additionally, I refuse to subject my daughters to Tiffany's relentless need to control when and in what manner we speak. Quite frankly, I refuse to have any conversation under these circumstances.

Conversely, when the girls are with me, Tiffany has NEVER had a problem speaking to them. Their phone calls are NEVER recorded and, in fact, the calls are oftentimes taken in a back bedroom and away from anyone in the house. If Katie or Megan say to me, "I want to have a private conversation with mommy," by God, they have one. If a call is missed, due to my conducting business on the phone, the girls will return that same call as soon as I've finished my business call. I encourage the girls to call their mother daily and if Tiffany doesn't call, which has happened occasionally, I remind them that they need to call her before going to bed. Saturday and Sunday mornings when their mother fails to call them by 8:30 I encourage them to call Tiffany and not wait for her phone call. I do not falter on this. It's a common courtesy that is not reciprocated in any form and the only ones who suffer are Katie and Megan.

To expound on the information you already have, information that Tiffany would rather you NOT know about, is that there is legal documentation noting that Katie has had bouts of serious abdominal pain towards the ends of the weeks the girls are in my custody and when they are preparing to return to their mother's house. It usually starts on Thursday and is carried through Friday, the day that the girls return to their mother. On many occasions, Katie expressed that she doesn't "want to go back" to her mother's house. On several occasions, I have had to remove Katie from school, due to vomiting and severe stomach pain. Her pediatrician did a battery of tests to rule out a number of things and came to one possible conclusion, which is that Katie may have stomach or duodenal ulcers. They are still trying to rule it out, but in the interim, she has been prescribed and is taking Prevacid on a daily basis, which is administered by the school nurse.

She does not take her medication home with her because when she started taking this medication and she was in her mother's care, she never got it. It was either "lost or "forgotten" and on a couple of occasions, Katie told me that "Mommy took my medicine. I gave it to her because her tummy hurt, too." How beautiful is that, sir? A nine-year-old child would be so concerned about her mother, she would give up the one thing that makes her own pain go away . . . and the sad part is that your client accepted the offer. To date, with Katie receiving the medication from the school nurse, her pain has subsided to a great extent and although there is pain at times, I try not to talk about it on the weekends, so she is not reminded.

With regard to the recorded phone calls, I will say this: if you are not able to persuade your client that she is doing irreparable damage to our daughters, I have no other choice but to take the next step. I will file an "ORDER TO COMPEL — Mother To Allow Private Conversations Between Father and His Children" while they are in her custody. The threat last year of doing so, and the recommendation of attorney Donna Jewett, was the only thing that convinced the Nelsons to comply with that excellent advice. By behaving in this manner, your client and her family are playing a dangerous game with our daughters' psyches, as well as their health. It needs to stop and it needs to stop now.

Although, the man answering Tiffany's phone was nothing more than the annoyance of a gnat. The Nelson Clan's quest to get me to "snap" is escalating, Mr. Everts, and you as legal counsel to a party in that family must do something to curtail their behavior. I will not initiate any physical engagement with anyone in that family if there is no imminent danger to me, as

I proved when Susan Nelson assaulted me in the corridor of the courthouse and again when Susan Nelson's husband assaulted me at the girls' school. For the record: The moment I feel I am being threatened with bodily harm, or I am assaulted by someone other than an elderly person, I will defend myself, sir, and no one wants that to happen, but by the recent number of attempts to provoke me it would appear that time may be near. This will be the third time you've been notified of attempted provocation by the Nelson Clan and I have yet to hear a response from you regarding the same. I would hope that this time you take the matter a little more seriously and would do your due diligence to see that it doesn't escalate any further than it has.

No one wants to wish they could "un-ring" the bell, once it is rung. I have no desire to ring any bell, but others it seems doable. All I want to do is make sure my children feel safe and are happy, but that is a difficult task with so many antagonists in their lives fighting against it.

Tiffany's former attorney, Donna Jewett bailed out in a big hurry for reasons obvious to me, but remain unknown to you because it appears you have very little knowledge of what you are dealing with regarding the Nelsons. You need to pull the reins in as quickly as you can before this spirals out of control for your client, thus making your job a very difficult one in the coming months. She is already in some hot water on another, and civil, level and will need to answer to some serious matters in the very near future.

I'm not trying to tell you what to do, or how to counsel your client, sir. All I am doing is offering up some suggestions that will help my children and may be of help to you. In the meantime, I will continue to do what is best for my girls and hope that you do your job by keeping Katie and Megan at the forefront of your representation of Tiffany Nelson.

Kindest regards,

Eric Di Conti

NOT THE LOVE OF MY LIFE

The Jockey would continue his representation of the histrionic Tiffany until late 2008, at which time he withdrew as her counsel of record. I mused he grew weary of waiting for the big fireworks show the Nelson clan had promised him. Since he had made a good deal of coin off of her and even procured a few bucks to line the pockets of his little friend, Johnny Zarzynski, it was time to pack up and insert a straw into someone else's blood supply. He and Zarzynski were like the brothers, Romulus and Ramous, suckling on the teat of their surrogate wolf-mother; the judicial system.

"I'M GOING TO STICK AROUND FOR AWHILE"

"To find something that is lost and to make your search meaningful, you must first believe that <u>finding</u> it is meaningful." – Unknown

February 2007

I now had to make a decision. Do I bail and be out of my job with Dynamite Custom Homes, or stick around, collect a check and try to get more information to hang onto in the event everything goes south? I needed a job to keep my kids and if I made a sudden departure, it would raise suspicions at every level. I spoke to a close friend of more than ten years about what I had found and showed him the documents I had copied.

Ryan Quinn, a licensed electrician and sub-contractor of Dynamite Custom Homes, was worried about the legal implications of my situation, as well. He had been working on the Tasha and Will Henstein residence, in the Mirabel Community, which was just up the street from Mark Acre's unfinished home. He had done the underground electrical work and after a great deal of hassle and my insistence, he was finally paid for the work he'd done. At this time, the house was sitting at about 85% frame, but since there was no more money left to build and only a couple of subcontractors paid, the house was "parked." The Hensteins were close friends of Paxton's, back in Montevideo, Minnesota, so the trust factor was high, but a year later that would change.

"What are you gonna do?" Ryan asked me.

"I'm gonna stick around for a while," I told him. "I have to for a few reasons; I need a job, I can't leave and raise suspicions, it's too tough to find another job right now, and if I stay I can gather more information on these pricks and still get paid. Besides, this operation is buried so deep it's gonna be tough to be exposed without someone like me going to the authorities, and that's what I plan on doing when the time comes."

Ryan agreed that I had made some good points. He was with me, but he suggested that I have an extensive background check done on him. Within a week I would find a person to do just that.

When the background report came back, I was handed a fifteen-page treasure trove with more information than I had ever dreamed of getting.

It contained Liens and Judgments against Paxton, which totaled thirteen, UCC filings, every known address from the time Paxton Jeffery Anderson was able to wipe his own ass without the help of his wonderful mother Sandra, every vehicle he had ever owned and registered in his name (two), his birth date of August 25, 1971, his driver's license number, and his home address on 7th Street in Montevideo, Minnesota. It showed he had never registered to vote. It also showed that other than the LLC's Paxton had attached his name to, he was careful to have nothing in his name since the late 1990s.

Of the LLC's filed with the Arizona Corporation Commission, he had come up with some very clever names. Among them were the names "Cash Cats Enterprises," "Stone Paxton" and "Paxton Stone."

Stone was the name of Paxton's son, the eldest child of four. The others were a daughter, Scout, and two more sons, Trip and Rhett, beautiful children with incredibly angelic faces. They carried on the demeanor and sweetness of their mother, Kelli, who I liked very much. She was one of those very attractive women with a huge heart, who worked so hard to make everyone around her comfortable. When you saw her with Paxton, you wondered what the hell she ever saw in the hillbilly. Thankfully the kids took after their mother and didn't fall into the shallow gene pool of their father.

The LLC name of "Cash Cats" is just funny to me for the one reason that the main objective of Paxton and Joey in business was to gather as much as they could, without actually working for it. In fact, in addition to his narcissistic handles of *Big Daddy, Daddy,* and *The Man,* Joey Plany had a few passwords that reflected his love for money like *Daddy Cash* and *Loot Man.*

The background report I had been given gave me a deep insight into Paxton Anderson, what he was several years prior, and what he had melded into. This was, not a scary guy, but rather a devious little prick who found a chink in the armor of the banking system and then figured out a way to systematically exploit it to his own advantage. All the while, he was creeping along like a viper seemingly undetected even though there were numerous liens placed against him; the largest of which came from the State of Arizona, Department of Revenue in November of 2006 to the tune of $312,777.94, more than a third of which was interest and penalties. Of course, the lien was in the name of Dynamite Custom Homes, so Paxton hadn't a care in the world.

I had also found that when payroll deductions were made from our checks the taxes were never paid and wound up back in the pockets of Mr. Anderson, but one more very interesting thing I discovered, through my nosing around, was that no matter what deduction was made from payroll checks the end user, or recipient, was always Paxton Anderson. This included wage assignments for child support obligations; mine included.

I would learn this very unfortunate lesson upon entering the courtroom one day, while I was being sued for arrearages by the unrestrained, histrionic, Tiffany Nelson. The Honorable Eddward Ballinger would enlighten me on this little known Rule in Arizona Family Law; Even though there is a Court Order demanding payment from an employer, it is still the obligation of the payer (Eric) to ensure the funds are being paid to the payee (Tiffany) and the payer (Eric) is still liable if those funds don't make it to the payee. The Rule also affords the employer the latitude of **not** being held accountable, whatsoever, for any funds **not** paid. I would find myself in arrears of some $500.00 that I ended up paying twice; once to Paxton, for his decision to liberate it from me, and once to Tiffany, through arrears' payments. Thankfully, the amount wasn't larger.

What sucks about this Rule is in the State of Arizona, one "can be incarcerated and held on a Purge Clause until the funds are paid." It's all up to the payee, which means all Tiffany has to do is get her attorney to write a complaint, drag me into court to answer the complaint and if I don't have the money, be taken into custody and held pretty much indefinitely, unless, of course, I could get a friend to pay the money that was owed.

A few months down the road the scenario I just described would become a reality, but not from failing to pay arrearages; it was due to not following an order of the Court (Judge Ballinger) in paying insurance premiums. I demanded to see proof that insurance was put in place when Tiffany claimed it was and was never afforded the proof, so I neglected to pay it. Well, actually, I refused to pay it, which, as I would find out was a pretty stupid mistake on my part.

In Court, Tiffany had claimed that insurance coverage for the girls was to be immediate, but there was no coverage for well over two months after her claiming so in court. The good Judge, Eddward Ballinger, probably taken in by the beauty of my ex-spouse, took her at her word and never felt proof was necessary. After all, why would this beautiful woman before him lie in a court of law? She's gotta be tellin' the truth.

The result was that since I had "failed to follow a Court Order," even after pleading to the Court for proof, I was held in contempt and taken into custody by the Maricopa Sheriff's Department. What added insult to injury was the fact that Tiffany was snickering the whole time I was being handcuffed and led out of the courtroom. I sat in a holding cell for a few hours and was then released when a close friend came to my aide and loaned me the money to pay the arrearages owed.

Judge Ballinger was a judge I respected for his ability to follow the law, but he fucked up big that day. His attention to detail was such that he never lost sight of what was being discussed, or was on his docket for that time frame; however, if you threw something else in the works, he would either ignore it, or direct you to file a motion to discuss it. This was, at the very least, frustrating. A month or two later, when his mistake was finally realized I never got so much as an apology, let alone hearing him admonish Tiffany for her indiscretions in his courtroom.

What I got from the Honorable Eddward Ballinger was a sniff and a "Hmmmm. How does a $300 credit sound, Mr. Di Conti? Does that sound fair?"

"It sounds insulting, Your Honor, considering Ms. Nelson lied in your courtroom, but this is your world and what you say in it goes. In light of that, I find it curious you would even ask me what I would find fair. I have no choice, but to accept what you offer and smile about it for fear of being held in contempt for not liking what I am being gifted."

Judge Ballinger just looked at me, shrugged, and signed the Order. It would not be the last time I would be in front of the good judge, Eddward Ballinger.

RISEN SAVIOR LUTHERAN CHURCH AND SCHOOL

"I'd rather enter once through the door of God, than a thousand others" – A version of a Bible Verse, however the door to this joint would prove to be a fairly toxic one . . . on several levels.

Mid-April 2007

A couple of months had passed and I found myself still tied to Paxton Anderson, Joey Plany and Dynamite Custom Homes. Although I was still conducting my fact-finding mission, the money situation bettered and things started falling back in line. It seemed as if Paxton's excessive spending on horses had subsided and I assumed he was back to being a human being again. As the money started coming in with regularity and didn't mysteriously disappear, subcontractors were getting paid again and in having these two previous issues resolved, my comfort level eased to a manageable level. I was able to function without continuously crawling around on my hands and knees, shaking like a frightened rodent and swearing incessantly.

An old project was about to start up again and it was right down the line of work I had been accustomed to for so many years. It was a Tenant Improvement, or TI, at Risen Savior Lutheran Church and School; the place of worship Tiffany had discovered and the first religious dwelling I had entered when I came to Arizona. It was also the place where Tiffany had first met Paxton Anderson. She swooned over his "accomplishments" as a builder and his pillar of excellence in the community.

A few years prior, Paxton had promised to build the church a school that would carry students through the eighth grade. He originally claimed for the school, a piece of property off Arizona Ave., near Hamilton High School in Chandler. The property was an alfalfa field that the church was attempting to buy, but it never came to be. The school would build a second level above the existing school that carried children, to that point, through the second grade. As was normally the case and certainly due to my background in this type of building, I would be in charge of the project.

It started normally in the offices of the first floor which needed to be completed in a "first phase," so parents had a place to go to enroll their child in the new school. Paxton had promised the church that the second level of the school would be completed, prior to the summer's end and before the start of the new school year, at the beginning of August. Like many of his promises, this too, dissolved into the red dirt of the Sonoran desert.

Early on, the project experienced delays, and once again, money began to disappear and sub-contractors were once again waiting on the promise of payment for their work. Paxton was back in business and I saw it coming.

The school director of several years, Linda Pauley (a huge advocate of the project and staunch supporter of Paxton Anderson), was my direct contact for the project. She was a big-boned, thick gal with a big heart who never wanted to see the bad in anyone and was deeply religious. She and I had a falling out when I took my girls out of the school there and enrolled them into Our Lady of Mount Carmel in Tempe, Arizona, but one day prior to the project starting, I entered her office and after a forty-five-minute meeting, we had repaired what had been broken. As Tiffany had stayed in contact with several of the mothers at the school, Linda was one of the first people to learn Tiffany had accused me of molesting my girls and physically abusing the three of them. She was also the first person to enlighten me about a mental disorder called "Histrionic Personality Disorder."

It was her opinion that Tiffany was afflicted with this disorder and as she went down a list of signs and symptoms of the same I, too, was convinced. Out of fifteen, or so, signs, Tiffany exhibited twelve of them. It was scary to hear, but relieving as well. Linda confided that she had pegged Tiffany shortly after she had met her; long before I ever moved to Arizona. She also confided that she never believed the accusation Tiffany had made against me. It was calming to hear.

Linda Pauley was always smiling, but the smiles I saw had the slightest hint of pain in them. I couldn't put my finger on it, but her smile always troubled me for some reason. Several times she went to the rooftop to pray the project went as scheduled. One time in particular, when the roof had been removed for framing the second level, it began to rain. Linda ran up to the roof and started to pray for the rain to stop, so the first floor wasn't flooded. Ironically the rain *did* stop and very little water ended up inside the school. I won't even speculate what happened up there, but I cannot rule out divine intervention.

On May 10, 2007, my phone rang and as I looked at the screen of my cell phone I saw it was Linda. I was told she had received an anonymous call from "a concerned parent" who didn't like the fact there was "a felon working at the school." She would get a fax the following day, stating the same. My worst fears were about to come true.

On May 11, 2007, a close friend of the histrionic Tiffany, Melissa Nordquist, along with, what I was told was, a few other parents walked into the office of Linda Pauley and demanded that I be removed from the school property, that they didn't want a pedophile around their children. Linda informed them that it wasn't possible, or lawful; to do such a thing since the allegations were unfounded and I was never charged with anything. Linda was also informed by Melissa Nordquist that a group of parents had pooled their money together and hired a private investigator to do an extensive background check on me. The parents then demanded and were granted, an emergency meeting to discuss the matter. When Linda told me of the impending background check, I gave her my social security number and my driver's license number and in fact, made a copy of it for her and gave her my California driver's license number. I told Linda I had nothing to hide and encouraged her to pass on the information I had just given her to whoever wanted it. The meeting took place that evening in the church hall.

Linda stood her ground and told the parents they would just have to live with the situation that their children were safe and there was nothing to worry about. I figured that the school would not even be in session and wasn't sure why they were making a big fuss, but I never considered "summer school."

The meeting between Linda and the parents ended in a stalemate and I was granted a stay of execution, but there was one stipulation that Linda agreed to; I would not be allowed into the restrooms when other children were present. I was once again, dumbfounded. One sick and twisted lie, from one sick (in my opinion) woman (Tiffany Nelson) to several others, and I was marked as a pedophile. I was crushed and heartbroken to hear this news from Linda. I came to the realization that I truly was a "marked man" in this community. I would ease the nervousness further by disallowing ANY construction personnel into the restrooms when they are occupied, even by adult males working at the school.

Linda, I would come to learn, when problems arose, would play both sides of the fence. She would gather information from one individual, take it to the other side and share it there. When she had gathered information at that venue, she would bring it back and share it with the party with whom she had originally been. Her biggest blunder would be that she trusted Paxton so deeply that he was the end user of all information she had gathered and whatever Paxton received was used with precision.

Any information Paxton gathered, even information that could potentially have an adverse effect on his relationship with the church he would pull an explanation out of his ass and make it sound so real and so logical, that there wouldn't be another question on the matter. Paxton is a master of diversionary verbiage.

His other trick is to continually speak and I mean speak without a break of more time than it takes to inhale a quick breath before he continued speaking. Consider this: during a conversation we were having, as Paxton was driveling about something I put my phone down for a little more than ten minutes. My cell phone sitting next me, I picked up a magazine and thumbed through it. I could hear a barely audible muffle coming from the phone as Paxton spoke. He never let up.

I picked the phone up and said into it, "Yeah, I know." And put the phone back down.

He continued talking for another fifteen minutes when I finally picked it up and said, "Paxton, I gotta go," and hung up the phone.

As long as Paxton was talking, the person he was speaking with didn't have an opportunity to interject at any level. If a subcontractor was questioning the whereabouts of his payment, Paxton spoke in circles and as Paxton spoke in circles, the individual would either give up on their inquiry or believe that they understood what Paxton was saying. Either way, Paxton won and that is just what he wanted.

Harry Harm was the church project's direct contact and the church's gopher, of sorts. He lived close by and when something was leaking, water was running, sprinklers didn't shut off automatically, the alarm went off, or someone just needed to get inside the church, or school, he would be the poor slob they called.

Prematurely gray, well actually he was prematurely "white," and looked many years past his true age. I would learn he was a mere year older than me. He had endured many damaging miles on that body of his. His shuffling gait and the forever forward-slumping shoulders that gave him the appearance of a man walking uphill added to my belief he was a man who was in his waning years.

Harry would turn out to be a little worm that reported every little bit of information back to Linda Pauley, which then went to Paxton. On the street, as a police informant, he would be known as a snitch and in prison, he would be known as the same; however, if he wasn't protected by the guards, he would undoubtedly have a "shiv" buried into his back. Once I figured him out, I realized why he looked such an advanced age; he never grew up from, or out of, being a worm and he was probably beaten up so many times, his nervousness and continually agitated state of mind aged him far more rapidly than if he was a normal kid and adult.

Bill Ensel, a 70-something, self-professed "Elder of the church," was always pushing up his glasses as they slid down his nose and ALWAYS had his face wadded up to one extreme or another; each "wadding," of his face, had several variations. I fantasized about each slightly different facial expression; both eyebrows raised seemed to suggest he had continuous bouts with extreme constipation, or an obstructed lower colon. One eyebrow raised always meant he would be leaving our presence soon and I mused that he had fouled himself and was in need of immediate cleaning. A wide-eyed gaze, with his mouth slightly open, meant he was about to raise his voice in either anger or excitement. He always interrupted our conversations for the slightest issues and would start speaking before ever getting close to you, but that look would always be there, so I knew what was coming. I guess this look would be that of a person who just stepped barefoot into a steaming pile of non-human excrement. This man had the oddest facial expressions I had ever seen on one human being in my life and I've done work at the Camarillo State Mental Hospital in California, so I've seen my share of weird expressions. Bill Ensel's expressions creeped a lot of people out, especially me.

Bill knew everything about construction and trust me, he would let you know about it too. He would show up onsite and with his whiney little voice start telling people how things are "going to be done." It wouldn't have been a bad place to be during construction if it wasn't for three things; Bill Ensel and his creepy wadded-up face, his knowledge in building, or lack of it, and his whiney voice echoing through the timber of the second floor. Bill claimed to have single-handedly built high rises in Chicago for a company and even went so far as to write letters on their letterhead! When I did some checking with this company, I was told he wasn't known beyond a minor league project manager and when I finally confronted him about it, he finally backed off until he saw a new face to tell his tales of heroics in the construction field.

Ryan Quinn, the electrical contractor on this project, despised Bill Ensel due to his incessant hounding of county officials when an inspection was needed. The inspectors were taken aback by *Bill* telling *them* what they were going to pass during an inspection and that if the inspector balked, he would threaten to sue the county. It was a bad mix that no one seemed to want to get in the middle of. We were stuck with the "step-child," as it were, of the church. One inspection was "failed" due to Bill's insistence an inspection did not need to be conducted on some underground electrical conduit. Before any inspections could be done, Bill had the trench back filled and compacted without ever consulting Ryan.

Ryan quipped, "I wish that asshole would go back, find the bingo table he was sitting at and leave me the fuck alone." I could do nothing but laugh.

The one interesting thing about Bill Ensel was that his daughter was a very close friend of Paxton's wife, Kelli, and later on, when everything started to fall apart, we would hear a good deal from him, including how much money the church had lost due to Paxton not fulfilling his promise. He would also keep us informed of Paxton's whereabouts once he made his exit out of Chandler, Arizona, to parts unknown.

Sub-contractors began coming to the church in droves demanding payment, or they would lien the project, and church officials were clamoring for an answer. They would tell these people that they had paid Paxton and there was nothing else they could do for them; "Please contact Paxton" they would say.

One miscalculation on Paxton's part was that his slight offhand technique and contract trickery would not work so well in this arena; this was not residential building. Since this was commercial work, that little Arizona law that disallowed sub-contractors to lien property "unless they were in direct contract with the owner," did not apply here, so when Paxton decided to start taking money from the church, "to pay subcontractors" and pocketed the money, things started to spin out of control.

I was right in the middle of it and didn't give a damn; I was going to enjoy this "fall from grace". I knew that what appeared to be back-to-normal business would be short-lived.

I gave the church every bit of information I had, on how Paxton worked so hard in not paying most of our subcontractors and the manner in which he duped people into doing work for Dynamite Custom Homes. I informed the church that Paxton had falsified invoices to the church and inflated the numbers to garner a larger check from them. I told them that Paxton had even attempted to have work done at the church by a residential contractor, but billed his work to the home of Jason Rongstad in the Superstition Mountain

Properties Community. With two billings Paxton would be paid twice for this work; once from the church and once on the house. Clever he was, but his cunning and adroit practice of thievery was about to come to an abrupt halt.

For a while, he was able to talk away much of what I had informed the church of, but they soon began to question the veracity of their personal "savior." The only information he *couldn't* talk away would be the information I would give church officials on his practices in paying, or not paying, our subcontractors; it was the existence of a paper trail and a lack of one, that couldn't be talked away.

Paxton was obsessed with the need to be the liaison between everybody and everything that needed to be discussed. His normal comment at the end of a conversation was "don't call so-in-so, I'll take care of it." He wanted to be the one to pass on any information and as long as he was involved with both sides of the conversation, he could formulate a defense on the fly if one was needed and as long as he was talking, he was extremely adept in defending himself. Because the church had more information than Paxton would have liked them to have, compliments of me, I became the bane of Paxton's existence and our already cautious relationship began to unravel. Another thing began to unravel at the church as well; my trust of Linda Pauley and Harry Harm. Each conversation I had with them would somehow get back to Paxton almost immediately and verbatim, as we had discussed each matter. With these conversations being repeated back to Paxton, I knew my days were numbered. He knew he couldn't chance more information, on his business practices, getting to the church.

I finally got the call from Paxton that I would be pulled off the project, "because parents are threatening to pull their kids outta the school if you're allowed to stay on the property."

"There's nothing I can do, buddy," he said. "The school is going to lose their enrollment and a bunch of money."

I knew this was coming, but I also knew he was full of shit. "If that's what has to happen then I'll deal with it," I said. We both knew what the real reason was and neither of us felt the need to bring it up. It was understood and there may have been a sense of safety for Paxton not to bring it up and ask why I had ratted him out. That would entail admitting his wrongdoings and he would never admit to anything.

"I'm really sorry, buddy. I'll be in touch." We hung up the phone.

I thought to myself, "Yeah, the only money they'd be losing is the money you're stealing from them, and with me out of the way you can clean them completely out, you fucking prick."

Though Paxton's involvement in homebuilding was a stealthy one, at Risen Savior Lutheran Church, his place of "worship," was outward. It had to be since everyone knew him by name and by sight. It was too tough for him to hide and quite frankly, I'm not sure he wanted to. He needed to be out in the open here, or the trust that these people had for him would be lost. He would be at the site almost daily for the usual back slaps, smiles, and laughs. The people here loved Paxton Anderson and the reason they did was that he promised to build them a school "at cost," using our workforce, no cost to the church at all. He would even throw in "a room full of computers," gratis. The "elders" (and I use the term loosely) flocked to Paxton and held him in the highest regard. Paxton's charisma was so unrestrained there wasn't a soul at the church who didn't see Paxton as the giver of all givers. He was just giving away money that didn't belong to him. People bringing their children to school would point him out to the young ones and to new members they would say, "Oh, there's Paxton Anderson. He's building us a second level to our school….for free."

I remember looking at these people and wondering how it was they couldn't see through this guy's bullshit. This prick was so arrogant that when confronted, he had no qualms in letting parishioners, church board members, and elders alike know what he was doing for the school, even while he was stealing from the very church he claimed to hold so dear. Paxton had one arm around these people in friendship, hand cupping their shoulder and the other hand would be lifting their wallets. He would eventually use the very issue of his "hard work" in bringing the church something no one else could. It would be held over their heads to make them feel guilty for ever questioning his sincerity. Paxton Anderson had a visceral view into most people's psyches and was so adept in his craft that he knew exactly what to say to deflect suspicion of any kind. He was a master of verbal misdirection and easily fooled most people.

He would cry, "How could you believe I would steal from you people, I'm building you a school with money out of my own pocket! Look, people, look what I have done for you!"

They would look around and see a building under construction, then look down the hallways of artwork completed by the children and smile at the thought of a completed project. They would envision halls filled with young children and happy parents smiling and praising God that Paxton Anderson had lived to fulfill the dream of a church; to have a learning institution, such as the one in which they were standing.

The church and school were thriving due to the revenue produced by the added students and worshipers to this House of God, Risen Savior Lutheran Church. All because of one man's vision to better the school that his own children attended, is *this* place. One man's promise to "give" so much of himself, is why these people followed Paxton Anderson and hung on every word that wisped across his lips and bristled the ends of his mustache, as he spoke. I liken the reaction that people at Risen Savior had towards Paxton to that of the followers of Jim Jones; a vast majority of Paxton's *followers* may have downed a Dixie Cup filled with cyanide-laced Kool-Aide had he handed it to them. Nine hundred did it for Jim Jones. Paxton was *that* good at talking.

The Risen Savior parishioners were a large gathering of people following, in a parade, their "messiah" wherever they were led. At the front of the parade was a short, overweight diminutive man blowing air into a little flute. As the breath of Satan's spawn passed through its chambers, bringing to life a melodic and mesmerizing tune for his people to follow, the silver-tongued Paxton Anderson made sure no one was able to see his face. He was trying not to smile as he skipped along.

Though the followers of Paxton Anderson would be warned incessantly, they refused to listen and would come to a very cruel and harsh realization that they were actually little lambs being led to slaughter.

"CHURCHES ARE A STRANGE BREED OF PEOPLE"

"Behold, I stand at the door and knock," – Revelation 3:20

First week of June 2007

I was out of a job and owed about $10,000 for work I had done and I didn't expect to see a penny of it. I called Assistant Pastor David Brinkman at Risen Savior. Pastor David, as he was known, was the one who had been attempting to make Paxton's debts good with the subcontractors through his discussions with the church board. He had been fairly successful thus far and I felt he was my best chance at getting paid, so I, too, was "knocking on his door."

Early on, ironically enough, my brother Marc and Pastor David Brinkman had a connection that was far too coincidental. I told Pastor Brinkman of my brother's first tour of duty, during the Iraqi conflict, and that it was spent aboard the USS Princeton CG-59. The Princeton acted as the air traffic control center and back up for the USS Nimitz, which she shadowed all over The Gulf. Chaplain Jacks, the Lutheran Chaplain serving aboard the Nimitz, was a close acquaintance of Marc's and also, oddly enough, a close friend of Pastor Brinkman. Chaplain Jacks, I was told, had a huge impact on David Brinkman and was ultimately responsible for him entering the seminary and into a life of serving the Lord. Small world, indeed.

Sadly, Chaplain Jacks' life would end suddenly, aboard the USS Nimitz. The victim of a massive heart attack.

To be brief, through e-mail correspondence with my brother during one of his tours in Iraq, as the battalion chaplain, I asked Marc what he thought of the idea of delivering the sermon at Risen Savior Lutheran Church, upon his return. Risen Savior being affiliated with the Missouri Synod, he jumped at the chance. The Missouri Synod is the more conservative of the two governing bodies of the Lutheran church. I asked Pastor Brinkman what he thought of the idea and he readily agreed it would be a great idea, but it had to be approved and arranged through the church board. It didn't take long for them to accept Marc into their church to deliver the sermon, which would ultimately be on "our salvation."

The following is from the sermon Marc delivered at Risen Savior in early 2006, however, I must first admit that I do not have the notes that my brother wrote for this sermon and in light of that, most of what you will read regarding the sermon is a paraphrasing of what was actually said. Marc, being a stickler for accuracy, would have my ass for not quoting him verbatim and chastise me for not making it clear these are *not* direct quotes.

For the record: These are *not* exact quotes. The reason I have Marc's words in *quotations* is merely for the effect and the verbiage is *close* to what he said, but the message is *exactly* the same and more importantly, it is what I remember. Marco – I hope the above disclaimer will keep me on your Christmas Card list.

After Pastor Brinkman introduced him, Marc walked to the podium.

"Good morning," Marc introduced himself again. "My name is Marc Di Conti. I am a Lieutenant Commander with the United States Navy and am currently assigned to the United States Marine Corps, 2nd Battalion, 5th Marine Division out of Camp Pendleton, California. I am also that battalion's Lutheran Chaplain and have just returned from Iraq."

"Being in an active war zone you are closer to meeting your 'maker' than anyone else in the world," he would preach.

He continued, "Every day is a time for salvation, but being in Iraq, in the Sunni triangle, is a time that these men should receive

Jesus Christ to ensure a place in heaven. I have cradled the heads of too many dying men and given last rites more times than I ever believed I would and many of those had not accepted Jesus Christ into their lives. The men fighting this war are the ones who need Jesus Christ, the most. The people among us, here at home, are in need as well, but the urgency isn't there and it should be. We go through life as we would if, say, we were riding a roller coaster. We grab the bar in front of us and hang on as tightly as we can, muscling through the twist and turns and ups and downs, not knowing what the next turn will bring, but certain the ride will stop. Like that roller coaster life *will* stop, but at the end of our lives, there is no bar to hang onto for safety; at the end of our lives, the only safety we have is salvation and the only way you can get salvation is through the acceptance of Jesus Christ. Now is the time for salvation."

Marc is a wonderful orator and can keep people hanging on every word as he speaks from his heart. I cannot count how many people came to me after the service and praised Marc for his service to God. They were amazed at the powerful message and how he delivered it and several people had asked the church to bring Marc back again, sometime in the future.

Pastor Brinkman had been at Risen Savior since the church had opened and though many felt he should have been made the senior pastor, many of the older parishioners felt that at thirty-five, or so years, he was too young to hold that position. They had hired some older, good-looking, charismatic guy from the mid-west to fill a vacancy left by a retiring, senior pastor. The new guy, after only a few months, was given the option to resign, or be fired after it was found that he was banging some gal, a newly divorced woman. A woman who had come to him for spiritual counseling. Unfortunately, his name escapes me because I would love to throw it in here. You just gotta love these self-professed holy-guys!

David Brinkman was once again, the go-to guy without the title. He had been kept in the loop much of the time and I had had several private sessions with him to inform him of Paxton's real motives at the church. I told him what was owed to me by Paxton and he said that he would make sure the church made the debt good and they appreciated me coming forward with so much information.

As fate would have it, his oath of confidentiality was a joke and much of what we discussed, in private, would also get back to Paxton, almost verbatim. The whole place was a joke and none of those wretched bastards could be trusted.

I spoke to my close friend, Ryan about it and his only comment was, "Church people are a strange breed of people."

"No shit."

Of course, the promise Pastor David Brinkman made to me, that I would be paid for what I was owed, went the way of every other dollar that floated through the joint. It would vanish into thin air and I would spend the next several months struggling harder than I have ever struggled before. If it weren't for the monetary generosity of Ryan Quinn helping me through the ensuing months, I'm not sure what position I would be in today. Nearly a year later I would joke that Ryan carried me longer than my own mother did during her pregnancy. And there may be some truth to that.

"MY NAME IS LINDA PECANIC"

"It's double pleasure to deceive the deceiver." – Niccolo Machiavelli

First week of June 2007

It was a day or so after Paxton had informed me that I no longer had a job at the church and a few days before I went to Pastor Brinkman. I had called Paxton to discuss payment for my services to that point. He basically told me that since I had told the church what was going on, with regard to the missing money, he would not be paying me a dime; that I had betrayed his friendship and in doing so, I had nullified any obligation he had to pay me.

"Are you sure about this, Paxton? Because I can tell you right now, you are making a huge mistake, if you don't pay me. You have no idea who you're fucking with and I will bury your fat ass." I told him he needed to be smart about this because what I know, will land him in a federal prison. He laughed at me and told me he didn't think I had anything on him.

In all of his arrogance, he refused to budge, saying he had the best attorney known to man. A graduate of Harvard Law School, David Tierney of Saks-Tierney in Scottsdale, was just as arrogant and, in my opinion, just as big a cockroach as Paxton Anderson. It may be true that the only people that Paxton paid with regularity and without fail was the Saks-Tierney Law Firm, as they were keeping about three steps ahead of everyone who happened to be after Paxton. Joey Plany confided in me that, be it true or not, the monthly bill from that law firm exceeded $35,000 and it was paid without question, or hesitation.

The following day, everything that I knew about the activity of Paxton Anderson and Joey Plany was written down in detail. I didn't leave anything out. I also produced a flow chart that explained how the operation worked and attached it to the three-page explanation of activities that these morons engaged in.

On, or about June 14, 2007, I walked into the Chandler Police Station. The same police station in which my former wife walked into and filed the police report, claiming I had molested my daughters. I walked up to the window and asked for a fraud investigator.

The woman asked, "What kind of fraud?"

"Bank fraud," I said.

"Well, give me what you have, and I'll give it to someone in that division."

"With all due respect, I'd like to hand them to a detective myself, ma'am. These are very important and I need to explain what's here, otherwise whoever reads it won't understand what they're looking at."

The woman rolled her eyes and said, go have a seat and I'll send someone down.

As I sat there and waited I wondered why Paxton had been such an idiot in his refusal to pay me what he owed me. He had amassed a small fortune in horses and the money continued to roll in. As long as he kept talking, lying and deceiving the people around him, his fortune would continue to grow.

Why would he risk losing everything, as well as risk going to jail, over an amount of money that totaled $10,000? Was he that stupid? Or did he truly believe he was that superior to everyone else and had no obligation to anyone, or anything, beyond his wallet. I decided that he *was* that arrogant and truly believed, in his heart, that he was entitled to whatever he was able to steal from people. If they were dumb enough to lose it, then it was his to take without remorse, or caring.

As I sat there, another thought entered my mind; They say a lie is difficult to retell the same way multiple times, but the truth can always be remembered, but Paxton was *always* able to remember what he told someone no matter what it was. Most often they were lies and his lies to these people would become, through diligent practice in his mind, the absolute truth. He made sure what he said *was* the truth and in telling the same lie over and over again, in his mind, it became the truth and therefore, easy to remember. Surely, this is the reason he argued with so much conviction and was usually able to get his accusers to question their own beliefs.

A voice interrupted my thoughts, "Can I help you?" This guy was obviously bothered by having been pulled away from whatever he was working on.

"Uh, yeah." I stood up and extended my hand, "I'm Eric Di Conti, and I have something you may be interested in. Is there somewhere we can talk privately?"

"Whataya got?" He asked, never offering a private room to talk. He was obviously bothered by my presence.

As I started to hand him the papers, I said, "I'm sorry, what was your name?"

Never looking up he responded, "Detective Skuggs." He took the papers from me and began to look them over.

"So, what is this?"

Once I explained what I had written and what the flow chart showed, some interest was sparked and he finally offered to sit and speak privately, however, once I was done going over everything, he suggested that what was going on, may be nothing more than what he called, "creative financing." I assured him that it was far more than "creative financing" and he should really look into what I was telling him.

"I'll tell ya what, I'll make a few phone calls and get back to you, but I can't promise you anything. It doesn't look like much to me, but I'll see if there's any interest from a few people."

I thanked him, but also told him that my next visit, if this goes nowhere with the Chandler Police, would be to Catherine Reagor from the local newspaper, The Phoenix Register. Catherine Reagor had been following the bank fraud epidemic and writing articles on the same for several months.

When I told Detective Skuggs that she may be interested in what I have and that I would be using his name, as my first contact and it was his feeling this was "creative financing," he changed his tune. He asked me to not "say anything to her just yet and to allow [him] to make [his] calls," to see if any interest is stirred. I told him I would give him forty-eight hours to get back to me before I called Reagor and I left.

Detective Skuggs called me the next day to say he called a few people and no one was "overly interested," but he was waiting on one more call from a woman with whom he worked closely at M&I Bank. That was the last time I spoke to Detective Skuggs.

On June 17, 2007, I was doing some side-work on a friend's house for some extra cash when my phone rang. I looked down and though I didn't recognize the number, I answered it anyway. I don't often answer the phone when I see a number foreign to me; at that time in my life, while going through a divorce it was normally just a bill collector. I usually let them go to voicemail. When bill collectors called, we would speak about money that I owed, but could not afford to pay, so the time spent talking about it would be time wasted. I would hit the "ignore" button and erase it later. However, I'm glad I answered this particular call.

"Hello?"

A woman's voice was on the other end, "Hi, I'm looking for Eric Di Conti."

"That would be me," I said, certain at the time it was another bill collector and pissed off at myself for having answered the phone.

"Hello there! My name is Linda Pecanic. I work for M & I Bank in the fraud division, and I got a call from a Detective Skuggs, at Chandler PD, saying you had spoken to him about a few things. He gave me your number."

I probably had the expression of a bird dog on a pheasant hunt; neck extended, ears pricked and eyes wide and fixed. My heart began to pound.

"Have you got a few minutes to talk?" She asked.

"Uh, Sure." My heart *was* pounding and I could feel it in my ears.

"Can you go over what you had told Detective Skuggs, at the police station, for me?"

I spent the next twenty minutes telling Linda exactly what I had told the detective and while I spoke, Linda said nothing. She just let me talk. When I was finished there was a long pause.

Hello?" I thought I had lost her.

"Oh, I'm still here," she responded. "Listen, can I call you back in a few minutes? I need to make a call before this continues."

"Sure," I said. "I'll be here."

Not five minutes later, my phone rang again. I looked down and saw it was from the same number.

"Hello?"

"Hi, Eric. It's Linda Pecanic again. Is there any chance you could come down and talk to us? There are a few people here that want to hear your story."

I said to her that I was a single Dad and had to pick my girls up from school. I also said I had nowhere to take them and that they would be in tow when I arrived.

"No problem. When can you get here?"

"Uh, I don't know. They get out of school at three o'clock. Where is your office?"

She told me how to get to M & I Bank at Central Avenue and Camelback Road and told me not to worry, that she would have things for the girls to do while we were talking.

The stage was set. I was about to embark on a journey that I never imagined taking place. I would soon be at the forefront of a federal investigation into the business practices of Dynamite Custom Homes, Paxton Anderson, and Joey Plany, but it had to start with the institution that was damaged financially by these guys before the Feds got involved, but they were coming.

I arrived at the M & I Bank building and met Linda Pecanic in the lobby around four in the afternoon. Linda was tall and thin, had a tougher-than-normal looking exterior for a woman, but also exuded a good deal of femininity. Her gait and demeanor suggested she didn't take shit from anyone and anyone who made the unfortunate mistake of giving her shit, would be summarily dispatched in one way, or another.

As I looked at Linda, another quick thought came to mind was that she probably used the "nice gal" angle, when dealing with some arrogant punk and as soon as she lured him into her little world and get him to soften up to her, she would have his testicles removed. And for the mere violation of questioning her authority, I cannot imagine she would have asked to have a consent form signed for the removal of the same.

Her handshake was as firm as any I had ever encountered and she was all business. I mused; this was a tough woman and obviously not to be trifled with. I could say that she didn't make me nervous, but I would be lying through my teeth.

In the following weeks I would come to find out that Linda had been married to the same man for thirty-five, or forty, years, enjoyed the outdoors, camping, motorcycles, and four-runners and was a proud grandmother of a little boy. I would also come to learn that the license plate of her vehicle translated to, "Dickless Tracey." I can assure anyone reading this that it fit perfectly.

Over the next eight months, or so, as she conducted her investigation, up to and including the time she handed it over to the FBI, Linda and I would become fairly close. She had learned a great deal about me and the misery I had been living since March 3, 2006. I showed her just about all the investigative reports made by the police, as well as the court documents that were laced with all the bullshit Tiffany had fed them. In listening to and digesting what Tiffany had done, it wasn't long before she, too, elicited some displeasure when her name came up and was fairly open about the fact that she didn't much care for my histrionic ex-wife, or what she had done to me and the girls.

I would come to admire Linda for her tenacity and passion for taking out these little cockroaches that have systematically destroyed a large part of the economy which, at the time of this writing, was in a shambles. The housing industry flourished for several years, but as cyclical as our economy is, instead of a slight downfall, compliments of people like Paxton Anderson, it plummeted and everyone suffered.

NOT THE LOVE OF MY LIFE

The elevator was one of two, side-by-side glass models which overlooked the atrium and they were quite fast after the first twenty feet of upward movement. The girls and I were looking out the back of the cab when it started to lift and within seconds the girls were giggling that their tummies felt weird. The plants on the ground level became mere specs to the girls; Megan commented on how small a man looked crossing the atrium floor.

The four of us got off on the eleventh floor, where her office was located. Linda waved a card across a scanner, which released a magnetic hold on it and allowed us into the reception area. I was surprised that there was a magnetic security lock on the front door of the reception area. We greeted the receptionist and passed to her left, to another door, which required another wave of the card across the scanner. The lock on the door made a clicking sound and Linda pulled it open to allow us in.

A few people who were working in a triangular bullpen of low-walled cubicles raised their heads and said hello as we passed by. Linda's office was at the opposite end of the entrance and to the left as we walked. She motioned us into her office where another woman sat. Linda first called a secretary into her office and asked her to get the girls some coloring books and crayons and some other items that would keep them busy while we talked.

Linda introduced the woman as a vice-president at the bank and wanted her to hear my story in detail as well. I handed over an envelope containing the copies I had made of the documents which I had found and taken to FedEx Kinko's several months prior. The vice-president was thumbing through the papers she was handed as Linda and I recapped our previous phone conversation. After a few moments, the vice-president interrupted us.

"Where did you get this?"

"Out of the filing cabinet."

"No this," she emphasized, as she held up the background check on Paxton Anderson.

"From the guy that did the background check," I responded.

"Who is he?" She asked.

"Does it really matter?"

"Well the average person doesn't have access to background checks like this. This is something that banks and police agencies get and I'm surprised you have one. I was just wondering how you got it."

"No offense and with all due respect, but I'd rather not say. We're already treading on unstable ground here and I'm not really sure who all the players are just yet."

"Point taken," she said and dropped it.

She asked me if she could have copies made of the stack of documents she was holding. I had no problem with it and the secretary was called back in. She took the documents and disappeared, closing the door behind her.

I had no conception of time as I continued to tell my story and with the girls still coloring away and playing with a couple of little stuffed animals, given to them by the secretary, I realized that it was getting dark. I had been talking away for nearly three hours and the girls hadn't even eaten dinner yet. I explained that the meeting had to end, that although I wanted to tell them everything I knew, my girls were of greater importance than Paxton Anderson getting clipped on a Federal beef. We would continue our discussion at a later date; possibly the following week when the girls went back to their mother.

One thing that Linda did ask me was why I was coming forward and if I was looking for any compensation for my cooperation. They wanted to make sure I wasn't just another disgruntled ex-employee. When I asked why they would ask such an odd question, Linda explained that when she spoke with Detective Skuggs, he told her that there may be nothing to my story and cautioned her that I "may be a disgruntled employee, who lost his job, and felt maybe I was getting back at [my] employer."

"Really? Well Detective Skuggs is an idiot if he can't read into what I handed him," I said. "Shit like this just can't be made up and if it were possible, I'd have written a screenplay on the subject instead of wasting my time, telling my story."

I was asked what I expected to gain by coming forward and I sensed they were alluding to whether, or not, I wanted to be compensated for my cooperation with the bank, so I asked them directly.

"Are you asking if I want to get paid for what I'm telling you?"

Linda responded, "Well, why else would you come forward unless you had something to gain?"

I remember thinking, "OK, this woman is completely out of touch and I'm not sure I'm really that crazy about her anymore. Does she not believe me? Jesus, would I have come all this way just to mess with these people's world?"

I shot back, "Listen, this prick clipped me for a little less than 10K. It's money he owes me for work on several projects. He didn't pay me and has no intention of paying me, so I figure that if what he owes me is worth going to prison over, I've got no problem with it. I expect nothing from you people. I don't want a dime. I just want you to know that you own a bunch of houses that you'll have to put on the auction block, once they're foreclosed on and you'll be left holding a very large bag."

I was somewhat insulted at this question but passed it off as nothing more than these two women jockeying for position and getting a feel for the terrain they were about to tread upon. I didn't know them and they didn't know me, and they, too, needed to be careful. I think they believed what I was telling them could have only been one, of two things; 1) a complete line of bullshit to make the life of my ex-employer/partner, because I felt I was wronged, or 2) what I was telling them was the complete truth.

If I was bullshitting them, I would be flushed out rather quickly, but if the latter were true, they had better be extremely cautious in what they said and what information they gave up or looked into.

I'm no legal expert, nor do I know how the banking system works, other than it can be breached quite easily and I can only guess at it. If someone brings a claim and they start looking into someone's personal files over that claim, they had better damned well be justified in doing so, or their own asses would be in the proverbial sling. I knew what I was bringing to the table was big, but they didn't. What they *did* know is that I had handed over a gang load of legitimate-looking documents, offered up legitimate-sounding information, and had a detailed explanation of how Paxton's operation worked. I think they saw the flaw in their system, as plainly as I had shown them, and they cautiously believed what I was saying was the truth. To some degree, they had to take me seriously.

I continued, "Look, the reason I'm here is that I don't like liars or thieves, and this guy is one of the best. He is world-class and if you ever meet him, you'll be asking yourself why people would say such horrible things about a guy as nice as Paxton Anderson. You could have this prick, dead-to-rights, but when you meet him, he'll have you questioning yourself and what you believe to be the truth."

Both Linda Pecanic and the vice-president shot glances at each other and just stared at me, probably not believing I was telling them that Paxton is so charismatic. I didn't really care, because if they ever got the chance to meet him, they would find out for themselves exactly what I was talking about.

Linda and the vice-president thanked me over and over again for coming forward and I thought to myself, "I've heard that before and it got me nowhere. I hoped this time would be different."

I gathered my girls and we headed home. As we drove down Central Avenue, Kate, knowing the Anderson family as a good clan, whose children she played with, asked me what Paxton had done. I merely explained that he had stolen money and that I had to say something to the people he stole from so they could make him stop stealing. It was a difficult thing to explain, especially because the girls knew Paxton and his kids and thought Paxton was generally a nice guy. I wondered how far this was going to go and if what I had given them was enough to raise some eyebrows. I would soon find out that the information I had given Linda not only raised a lot of eyebrows, but it also raised the hackles on the back of many necks . . . and embarrassed many more.

When I learned that the loss exposure to M & I Bank was in the neighborhood of forty million dollars, it finally hit me; for the last several months I had been holding a book of matches in one hand and cradled in my other arm, a can of gasoline. During that entire time, I didn't even realize the enormity of it. The life of Paxton Anderson was about to change and the precursor to a forest fire was smoldering in the office of Linda Pecanic.

"HE WOULD HAVE EVENTUALLY BEEN CAUGHT"

"A vandal, vomited from Hell, who worships no God, but gold." From an address of the San Luis Potosi priests in Monterey, Mexico, 1846

Late 2007

Though Linda and I spoke on a regular basis, it wasn't until several months later that was finally contacted by the FBI and asked to come in for an interview at a Post Office at 16th Street and Buckeye in Phoenix, just west of Sky Harbor Airport. I flashed back to staring at Joey's face and listening to him tell me how a vast majority of the money was used for horses, I again felt sick to my stomach.

I walked into the Post Office and was met by a Federal Agent with the US Postal Service, who ushered me upstairs, where another agent with the FBI, was waiting. The two agents, "Pat" and "Amy" introduced themselves and before I sat down, I was asked to provide identification, which I gave them. After the small talk and feeling-out process was over, we got down to business.

One of the agents told me that she had worked with Linda Pecanic for a number of years and explained that Linda told her I had some information they might be interested in. I didn't waste any time and dived right in.

The whole process started when Paxton found a person with good credit and a fair amount of money in the bank, 401K, etc. Early on, he used his mother, Sandra Anderson, one of his sisters, Marti, his father, childhood friends, or whomever he could find that would fit the needed criteria to eventually qualify for a loan that amounted to a couple of million dollars. After the waters were tested, however, Paxton enlisted the help of a fairly charismatic cockroach name Greg Sanchez who would lure unwitting lambs into a pen for fleecing and the eventual slaughter, by Paxton.

The information I have on the process of how they worked the system is from Joey Plany explaining to me, in detail, how they did it and what I know to be true from my personal experience.

Here's how it worked:

A plot of land was found in an upscale community such as Mirabel in north Scottsdale, Superstition Mountain Properties at the end of Hwy 60 on the eastern edge of the Phoenix valley, on the road to Globe, Arizona, or Fire Rock in Fountain Hills, Arizona at the east end of Shea Road just past the famed Mayo Clinic. Once the piece of property was found it would need to be appraised for a construction loan. To the naked eye, everything was business as usual; however, this would be the last time a plot of dirt would see any lawful activity.

Paxton had a couple of appraisers which he used exclusively and who, once the value of the land was determined, would double the appraised value and submit their findings to the bank. Sometimes he would use both of them, at different times, to get a "second opinion" as a back-up appraisal, if any questions were ever raised. The appraisers were paid, not the normal $250 to $400 for an easy, no-hassle, appraisal these plots of land would normally garner, but rather a whopping $2,500.00, in cash, for each piece of dirt they reported on. They were paid this very large sum because they were doubling the value of the land. If the plot in any given community was valued at $500,000 they would essentially double it to $1 million. If the land was worth $800,000 the appraisal may come in at $1.6 million and so on.

Some of the time these appraisers would even report to the County Assessor's office to report their appraisal. This would be an added insurance if, anywhere down the line, the bank's underwriter decided to question the validity of the appraised land and called the County Assessor to confirm the value. The underwriter would be given the exact, or close to the exact value that they were staring at on the loan application. The underwriter would then compare the requested loan amount to the Schedule of Values of the intended project.

The Schedule of Values is nothing more than a list of tasks, such as grading, foundation, framing, plumbing, electrical, mechanical, etc., all the way up to and including the finishes in the home, which must be submitted for review during the loan process to ensure the bank that all the money being borrowed will be used for construction and that money will be sufficient to complete the home. If the numbers added up, which they always did, the underwriter was satisfied that they had some security for the loan. This would usually lead to an approval for a construction loan for 90% of the appraised value; common in the industry.

The beauty of this scheme is that Paxton also had a banker, on the inside, working with him. He used exclusively, one branch of Marshall & Isley Bank, or M & I Bank, as it is commonly known, at the corner of 48th Street and Warner Road, in the Ahwatukee area of Phoenix. This banker would be paid a much larger sum of money to "turn a cheek" when one of Paxton's loans came in. The sum I had heard, more than once, was twenty-five thousand dollars, in cash, for each loan that was pushed through with no problems. This banker was even witnessed by me, accepting an envelope from Joey Plany in the branch office, which included a lot of smiles and backslapping.

Once the loan was secured, Paxton had enough money to start construction on the home, as well as a lot of play money, compliments of M & I Bank. If the loan came in at $1 million, $500,000 would be used to "start" building a home and the other $500,000 would be used elsewhere.

At the top of the Schedule of Values is a rarely questioned figure that is called "Soft Costs." This little gem is worth its weight in gold and Paxton loved this particular little cell of the Excel spreadsheet.

"Soft Costs" are supposedly all the out-of-pocket expenses, such as design, architectural plans, permitting, etc., which had been incurred up to the point of loan approval. Upon ground-breaking, or once the grading of the lot has started, these funds are usually paid out immediately. The sums of money are normally in the $200,000 range. That amounts to instant cash, even though that number is greatly inflated and the "claimed" costs were never incurred to that degree. Once a tractor had been delivered to the home site, Paxton received the soft cost money from the bank with no questions asked. That little cell in the spreadsheet was fool-proof and was guaranteed every time.

Once construction on the house had begun is when the in-fighting and wrangling started, as well. With the grading and slab completed, bank inspections done and reported for approval of payments to Dynamite Custom Homes the real party started. It was the second part of the well-crafted plan and he had to have one, because the $500,000, or so, was enough to get the house to the completed framing stage, and then little else was left to actually finish the house. It would be obvious to even the dimmest of laymen that $500,000 could not build a $2 million house.

All Paxton had to do was get the house framed and roof structure set in place and he could, with our client, go back to the bank and re-finance the loan from a "construction loan" to a" home loan." All the while, our client still believing he, or she, would have a brand new custom home within a few short months. With a framed structure standing on the property, in many cases, a new loan could be garnered for a percentage of appraised value of the home itself, as if it were finished.

All of the figures on the "Schedule of Values" were drastically deflated to reflect the needed funds to build the home was minimal and could be done for less than a million dollars. On the Schedule of Values would be ridiculous numbers like $8,000 for a roof that would cost $25,000, or $15,000 for all the kitchen cabinetry that would actually cost $60,000, or $11,000 for finish plumbing fixtures that would cost $55,000. The earlier tasks (grading, all underground work, slab, and framing) would be closer to the actual costs due to the need to complete the house to framing, so refinancing of the original loan could happen.

Bigger bank wires were soon to come and Paxton's cut would increase with those wires, but of course, the house would not see but a fraction of that money.

At that point the house would essentially be "parked" and only minor work being conducted to make it appear to the homeowner/borrower that work, albeit slowly, was continuing. Eventually, work would stop completely and the sound of hammers and saws would be replaced by the Arizona wind whistling through a shell of a home; open to the elements. This was the time that Paxton backed away and informed the homeowner/borrower that they were on their own and if they didn't find a way to pay the banknote, it would be subject to foreclosure.

One such poor bastard was Bill Bailey, who allowed Paxton to build a home using his signature and credit history to garner a construction loan for a custom home in the Fire Rock community of Fountain Hills, located at 9445 Desert Wash Trail; Lot #11, building permit #05-234.

Of the several homes I had a hand in building, I know of only one that was ever completed. Located in the same Fire Rock community as Bill Bailey's home, this particular home was at 10240 N. Fire Canyon Drive; Lot 14, building permit #05-68.

Originally Greg Sanchez secured the loan on N. Fire Canyon Drive and when it was finished Paxton's mother, Sandra, "bought" the home. Even though she was unemployed and had no way of qualifying for a loan to buy this home, Paxton gave her a "job" and employment history at a company called Flagship Development. After Dynamite Custom Homes was dissolved due to so many people being owed money and my resignation as the "Qualifying Party" for the contractor's license, JR Custom Homes became the new front for Paxton's fraudulent activity. However, this too, would eventually roll up the mat, due to owing sub-contractors money and Flagship Development became the torch bearer.

The way Paxton got around employment verification for his mother was to unplug the JR Custom Homes fax line, plug in a regular phone, and use it as the business line for Flagship Development. The paycheck stubs were easy to dummy up by figuring out what size of font and letter style the payroll company used. Once that was determined, it was a matter of formatting it as closely as possible and producing a pay stub showing she was paid a heinous amount of money. When the bank called the JR Custom Homes fax line to verify Sandra's employment, they were happy to hear that Sandra Anderson had a job and had been "employed" there for several years; she was also a model candidate for a loan of this size.

Of all the homes that were being built by us, one question constantly nagged me; how'd he get the money? Once the pay applications were submitted, bank inspections were completed and money wired, the money NEVER made it into the hands of the person for whom the house was being built. It didn't make any sense and I was perplexed as to how the hell he did it.

Common in the construction industry, once a task was completed, the General Contractor would submit a payment application to the bank holding the note and a bank inspection would be made to ensure the work had been done before payment was issued. However, *normally* the payment would go to the homeowner for disbursement and *not* the General Contractor, as was the case in each of Paxton's deals. The funds, wired from the bank, were deposited directly into the account held by Dynamite Custom Homes, JR Custom Homes, and eventually Flagship Development. No matter how much I wracked my brain, I just could not figure out how the money bypassed everyone and went straight into our account. Joey Plany would solve that mystery for me.

With every loan that was processed, a copy of the loan documents would be sent to our office and in those loan documents, was literally everything a person needed to engage in fraudulent activity. The biggest and most important item out of all the information contained in those documents was the borrower's signature; it was also the dagger that would be buried into their hearts, once all the money from the loan was gone, the house was "parked" and unfinished, interest payments due, and Paxton Anderson gone.

At Paxton's direction, Joey Plany would make a copy of the borrower's signature, cut it out and tape it to the payment application. From this point, another copy would be made of the altered document and what the copier spit out was a clean copy of an approved pay application ready for submission to the bank. The document would then be faxed to the bank for processing. The borrower's *signature* proved that he, or she, had reviewed the application for payment and agreed to its content and claims of completed tasks.

Unfortunately, in this day and age, facsimiles are accepted just as readily as a wet signature and are rarely questioned. In the event that any of Paxton and Joey's, "cut-and-pasting" techniques faltered and was questioned, I'm certain it would have been a cue to pack up and hit the skids, but it never happened. Even understanding that they had cut-and-pasted the borrower's signature didn't explain why the borrower never got the cash. Although Joey Plany never admitted it, he eluded to the fact that with the precision used in their cut-and-pasting technique, they might have also procured an affidavit, of some kind, on which was the borrower's "signature." What this did, is grant the General Contractor permission to handle the money. It also gave them full reign of the funds from the payment application, once they received the money. Paxton would then be responsible for distributing the same to each respective subcontractor, which would usually never happen because each subcontractor was "fired" over shoddy work. With the loan in place and money rolling in by the truckload, the bleating of the slaughtering of lambs was close behind.

With a bank manager on the payroll and in his back pocket, Paxton could do just about anything he wanted. He had access to pretty much everything, but the bank vault itself and even that, I don't believe, would have been safe had Paxton been given the opportunity to enter it. He would have somehow found a way to get someone's signature allowing him to empty it at his leisure and with the same self-assured arrogance, he would walk into the bank, load a cart with all the cash the vault could hold and with his signature Barney Rubble walk and Fred Flintstone laugh, stroll out of the bank as if he hadn't a care in the world.

It was genius how Paxton Anderson was able to put this whole plan together, gain the complete trust of his friends and then his acquaintances, through Greg Sanchez, and once all his proverbial ducks were lined up, he would destroy their world with the precision of a surgeon. All the while he would continue to engage these people with the niceties of an old woman in church until the money was gone.

His most amazing feat was that although he was controlling literally everything, he was not connected in any way, shape, or form to *any* of the loans. Paxton instructed Joey Plany to prepare all the docs for payment and to forge all the signatures by his "cut, paste, and copy" technique. Paxton was the guy after I notified him of a completed task, who instructed Joey Plany to set up the bank inspections of projects and readied themselves for the pending bank wire. Paxton was the one who instructed Joey to pay certain sub-contractors a percentage of what they were owed to keep them "interested" in gaining the rest as long, as they played Paxton's game.

Joey took all the calls from disgruntled sub-contractors wanting money and passed on the information to Paxton, who made the decision to act or ignore them. Although many knew the name of Paxton Anderson, he was a virtual ghost to anything, or anyone, living in the real world. The way Paxton worked reminds me of a line in the movie, "The Usual Suspects" in which Kevin Spacey, who would go on the win an Oscar for his role in this movie, said to Chaz Palminteri, *"The biggest trick the Devil ever played, was convincing the world he didn't exist."* Though he truly didn't "exist" in any of the bank transactions, the vast majority of those who knew Paxton Anderson would contend that he was the Devil. I knew him well and after finding out what I did about Paxton, I am among the "vast majority."

Another aspect to be considered, in all of these bank transactions is the existence of an animal called a "Mortgage Broker." These individuals are what enabled Paxton to get rich on his clandestine travels through the home loan and construction loan market. He read the tea leaves well and once he put his plan to work he found it was fool-proof. Or nearly so.

As I sat in the conference room, telling my story to this Postal Inspector and agents for the FBI, I commented on what a genius plan Paxton had devised and executed. I remember chuckling, shaking my head from side-to-side and looking down at the tabletop, as I spoke. One of the lead FBI agents investigating this case snapped, "He would have eventually been caught."

I calmly looked up from my gaze at the table and said to her, "No, he wouldn't have, Amy. With all due respect, he would have continued until he was done robbing people in Arizona and moved on to another state, to pick up where he left off here. This guy is a smart sonofabitch."

"How can you be so sure?" She asked smugly.

"Because banks don't hold loans," I responded.

"They may hold them for a while, but there's always a mortgage broker out there looking to make a buck and when he finds a buyer for the loan, that loan is passed on to some other banking institution, and then it's passed off again and again and again. As long as there are brokers interested in buying loans, so they can sell them to someone else, that loan will be purchased. By the time the building of the house is into its twelfth, or fourteenth month, that loan may have seen five or six banking institutions. The longer the loan is alive and interest payments are being made, mortgage brokers will sell it off. Then when the time comes that the payments stop and people begin to look into the cause of the collapse, somewhere down the line one of those banking institutions will have gone out of business and what you're left with is some poor bastard with his mouth hanging open, holding a small stack of worthless papers that no one will touch."

"Amy" just stared at me as I continued.

"The only way Paxton was going to 'get caught', as you say, was by making a mistake; a gross miscalculation on his part. That miscalculation was **me**. He didn't count on me having a conscience and morals, or that I would ever rat him out. Without me coming forward, you guys would be working on something else."

She never countered; probably because she knew I was right and couldn't respond.

I would speak to federal agents on this case, numerous times to give them various documents that I came across, or e-mail I happened to find that had been forgotten about. Each time I came across something I would call "Pat" and inform her of my find. Most often, we would meet so I could hand it over to them.

"EMERGENCY MOTION TO REMOVE WITNESSES"

"The stone in the water knows nothing of the hill, which lies parched in the sun." - African proverb

August 22, 2007

In August I was dragged back into court once again. I think that Tiffany was making another attempt at modifying custody of our children and she had what she thought was a silver bullet. Tiffany is all about control and when she doesn't have it, she goes a little crazy. For nearly a year and a half, she had some control, but had not attained complete control. When she lost her bid to have me removed from the lives of my daughters, by her accusations of sexual and physical abuse, all she could do is try to make me snap so she could say, "See? I told ya so." That little plan never materialized, so what she did was to make sure she could keep me on the ropes, and every month, or so, I was back in court to answer another complaint.

Once the news of my parting ways with Paxton was out, they somehow got in touch with each other. I'm not really even sure who called whom, nor do I care. It is just a known fact that they were in touch. Paxton knew the information I had on him could be detrimental to his livelihood of liberating funds from banking institutions and leaving unsuspecting friends responsible for repaying those funds. He needed to stop the bleeding and if he could slow me up for a while, he might be able to salvage some of what I had damaged; and I had done some serious damage at Risen Savior.

The "old" Paxton whose normal reference to Tiffany was, "the fucking douche bag," or "dirty c**t." With his current situation, he had apparently shed those feelings and was now the "new" Paxton, willing to testify that I was an unstable person, not fit for parenting two young girls. Pretty amazing statement for a guy who openly uses either the "C" word, or "pussy" when speaking to his five-year-old daughter, Scout, after she used the restroom.

Paxton Anderson would ask, "Scout, did you wipe your c**t?" Or "Scout, did you wipe your pussy?" To a five-year-old! It was very sad to watch this and I realize Paxton saw nothing wrong with the manner in which he spoke to his daughter. It was the way Paxton spoke; that was all there was to it. I had even heard him, on a few occasions, speak to his wife in the same manner and refer to her as a "dumb c**t" to her face.

Regardless, it was clear what Paxton was trying to do here, I loved the fact that he and Tiffany had teamed up for this one. In my opinion, considering what the two of them were made of, it made them both look foolish.

When I had read the names of Paxton Anderson and Joey Plany on Tiffany's witness list, I called Linda and told her what was going on. Like me, she wasn't surprised given the character of people such as these two. I asked her if I could inform the judge (Ballinger) of what was going on. She was hesitant but agreed to allow her name and contact numbers to be used in the motion I would submit, requesting the removal of Paxton and Joey.

I sat in front of my laptop and banged out the Motion below to have them removed from the witness list. Up until that point, Paxton had no idea of the level at which I had taken the information I possessed. Tiffany would change that for everyone who was worried about the investigation becoming common knowledge.

Below is the exact transcript as it appears in the public record.

Eric Di Conti
44191 West Sedona Trail
Maricopa, Arizona 85239

In Pro Per

IN THE SUPERIOR COURT OF THE STATE OF ARIZONA
IN AND FOR THE COUNTY OF MARICOPA

In Re the Marriage of:	) Case No.: FC 2006-050978
TIFFANY NELSON,	)
Petitioner,	) *EMERGENCY MOTION*
	) *TO REMOVE WITNESSES*
ERIC DI CONTI,	) *FOR TESTIMONY*
Respondent	)
	)
	)
	) DATED AUGUST 22, 2007

(Judge Eddward Ballinger, Jr.)

_____

Your Honor,

There are two witnesses on the Petitioner's list of witnesses that should be removed. The names of these individuals are <u>Paxton Anderson</u> and <u>Joey Plany</u>. These two individuals, if they even show up, are two people I worked with very closely for some 15 months and became aware of many fraudulent practices used by them. During the months of April and May of this year, I exposed many of their fraudulent business practices, fraudulent bank activity, and misappropriation of bank funds to several people close to them, including M & I Bank Corp. Mr. Anderson and Mr. Plany lost several contracts due to my giving up this information and exposing these practices. They both vowed to get back to me one day and it seems they feel they have found a way by aligning themselves with Tiffany Nelson. Their veracity is, at *the very least, questionable and would say anything to retaliate against me for exposing them.*

Further and more importantly, due to my giving up this information, there is currently an open and active investigation by the F.B.I. and by M & I Bank, Corp. The loss exposure for M & I Bank is somewhere between $10 and $20 million dollars due to the practices of these two possible witnesses. Paxton Anderson and Joey Plany were also involved in several fraudulent bank loans with First Magnus Bank who, as Your Honor may know, filed for bankruptcy last week due to these same practices. I exposed those fraudulent loan submissions as well.

If these two individuals are allowed to testify as witnesses for the petitioner, in order to discredit Mr. Anderson and Mr. Plany, as it will be necessary to expose them as hostile toward me for exposing them and their activities. The only way to do this is to address the fact that there is an ongoing investigation being conducted. The last thing M & I Bank wants is to do is have this investigation exposed, as it will severely and adversely impact the integrity the same. It could also jeopardize the safety of several people involved if this investigation were to be made known to these two individuals.

I have spoken to Linda Pecanic who is head of Securities and Fraud at M & I Bank, Corp. regarding this matter. I have been in contact with her from the start of this investigation and she in turn has spoken to agents in Tucson and Phoenix on this matter. With great reservation, I have been authorized by Ms. Pecanic to give Your Honor her phone number for confirmation of the above. She wanted it very clear that, although she will speak to Your Honor, she must be extremely cautious in what is said. Ms. Pecanic will inform the Court that it is imperative the information she gives you is off the record, as far as the witnesses are concerned. Ms. Pecanic will acknowledge that there is an open and active investigation as well as, acknowledge that these two individuals, in no uncertain terms, can know nothing of this investigation; that it would, in fact, jeopardize everything M & I Bank, Corp. and the federal government has worked for thus far.

Due to this information being copied to the Petitioner, it also must be known that any other persons passing this information on to Paxton Anderson, or Joey Plany, or informing them that they are the subject of an intense investigation, will be interfering/ tampering with an active and ongoing federal investigation and again, it could prove detrimental to the safety of several individuals close to this investigation.

For the above reasons, it is respectfully requested that the Court disallows the presence and the testimony of these two witnesses (Paxton Anderson and Joey Plany), that it will severely impact an ongoing investigation by the F.B.I. and M & I Bank Corp.

I will concede to little more than the fact that Joey Plany conducted payroll duties during my employment and he was in fact responsible for making support payments to the Clearinghouse. Several of which he missed, or was late in the making, due to his lack of understanding of the Child Support System.

Linda Pecanic's phone numbers, for Your Honor's use, are as follows: Office (602) 27#-#### (Push "0" as soon as the recording comes on), and Cell (602) 31#-####

Respectfully submitted,

Eric L. Di Conti
Dated this 22nd day of August, 2007

A copy of the foregoing hand-delivered
Or mailed this__ day of_____, 2007 to:

Honorable Eddward Ballinger, Jr.
Arizona Superior Court
Northeast Regional Court Facility
18380 N. 40th Street
Phoenix, Arizona 85032

Steven Everts
Udall, Shumway & Lyons, P.L.C.
30 West First Street
Mesa, Arizona 85201-9392

The following Monday, as I was at Our Lady of Mount Carmel School to pick up my girls, my cell phone started ringing. The screen told me it was a call from Linda Pecanic.

"Hello?"

"Hi, Eric. You'll never guess who I just spoke to," Linda said.

I didn't want to play, "OK, I give up. Who?"

"Paxton Anderson."

The name stopped me dead in my tracks, my body ever-so-slightly leaning forward, "Are you shitting me?" I was probably yelling into the phone.

"I just got off the phone with him. You were my first call."

"What the hell did he want?" Then it hit me, "And how the hell did he get your number?"

"I'm looking at the Motion to Remove Witnesses on line right now," she said. "He told me to pull it up and read it."

"What the hell did he want?"

"He wanted to know if he was under investigation and if I knew you."

"What did you tell him?" I asked still trying to digest this development and straining to figure out how in hell he found out about the motion to remove him.

"I told him I didn't know what he was talking about, I didn't know who he was and I had never heard of Eric Di Conti."

My voice raised a few decibels, "Are fucking shitting me?" I just couldn't believe what I was hearing. Then it dawned on me. Tiffany told him! I just couldn't believe that Tiffany would be that stupid to inform Paxton that I had, 1) written the motion and 2) blown the cover of a federal investigation. She would have been putting her ass in a serious sling by allowing Paxton to be privy to this investigation.

"How, in God's name, did he find out about it?" Hoping I was wrong and there was another reason for the information leaking out.

"How do you *think* he found out about it, Eric?" Linda asked me very sarcastically.

She had warned me that Tiffany would take this information and go right to Paxton with it and I told *her* that Tiffany wouldn't be that stupid. Jesus, was I ever wrong. There *was* only one way that Paxton could have found out; Tiffany.

Tiffany either *gave* Paxton a copy of the motion or *directed* him to the public records to view the document. If the latter scenario occurred and she was ever called to answer for her actions, she probably felt she could rationalize, in her feeble little mind, she hadn't outwardly informed him, but rather directed him to where he could find this information.

I fantasized about Tiffany being hauled before a federal judge to answer for her involvement in interfering with a federal investigation, by tipping Paxton off.

I fantasized about a federal judge looking down on Tiffany and making the following statement; "Ms. Nelson, it has come to this court's attention that you played a very big part in interfering with the investigation of Paxton Anderson, which was being conducted by the Federal Bureau of Investigation. In fact, Ms. Nelson, there was no possible way Mr. Anderson could have found out about this investigation had you not wanted so badly to repay him for his testimony against your former husband, Eric Di Conti. Would please explain to this court what it was that you were thinking when you decided that this was the right thing to do?"

The judge excuses Tiffany and tells her not to leave town, that she would be contacted to appear before the court again. My thoughts were interrupted by someone calling my name and my fantasies faded back into reality.

"Eric! You there?" Linda finally got my attention.

"Uh, yeah. Sorry. I was just thinking about something," I said.

"Look, just keep quiet for a while. Don't talk to anyone else about this. Maybe it'll blow over."

"OK. Sorry about all this." We bid our good-byes and I hung up the phone.

As Paxton had known nothing of my actions thus far, he was that proverbial "stone in the water," as described in the quote above, but thanks to someone who thought she was smarter than the rest; he was just introduced to the hill laying "parched in the sun." His world was going to be pretty attention-grabbing, but we had hoped it wouldn't be so soon.

Whatever the case, and as bad as it seemed at that moment, there was an upside to the whole scenario; she had just interfered with an investigation that was just about to turn federal and that isn't a good thing. At least I had some satisfaction, with which I could gloat.

Another interesting development in Paxton Anderson being informed of this investigation was that, at the time of this writing, he was rumored to have retained the same attorney, United States Representative, Gary Condit retained in 2001 when a scandal of an affair between he and an intern named Chandra Levy surfaced. This has not been confirmed, but it would stand to reason that he would need a damned good attorney to represent him.

Gary Condit, you may remember, represented California's 18th congressional district and was a senior member of the House Permanent Select Committee on Intelligence. His intern, Chandra Levy, went missing on May 1, 2001 and seven days later, on May 8th, it became common knowledge she had been having an affair with the Congressman. The married Condit finally admitted to the affair but was never named as a suspect. Many believed he should have been. Four-and-a-half months later, on September 11, the case would be overshadowed by the attack on the World Trade Center. Sadly, her remains would be found on May 22, 2002, three weeks past the one-year anniversary of her disappearance. The homicide, as it was ruled by the coroner, remained unsolved and was classified as a "Cold Case" for some time, however I believe a man was finally jailed in connection with her murder. Hard to say if the guy was set up by our government to save it from further embarrassment, or he actually did the deed. Gary Condit has pretty much disappeared from public sight.

"WERE YOU INVESTIGATED BY CHANDLER POLICE?"

"No matter how long you beat on a wall, it's not going to turn into a door" – Unknown

August 2007

I had spent the past three and a half months looking for work and in that time, what I had found was the State of Arizona had new rules for employers looking to hire employees. Construction has, for many years, been known to hire illegal aliens for their eagerness to work, their oftentimes hard work, and the hard fact that they accept lower pay than those born on US soil. Construction contractors were now employing a new tactic in hiring to avoid enormous fines if they were found to have hired undocumented workers; a background check. Many of these contractors, probably due to their long history of hiring practices, conducted extensive background checks that delved deeper than the cursory checks others employed.

I have a very long history in construction that dates back to the late seventies and have climbed the ladder in the industry to a level near the top. I excelled in this industry and although my manner and practice of getting things done were, to say the least, unorthodox, I had a reputation for doing just that; I got things done. There were only two kinds of people that I dealt with, those who revered me and those who despised me. The ones who despised me were those who lied to me or didn't do what they claimed they would do. To these individuals, my response was swift and harsh and nine out of ten times, they would not repeat the error.

I was fiercely loyal to those who made my projects run smoothly and would use them again and again, many times without ever getting bids from other sub-contractors for those projects. I trusted them and they repaid me with a near-flawless completed project, often with short punch lists.

Since the start of the fiasco that surrounded my divorce and the months that followed, this was the first time I had to conventionally search for work. I did so by using Monster.com and in doing that, I had a wide range in which to search the Phoenix area. I submitted over forty resumes to construction companies of all sizes and most of them never responded. Of those who did, either by electronic response or telephonically, offered their regret that I didn't "have the experience" they were looking for, or were "unqualified for the position" I was applying for. With over twenty-five years in the industry and attaining the level of Construction Manager, running the Tenant Improvement division, for a major company, I was surprised I didn't have what they were looking for. I was more than qualified to hold a position of Project Manager, or Construction Manager, in any construction company in the country, but for some reason, I now found myself "unqualified."

It wasn't until August of 2007, during an interview, I was let in on a little secret by a manager of a fairly large construction firm who will remain nameless. I'm just thankful he let me in on the secret. He happened to know a friend of mine and confided in me that when my name was run through the background check, I came back with some red flags.

"Well, actually a major one," He said.

"What the hell are you talking about?" I asked, "What 'red flags'?"

"Were you investigated by the Chandler Police Department in March and April of 2006?" He asked.

"Fuck!" I was back in the vacuum I hadn't felt for a while. "There is no fucking way you can be serious!" I was livid.

"Well, were you?"

"This is bullshit."

"Just answer the question." He seemed as if he wanted to help, hoping it was a mistake.

"Well...."

He interrupted, "Hey, I don't really give a shit either way," he said. "You're a good guy and that's all I need to know, but human resources have their own way of fucking things up around here and unless I was the president of this shit-hole, I can't get past them. Since I'm not the president, I was just wondering if it was a mistake. Cuz if it is, then we can work around it and get a copy of the report. Ya know?"

"Fuck it. I'm outta here." I'm certain my head was down when I walked out of the building and to my car. I don't remember if I even acknowledge the receptionist as I walked past her, but I remember hearing, "Have a nice day."

"Yeah, thanks," I remember thinking. "What better day could I have than the one I'm having?"

As I pushed the door open the din of passing traffic filled my ears. It was a long walk to my car which was parked across the lot, about a hundred yards from the front door. When I got to my car and slid my key into the door lock, I could see the distorted reflection of myself in the driver's side window and wondered who it was I was looking at.

I wasn't the man in the glass that I remember seeing, so many years before this one. This man appeared to be broken and much older than the man I had seen even earlier that morning. I pulled the car door open and positioned myself to slide in just as a plane, from nearby Sky Harbor Airport, barreled overhead. I looked up for a moment and wondered where it was headed and imagined the people inside it, being happy they were going somewhere fun and away from the reality of the Phoenix Valley. I wanted to be with them. I wanted to get away from this reality, as well. I got in and as soon as I closed the door, all that was left of the noise was the faint whine of the US Airways jet engines; the noise from the traffic was virtually gone. When the noise from the plane had faded away, but for the sound of my breathing, I was in complete silence. All I can remember thinking about was each one of those rejection letters, or phone conversations, which I was informed I wasn't qualified or didn't have the experience needed for employment. I replayed it over and over in my head and I couldn't make it stop. I finally knew the real reason that I wasn't "qualified."

Of the times I heard, "I'm sorry" and "good luck," "we'll keep your application on file," and other bullshit lines I heard and could never figure out why. I now knew the exact reason why and it was another humbling experience I had to endure. I then realized the embarrassment of it all. As I was applying for employment I was giving these people permission to delve into my past; giving them full access if they so desired. What they came away with was the belief that I was a pedophile and there was no way in hell, I would be employed with them; the liability was too great. No one in their right mind would take the chance even if they *did* read the police report all the way to the end where the words, "Accusation Unfounded – Case Closed" were written. The average person would think, "If the accusation was made there must be *some* truth to it."

Later that day I would call my friend at UDC, who still had close ties to the brass at Northrop-Grumman and asked him to have a security check run on me. Two days later I received the e-mail below:

Print – Close Window

From:	############
To:	"*Eric Di Conti*" <#########@yahoo.com>
Subject:	*Northrop Grumman Access*
Date:	*Thu, 16 Aug 2007 10:20:32 -0700*

Hey Eric,

After we spoke I had a scheduled meeting with one of the Heads of Security here at Northrop-Grumman. I ran down the scenario we were talking about and what he told me was that preliminarily, if there was a background check done on you (which there would be) and you had ANY kind of questionable activity in your past, investigations of violence, and especially if you were investigated for sexual assault on a child, you would not be given a clearance higher than that of a laborer. He said he didn't think he would allow you to work here in the capacity that you did before when you worked as a PM on the Air Combat Design Center. He said he would have to really look closely at the situation and make a decision, but he would be leaning toward a "No Access" decision.

Now that's just coming from a discussion I had with the guy on a superficial level. Nothing more than a preliminary statement. Anything could happen, but I think he was being cautious in saying that he would look closely at the situation, but I think he would have already made up his mind once he saw that you were investigated for sexual abuse. You're pretty much fucked, my friend. Maybe you can get a job at a company driving a truck, they only look at your driving record. Just kidding. Sorry to give you the bad news.

Keep your chin up.

Rick

I was damaged goods and no one wanted me around.

DEFAMATION OF CHARACTER LAWSUIT

(**Amended Complaint – The Judge wanted me to "strike" a few things in my complaint, so I did just that; I added a strikethrough and refiled my complaint.**)

Note: This following document is exactly as it was entered into the record in Maricopa Superior Court. Nothing has been changed and again, though this would become public record, I used the wisdom and teachings of my old friend Fernando Vargas as I wrote. Again, this is Public Record and can be verified through the Courts.

October 16, 2007

Eric Di Conti
44191 W. Sedona Trail
Maricopa, AZ 85239

In Pro Per

IN THE SUPERIOR COURT OF THE STATE OF ARIZONA
IN AND FOR THE COUNTY OF MARICOPA

In Re To Civil Suit: ERIC L. DI CONTI, *Plaintiff.* Vs. TIFFANY A. NELSON SUSAN B. NELSON-STEPHANSON *Defendants.*	))))))))))	Case # CV 2007-003198 <u>Amended COMPLAINT:</u> DEFAMATION OF CHARACTER; LIBEL; SLANDER; INDIVIDUAL'S RIGHT TO PRIVACY; FRAUDULENT CONCEALMENT OF MARITAL ASSETS AT THE TIME OF DISSOLUTION (ARS-12-653.01.1; 12-653.01.2; 12-653.01.3; 12-653.01.5) Date: October 15, 2007 ~~Honorable Ruth Hilliard~~ Honorable A. Craig Blakey II

The following is the "Amended Complaint" per Minute Entry of Honorable A. Craig Blakey II dated September 26, 2007. All changes are in, "italics" and <u>underscored</u> for identification of the same. Also included are changes to items that were dismissed by Judge Blakey, identified by a "strikethrough."

A Civil Complaint/Law Suit has been filed against the above-named defendants, Tiffany A. Nelson (daughter) and Susan B. Nelson-Stephenson (mother), by Eric L. Di Conti (ex-husband of Tiffany A. Nelson) for Defamation of Character, Libel and Right To Privacy.

These are the facts and they are undisputed:

<u>*Item 1:*</u> *(See Exhibit 2) On March 2, 2006, at 7:32PM through an armed process server (armed- due to Ms. Nelson-Di Conti's claims that Mr. Di Conti was violent, thus the need for protection), Tiffany Nelson-Di Conti served her, then husband with an Order Of Protection. The Order of Protection (Case # CC2006023696000), stated that there was physical and verbal abuse being committed against Ms. Nelson-Di Conti and their two daughters, Kathryn E. Di Conti (7 yrs.) and Megan E. Di Conti (5 yrs.). There was also an underhanded inference of sexual abuse in the Order that stated "rubs," and "rashes," were seen on the insides of one of his daughter's thighs. This Order was filed erroneously and without cause, as there was never any history of violence against either party in the home. The Order of Protection Hearing was set for March 27, 2006 at 10:00AM at the Maricopa County Superior Court, McDowell Mountain Facility in Courtroom 101. Presiding over the hearing was Comm. Susan M. Brnovich, who dismissed the Order against Mr. Di Conti, stating "there is no proof by preponderance that any domestic violence has occurred," and that the case before her was, "Not appropriate in this arena." The Minute Entry shows the conclusion of the hearing at 3:54PM.*

Even though the order was dismissed after 25 days, because of Ms. Nelson-Di Conti's manipulation and evasion, Mr. Di Conti did not speak to his children for another four (4) days, which, when he finally did, was telephonic. By Mr. Di Conti's account, the girls were surprised to hear from their father as they were under the impression that, according to the story Ms. Nelson-Di Conti told the girls, he had "moved to California because [he] didn't want to be [their] Daddy any more." On

April 4, 2006, an "Accelerated Motion For Expedited Order To Compel Mother To Permit Father Access/Parenting Time And Request For Telephonic Conference" was filed with Judge Eddward Ballinger, Jr. It was another five (5) days past that, due to more manipulation and further evasion by Ms. Nelson-Di Conti, he was finally able to see his children, but that visit, which lasted one hour, was in a public place, at Peter Piper Pizza in Scottsdale, under the supervision of one Pamela Chambers, counselor on the court roster. This was at Mr. Di Conti's request and his cost. Mr. Di Conti requested Ms. Chambers' presence and supervision due to the continued claims, by Ms. Nelson-Di Conti, that there truly was a problem of abuse and molestation. Mr. Di Conti wanted a professional there to witness this visit, and three (3) other visits following this one, to dispel any of his estranged wife's claims. Ms. Chambers filed a report with Mr. Di Conti's counsel, Michelle Kunzman and DeAnn Gillespie, of Gillespie and Associates.

<u>Item 2:</u> Per Order to Dismiss ~~During the Order of Protection Hearing, Ms. Susan Nelson-Stephenson testified on direct examination by Donna Jewett, that on one occasion a few years back, because his daughter (Kathryn) "interrupted him," she witnessed Mr. Di Conti grab her by the arm, picked her up, and dragged her into to her room. She testified that this act was so violent that Kathryn's "little toes barely touched the ground," as she was taken to her room. She stated that Mr. Di Conti's daughter screamed the whole time for her grandmother's help. This incident never happened the way that Ms. Nelson-Stephenson testified while under oath. Although there was a similar incident, there was never any such physical contact between father and daughter. Remarkably, when cross-examined by DeAnn Gillespie, Ms. Nelson-Stephenson could not remember the date, month, year, or even the season in which this happened. She could not recall who was present, nor could she recall where anyone was standing when this supposed incident took place. She could remember absolutely nothing of any details about what she had just testified to under oath. She was given~~

~~time to collect her thoughts in an attempt to recall any facts of this incident and she was virtually unable to. She was reminded by Ms. Gillespie that if this was such a violent and horrific act against her granddaughter, as she claimed it to be, surely she would remember very distinct details of the same and probably should have contacted Child Protective Services, which she did not. The very obvious reason for her inability to recall anything is that she fabricated the incident, in open court, in an attempt to help her daughter keep the Order of Protection in place. She knowingly, deliberately, and willfully lied about Mr. Di Conti's actions and did so under oath and before God. Simply put, she committed perjury for the sake of her daughter and in the process attacked Mr. Di Conti's character and reputation, as a father to his children.~~

Item 3: (See Exhibit 3) On March 3, 2006, at 10:58AM, Tiffany Nelson-Di Conti, with her friend Ryanne Ritter, walked into the Chandler Police Department and knowingly filed a false police report (Report # 06-02-5810), accusing Mr. Di Conti of molesting of their two daughters, Kathryn E. Di Conti (7 yrs.) and Megan E. Di Conti (5 yrs.). Ms. Ryanne Ritter (family friend) accompanied her at Ms. Nelson-Di Conti's request. It was also stated that there was physical abuse against her and the children. In the initial interview, taken by Officer Philip Besse (#00252), Ms. Nelson-Di Conti was quoted as saying that their sex life was non-existent due to Mr. Di Conti's "inability to perform," inferring that his preference was for young children and not that of an adult woman, when in fact, their sex life was quite active for much of their marriage. Ms. Nelson-Di Conti also admitted, in this report, that she had taken, without permission, a very private letter that Mr. Di Conti had written his father several years before, made several copies of it, and passed them out to friends in an attempt to bolster her claims of abuse.

Item 4: Ms. Nelson-Di Conti stated that Mr. Di Conti had molested his older daughter (17 yrs.) and had nightmares about *this act, which he supposedly confessed to another woman, who wrote a letter to Ms. Nelson-Di Conti about this incident. The incident of the alleged "dream" never happened and if such a letter exists as it is stated, this woman will be named in a lawsuit, as well. Officer Besse informed Ms. Nelson-Di Conti that she would be required to take the children in for a "forensic interview and medical examination," that she would be contacted by "CPD." The police report was turned over to the Chandler Police Department Detective John Beekman (#00288) of the Sex Crimes Division and an investigation was subsequently conducted on Mr. Di Conti. The girls were never taken to be examined by the forensic specialist.*

<u>Item 5:</u> (See Exhibit 3-Follow-up Report) On March 14, 2006, a second interview with Ms. Nelson-Di Conti was conducted by Detective Beekman, during this interview Ms. Nelson-Di Conti contradicted her original claims of physical abuse, stating that Mr. Di Conti had "never been physically abusive to [her], or the girls" and "never really touched [her]." Ms. Nelson-Di Conti was informed that the department's investigation found her claims baseless. The investigation was closed

<u>Item 6:</u> During the period of this investigation on Mr. Di Conti, and sometime prior to the second interview with Chandler Police Department, Ms. Nelson openly accused Mr. Di Conti of physical abuse and/<u>or</u> sexual molestation, on numerous occasions, to several individuals close to their family, <u>including the Ritter Family, the Sheppard Family, the Gerbich Family, the Nordquist Family, the Blessing Family, the Collins Family, the Woodford Family, Mary Houseman, Linda Pauley, Director of Risen Savior Lutheran School, and many others.</u>

<u>Item 7:</u> (Included in Exhibit 1)During one visit to the home of Patricia and Bill Sheppard, in Oakwood Hills, in the presence of the Sheppard's and Ritter's, she also accused Mr. Di Conti of sexually assaulting the 7-year-old son of close family friends;

Ryanne and Charles Ritter. Both the Ritter's and Sheppard's are willing to testify to the statements made by Ms. Nelson-Di Conti

<u>Item 8:</u> (Included in Exhibit 1)There was also an inference that the children (Emma and Aidan, 4 and 3 respectively) of Ms. Ritter's brother, Shawn Sheppard, had been molested by Mr. Di Conti, as well.

<u>Item 9:</u> (Included in Exhibit 1) The Ritter's were given a photocopy of the private letter Mr. Di Conti wrote to his father to read, which they did. Handing out the ill-gotten letter, Ms. Nelson-Di Conti took from her husband, was to, once again, bolster her claims of abuse. The Ritter's are willing to testify to this account. <u>Tiffany Nelson was ordered by the Court to return this letter to Mr. Di Conti, but what Mr. Di Conti received was a "copy" of the letter in pristine condition which would indicate that she is still in possession of this private letter.</u>

<u>Item 10:</u> (Exhibit 1) Ms. Ryanne Ritter has written and signed an affidavit, which outlines her knowledge of Ms. Nelson-Di Conti's conduct and the accusations against Mr. Di Conti. She was present at several meetings with Ms. Nelson-Di Conti's attorney, Donna Jewett, and privy to a great deal of information given out by Ms. Nelson-Di Conti. A preliminary investigation (Malfeasance) was conducted by Ms. Jewett's husband who is a detective with the Phoenix Police Department in the Sex Crimes Division, at Ms. Jewett's request. He reported back to Ms. Jewett while Ms. Nelson-Di Conti and Mrs. Ritter were present, in her office. He advised Ms. Nelson-Di Conti against filing any report against Mr. Di Conti, as it would be "baseless" and the investigation would be "attached to his name for the rest of his life." Ms. Jewett informed Ms. Nelson-Di Conti that if she did, in fact, file this report and Mr. Di Conti "found out about it and made a stink," she "would lose her kids." Ms. Nelson-Di Conti was informed that the court system does not look kindly on baseless and unfounded accusations, against spouses, during a divorce. In addition to her affidavit, Ryanne Ritter is willing

to testify to all aspects of her knowledge of Ms. Nelson-Di Conti with regard to this matter.

Due to Ms. Nelson's constant denial of ever disparaging, or defaming Mr. Di Conti, it is absolutely noteworthy here that, knowing Ms. Jewett very specifically advised her client "Not to file the police report," citing the very serious repercussions for doing so; on the morning of Monday, October 23, 2006, at about 9:30am, Mr. Di Conti informed his now ex-spouse that he did, in fact, know that the police report existed, was in possession of a copy of the same and offered to send her a copy, as well, to refresh her memory of statements that she made. That very afternoon, after Ms. Nelson contacted her on this matter, Ms. Jewett filed a "NOTICE OF WITHDRAWAL" as Ms. Nelson's legal counsel.

Mr. Di Conti subsequently mailed a copy of this report to Ms. Nelson's home, located at 2211 W. Olive Street, Chandler, AZ 85248, the following day.

<u>Item 11:</u> (Included in Exhibit 1) Mrs. Ritter has also been present when Ms. Nelson's mother, Susan B. Nelson-Stephenson, made claims of abuse against Mr. Di Conti, to others, <u>in that she recounted the same story she told in the Order of Protection Hearing about how Mr. Di Conti dragged his daughter through the house and to her room. She also claimed that Mr. Di Conti is a violent person and unstable, which mirrors her daughter's statements about Mr. Di Conti</u>. Ms. Nelson-Stephenson has openly claimed <u>to the Ritter and Sheppard families on more than one occasion</u> that Mr. Di Conti is a "bad person" and should not be trusted. It is curious that Ms. Nelson-Stephenson was very surprised to learn that her daughter had claimed Mr. Di Conti molested any children. She said she was never made aware, by her daughter, of any problems of this nature. The Ritter and Sheppard Families are willing to testify to this account.

<u>Item 12:</u> In addition to the police report and Order of Protection, claiming physical abuse, Ms. Nelson has also openly made many public claims of physical abuse (Domestic Violence)

to friends close to their family. One such accusation was one that she claimed to have been so severely beaten she "could not leave her house for two weeks." A very close family friend and long-time neighbor in Orange, California and now a resident of Chandler, Arizona, Janine Walker, was confronted by an acquaintance (Erin Woodford) sometime in late 2004, or early 2005, on this particular incident. Janine Walker claims that in all the years she has known the Di Conti's, she has no known knowledge of Tiffany ever being abused, in any way, by Mr. Di Conti. Janine Walker is willing to testify to the questioning she received and to the content of the conversation with Erin Woodford.

<u>Item 13:</u> (Included in Exhibit 1) Ms. Nelson-Di Conti's claims of domestic violence continued throughout 2005 and into 2006 and at one point, several of her friends held an "intervention" at Paradise Bakery located at Alma School and Queen Creek, in Chandler, to get her out of the house and away from Mr. Di Conti. Ryanne Ritter was contacted by Susan Blessing and asked to attend this meeting with another friend, Melissa Nordquist. She was told that there would be several women there. Mrs. Ritter declined. It was understood that these friends had secured a room, for Ms. Nelson-Di Conti and her two daughters, in a shelter for battered women. <u>Ms. Nelson-Di Conti</u> declined to go to this shelter, saying she would take care of it herself. Presumably, she declined due to the fact that these shelters are run by professionals and one look at Ms. Nelson-Di Conti would verify she had never been a victim of abuse and her lie would be revealed. <u>Ms. Ritter is willing to testify to this account.</u>

<u>Item 14:</u> (Included in Exhibit 1) Unbeknownst to Ms. Nelson-Di Conti, at the time of this "intervention," a neighbor and close friend of the Ritter's, Mary Krauseman who also resides in Oakwood Hills, was seated in the booth directly adjacent to where Ms. Nelson-Di Conti was seated and overheard much of the conversation. Ms. Krauseman is willing to testify, under

oath, of her knowledge of the conversations she overheard on this day, as well as give her account as to the disparaging remarks made by Ms. Nelson-Di Conti about Mr. Di Conti and Ryanne Ritter.

Item 15: In the days following the Order of Protection being served, Ms. Nelson-Di Conti, made copies of the Order and distributed them to parents at the children's school, Our Lady Of Mount Carmel School and Church, in Tempe. It is understood that with the photocopy was an attachment that identified Mr. Di Conti as a pedophile. There are several individuals that remember this incident and are willing to testify to that account. Mr. Di Conti is still seeing, and feeling, the effects of this from his parents a year after these events started. To this day, several parents still shy away from Mr. Di Conti as he approaches, in the corridors, on the school campus.

Item 16: Mr. Di Conti was in the process of gaining employment with a valley residential contractor, with whom both Mr. Di Conti and Ms. Nelson-Di Conti were acquainted. Sometime in February, 2006, Ms. Nelson-Di Conti approached one Paxton Anderson, owner of Dynamite Custom Homes, LLC outside the school office of Risen Savior Lutheran School, _where daughters, Kathryn and Megan attended school, prior to transferring to Our Lady of Mount Carmel_. Ms. Nelson-Di Conti told Mr. Anderson that he should not hire Mr. Di Conti, as he is a "bad person" and would "give a bad name" to Mr. Anderson's company.

Subsequently, Mr. Di Conti was denied employment by Dynamite Custom Homes. It took several months of conversation between Mr. Anderson and Mr. Di Conti, whereas Mr. Di Conti had to prove that he was worthy of employment with this firm. Mr. Di Conti finally gained employment with Dynamite Custom Homes, LLC, some six (6) months later, and is still employed there now. Mr. Anderson is willing to testify to the content of that conversation. _To update this "Item," Mr. Di Conti no longer works for Mr. Anderson. In April of this year, 2007, Mr. Di Conti found that Mr. Paxton Anderson was_ *involved in and committing Mortgage Fraud and after gathering as much information as he could regarding the fraud, Mr. Di Conti, in June, 2007, contacted Chandler Police Department regarding the same. The same day, a detective there contacted M & I Bank Corp who held many of the bogus loans. Mr. Di Conti was contacted by the head of the Securities and Fraud Division within the bank who then requested a statement from him. A full investigation was then opened by the FBI. At the time of this amendment, M & I Bank has concluded its internal investigation and an open and active investigation by the FBI is continuing on this matter. In Mr. Di Conti's role of being the "whistleblower," Mr. Anderson has turned against Mr. Di Conti and aligned himself with Ms. Nelson as her proponent. He has even appeared on Ms. Nelson's witness list to testify against Mr. Di Conti in a custody battle between Mr. Di Conti and his former spouse. Once Mr. Di Conti saw Mr. Anderson's name on the witness list, he filed a motion to have him removed due to the possibility of the investigation being jeopardized. Tiffany Nelson subsequently forwarded a copy of the motion to Mr. Anderson, making the then-secret investigation by the bank and the FBI, known to Mr. Anderson. Quite simply, Ms. Nelson interfered with a Federal investigation in order to try to help her cause. The FBI is currently looking into the damage that Ms. Nelson may have caused by her interference. Additionally, Ms. Nelson has brought in an acquaintance to help her find any damning evidence she can on Mr. Di Conti. This person's name is Kristen Ayres and is employed by M&I Bank. Ms. Ayres contacted the lead investigator at M & I Bank and claimed that she knew Mr. Di Conti, watched his children on several occasions, and claimed that Mr. Di Conti was a "loose cannon" and "unstable." Mr. Di Conti has never met this woman, nor, by his daughters' account, has she ever watched his children as she had claimed. Ms. Ayres also admitted that she had given Mr. Di Conti's name to a "friend at the FBI" so that person could look into Mr. Di Conti's background. Ms. Ayres was subsequently told by investigating officials to stand down and keep her distance from Mr. Di Conti and Ms. Nelson, as it could be a ticket out of her employment with M&I Bank and that she, too, was interfering with a Federal investigation.*

Item 17: On several occasions, Ms. Nelson-Di Conti requested from Linda Pauley, director of Risen Savior Lutheran School, a letter stating that Mr. Di Conti is an "unfit parent" and "should not have custody of his children," due to his "violent" outbursts. The most recent request for this letter was sometime between November 2006 and December 2006. On every occasion, Ms. Pauley has denied this request. *It is notable that sometime in May, 2007, Mr. Di Conti was managing a construction project at Risen Savior Lutheran Church and School which entailed adding a second floor to the existing dwelling. Two months after this "Complaint" was filed and a day, or so, after Ms. Nelson and her mother Susan Nelson were served, a phone call came into the Church office and more specifically to Linda Pauley (See Exhibit 5). A man who would not give his name and wanted to remain anonymous but expressed his concern there was a felon on campus. Once it became widely known that Mr. Di Conti was on campus, two parents who are close friends of Ms. Nelson's (Tamara Gerbich and Melissa Nordquist) banded together with other parents at the school to have Mr. Di Conti removed from the project and away from the children at the school, citing that Mr. Di Conti was a felon and pedophile. There was a "borderline emergency meeting" held within days of the initial phone call involving Ms. Pauley and several parents who demanded Mr. Di Conti's removal. Though Mr. Di Conti was not initially removed due to the implications of a lawsuit, there was a continuous fight with parents at the school throughout Mr. Di Conti's tenure on this project. After the pressure from parents became too great Mr. Di Conti was finally removed from this project, citing reasons other than the allegations by parents, but this was not before a rule was implemented by school officials that while Mr. Di Conti was on campus "no adult male can be in the restroom when the same is occupied by small boys." Though this is completely irresponsible on the part of Risen Savior Lutheran Church and*

School, this action is in direct relation to the beliefs and actions of two friends of Mr. Di Conti's former spouse that stemmed original accusations made by Ms. Nelson to those individuals. In being removed from this project, Mr. Di Conti subsequently lost a great deal of income totaling around $175,000.00.

Mr. Di Conti's search for employment, after his removal from that project, has been a frustrating and arduous one, as he has been met with several rejections due to background checks of public records being conducted by many prospective employers. What is causing the rejections is the fact that when the background check is conducted and as this police report is public record, the investigation by the Chandler Police Department surfaces and what the prospective employer sees is "Sex Crime, Child Victim"; the hope of employment is summarily dashed. Because Mr. Di Conti cannot find employment to satisfy his needs and the needs of his daughters, nor can he afford to make the necessary monthly child support payments, he is in constant fear of being incarcerated, at Ms. Nelson's request, by Judge Eddward Ballinger, Jr. The current support payments are in the amount of $410.00 and since Mr. Di Conti has not found viable employment to satisfy those payments the threat of a bench warrant is constantly looming. The only reason that Mr. Di Conti cannot find employment in his field and has not been able to do so for over three (3) months is due solely to the false police report and rumors started by Ms. Nelson and Susan Nelson-Stephenson

__Item 18:__ (Included in Exhibit 1) Sometime in mid-2006, at a luncheon with Ryanne Ritter and another friend, Amanda Eisenfeld, Ms. Nelson made a statement that she could show her friends how to skim money out of the household account and hide it in another. Her statement was, "I've been doing this for years and Eric is so stupid, he has no idea how much money I have. Besides, if the marriage doesn't work out, you'll have a nice little nest egg when it's all over." Mr. Di Conti has four (4) years of Ms. Nelson-Di Conti's subpoenaed bank statements (while they were married) that show excessive spending and large deposits *from sales of homes into her account. These statements also show that the following day, Ms. Nelson-Di Conti would walk into the bank and make a "branch withdrawal," in the form of a Cashier's Check, for a large portion of the initial deposit and walk out. Presumably, this money was deposited into another separate account. <u>Tiffany Nelson-Di Conti has stated to Ms. Ritter that "a while back" she withdrew some $80,000 from her account and she "hid at least $40,000 each, in the accounts of [her] brother Timothy Nelson and [her] mother," Susan Nelson-Stephenson. Mrs. Ritter said that Ms. Nelson claimed that if it ever came up she would claim that it was a "business loan being paid off and Eric couldn't touch it." There is proof of a withdrawal in the exact amount that Ms. Nelson-Di Conti boasted of in the amount of $80,000. That transaction took place on November 8, 2004, under the heading "Withdrawal Made In A Branch/Store." Incidentally, this transaction was made exactly three (3) months to the day after Ms. Nelson-Di Conti packed as few belongings and while Mr. Di Conti was at work, secretly moved to Arizona with their two daughters. Mr. Di Conti did not see his children for nearly two months and over the next 15 months was forced to commute back and forth from Orange County, California to see his children. With Ms. Nelson-Di Conti's promise to "be a family again and not get a divorce," Mr. Di Conti finally found employment and relocated to Arizona on October 7, 2005. Nearly five (5) months to the day after Mr. Di Conti's arrival, his former wife began to carry out her plan of destroying Mr. Di Conti.</u>*

  <u>The practice of withdrawing funds from their marital account (See Exhibit 6) happened on more than one occasion over the course of their marriage (the earliest of large withdrawals, or transfers, on record was three (3) months prior to Ms. Nelson secretly leaving the state of California and spiriting away Mr. Di Conti's two young daughters): on April 29, 2004, an "online transfer" was made in the amount of $54,500 from Wells Fargo Checking Account # 784055857, which was transferred out of the marital account and into Wells Fargo account #6621936160; on November 8, 2004, "Withdrawal Made in a</u>

Branch/Store" in the amount of $80,000 Wells Fargo Checking Account # 784055857 (described above); ten (10) days later on November 18, 2004, a "Withdrawal Made in a Branch/Store" in the amount of $53,763.59 Wells Fargo Checking Account # 784055857. The whereabouts of these funds are unknown at this time; on January 31, 2006, One (1) month and three (3) days prior to the Order of Protection being served on Mr. Di Conti, an "Online Transfer" was made in the amount of $75,000 Wells Fargo Checking Account # 784055857 and into Wells Fargo account #6621936160; and the final "major" transaction on March 1, 2006, entitled "Withdrawal in a Brach/Store" in the amount of $68,677.38 Wells Fargo Checking Account # 784055857. Mr. Di Conti, who had NO access to this account, was unaware of any such savings account that held more than a few hundred dollars that his spouse claimed this account held. The total of all of the above transactions by which Ms. Nelson secretly withdrew joint marital funds from the bank and hid them is $331,941.00. It is easy to see Ms. Nelson's true intentions by the mere admission of her activity to her former friend, Ryanne Ritter, and just by looking at her bank transactions and activity of spending the same.

Incidentally, prior to the final withdrawal of funds from the joint marital account of Mr. Di Conti and his former spouse, Mrs. Ritter was present when Tiffany Nelson's attorney, Donna Jewett, told her to "clean out the account before Eric can." Ms. Jewett also advised Mr. Di Conti's former spouse that Mr. Di Conti is entitled to half once it was known that she withdrew the monies from the joint marital account. The final withdrawal will show Ms. Nelson-Di Conti did as she was advised, but for a little over $7,500, no money was ever returned to Mr. Di Conti and certainly not half of what was skimmed from their joint marital bank account, over the years prior.

Although Mr. Di Conti's name does not appear on this account number, it is imperative to advise the Court that Wells Fargo Checking Account # 784055857, in which ALL monies were deposited, including Mr. Di Conti's weekly pay, was the *joint marital account of both Ms. Nelson-Di Conti and Mr. Di Conti and that all monies deposited into the same should be viewed as such. It is also imperative to advise the Court that Mr. Di Conti had every intention of bringing the issue of missing marital assets to the forefront during their divorce proceedings, but as he was advised it would cost him upwards of another $10,000 to continue into trial, Mr. Di Conti could no longer retain his legal counsel, and that he should attempt to recoup these funds in a civil action under the heading "Fraudulent Concealment Of Marital Assets At Time Of Dissolution," at a later date.*

It is noteworthy to add that Wells Fargo Bank records will show that in the most recent transaction made, Ms. Nelson-Di Conti walked into a "Branch Store" and made a final withdrawal in the amount of $68,677.38. The date was Wednesday, March 1, 2006;

One (1) day prior to the Order of Protection being served on Mr. Di Conti. The whereabouts of these funds, or any other funds Ms. Nelson-Di Conti skimmed and hid, are still unknown. (Oehne vs. Oehne; 10 Kan App 2d. 73, 691 P2d 1325, 1984 and Burris vs. Burris; 904 SW2d. 564, 1995).

There are numerous other "Online Transfers" and "Branch Withdrawals" made in smaller amounts with headings of "Business Loan," "Allowance for our beautiful wife," "Harrison Bogart," etc., presumably to make her activity harder to detect, but by the mere fact of her admissions of her activity to her former friend Ryanne Ritter and by the reflecting behavior described above shows the behavior of Tiffany Nelson-Di Conti and her mother, Susan Nelson-Stephanson was outrageous, willful and wonton.

The actions by these two women have caused Mr. Di Conti to be severely damaged financially as the money which was realized through the sale of real estate properties should have been shared equally by both parties, but instead, only one person enjoyed the good fortune that came from a profitable real estate market in California. In the end, the extreme and implicit trust that Mr. Di Conti placed in his former spouse to care for their two daughters and take care of the household expenses while he worked as hard as he could to provide for his family, proved to be a monumental blunder on his part. After he was served with the Order of Protection Mr. Di Conti was left with a negative bank account and nowhere to go, but to sleep in his vehicle for two days, until he could borrow some money to pay for a hotel room. He remained in a "pay-by-the-week" In-Town Suites, located at Guadalupe and Arizona Avenues in Mesa for over six (6) weeks until he was able to find a suitable and viable residence for himself and his daughters while they visited.

Item 19: *(See Exhibit 4) Mr. Di Conti has in his possession an E-mail sent by Ms. Nelson on February 22, 2007, after once again responding to Ms. Nelson's statement that she does not "lie," referencing her outward claims that Mr. Di Conti molested children and physically abused her and their children, stating that Mr. Di Conti "NEVER LAID A HAND ON ME." A complete contradiction to prior claims of abuse,* *to the Chandler Police Department.*

There is also "Intentional Infliction of Emotional Distress" by the mere fact that Ms. Nelson continues to disparage Mr. Di Conti at every opportunity and the fact that he continues to feel the effects of her actions and behavior since the day Ms. Nelson filed a false police report and Order of Protection without cause. Ms. Nelson has had absolutely no regard for Mr. Di Conti's name, integrity, or standing in the community and has made every attempt to tarnish the same by her accusations and behavior and should be held accountable for the same.

In conclusion:

Mr. Di Conti plans to call several witnesses to testify against his former spouse, now Tiffany Nelson, for her claims of abuse, both physical and sexual; for invading Mr. Di Conti's Right to Privacy; in illegally taking a private letter written to another and invading his Right To Privacy by making copies of the same and distributing it to close acquaintances; for invading Mr. Di

Conti's Right To Privacy in claiming he was unable to perform sexually with his spouse, due to his <u>alleged</u> interest in children, rather than adults.

Mr. Di Conti has numerous pieces of E-mail sent from Ms. Nelson with contradictory content and denial of her accusations. Mr. Di Conti also has a digital video of Ms. Nelson-Di Conti's testimony and the testimony of her mother, Susan Nelson-Stephenson, at the Order of Protection hearing, where she claims to have been physically abused by Mr. Di Conti, as well as, her testimony of claims that their children were sexually assaulted by Mr. Di Conti.

Also, in his possession, as well as Ms. Nelson's possession, is the false police report she filed with these same claims against her former husband. Mr. Di Conti will bring several sworn affidavits by which the court will clearly see a great injustice has been done to Mr. Di Conti, by his former spouse, Tiffany A. Nelson <u>and her mother Susan Nelson-Stephanson</u>. Tiffany Nelson's complete disregard for Mr. Di Conti's privacy and the cavalier manner in which she methodically destroyed his name within the community he resides in must be addressed. This was a most malicious act that Ms. Nelson-Di Conti carried out on her husband and can not go unpunished. She, <u>nor her mother, Susan Nelson-Stephanson, have ever expressed any concern or</u> apologies to Mr. Di Conti but rather stated that these events never took place. Tiffany Nelson feels that there is nothing worth speaking about, but Mr. Di Conti feels she must be held accountable for her indiscretions and her unwarranted attack on his character. Mr. Di Conti also feels that the actions of her mother must be addressed in a manner conducive to the court's process.

~~In addition, Mr. Di Conti feels that Donna Jewett, attorney for Tiffany Nelson-Di Conti, and her husband [NAME UNKNOWN], allegedly a detective in the Sex Crimes Division of the Phoenix Police Department, should be reprimanded for their part in the initial investigation of Mr. Di Conti, thus invading his privacy, as well. Ms. Jewett used her husband's status in the police department as a tool in determining how~~

~~strong a case she actually had in moving forward with a divorce case. Donna Jewett's husband committed malfeasance in using the property of the Phoenix Police Department to investigate Mr. Di Conti preliminarily out of the jurisdiction where the alleged incident took place and without probable cause. The court is respectfully asked to order a discovery hearing on this matter and then carry over to trial, a civil suit filed by Mr. Di Conti against Ms. Tiffany Nelson (nee Nelson-Di Conti) and Susan Nelson-Stephenson.~~

Attached to this "Amended Complaint" is (EXHIBIT 1) a copy of Ryanne Ritter's Statement which contains firsthand knowledge of Tiffany Nelson's admissions, acknowledgements of her actions and first hand accounts as a witness to many of Ms. Nelson's statements and behavior, as well as knowingly filing a false report with Chandler P. D. and Order of Protection with the Maricopa County Courts, (EXHIBIT 2) a copy of the Order Of Protection containing false accusations, (EXHIBIT 3) a copy of the false police report filed by Tiffany Nelson, (EXHIBIT 4) a copy of the E-mail Tiffany Nelson sent admitting Mr. Di Conti had never touched her, (EXHIBIT 5) a copy of the E-mail regarding the conversation with Linda Pauley regarding parents at Risen Savior Lutheran School wanting Mr. Di Conti removed from his job at the school, (EXHIBIT 6) a copy of Tiffany Nelson's Bank statements showing the numerous withdrawals totaling well over $300,000 that show "Fraudulent Concealment of Marital Assets, including the $80,000 withdrawal that Ms. Nelson boasted of, These withdrawals are highlighted for effect, (EXHIBIT 7) a copy of an E-mail to Tiffany Nelson regarding her use of derogatory statements about Mr. Di Conti in front of their daughters, (EXHIBIT 8) an affidavit from Ryan Quinn who overheard a conversation between Mr. Di Conti and Ms. Nelson wherein she was berating Mr. Di Conti in front of the children, (EXHIBIT 9) a letter to Susan Nelson-Stephenson admonishing her for telling Mr. Di Conti's daughters that he "hit" their mother "all the time". (EXHIBIT 10) a copy of an E-mail Mr. Di Conti received from a former employer regarding his now being

<u>*unemployable due to the police investigation for "sex crimes against a child."*</u>

Respectfully submitted.

Eric L. Di Conti
Dated this October 15, 2007

Original filed with the Clerk of the Court and Copy hand delivered/mailed this ___day of_____2007, to:

Hon. A. Craig Blakey
Maricopa County Superior Court
201 W. Jefferson
Phoenix, AZ 85003-2243

John McKindels for
Susan Nelson-Stephanson
1108 E. Greenway, #1
Mesa, AX 85203

Tiffany A. Nelson
33030 N. Sandstone Drive
Queen Creek, AZ 85243

It is noteworthy to reiterate what was mentioned in Item 10 of this complaint, regarding the withdrawal of Donna Jewett as Tiffany's Counsel of Record. To recap; up until October 23, 2006, Tiffany had no idea that I knew, and had known, about the police report she had filed with the Chandler Police Department. Again, I became privy to that information during the conversation with Ryanne Ritter several months before, while I was residing at the Inn Town Suites.

That morning in October, at about 9:30AM, I had called Tiffany for reasons I can no longer remember, but midway through the conversation Tiffany said something to set me off and I shot back at her that I was aware she had filed the police report. I remember there was dead silence on the other end of the phone and after a few seconds, I asked if she was still there. A few more seconds passed before she acknowledged she was. I'm certain she was trying to come up with a response and when she did, I was shocked.

She claimed she didn't know what I was talking about and if there was a police report, she knew nothing about it. I probably used a few expletives before I regained my composure, but I told her that I would send her a copy of the police report to refresh her memory. It was very quiet on Tiffany's end of the line and due to the fact there wasn't much left to talk about, the call ended shortly after that. I expected that, within minutes, Tiffany was on the phone to Jewett's office trying to secure a plan to combat the new weapon I now had.

A few days later I would receive, in the mail, a document filed with the court that read simply, "NOTICE OF WITHDRAWAL" that stated, for the record, that Donna Jewett was withdrawing as legal counsel for Tiffany Nelson. The date of the filing was the afternoon of October 23, 2006; the same day I let Tiffany in on my secret. As I had expected, she called Jewett's office immediately after we spoke and I can only guess that Jewett reminded Tiffany she had warned her this may happen and then informed Tiffany that she was on her own; good luck in your future, honey. It was nice to get a gift like this in the mail.

The following is the document I received that day.

ERIC L. DI CONTI

DONNA FARAR JEWETT, SB#12999
JEWETT ♦ PRZESLICKE, PLLC
8121 E. Indian Bend Road, Suite 126
Scottsdale, Arizona 85250
Telephone: (480) 949-6500
Facsimile: (480) 607-5241
Attorneys for Petitioner

IN THE SUPERIOR COURT OF THE STATE OF ARIZONA

IN AND FOR THE COUNTY OF MARICOPA

In Re the Marriage of:

TIFFANY NELSON,

    Petitioner,

    and

ERICCO DI CONTI

    Respondent.

FC2006-050978

NOTICE OF WITHDRAWAL

(Assigned to the Hon. Ballinger, Jr.)

NOTICE IS HEREBY GIVEN that Donna Farar Jewett in accordance with Rule 9, Rules of Family Law Procedure, hereby respectfully submits a Notice of Withdrawal as Counsel of Record for Petitioner. Counsel undersigned will no longer represent Petitioner. Counsel undersigned avows that there are no pending hearings, trials or other proceedings before the Court.

Petitioner's last known address and telephone number is:

Tiffany Nelson
221 W. Olive Street
Chandler, AZ 85248

RESPECTFULLY SUBMITTED this ___ day of October, 2006.

JEWETT ♦ PRZESLICKE, PLLC

DONNA FARAR JEWETT
Attorneys for Petitioner

FRY'S FOOD AND DRUG

"Even a blind squirrel will find a nut every once in a while" – Spiro Psaltis at Santa Anita Race Track after I hit an elusive Trifecta.

November 2007

While the prospect of employment in construction was dead, I was still in desperate need of a job and for some reason, I walked to Fry's Food and Drug, at Southern Avenue and Rural Road in Tempe. I had never had any inclination to work in a supermarket, but at this point, I couldn't be picky. I asked if they were hiring and told them I could do just about anything. The gal I spoke to, gave me the number of a guy who worked in human resources and set up interviews. I called him, told him about my background in construction, and for whatever reason, he wanted to sit down with me and speak further.

To make this process as painless as possible for the readers; with my background in management, I was hired as a Grocery Manager and would start my training at a store in Apache Junction. The store was on the east side of the valley and in a place where one would have to gather six to eight people to make a full set of teeth. Not *find* a full set of teeth, but rather *make* a full set of teeth. One drawback to being a manager at Fry's Food and Drug was that I was one of about five people in the store that was paid on a monthly basis. My compensation had never been spaced out further than every-other-week and most often, in construction, compensation was paid weekly, so having to budget for a full month was not something I was looking forward to, but I had no choice.

Apache Junction, Arizona, at the time of this writing, was the methamphetamine capital of the state, and with the use of methamphetamine comes the loss of teeth and oozing, open sores from the constant picking at the user sees, but is not there. There were people who looked to be in their late-forties, but when I checked ID, for a liquor purchase, though there were obvious similarities in their physical features, the birth date would put them in their late-twenties. Meth is the devil and using it will guarantee a trip into the inner sanctum of hell. In the short time I was in Apache Junction I had seen and had witnessed, firsthand, the descent of several people into that *hell*.

I was promised my work hours would be daytime, which was amenable to my schedule, since I had two little girls to tend to, but I would find that what I was told, was about as far from the truth as one could imagine; my day started each night, between 10pm and midnight and ended, between 8am and 10am each morning.

Once again I was in a quandary and had nowhere to turn for the care of my girls, but to a couple of girls at Mount Carmel Church. They were students at Arizona State University and had agreed to come to our house an hour before I had to be at work and would sleep on the couch until I returned home the following morning. It was a great set-up for me and them, but it would be dashed when Tiffany and The Jockey started filing petitions with the court, asking for it to disallow any "over-nights," of any kind if I wasn't there. "Motion Granted" and I was once again screwed. What ended up happening was on my custodial weeks, I would have to turn the girls over to their mother at six o'clock each night I worked and could retrieve them from school the following day at 3pm. It was all I could do not to go crazy and lose complete control, but again, that's exactly what Tiffany wanted me to do and I had two little girls to think about. Kate and Megan were the only people who kept me going and I knew there would eventually be light at the end of the tunnel; I just couldn't see it yet.

The grocery industry is a jacked-up world. There are those who belong there and those who do not and I met very few who did not; I was one of those who did not. If you don't ever have to enter this realm of craziness, don't do it. It'll only make you jaded and feel the need to grow your own food. It may even steal your soul. In the eight months I endured in this cult, I met a cast of characters that would rival the HBO series "Sideshow" and may even eclipse the number of freaks by double. I won't go into each and every employee, but a few stood out.

The first store manager I met was Diane Latta. She was actually very pretty with clear blue eyes, but that's where her femininity stopped. Whenever she walked, her swagger closely resembled that of John Wayne and I immediately noticed she demanded, not respect, but *fear* from her employees. She had the oddest of midsections. It wasn't a distention of her abdomen, but rather a flap of fat that hung down over her belt. She didn't even bother to suck it in but was content having it hang there as if another appendage. Her mouth rivaled any longshoreman alive and used the "F" word like a comma.

Diane Latta had a reputation of lashing out for no reason and meted out severe punishment to those who she felt crossed her, or didn't pull their own weight. She did little on her own and would delegate each and every little task of every employee at the store. There wasn't a day that went by that I didn't hear about someone crying, or being given "shit duty" somewhere in the store. Those who knew her well steered clear at all cost, but many didn't have that luxury.

I approached her one day and asked something about the baler. A machine that crushes boxes and allows an individual to pull baling wire through holes and once they are tied off, releases the pressure and dumps the bale onto a pallet.

"I don't fucking know. Go ask the retard," she responded.

"Excuse me?" I asked.

"What the fuck? I said go ask the retard. Can't you fucking hear?"

"And who might that be, Diane?"

She told me the name of a woman who was mentally challenged and also, I would come to realize, one of the hardest workers in the store. She did everything she could to make Diane proud of her, but all Diane ever did was take advantage of her loyalty and gave her every "shit job" no one else wanted to do. I was disgusted by her reference to this poor woman but said nothing. I went off to find her.

Another incident, I witnessed firsthand, involved a young African-American man whom I liked very much. Garrett worked in the produce department in the Apache Junction store. He was another of those who didn't belong in this industry. He just didn't fit the mold, as he was well above average in intelligence and extremely well-spoken and I just couldn't grasp the idea that he would be stuck in these doldrums of a career in the grocery industry.

Don't get me wrong. I am not inferring that all people in this industry are unintelligent or not well spoken. I am merely pointing out that an overabundance of people in the grocery industry are High School graduates, who got caught up in the steady work of a stable industry, the weekly pay, and incredibly good benefits. Many of those I worked with and got to know, confided that this was their first job out of High School and before they had realized it, they were celebrating their twenty-year anniversary at Fry's Food and Drug. Five others told me that they had, through a friend, accepted employment as a "summer job" and never left. All but one had already been enrolled in college the following fall, but "just never went." The other individual was taking a year off before enrolling in college to pursue a career in law. He never made it.

To me, it is a little noticed phenomenon that these grocery stores can lure people to them, and then once inside, everything on the outside ceases to exist and the desire to leave comes only when gray hairs begin to sprout on one's head, only then, it is too late. This is the time in which many realize they have been vacillating for the better part of their adult lives and few have attained a level higher than that of a department head, which equates to about a dollar and hour more per hour. What this phenomenon breeds is people who are looking to be led; someone to tell them what to do, just as they did so many years before as an eighteen-year-old kid. The ones who make it past the position of a department head and go on to be Front End Managers, Grocery Managers, Assistant Store Managers, Store Managers, and beyond are those who know how to either work the system, or kiss some good ass. If you're a "yes man" then you will go far in the grocery industry. A few are not ass kissers and got there by their own means, but most are; I've seen it with my own eyes.

Another odd little thing I'll call a "phenomenon," is the fact that virtually everyone within the confines of the store walls are terrified of anyone from corporate. If you walk into any grocery store and sense that everyone seems to be in a bad mood, then you're probably witnessing the frenzy prior to a visit from a District Manager, or a person higher up the food chain.

These "corporate" people thrive on the fact that they are feared and use that hold at every opportunity. One such District Manager, a woman, will walk into a store and move through it as if she is royalty. Never taking her purse off her shoulder, she will yank items off displays and toss them aside [sometimes onto the floor], as if they are clutter and in need of the "maid" to get the object out of her sight. I rarely saw her smile and when she did, it was of a very condescending sort. People seemed to hold her in such high regard, for the one reason that if the store could pass her test, they have attained some sort of greatness. I guess you could say that of all the District Managers this woman was the most feared, but I just saw her as a commoner, a bitch with a low self-esteem who needed the glory of being feared to feel better about herself. I enjoyed the show whenever she came into a store.

Another amazing trait in the grocery industry is the literacy of those vacillating in it. In reading e-mail back and forth from Grocery Managers, to Managers, to District Managers, to the "big boys" in the corporate offices, I have never seen such a vast display of atrocious spelling and grammatical errors, as I have seen and read in the e-mail these folks sent. Most of which I cannot fathom how it was the individual had, prior to hitting the send button, re-read their text and felt it was good enough to send off to their peers for review. Responses to statements like, "I haven't did that yet" and "I putted [sic] it back already" and "I specially [sic] want to thank 'so-and-so' for doing their job really good" and "I asked there whole staff to do it, but no one did nothing." These are actual sentences from those e-mails.

I could go on and on, but I would get an insatiable urge to slit my wrists and I'm just not up for that right now. When I refer to the literacy of many of the people in Fry's Food and Drug Company, I use the term loosely. Of course, there are some very intelligent people employed by Fry's, but most are tucked away in the corporate offices and rarely seen.

With regard to Garrett, in produce, I was looking for Diane one morning and found her staring at Garrett from the adjacent bakery department, shaking her head. I walked up to her and stood to her right.

"What's wrong?"

"Them," she responded.

"What do you mean 'them,' Diane?"

She nodded her head toward Garrett and said, "Those people. Don't you think they should leave the produce to the Mexicans? They just don't look right handling that stuff." Her inference was such that since Garrett was black, he should be working elsewhere in the store and not in the produce department; "Mexicans picked the stuff" and therefore "should be handling it" at this level, as well.

I was sickened by a reference such as this, coming from a Store Manager, but not surprised by what she said. In hearing stories about her I had finally witnessed, firsthand, her miserable leadership skills; it was par for the course. I finally reported her to human resources and filed a formal complaint against her; citing, not only the incidents described above, but other complaints that subordinates had come to me with.

I had heard rumors throughout the company that she had been reported numerous times before and nothing was ever done about it, beyond transferring her to another store. In looking back at how the brass at Fry's ignored everything beyond a homicide, I am not surprised to this day.

She had supposedly racked up some fifty complaints (This number was never confirmed) at one store and instead of relieving her of her duties as a Store Manager, they simply transferred her to Apache Junction. Once she had racked up enough complaints in Apache Junction, she was transferred to a store in Queen Creek. I had always wondered how it was that she had kept her job for so long and mused that she must have had pictures of the CEO of Fry's

Food and Drug wrestling with barnyard animals, or something of that sort.

With this particular individual, it was all about hiding and ignoring cancer. In my untrained and completely unprofessional opinion, Diane Latta is cancer with some serious issues and always will be a cancer no matter where she goes.

While filling in at another store in Mesa, Store #23, I was able to see and understand that Store #65 was not an anomaly and the craziness reached other stores, as well. This particular store, which was open twenty-four hours a day, mirrored the others in the cast of characters, sans anyone like Dianne Latta, with a few slight variations.

One person, in particular, was a guy who worked only in the frozen foods section and never ventured to any other section of the store unless absolutely necessary. The most noticeable physical characteristic of this guy was the fact that he had several oozing sores on his arms which he picked at incessantly, continuously, and without regard for whoever happened to be standing nearby and within his line of sight. However, this was just a minor irritation to my eyes, when measuring the level of disgust, compared to what lay ahead.

This individual, who will remain nameless, followed no orders, rules, or protocol. He ran his own ship and cared little for anything else around him. He lead a small group of one, or two, other employees in harassing another employee who had some serious bouts with his own physical hygiene; he rarely showered or changed his clothes. Even though John's appearance was rather slovenly and with him, came a putrid stench, he worked until he was told to go home and never complained. He worked his ass off in whatever aisle he was assigned to and stocked the shelves. Unfortunately, John was the recipient of some pretty mean jokes and his tormentors were unrelenting in the name-calling. The individual, with the oozing sores on his arms, would refer to him by names such as "stinky" and "smelly" and never missed a chance to tell him how badly he needed a shower. I found it odd that this guy, who sounded quite effeminate when he spoke and by the way he carried himself, he could very easily be mistaken for someone who is gay, would be so unrelenting in his harassment of another human being. Maybe he *is* gay, was harassed himself, and wanted to "get back at the world." Whatever the reason, there was no need to act out in the manner he did. I had had several conversations with this person asking that he stop, but my requests fell on deaf ears.

The fact is, John *did* need a shower and *did* smell quite badly, but he was also one of the nicest people in this particular store and I got on quite well with him. We talked often and I always addressed him with a "Mister" before his name, and when I asked for something to be done, I ended the request with, "Thank you, sir." John reciprocated the respect when he addressed me, as well, and was grateful that there was someone like me to treat him with some dignity.

John seemed to be well read and was very knowledgeable in several areas. I was surprised to find he had been working for Fry's for some fifteen years, or so and that Fry's Food and Drug is what he found, as a second job, while he was teaching at a local college. I'm not certain what caused him to leave his employ at the college, but like so many others working for Fry's, he never left the grocery industry. I never asked, and he never offered up that information.

He confided in me that he hated being harassed, but that no one would do anything to stop it. The one thing that worried me was the real possibility that he could one day snap and if he decided to bring his cache of guns, which he boasted of, to work there would be a lot of bodies piled up throughout the store. My worry wasn't for me, because due to John being genuinely partial to me, I believe my life would be spared. My worry was for John's tormentors and reflecting back on what happens to "bullies" in our society, the attack would probably be quite vicious. Not that I feel they wouldn't deserve it, or that I wouldn't feel bad for them if they wound up on the business end of a gun, but because they would have family that would be saddened.

John's tormentors were, and are probably still *are*, assholes and should be held accountable for their actions, but no one in the store's upper management would do a thing to stop the harassment. As callous as this may sound, looking back on it today; it wouldn't bother me in the least to hear that these guys had been shot and killed by John.

When he wasn't harassing John, he was in his frozen food aisles. Each night when the "frozen load" came in, he would systematically pull everything from the back of the store and place the frozen items in the respective aisles, which took about two hours to accomplish. Once these items were on the floor and lying in the aisles, he would take his first break which lasted about thirty minutes. When his break was over he would go back to one of the aisles and begin pulling items from each cardboard case/container and placing them in their proper locations in the freezer. In a couple of hours, he would be due another break and would take it accordingly; a large portion of the frozen goods still on the floor and marking a passage of time at four hours, thawing. You read that right; probably seventy-five percent of the frozen goods have been thawing for over four straight hours.

His break lasts another thirty minutes and then he returns back to stocking the frozen goods. Let me add that during the time the food should be going into the store freezers and he is supposedly back from his breaks, this individual is doing more running around, playing grab-ass, and making phone calls than he did spending time trying to keep the merchandise from thawing out. Another two hours had passed and he was again on a break. The time the "frozen" food has been thawing reached nearly six hours and he still wasn't concerned. By the time his shift was over much of the food had been completely thawed out and some of the food had even warmed, which means bacteria would be present and able to grow. The bad part about that was the fact that there was a great deal of meat and poultry that had completely thawed and then been put back into the freezer. This practice violated just about every health code there is, but this isn't the worst part of his work ethic. Remember those open and oozing sores that were the focus of his incessant picking?

Often times there would be boxes of whatever, that had broken open and the contents spilling out. With my own eyes, I would watch as he, with his hands, pick up the now thawed food and place it back in the box from which it spilled, carefully closing the box back up and placing it on the shelf. These are the same hands that he picked his oozing sores with and which he never washed. I reported this practice to one of the managers and was advised as such; "Don't worry about it." I then went higher than that manager, within the store, and was met with the same, "don't worry about it," attitude.

I was so moved by this filthy and disgusting practice, with the exception of ice cream (because it cannot leave its container), I have never purchased a frozen food product from Fry's Food and Drug since. If I were asked to give my opinion to anyone on whether they should buy frozen foods from Fry's Food and Drug, my answer would be a very clear, explicit, and unequivocal "Absolutely not!"

I know it doesn't happen at every store, but with each trip into Fry's Food and Drug I am reminded of seeing this individual handling thawed-out food with those wretched hands and cannot shake the memory of it. I also cannot say with certainty that anyone has become ill due to these practices, but I won't be taking any chances myself and in my opinion, neither should anyone else. This would be especially true when there are people like the one described above, picking sores, oozing with pus, and then handling food with the same fingers; food the public would eventually consume and never know what repulsive contaminant fouled that same food.

Thankfully, I was transferred out of Store #23 and to another store after only three weeks. While they looked for a store to place me; one where they felt I fit, I bounced around from store to store until I finally settled at Store #15. This would also be the last store I worked at for Fry's Food and Drug.

Store #15 is located at Val Vista Avenue and Baseline Avenue in Mesa, Arizona. Tom Middaugh was the Store Manager and had been at this fairly slow store for the better part of five years. Other than for disciplinary reasons, it was an odd occurrence for a manager to stay longer than a year, or two at the most, at any given store. I was told, Managers and Assistant Managers are sometimes transferred without reason, but for the most part, it is the Managers who most often leave for other horizons, within the company.

Tom Middaugh, I was told, was the poster boy for the unwanted "step-child." When I met him, I realized why. He was left at this store, probably because there was nowhere else to put him. Tom was an extremely meek guy who did not like confrontation of any kind. If there was a problem, he would have one of his underlings mete out discipline; verbal or otherwise. He seemed afraid of his own shadow and rarely gave a directive to anyone. When he did, he seemed to want to apologize for it. I once complained about the way a gal named Laura, in shipping and receiving, treated some of our vendors, and when he walked back there, he was summarily reprimanded by *her* for questioning her authority, in her little world and he left as quickly as he had come.

I was shocked that a manager would take such tongue-lashing when normally the manager of a store was God in his, or her, own mind and usually took shit from no one. I made a sign and posted it at the receiving desk and door that read: THIS IS LAURA'S WORLD, YOU JUST HAPPEN TO BE LIVING IN IT. Laura loved that sign and make no mistake in understanding that literally everyone took that sign very seriously.

At Fry's Food and Drug, even sexual harassment was usually swept under the carpet; however, one young man was let go while he was still on probation for allegedly making inappropriate comments to one of the cashiers while he was in training.

He confided in me on one occasion and boasted of having this young woman being infatuated with him and that she had bared her breasts for him in the employee lounge on the second floor. He also made boastful claims that he'd given her a ride home one night.

My instincts of being accused of something I had never done, took over and I asked him, "First of all what the fuck were you thinking, by letting it get to a point in the lounge that she showed you her breasts, if that's what really happened? Secondly, why the hell would you give her a ride home with no one else in the car? Do you have any idea what kind of position you put yourself in by doing that?"

He just stared at me, so I continued.

"Let me tell you something, Einstein. I know this gal, not well, but I know her well enough to question your claim that she showed you her tits, but just for shits and giggles, let's just say she did and I'll give you a little lesson to chew on."

I was on a roll, "You're a manager in this store; a low-level manager but a manager, nonetheless. She is a subordinate of yours and by you allowing this to happen, you're putting your ability to lead in a very precarious position. Now, if there's a problem involving her, you won't be able to reprimand her. You know why? I'll tell ya why; because there's the possibility of having the little incident in the lounge, coming back to bite your tired ass. If it really happened, like you say it happened, she has you by the short hairs and there's not a thing you can do about it. The next big mistake you made was to allow her into your car because if she gets pissed off at you for any reason in the future, she can use that "ride home" to say that you sexually assaulted her, but was too scared to come forward because she didn't want to lose her job. You see where this is going, you moron?"

He still just stared at me and then tried to say something, but I held my hand up and stopped him, so I could continue my sermon.

"The third thing you did wrong was to tell people about it because if it *did*, or *didn't* happen, either way, you've now embarrassed her and she pissed. When a girl gets pissed, you've got a major league problem on your hands and it is tough to make the problem, of a pissed-off woman, go away. You're pretty much fucked at that point."

Yeah, but," he said.

"Stop! Let me finish, Turbo." I didn't want to be interrupted while the Ritalin is still in my system, because if I stop at this point my brain was going to lock up on me and I'd have been pretty much useless. I finished up my reprimand by ending with the following.

"The worst mistake you made was to tell *me*. I am a grocery manager here and *you*, my maladjusted little friend, would be *my* subordinate and that puts *me* in a precarious position of knowing something that should be reported to those higher than me."

His eyes widened.

"Do you feel like you just stepped on your own dick? I sure would."

I finished up. "I hope no one asks me if I know anything about this, because I'm not going to lie for you. I hope, for your sake, this dies right here because if it doesn't I can pretty much assure you that you're going to be escorted outta here." I turned and walked away.

As it turned out, I was approached about a week later and was asked to file an incident report, which I related the conversation the two of us had. He was summarily relieved of his duties at Store #15 and Fry's Food and Drug, after only three and a half weeks.

Another odd characteristic, which I was told was inherent in most grocery stores, is that Grocery Managers, although third in the line of hierarchy, were the most abused when it came to hours worked. I cannot speak for any other grocery chain, but at Fry's Food and Drug the Grocery Manager is expected to work as many hours as the store manager tells them to work. Although the company policy states that all managers are required to work "no less than ten hours a day," it was not uncommon for one, myself included, to pull twelve, fourteen, and sometimes fifteen and sixteen-hour shifts. And we did so, without so much as a "thank you," from the store manager, or assistant store managers; you just did it without question.

This practice was the only way that the managers could get as much work as they can do without ever having to have those hours show up as labor costs. It took only one or two times of this before I did my ten hours and walked. I wasn't about to allow these pricks to abuse me the way they did other employees. I was stopped many times, as I was on my way out of the store, and told that I couldn't leave, that there was more work to be done.

I stood my ground and said, "I've already put in eleven hours and I'm going home. See you tomorrow."

There wasn't a single manager who wasn't shocked that I left, without so much as a sniff. They were left standing at the entryway, watching me walk to my car, knowing there was nothing they could do to stop me. I would be approached by several employees the next day saying things like, "Wow! You just walked out? That's awesome, but I could *never* do that."

Each time I did this, the manager's attempt at showing his, or her, power was cut short and was done so in full view of their respective employees. I had done my own training of the tormentors of the store and it wasn't long before their attempts at stopping me from leaving, after my ten hours of work, ceased completely. They couldn't take the fact that someone would actually stand up to them and would rather let one person go and keep the rest in line, or "fear," as it were.

I was so amazed that a vast majority of the employees at Fry's Food and Drug were in fear of management and of losing their jobs. Terrified would be a better word. These people tremble and cower if they were approached by anyone in management and especially if a District Manager making his, or her, rounds of the stores in their district approached them for any reason. It was sad to see these people, who appeared to me anyway, had lost their dignity and sense of who they were. What I saw while I was in the employ of Fry's Food and Drug, with the exception of management, was a bunch of individuals that had done what they were told for so long that they had forgotten how to say "no."

There is an extremely powerful scene in the movie, The Shawshank Redemption, where some prisoners were wondering why another inmate, played by James Whitmore, snapped when he was informed that he was being paroled. He held a knife to the neck of another inmate, nearly cutting the throat, so he could stay in prison. Morgan Freeman made a very simple statement to explain it. He said, "He's institutionalized."

Freeman's character went on to explain that Whitmore's character had been in prison for so long that he didn't know anything beyond the walls of the prison, nor did he want to be outside those walls. Whitmore's character had become a "spoke on the wheel" of the prison and without him, he felt, it couldn't function properly. Take a spoke off a wheel of a bicycle, see how long the wheel stays true and round.

It may have been the fear of the unknown for this prisoner, or as Whitmore's character explained that he was a "big man inside" and in addition to him feeling he couldn't make it on the outside, no one would know him. He was afraid of what he may find outside the walls of Shawshank Prison. Anyone who saw the movie knows what happened shortly after he was paroled and left the safety of the prison walls.

I cannot help but view ninety-five percent of the employees, whom I had met, as "institutionalized" by the grocery industry. Nearly all of them can get out, but they don't want to because they're afraid they won't be able to make it anywhere, away from their familiar surroundings.

The managers take full advantage of this phenomenon and work on the employees, systematically picking on the weaker ones to do the little tasks they need to complete, which are never-ending. In an eight-hour shift, a cashier could very easily *never* see a cash register if he, or she, is running little bullshit errands, around the store, for a manager. Unless the cashier, or for that matter, anyone else in the store, stands up to a manager they will become a trained monkey in no time at all; and many have.

The employees truly *do* become very much like trained animals willing to do anything for their "masters" with the hope of some sort of recognition. The act of giving someone any kind of accolades, or recognizing that an employee had gone above and beyond, is normally absent from the personalities of managers; you were expected to do what you were asked and like it; it was for the company. I cannot count the number of people who confided in me that they have nowhere to go, saying to me "I ain't got no education and won't be able to find another job, making as much money and the benefits are good." Sadly, this was probably very true. Many of these people *don't* have anywhere to go, the management knows it and capitalizes on it. They *are* "institutionalized."

It was obvious to me and those with whom I worked that I didn't belong in this environment. I was approached countless times and asked what I was doing in Fry's; that I was "above this place." They were amazed themselves, that I would continue my employment at Fry's and suggested I get out. So many times I heard the words, "You don't belong here. You should get out before you end up like me." A sense of sorrow washed over them as they spoke. The fact was, I couldn't get out until I found another job that allowed me to work during the day and I wouldn't find one until June of the following year.

All that was written above aside, the worst part of the eight months I spent in the grocery industry was the fact that much of the time, my two daughters were away from me. I kept going back to the custody issue and needing my girls near me more than a few hours a day. Not that they were away during the night, as we would be apart if I had a day job, but the fact that good 'ol Tiffany jumped in and dragged me back into court demanding that the girls could not be watched by a sitter overnight.

It's a normal and common practice for people to have sitters, while a parent was at work, but this arrangement dealt with "overnights" and Tiffany used my unfortunate situation against me. With her histrionic theatrics, the judge melted in front of her and ruled that I could not have anyone stay with the girls, that they would be cared for by their mother since she was available. I had to get out of Fry's Food and Drug as soon as I could.

"I'LL PUT YOU ON THE MAP MYSELF."

"If you want to make God laugh, tell Him your plans."
- Louis Mandylor

February 2008

Little, of any real significance, occurred in the eight months I was at Fry's Food and Drug, but in early February of 2008, an acquaintance, with his son-in-law, flew into town. Kim and Steve owned a winery located in the famed Marlborough County at the north end of South Island, in New Zealand. We had talked about their winery breaking into the United States market and specifically, Arizona and I began doing some research to have our talks realized. I set up a meeting with a wine distributor in the area, called Classico Fine Wines and Spirits, owned by Dario Soldan. I met Dario through the Cellar Master at A.J.'s Fine Foods in Scottsdale. Dennis Wells had the opportunity of sampling a couple of the varietals, produced by them and had spoken to Dario about the quality of the wine. Dennis passed on Dario's contact information and I called him a few days later.

I told Dario of the intended trip to Arizona by Kim and Steve and set up a meeting for the four of us to taste some wine, with the hope that Dario was as impressed as Dennis was with the wine. Kim and Steve brought several bottles of each of the wine varietals they produce.

Kim and Steve arrived at Sky Harbor Airport in the early evening, that February. I was there to meet them and took them to their hotel. The following day was the meeting I had set up with Dario and Steve wanted to prepare for it; he got right to work. Later that night I returned to pick them up for a quick bite to eat at Z-tejas at Ray and the 10 Fwy in Chandler where we had a quiet dinner and discussed our strategy for the meeting. I returned them to their hotel and went home excited about the possibilities of the following day.

Dario seemed impressed with two of the four but stated that he would be interested in carrying all of them. As we left the meeting and tasting, the three of us were extremely ecstatic that we had just landed a huge opportunity in the State of Arizona. That night I picked them up and we went to Scottsdale to pick up a good friend of mine, whom I'd met at a Starbucks Coffeehouse, just a stone's throw from the A.J.'s Fine Foods; the same store in which Dennis Wells worked. The four of us celebrated that night, at Caffé Boa on Mill Avenue, in downtown Tempe.

Kim returned to New Zealand with high hopes of a big return from the State of Arizona and getting their name known to wine drinkers. Steve traveled on to New York for a scheduled meeting there.

Early one afternoon, I received a phone call from Kim and he gave me the news. After the promise of big orders from Classico Fine Wines, it turned out that Dario only wanted a few cases of Sauvignon Blanc. My euphoria deflated, I told Ken what Dario was doing amounted to opening a clothing store and carrying only shirts; no pants, no belts, no shoes, no socks. Dario was playing it safe, I guess, but I wanted to make sure he would be aware of the mistake he had made.

In that conversation, I told Kim that if Dario wasn't interested in taking on their winery, I would do it.

"What do you mean, Eric?" He asked.

"What I mean is that if Dario is so stupid, he doesn't know what a huge opportunity this would be for him, then I will sell your wine.

I don't know how it works, but I'll look into getting a license to sell wine in this state and I'll put you on the map, myself. Fuck Dario."

Kim just laughed and I wondered if he really believed I would do it, but a month later, I had started the process with the Federal Agency of the Alcohol, Tobacco, and Tax. My quest was underway and I had brought a friend into the picture to join me in this venture, who would handle all finances. I would handle acquiring the accounts, but we first had to get a license and that, I would find, was a long and arduous process, especially when one has been investigated for sex crimes against a child.

Sometime in April of 2008, I had met and taken to, rather quickly, another Fry's employee named Jeff McCue. In passing, I had told him of my plans to get out of the grocery industry and start selling wine. Jeff's eyes lit up and told me he had the same type of story I had heard so many times before, about wanting out of the doldrums of the industry that he had been stuck in for so long.

He told me that his mother had worked for Fry's for many years and through her, after getting out of the Navy, he had gained employment there. We talked about his background for, what turned out to be, the rest of the night, I remember it getting light out when we finally stopped talking about his family's long history at Fry's, many of the employees there, wine, and the ultimate dream of walking away from the place most viewed as purgatory. Jeff had admired me for coming to this God-forsaken place later in my life and not when I was eighteen years old, as so many others had; I at least had a shot at getting out.

The following night, Jeff approached me again and asked me how fast I wanted to grow with my distribution. I looked at him and said that I wanted to grow as fast as I could, but that I didn't want to bury myself and not be able to give proper service to my clients. He smiled and said that he could help.

"Well, my Dad has a lot of connections in the restaurant industry. He used to own a restaurant in New Mexico and still has a bunch of connections there and here in Arizona. We could really help you with this."

He wanted to know if I would be willing to speak with his father about the possibility of joining forces; it would be a way for him to get out of Fry's for good and allow his father a decent retirement and away from selling copiers.

I looked at him and realized he was sincere in his belief that they could help. I told him that I would speak to his father and that if he had the connections that he claimed he had, we may be able to work something out. Hell, what could it hurt? A guy with connections in the restaurant industry could certainly help. We agreed to meet at the end of the week at his father's house, in Mesa.

Jeff McCue's father, Greg, was a nice-enough guy who looked to be in his early sixties, the stereotypical Irishman who enjoyed a good whiskey and loved a good cigar. We talked for a few hours and when I left his house I truly felt that there was some promise in bringing them in.

That night, at Fry's, there was a lot of talk about selling wine and little else. Jeff was so excited that he could speak of nothing other than his exit from Fry's and never looking back. He had said his wife had already begun looking into a wine tasting seminar for all of us to attend. Although my palate was already somewhat honed in wine tasting, as I have been drinking wine since I was 10 years old (it's a cultural thing), I would be their leader in this new realm.

In June, I would finally leave Fry's and once again find work in commercial construction with a small firm that didn't do extensive background checks. Woodruff Construction paid me a little more money than I was making at Fry's, but more importantly, I was working days, which meant my girls were back with me full-time, on my custodial weeks. I was happier than I had been in a very long time and my dream of selling wine for Kim hadn't faltered in the least; Jeff, his father, Greg, and I kept discussing and working on the planning of the business. My partner was in the loop the whole way and was a little concerned that I hadn't done a background check on these new guys to see if they really did have the connections they said they did. I assured her that if they didn't it would be apparent as soon as we got underway and we could deal with it at that time.

We had discussed splitting the profits equally after all bills were paid and for me having the New Zealand connection, 10% off the top would come to me and the remaining money would be split four ways. It amounted to about twelve and a half percent of the net profits, which was a decent amount of money considering what other wine salespeople made in this industry. Mary felt it was too much, but I felt if they could do what they said they can, it would be worth it in the long run.

I had told Jeff, who knew absolutely nothing about wine, that if we were to do this, he and his father would have to learn everything there is to know about wine and the industry, on which he was about to embark.

"That includes knowing how to make the wine, Jeff. You and your father have to know the fermentation processes of each varietal and know it well," I told him.

"Read everything you can and know the process of malolactic fermentation; it's big in the industry and if you don't know your shit, you can't sell it. I won't *allow* you to sell it if you don't know what you're selling. You also need to be able to ascertain what you're tasting; the smells and different fruit you recognize on the palate. There's a lot to learn."

I ended with, "and you had better know how to pronounce each and every varietal of wine, whether we sell it or not. I will not have anyone looking like an idiot; it's a reflection upon me."

The catalyst for that last statement was hearing his mother call Sauvignon Blanc, "sava blanca" and Jeff referring to Pinot Noir as "*pee-note nor*" and Cabernet as "*cab-er-net*" and not "*cab-er-nay*" I cringed at the thought of him selling Kim's wine, mispronouncing the whole lot and looking like a complete imbecile. Our business would die in an instant.

Jeff agreed that he needed to work on this and start immediately, which he did by printing off the correct spelling of each wine known to man and the pronunciation of each. It would soon be obvious that didn't help much; he couldn't get himself to correctly pronounce much beyond the word, "Chardonnay."

In the meantime, Jeff's wife, Tammy, had set up a wine tasting, at a cellar in Tempe called PurVine. The director and winemaker for this small winery was John Allen Burtner.

John Allen is a big bespectacled man with wavy hair and a deep voice; his demeanor is deliberate and gentlemanly. He came to Arizona, by way of Napa Valley, but originally hails from Texas and his southern accent was obvious, but not to the point that hearing it was like nails-on-a-chalkboard. He is a Texan through and through. PurVine would eventually close its doors in May of 2009 and John Allen Burtner would head back to Napa Valley and continue his passion for winemaking.

Tammy said that the attendees would all be "restaurant people with connections," which was exciting to me; I would finally meet these "restaurant people."

I was about twenty minutes late in getting there, as I had a construction meeting I had to attend and I was also packing my bags for a trip to California to attend the funeral of a friend.

As I walked in, I apologized for being late and once my eyes adjusted to the light, I noticed there was a beautiful charcuterie board with a spread of salami, cheeses, nuts, and dried fruit laid out on a table. In the room were Jeff, Tammy, Greg and his wife, and two other people: a husband and wife team, I had met previously. I immediately remembered these two as a couple introduced to me at Greg house, as "long-time family friends."

These two individuals didn't strike me as worldly people, as conversing with them was straining, but they were very nice and I enjoyed their company. We discussed, very briefly I might add, my impending wine venture with Jeff and Greg McCue and I discovered their knowledge of wine was limited to, "wine is like grape juice with alcohol in it."

"Uh,. . . . .yeah. Kinda. . . . . . .like. . . . . . . .that," I remember responding to them, probably with my face waded up in agony of having to actually agree with their assessment of wine.

As long as the conversation didn't go beyond their knowledge of the immediate surroundings they were fine, but I couldn't find much else to discuss with them. As my brain was assessing the new environment I was standing in, I also remembered that this couple had a daughter and son-in-law who owned a Bar-B-Q restaurant in Gilbert.

The time it took for me to walk in allow my eyes to adjust to the drastic lighting change from bright sunlight to a darkened tasting room, was just a few seconds, but I was seeing everything in slow motion, at this point, it seemed an eternity. I swallowed hard, scoured the area for a new face, but to my dismay, found none.

I asked myself, "Is this the *restaurant connections* they had been talking about? Please, God, tell me there are others here!"

I glanced at John Allen, who looked as if he was bothered by something and then noticed that virtually everyone had a full glass of wine. A *full* glass of wine, for the love of God! Here I was at a wine "tasting" and it appeared to be more of a cocktail party than a wine tasting. Wine tastings are called such for the very reason that the individuals are there to *"taste"* the wine, not **drink** it. I was trying to rationalize with myself, as to the reason for full glasses of wine, but knew in my heart that there was no other reason for the full glasses of wine, aside from the fact that these people, whom I was about to embark on a business venture, had demanded they be poured full glasses.

I envisioned the following scenario:

The lecturer greets everyone and after making all the proper introductions, explains the number of wines to be tasted and how each was made; hand-picked grapes, machine pressing, yeast introduction, oak barrels as opposed to stainless steel, length of time in barrels, etc. He introduces the first wine and then, in the proper manner of a tasting, pours a small amount into each glass to fill the bottom. What probably happened next gave the lecturer a full understanding of the ignorance of the people before him.

"Hey! What's this?" One would ask.

"Excuse me?" John would respond.

"What's this? Ain't you gonna pore us somma that wine?"

"Uh, well, I did."

"Well shee-it, that ain't no pore-in. Gimme some more. This ain't enough getta dung beetle drunk, boy. Com' on, now, filler up."

"Uh, well, OK." And so, due to his being outnumbered by a small, but angry, hillbilly mob who paid fifty bucks a head to be there, everyone's glass is filled. It was a horrible thought, but a very real possibility given the stature of the attendees.

My worst fears were realized when, to my horror, I saw one of the "restaurant people with connections" heading for the lecturer for a refill of wine. As she was walking toward him, she noticed that a drop of wine had escaped and was traveling down the outside of her glass. To thwart the possible loss of wine, this hillbilly raised the glass to her mouth and licked away the drop of wine that, by now, had traveled nearly to the belly of the glass.

I was absolutely mortified and nearly let out a scream at the sight of this barbaric act, but like in a dream where one cannot scream, I was silent. There are many forms of alcohol abuse, and **this** is certainly one of them.

Imagine a cow licking a pane of glass placed in front of you; the tongue flattened out, with the taste buds smashed against the glass. Following the tongue a line of saliva, sloshing and bubbling, leaving behind a trail of slime where the tongue had passed.

Imagine the above and you will have a very clear vision of what I witnessed that afternoon. The repulsiveness of what I saw had caused recurring nightmares.

I wanted to turn and run out of the place, but at that moment I knew I had to stay. In the wine community, there is a brotherhood of sorts and it is taken very seriously. We stand by each other at all cost and with the lecturer alone in a room of rabid, seemingly inbred, pseudo-intellects, I knew he couldn't be left alone to fend for himself. Leaving would be like throwing a kitten into a pit of wild dogs. A baby harp seal to a gang of Eskimos. Dropping off a young boy at Neverland Ranch. He needed me.

As he continued his teaching, I sensed that due to my presence, he had eased a bit.

At one point, the glass licker turned to her husband, pointed to the spread of food on the table, and said, "Eat the meat and the good cheese. This cost a lot of money and the wine don't taste so good, so we might as well get our money's worth."

Jeff McCue ended up getting drunk and giving his advice on what food should be eaten with a bottle of "Ziffadel." He was trying to pronounce *Zinfandel*, but he failed to use the letter "n" in the name. One would normally pass off this mispronunciation as Jeff being drunk, but knowing that he truly didn't know how to pronounce it, he just looked stupid. The fact that he claimed the perfect complement to a bottle of Zinfandel is salmon, made him look even dumber. As he explained his culinary technique in preparing salmon, which was the equivalent of adding ice to a 1959 Boudreaux, I just shook my head in disbelief.

John Allen just stared at him, then at me, and back to Jeff. His only comment, laced with his Texas class and charm, was, "I'm not sure *why* you'd drink a Zinfandel with a salmon steak, but that's something I'd never do. It just ain't right."

All I could do is wonder what I was getting into with these people. Though this incident had taken place in early September, I knew then it was also the beginning of the end for this venture. I couldn't work with these people and knew that if I did, the business would soon fail; my immediate need was to distance myself from them and to that end, the McCue's would soon be acquainted with this reality.

Unfortunately, my fears were realized sooner than I anticipated. As is usual with a "perfect storm," bad business dealings with the wrong people, others not paying their bills for wine that was delivered, restaurants suddenly going out of business, and finally an unexpected accident that put me in a hospital's Intensive Care Unit for weeks, thus allowing a *fox in the henhouse* without supervision, ended the business. By the time I was able to get a handle on things again, the entire operation had imploded. I was back where I had started and had nothing to show for it, except for being deeply in debt.

"STEVEN EVERTS REQUESTS ATTORNEY'S FEES TO BE PAID"

"Off the pig, bite the bullet, pay the piper, lock and load, eat shit and die and other fairly quick answers to your sleazy, open-ended questions." – Hunter S. Thompson

May 2008

I was once again, dragged back into court in late May to answer to The Jockey's request that the fees, which over the past eighteen months, had been racked up by *The Love of My Life*, be paid by me. These sleazy little cockroaches just don't stop at anything. If they can charge a buck to get a dime out of you, by God, they'll do it.

The cast of characters was the same as always; Eddward Ballinger was sitting atop his throne but resembled more of a court jester by now. Tiffany was next to The Jockey with her little stack of papers, pen in hand, and sitting with her back, board straight.

I always admired the way she could sit so straight and look so prim and proper. For as long as I can remember, she has always sat in that manner. Queens sit like that. People of royalty sit like that. Not commoners like *The Love of My Life*. But then she had always said that she was born, two hundred years too late and believed herself to be royalty, "in another life." If it were my guess and she really was connected to royalty "in another life," I would say she wasn't actually "royalty," but rather may have been more *near* royalty, than anything else. A chambermaid for the royal family, perhaps, emptying bedpans and such. Ho hum, I may be a little jaded, but it sure is nice to think about.

Tiffany and the Girls – Tiffany always wanted to be considered royalty, but unfortunately for her, this is the highest level she ever realized.

As I looked at her now, sitting to my left and just beyond The Jockey, in his father's ill-fitting suit, I saw her in a completely different light than I had before. She sat with her back in the same board-straight manner each time we were together in court. And each time we were in court because I could not afford an attorney, I was usually the one who got his ass handed to him. It finally dawned on me! Court appearances are where she was able to shine her brightest; her "crowning" moment. It was as if she were waiting to be crowned and she needed to sit up straight for the coronation! Her getting her way and walking out of the courtroom, a victor, was her proverbial "crown," so to speak. It's a weird analogy, but it works for me. I also realized that it was just Tiffany's way of feeling better by showing the world her pseudo-aristocratic, pedigree. Only those close to her, very close to her, knew the real truth.

Tiffany's "special needs" mother, Susan, was at the back of the courtroom with her husband, Greg who still only spoke when he was given permission to do so. All he ever did was glare at me, with some perverse hope of frightening me in some way. I hadn't seen these two, Susan and her hapless puppet, in a couple of months, but I noted they had changed. Susan looked as if she was enjoying her retirement and was getting well acquainted with a fork; she had gained a good amount of weight. The same old white pants, she always wore, were completely filled out and busting at the seams. I had a transitory fear of being in front of her if the button on the waistband gave way. It would surely put someone's eye out and I didn't want it to be mine; I kept my back to her. I could handle the pain of the shot to the backside, but my eyes are too important to lose. Greg's common red face and bulbous nose now appeared brighter and bigger, respectively. His enjoyment of cheap grapes was catching up to him.

Judge Ballinger called the court to order and the hearing began. The Jockey wanted to submit, as exhibits, his billing over the past several months and in addition, submitted a bunch of other crap he had subpoenaed from Fry's Food and Drug. I guess he was trying to prove that I had a job and could pay his fees.

Everts asked the judge if he could question me, which he was given permission to do. The Jockey asked me stupid questions about whether, or not, I was working at Fry's Food and Drug. My answer to him was that I was and he knew this because he has all of my employment paperwork in front of him.

He asked me how much I made and I told him but reminded him that he had that information, as well. It went on and on and as it did he was proving to me that he truly *was* an imbecile with a shingle from some university, hanging on his wall that says he can be one.

My answers to The Jockey were always short and often curt and it was kind of fun to see him get fired up when he wasn't getting me to quake under his questioning. I always knew when I was pissing him off because his voice would raise and start to squeak on certain words. At one point, during this line of questioning, I asked him if there was a reason he was angry.

"I mean, did I do something to make you mad?" I asked. "Because you seem irritated for some reason." I shot a coy little smile at him, which made his face turn red.

All he could squeak out was, "Nothing further, Your Honor."

The Jockey then got down to telling the court what it was that he and his poor, deprived and abused client wanted in the way of attorney's fees. I was disgusted by these two depraved dirt bags and the evil way the court works. If you are a degenerate, the only way to win at this game is to be as immoral and corrupt as you can be and the two individuals to my immediate left were, in my opinion, just that.

Ballinger asked about my position on how I felt about what the opposition wanted from me.

I asked Judge Ballinger if he would kindly rule that Tiffany and The Jockey stop harassing me, by continually dragging me into court when their hemorrhoids flared up and wanted to blame me for the malady. Although it would have been damned nice to ask in that manner, my request was not in those exact words and was actually along the lines of asking the court to issue an order that if they wanted to file a motion, make sure it was an important one and not a frivolous waste of the court's time.

Ballinger responded, "Well, it's not a waste of time to *them*."

I was stunned by his response. "Your Honor, it is harassment, plain and simple."

"I don't see it that way and I don't think they do either."

I thought to myself, "Is this guy kidding me?"

"Your Honor, with all due respect to the Court, I have been harassed and tormented by the claims this woman has made over the past two years, and all of it, in this very courtroom, before Your Honor. I have been accused of molesting my children and had police investigations conducted on me, endured the repercussions of the malfeasant conduct of the Phoenix Police Department because Tiffany's original lawyer is married to a detective in the Sex Crimes Division. I have been denied employment due to the background checks conducted by prospective employers, as soon as the police investigation surfaces. The woman to my left has skimmed in excess three-hundred thousand dollars from our marital account over the course of six years and I have been left with literally nothing to my name." I paused to catch my breath.

Well, not really. A more accurate statement would probably be that I "paused" because I wanted to read Ballinger's reaction to what I was saying. I wanted to make damned sure I wasn't pissing him off and land myself back in handcuffs. It was a highly possible scenario given his past reactions. I saw nothing that would indicate there would be an adverse reaction if I continued, so I did. . . . . . cautiously. For a bit of theatrics on my part, I dropped my head and stared at the tabletop for a quick moment and when I raised it back up I continued.

"Through all of this, you continue to side with a woman who is obviously disturbed beyond words. Now I find, because I can't afford an attorney, due to my low wages and the *inability* to afford one, I am punished further by being ordered to pay a large portion of Ms. Nelson's attorney's fees? I just don't get the reasoning behind this ruling, or how, or why the law affords this type of ruling. Can you explain it to me?"

I know I winced and squinted my eyes as I waited for him to call the bailiff because I was questioning his authority again. I cannot tell you how relieved I was that he never did.

Judge Ballinger's only response was, "I cannot advise you beyond telling you, you should get an attorney."

"Excuse me?" I asked.

Did I hear this prick right? That's all he's going to say in response to my statement? He repeated his statement that I needed an attorney. It finally registered that he was not going to give me any kind of explanation at all. I almost coughed up my spleen.

As I sat there with my face, once again, wadded up as it normally was during the good judge's rulings, I desperately wanted to say, but only thought to myself, "No shit, asshole! But how does one do that without any fucking money?" I will never understand this reasoning and all I can attribute it to is the *good ol' boy* system; if you walk into court without an attorney, I'll make sure you pay dearly, for that indiscretion.

My monthly support stayed where it was and included in it was nearly ten thousand dollars in fees that The Jockey was awarded. The monthly payment amounted to $180 towards The Jockey's fees, but worse still, was that it would be set as an arrearage, with The Clearinghouse. This meant it would be accruing interest on the total amount owed. It also meant that at any time the state could come in and seize any money in my bank account. These people didn't care. Even though I took issue with the way the Court system worked, I wanted to make sure my kids were taken care of, but all I was to these people, was another scumbag "deadbeat dad" who was trying to avoid paying child support.

On a side note, early on I had wondered why it was that as soon as The Jockey became involved with this case, I was getting my ass handed to me with regard to ridiculous rulings in the favor of *The Love of My Life*, on a whim I went on line and plugged in The Jockey's real name, Steven H. Everts. I didn't find out much past the fact that he was an attorney licensed in Arizona and Utah, but one thing caught my eye that, to this day, I have no idea how I found it, nor could I find it again; I'm glad I saved the document to my computer.

Back in 2002, The Jockey was admonished for improprieties in a division of the court where he also sat on the bench as a *Judge Pro Tempore*. In short, what happened was that he was representing a person in the same courtroom where he sat on The Bench from time to time.

It was determined, through his connection with this particular courtroom, where he was the preferred Judge Pro Tempore while the REAL judge was away that he was getting preferential treatment. As such, he had several ridiculous rulings that never should have *gone* his way, or *go* his way. These rulings came from the judge he *sat in* for, in the very courtroom he was pleading his case.

The truly beautiful side to this story was that his opposing counsel was none other than DeeAn Gillespie, the beautiful saint who represented me, opposed Tiffany and Jewett, and pulled me from the bowels of hell.

DeeAn too had wondered how it was that this miserable little rat, in the ill-fitting suits, was able to get the judge to rule in his favor, when the facts of the case were so obvious that the ruling should have gone the other way.

As it turns out, if Divine intervention wasn't a huge factor, fate was. One day, DeeAn just happened to be in that particular division on another matter and glancing down noticed an opened file with several names on it; beside the names were dates. The file, as it was, was not in the place it is normally kept, but due to a clerk's error, was left out in the open. The file contained the list of names of each Judge Pro Tempore who sits on The Bench in that particular division.

How surprised she was to see several entries on the list that bore the name, Steven H. Everts! The light bulb went on and she knew immediately why she was coming up short on many of the judge's rulings. It sure-as-hell wasn't because she was being out lawyered by this iniquitous little criminal; DeeAn Gillespie was one of the best in the business and just didn't have things go against her that easily and certainly not when things weighed so heavily in her favor. Even if they weren't, she found a way to win, but here, it was different and there was no plausible explanation.

DeeAn walking into this setting was like placing a $100,000 bet on a fighter who was sitting as a 30 to 1 favorite. It was a guaranteed payout for the one placing the bet. Then, right before the opening bell, you find out the fight was fixed and your boy is taking a dive. Before you could change your bet…….DING!

Too late! The bell to start the first round sounds and you're fucked.

Cries of, "We was robbed!" don't work here. In *this* courtroom, there lives a den of thieves, who will steal your soul if you're not careful. You may as well book passage on the Titanic, if you're going up against Steven H. Everts, in *this* courtroom. This may be the only courtroom in the land where The Jockey could suffer from a *superiority* complex, so long as no one found out where the kryptonite was kept. He could sit in his tree and when some unsuspecting animal passed underneath, he could pounce like a sneaky leopard, onto their backs and maul it to death. His Machiavellian tactics were commonplace here and nothing was as it seemed, ever.

Unfortunately for Steven H. Everts, his kryptonite was DeeAn Gillespie's eyes. She immediately filed an appeal to the judge's ruling, in Maricopa County Superior Court, Case #FC2002-094853, which was subsequently overturned on that appeal. The Appeal, No. 1 CA-CV 04-0343 was reviewed and a twenty-nine-page opinion was handed down by the Appellate Court which stated improprieties did, in fact, exist in the courtroom, during the case. Both the judge and The Jockey were admonished for their conduct. By all means, look it up.

Steven Everts, Esq., would love for this to go away and he would *hate* that I have resurrected this ruling and his indiscretions, but one thing he cannot do is deny this truth.

I had this information, as well as a copy of the twenty-nine-page opinion, for some time and I wanted to bring it to the forefront of my argument, wondering if the reason I had so many rulings go against me, was due to The Jockey sitting on the same bench as Ballinger. I didn't bring it up for two reasons; 1) the opportunity never arose for me to do so, without seeming adversarial, but more importantly, 2) I didn't want to wind up in handcuffs if Ballinger felt I was showing him disrespect, by asking him this pointed question, in his courtroom.

Oddly enough, I do have some semblance of self-preservation. One day maybe I can find out. Hell, the Opinion and Amended Order handed down on November 9, 2006, is now case law and I could refer back to it at any time in the future. To be sure, I'm not in any rush to do so at this particular juncture.

"WE NEED TO DISCUSS THE RESULTS OF. . . . ."

"The harvest is past, the summer has ended, and we are not saved." - Jeremiah, 8:20

May 2008

    A little more than two years had passed since my life had been turned upside-down by the accusations of abuse and molestation of my two daughters. I continued looking for work in the construction industry but was still met with a great deal of reservation and resistance by prospective employers. The reservation usually turned into a flat denial of employment. My frustration of not being able to find work in my field, where I could make a decent living, was growing and with it, grew my resentment of the histrionic, *Love of My Life*.

    As I have explained in the previous chapter, at every opportunity, Tiffany and her attorney continued to harass me, by dragging me back into court each, and every, time they felt there could be a few extra bucks made, or if they felt they could break me. Each and every time, they failed to break me, but even though they failed in that respect, the billable hours of The Jockey would pile up, as well. Every couple of months, The Jockey would request attorney's fees to be paid by me and the good judge, Eddward Ballinger, would oblige the little guy and his wretched client.

By this time, the fees of Tiffany's attorney had swelled to over forty thousand dollars and with that total, I thought about what she had really gained in all of this. In the year and a half since I prematurely requested a modification of child support, she received nothing more than a few extra hours with our daughters, while I was working nights.

Forty thousand dollars and a great many hours wasted in a courtroom were beyond comprehension when that money could have been better spent on the girls, instead of filling the pockets of some loathsome little prick, in an ill-fitting suit, with a law degree. It just didn't make any sense, but in this great country of ours, this is the way the legal system works.

With no work in the construction field in the foreseeable future, I filled out the federal forms for a liquor license in the State of Arizona. The application was fairly detailed in that they wanted to know, which was pretty much everything about me and my background. They wanted to know each residence I lived in over the past five years, which was a list longer than I could formulate in my head. Usually, one would have one, or two, maybe even three, and very seldom, four addresses they had used in five years, but I had something like eight addresses I had used in the five-year span they were asking for. This counted the hotels I had made my home for several months, the couches I had slept on, houses and apartments I had moved into, etc. With each one, I had filled out a change of address form with the United States Postal Service and each one would be one file. In dealing with the federal government, I couldn't withhold any of them.

The claim of this governmental agency, Bureau of Alcohol, Tobacco and Tax, was that they could turn around an application for a liquor license in, "ninety to one hundred and five days." Why this window of success was used, is beyond me. "Ninety to one hundred and five days" just didn't compute, or make any sense. They couldn't have been that inundated with people clamoring for a license to distribute wine in this state, but when I phoned their office and questioned the time line they were using. They didn't even flinch.

"It is what it is, sir." I was told by a very angry-sounding woman. She sounded as if she was suffering from rabies and probably foaming at the mouth as she spoke to me.

"It is what it is." I re-ran those words, over and over again, in my head. I recounted the last two years of my life and it dawned on me that she was right; "It is what it is." Now; what am I going to do with "what it is"?

A quote I had previously written in my little spiraled book shot back into my head, ***"In our life, only ten percent consists of what happens to us. The other 90 percent is how we respond to it."*** The rabid woman was absolutely right, in her assessment of my situation and the situation of all the others seeking her help. The question is; what was I going to do with it?

My intent was not to piss anyone off, so I did nothing; I decided I would simply wait it out. After all, I had no choice and since I felt there was an outside chance that the police investigation may be overlooked, I wasn't about to raise any eyebrows to cause them to want to dig deeper to make my life miserable. It was a short-lived expectation.

Early one afternoon, around the *eightieth* day, the call came in from the investigator working on my file. "Hello, Mr. Di Conti?"

"Yes, who is this?" I asked.

She told me who she was and explained that she had been working on my application for the federal liquor license and wanted to confirm my address, as well as all the previous addresses, my social security number, date of birth, marital status, and a few other things. I thought to myself that this was easier than I had imagined. I was skating through this process in less than the minimum of ninety days they said it would take. She then dropped the bomb on me.

"OK, Mr. Di Conti," she said with a heavy sigh. "We need to discuss the results of your background check."

I knew it was too good to be true, because the taste I had in my mouth, at that very moment, told me that I had just bitten into a shit sandwich.

Energetically I said, "Perfect," but cautiously, I asked, "Where do you want to start?"

This woman was a no-nonsense, venomous, stab-you-in-the-face-with-a-fork employee of the United States Government and she was all business.

"Where do I want to start? She asked. "How 'bout I start by asking you if there's anything you want to tell us?"

I thought to myself, "Us?" I became paranoid. "Jesus! These bastards are like the fucking IRS! 'Us?' I'm screwed."

"I'm not sure I understand your question, ma'am." I was buying time to figure out a good answer.

"I thought my question was rather clear," she shot back. "What don't you understand about it?"

"Well for one, what is it you want to hear? You did the background check, so I imagine you have everything you need to know in front of you. So, with all due respect, I guess my question to you is what is it *you* want to tell *me*?"

What followed was a terrible silence and all I could hear was faint breathing on the other end of the phone. I imagined the veins in the woman's forehead were bulging and pulsating, her pupils fixed and dilated, and her blood pressure was most likely, leaning toward an aortic aneurism. I'm certain she had to wipe away a great deal of sweat from her brow, which, by this time, was dripping onto the papers she was reviewing and causing the ink to run.

She mumbled something into the phone, but I didn't catch it, probably because as she spoke as she was wiping the foam from her lips and chin. The towel she used may have been snagged by the gnashing of her teeth, as well. I imagined her breath had the stench of death on it; maybe that of a small animal she snatched up, which had been scurrying across the parking lot on her way into the office.

"Excuse me?" I asked as politely as I could. "I'm sorry, ma'am. I missed that."

Her response was so frightening I nearing fainted. As she spoke, she was breathing heavily and every breath was accompanied by a single word in her response. She was so deliberate and so forceful in her speech that it took a whole lungful of air to get out each word that she growled. As she completed one word, she inhaled deeply and spoke the next word, using every molecule of air she had in her lungs, to force air across her larynx. It was like watching a horror movie when some poor, loathsome bastard picks up a ringing phone, in a home that just had the power cut off, and hears a breathy voice on the other end, telling them they're about to have there heart ripped out.

"Mr. . . . . . . .Di Conti . . . . . .I . . . . .am. . . . . not. . . . . . .playing. . . . . . . games. . . . . .here." She continued, "I. . . . . asked . . . . . .you . . . . .a. . . . .question. . . . .and. . . . .I. . . . . expect . . . . .an. . . . .answer."

I was horrified by her Freddy Kruger demeanor and although I don't remember, I may have started crying at this point. Thankfully our brains block out traumatic episodes, such as these, thus saving us from going completely mad.

After I composed myself, I explained I was new to this and wanted to cooperate, but due to my ignorance, I needed *her* help. She seemed to ease up a bit, but I knew she still had her incisors hanging out there; just in case.

She took the lead. "Mr. Di Conti, please tell me about the incidents surrounding the investigation by the Chandler Police Department back in March of 2006."

"Oh, *that*?" I jokingly thought, but in actuality, I was thinking, "FUCK! I knew this was coming."

I was once again back in my vacuum and ready to eat a bullet. I expected that it would surface, but hoped it wouldn't, and hearing those words again caused me to freeze. I must have taken a long time to answer because she asked me if I was still with her.

"Yes, I am," I said. "That was something my ex-wife claimed in order to. . . . .what she thought was the easiest way out of our marriage." It was obvious I was on the defensive.

I'm sure my voice was shaking, as I continued. "If you just turn to the back page you'll see that investigating detective wrote her claims were unsubstantiated and that the case was closed. I was not arrested, or charged." Now *I* was the one breathing heavily and I couldn't catch my breath; sweat beading on *my* brow. I waited for what seemed like several minutes for her response.

"Yes, I read that. What do you think motivated this accusation?"

"I wish I knew, but I swear I don't know."

"Well it's too bad because this will hold things up for a while. We always have to look deeper into the background when these come up. True, or not. I'm sorry."

She told me that the process will add several weeks, "if not months," to the background check and that she would be back in touch with me.

As I hung up the phone, I felt like I had just been beaten up. I was so tired, I was barely able to move, so I just sat there, staring at the wall in front of me. I closed my eyes and wondered why I was allowing myself to go through this; allowing these people to dig into my past and see the horrible lies, the abomination of a woman, claimed I did to my daughters. I was disgusted with myself and with the system, which I was relying on to allow me to make a decent living, without worrying about being laid off.

I laid my head back and as I drifted off to sleep I thought back to a conversation I had with an employer several years back.

George Adams owned a recycling yard in Anaheim, California and in a few years, his business swelled to a small empire. A few years after that, he became what he is today; a major player in metal recycling. Certainly among the largest and very well respected. George is a few years older than me, but his work ethic, stamina, and business sense are impressive beyond words. I have always respected George for what he was able to accomplish, but I respect him more for the wisdom he possesses.

George and I were returning to California one day, after a trip to Mexicali, Mexico. Adams Steel owned a non-ferrous metal recovery plant just outside of Mexicali, at the Ejido de Emilliano Zapata, where George's brother, Mike, had designed and built a conveyor system to extract non-ferrous metals from a landfill, used by a company operating a shredder, or hammer-mill.

The Mexican company took only the ferrous material from the shredder and dumped the rest into the landfill. The non-ferrous metal recovery operation was built adjacent to the landfill. I was tasked with overseeing the plant and would go to Mexico every week, or so, to check on the operation. Every now and then, George would accompany me on these trips. This was one of them.

During one of our many conversations, George told me of a story he had heard many years before, but its meaning still held true no matter who you are, or at what point you happen to be in life. It had to do with the various problems we all have and how we deal with them.

This was a story of a man, sitting atop a hill, contemplating his life and the problems he faced. While sitting there, he could see a train in the distance and just watched it as it chugged along, smoke billowing from its smokestack. He followed, with his eyes, the path of the tracks and saw the tracks crossed over a rickety little bridge. Under the bridge was a raging river.

It dawned on this man that the bridge was too small to hold the weight of the train and he instantly knew he had to warn the conductor of the train. He jumped up and started to run toward the train, hoping to cut off the path of the train. As he ran he could see the train was moving far faster than he had imagined and he may not make it in time. He tried to run faster, but his legs, growing wearier, would not carry him fast enough. He finally stopped from exhaustion; heaving air into his lungs. As the man watched in horror, the train barreled down the incline toward the little bridge. The man, sure he was about to witness a disaster, stood and watched helplessly. As the train reached the bridge and the first car had its full weight on it, the man winced at the impending crash. However, there was none.

The first car passed without incident, then the second car, and then a third. Each and every car passed over that little bridge with its full weight on the structure, and nothing happened. The man stood there in disbelief, as the last car of the train passed over the rickety bridge and the raging water below it, without so much as a creek from the little bridge.

It occurred to him that the bridge was, in fact, strong enough to hold the train, as long as the weight of each car was dealt with individually. Conversely, if the whole weight of that train had been on the bridge at the same time, it would have undoubtedly crumbled and fallen into the raging water.

The man pondered what he had just witnessed and realized how symbolic the incident was. The bridge symbolized *him* and the train, all of his *problems*. The river easily symbolized his *destruction and ultimate demise*. Like the bridge, if he just dealt with the weight of one problem at a time and did not try to carry the weight of the whole lot, simultaneously, he would not be defeated and crushed under the weight of his problems.

After George Adams told me that story, I pondered my own life's problems again and saw them in a different light. I will always be grateful to George and the many talks we had, on various subjects. George was always able to explain things in such a way that I could understand and that made sense. Through the wisdom of George Adams, I believe I became a better man.

I was awakened by the ringing of my phone.

I picked up the phone and answered it. It was Jeff McCue. All I could think of was, "Kill me now!"

"Hey, Eric! How about we sell cigars with the wine? My Dad knows a guy who rolls his own!"

All I could think of was some obese little hobbit, standing about 5'2", with dark spots of dried spittle gracing the front of an ill-fitting, thread-bare, striped shirt; a V-neck underneath. His filthy, fat fingers pressed tobacco together and forced it into an exterior leaf of tobacco, occasionally reaching up to pick his nose and then return to his task.

"Not now, Jeff." I hung up the phone.

"WE'D LIKE TO EXTEND YOU AN OFFER"

"We all try to make something of our lives and some are just luckier than others." – Jimmy Buffett

June 2008

Knowing how desperate I was to get away from the grip of Fry's Food and Drug, Ryan Quinn had called me in early June saying there may be an opening for a Project Manager with a small company in Tempe, called Woodruff Construction. The company he was working for at the time, Civaterra, was a sub-contractor to Woodruff on a Post Office renovation. Ironically, this project was at the same place where I had been interviewed by Federal Agents, of the US Postal Service and the FBI, on the Paxton Anderson case. Small world.

He gave me the number of a Mark Johnson who worked for Civaterra but was working out of the Woodruff office. It was a weird set-up, but I didn't care and didn't ask any questions. I made the call and was asked to come to the office that afternoon to meet with Mark. I found it odd that I would be interviewed by Mark Johnson and not a representative of Woodruff Construction, but if it was an opportunity to get back on more workable schedule than I was on, I didn't care who interviewed me.

NOT THE LOVE OF MY LIFE

I walked into the office, which was located on University Drive, in Tempe at about two o'clock the same afternoon and was greeted by Mark, who looked to be well into his fifties. He directed me into the front office. Behind the desk was a young kid who stood up and introduced himself as Wade Woodruff. We all sat down and started the interview, which is normally a bunch of bullshit and a feeling-out process, to tell each other how great we are and what we've done in the industry. Although affable, Mark didn't strike me as an impressive guy with a great deal of knowledge in the industry, as he seemed to let Wade, both ask questions of me, and answer questions I had for them. If I asked Mark a question, Wade would answer it. Wade, on the other hand, struck me as well beyond his thirty-two years and was extremely knowledgeable in construction. He spoke with the authority of a man who had been in the industry for several decades and I was extremely impressed with him.

The interview lasted maybe thirty minutes before the subject of money came up. They wanted to know what I was looking for in compensation. I was very direct in what I "wanted," but also let them know that in the ease of the current economy, it wouldn't be in the best interest of anyone to be too greedy. I deferred to them, saying, "I trust, if I am extended an offer, you will be fair in compensation." The interview ended shortly thereafter.

No sooner had I walked out of the Woodruff office and was sitting in my car than my phone was ringing. It was Wade Woodruff.

"Hi Eric, we like to extend you an offer."

I was ecstatic but held in my excitement. We discussed compensation and the package that came with it, incentives, allowances, etc., and when we were done, it was decided I start the following Wednesday.

On Wednesday of the following week, I entered the office of my new employer and was shown to my office. Mark Johnson came in and explained that I would be handling, with him, work being done at the Kyrene School District, which included the Ahwatukee area of Phoenix and parts of Chandler. The school district's main office would be my first stop where the weekly meeting took place to give an update on the progress of construction. Lagos, Esperanza, and Colina Elementary Schools, in Ahwatukee, were the three projects for which I was directly responsible. At Colina, a section of temporary classrooms was being razed and a new, permanent one was to replace them. This one would be attached to the main building. Lagos and Esperanza had minor interior work, but a larger scope was to take place with regard to concrete work and main water lines. My base camp was at Colina.

Dave Wheeler was the head of construction for Kyrene and I reported directly to him. Dave was a good guy who rarely got his blood pressure raised and when mistakes were made he always helped with a remedy. He was always there to help, no matter what time, or day, it was.

About two months into my involvement with Kyrene School District, I was informed, by Dave Wheeler, that all of the background checks on workers at the three schools had not been completed and that Woodruff would have to conduct them immediately. I froze when I heard those words come out of Dave's mouth.

"Here we go again," I thought. Here I was working at a school with children running around, I had a police investigation, with a title of "SEX CRIME – CHILD VICTIM," hanging onto my backside and a background check was about to be conducted. This was not a position I wanted to be in if I wanted to keep my job and the way it looked, I was going to be shown to the door like a drunken, homeless man who happened to stumble onto the golf course, at Augusta National Golf Club, during The Masters Tournament. I was sweating like Luciano Pavarotti and with good reason.

I knew I had to make a decision on what I was going to do. Do I pull Dave aside, tell him what he may find, and hope he doesn't reel back in horror? Do I go into Wade's office, close the door, come clean, and hope he doesn't feel it would be better to do some immediate damage control? Do I call a meeting with Wade and Dave and tell them together? I started to panic.

Two days had passed and I still hadn't decided what to do, but my time was running out. I had already been asked to provide my signed consent form to Woodruff, so they could run the background check, but I hadn't turned it in. Obviously, I didn't want to turn it in and truly hoped that because I was a Project Manager, and not on site all the time, they wouldn't *really* need it. I knew that the district didn't care who had what title, nor did they care how many times an individual stepped onto their campus. They wanted to know who it was that would be around the children they were supposed to protect. Yeah, I knew better; I was stalling.

I finally decided to take my chances and as horribly inconvenient as it was, I had to do the right thing. While we were both on-site, I pulled Dave Wheeler aside and confide in him.

As I spoke, Dave listened intently to my story. His stone-faced expression never changed and when I was finished he made a simple request. He said he would like to see the police report and anything else that would corroborate my story and bolster the fact that the police investigation never went anywhere and that it was thrown out by the courts.

He, too, wanted to nip this in the bud before anything came up and could, at the very least, if anyone made a stink, let the brass know he was aware of my situation and had viewed all of the documents on the matter. I then spoke with Wade Woodruff and told him my story. He was just as supportive and assured me that we would work through this little dilemma.

Thankfully, I did come clean, as I'm not sure where I would have landed, had I not said anything. The move I had made was a good one and as inconvenient and embarrassing as it was, I'm glad I made it.

I enjoyed working with Dave very much and hope one day, if he doesn't happen to read this book, I can thank him personally for all of his help and understanding. If he does read this book, "Thank you, Dave!"

A few months later, after being asked by my friend, Charles "Chili" Davis, to aid him in completing a project he was doing in Peoria, Arizona, I was removed from the Kyrene School project. In the long run, it was probably a good thing, as there are always parents who decide to conduct their own investigative background checks and God forbid, a parent pulled my name from the Chandler Police Department and came into the school office, waving it over their head. I'd have been a little bitter, I think.

NOTE: As it is with this entire book, the following is as close to the truth as it can be and any reference to individuals associated with the Chili Davis project are OPINIONS, personal or otherwise. Conversations that took place with individuals are as close to verbatim as I can be, but the content is the absolute truth. Analogies and musings are just that; analogies and musings.

The shell of the Chili Davis Premier Baseball Club, a training facility for little leaguers all the way to big leaguers, was being built by Moline Construction and the work, in my opinion, was shoddy at best and reeked of unethical business practices.

Moline Construction had entered into a "Lump Sum" contract with Chili Davis Premier Baseball which if executed normally, would have cost a total of whatever the contract price was; no more and no less. The scope of work would have been detailed in the contract and construction documents and each task assigned a numeric value on what is called a "schedule of values," much like the Schedule of Values we used for custom homes.

In this particular contract, for instance, the concrete tilt-up work was bid by a tilt-up company, which will remain nameless, and had a value of $585,000, which was accepted as a fair price. However, when the work was done, a company by the name of Arizona Site Works did the work for far less amount of money, and to make matters worse, they were not licensed to do tilt-up construction. It turned out that the owner of Arizona Site Works was a close friend of Dave Moline. Though this practice is unethical and frowned upon, it is not illegal.

There were many other questionable practices of Moline Construction that I brought to the forefront and made Chili aware of what these people, including his partner, Craig Maggi, were doing. A man named Tom Steimel was hired, by Craig Maggi, as a construction manager, but it was learned, well after he removed himself from the project, that he was never licensed to conduct business as a construction manager in the State of Arizona. Craig had coached Steimel's son in Little League several years back, so there was a trust factor associated with that relationship and when Craig discovered that Tom owned a business managing construction projects, he recruited him immediately. The problem was that Tom Steimel, other than two, or three occasions, never showed up on-site for any meetings; he sent his daughter, who had no experience in the field at all. He would charge the project for his time at those meetings and throw in mileage for good measure. His involvement in this project was a joke and when I perused his billing I saw a great deal of red flags, which I passed on to Chili.

Moline Construction was notorious for misreading the plans and then complaining they were not drawn well enough to read and would issue a change order for the corrective work. Craig Maggi would sign many of these change orders without question and once that happened, Moline could collect monies for this work and never be held accountable for their mistake. That is, until I came onto the scene.

I made note of the steelwork that was obviously erected, in my opinion, by a bunch of misfits, as the butt joints of the I-beams were not straight and not seated cleanly. The joints were touching at the bottom and had a gap at the top of about an inch. This would suggest the beam was installed upside down, the camber toward the ground and not toward the ceiling as is the normal and common practice. A camber is, in layman's terms, a slight arch in the beam, and all camber are set at a 360-degree radius, meaning if you put a bunch of I-beams end-to-end, with the camber facing outward, the beams would eventually form a circle. Cambers are used for downward load in a structure. In the application used at this facility, in which a mezzanine was constructed, the beams should have been set in place with the cambers up to carry the load of the steel and concrete structure that was to be set on top of it. It was never done.

To make the installation more laughable, none of the bolt holes lined up and it appeared that instead of taking the beams back down and reversing the camber, so the holes lined up, they just welded them in place and walked away. In other places, at the connection and ledger plates, the proper nuts and bolts weren't even used, but rather, whatever they had in arm's reach ended up being put in place. Many of them were never even completely tightened down. I had another steel contractor on site who was amazed at how badly the steel was set in place and was even more shocked that it passed any inspections. The original steel contractor, Apex Steel, even used what looked to be, scrap pieces of steel to bridge gaps where full pieces of steel should have been. These areas were finally corrected, once I made a stink about them.

I finally called GFG Structural Engineers, in Scottsdale, and spoke with Mike Gordon who drew the details and headed the structural overseeing of the project. I voiced my complaints and concerns, which brought him to the site the following day. He was clearly miffed that anyone would question his details, now that the steel was in place. He looked at all of the areas I had concerns with and basically told me that "as long as it's standing," he "didn't have a problem with it." Now *I* was stunned.

Here's a guy, with a degree in engineering, who didn't care how anything was installed on this project, as long as the building didn't fall down. He had a perfect "out" for himself and his firm, as there was a little note in the plans that called for "bolts, *or* welds." Hell, whatever works, I guess. I have been asked, several times since then, if I knew of a decent structural engineer and my first answer has always been, and will always be, "Don't use GFG Engineering if you care about what your building looks like." I would then recount the conversation I had with Mike Gordon that hot summer day.

At the rear of the building was a pretty cool little patio-type deck with a steel staircase and concrete-filled stair treads. Whoever designed the staircase never shot final elevations before building it, because when the staircase arrived at the site it was about five inches short in elevation. When it was set in place, the bottom stair never made it to the footing it was supposed to sit on. Once it was leveled up, where the treads of the staircase were parallel to the ground, the last step was five inches away from reaching the point it was supposed to reach.

What Moline did to correct the mistake was about as junior varsity as one could get. They decided to form up around the footing and make another step so it did fit, but they erred when they again misread the plans and where the drawings show a "control joint," formed a landing that didn't comply with the American Disabilities Act. They subsequently complained the drawings were incorrect and issued a change order to correct it. At my urging, this one was not signed and was eventually corrected by Woodruff Construction.

Even Wells Fargo Bank, who held the loan on the project, jumped into the ring of assholes, as I brought to the forefront some of the crap they were pulling, as well. More specifically, a guy named Joe Giordano.

Joe was a little guy, with an obvious Napoleonic complex, who liked to call the shots in a meeting. He demanded that things be done so the bank was kept happy. He didn't care how the project got done, either, just as long as it got done. He would cut checks to Moline Construction before any payment applications were ever signed by Chili Davis and would cite the Arizona Prompt Pay Act, as his reason for doing so. He was way out of line and I think, deep down, he knew it. He was just another individual who did anything he wanted, as long as no one called him on it. I would be the first to question his ethics and his distaste for my involvement was immediate. I would learn later that he had confided in Dave Moline that the best thing that could happen to the project was that I be removed from it.

While I was going over payment applications and comparing them to work that was completed and paid for, I realized that the payment for work completed, in my opinion, grossly outweighed the work actually completed. This threw up a huge red flag and I wanted to know why.

Once a payment application is submitted to the bank, it will not disburse payments on that application until one of its people can verify that the work was actually done. Banks usually hire a third-party inspection company to verify this work, which then submits a report on the same. In this case, Wells Fargo hired a group that went by the name, Swinerton, to do these inspections. When the bank is satisfied with the inspection report, funds will be disbursed for the same.

As I started digging around, I found that the young lady who was inspecting the work for Wells Fargo Bank, was a former employee of Wells Fargo, which wasn't a big deal, but then I discovered something that infuriated me. Prior to leaving the bank and going to work for Swinerton as a bank inspector, this young lady actually *worked* on the loan for Chili Davis Premier Baseball! I was furious beyond words.

No wonder these applications were being shoved through the system and paid at such an alarming percentage.

The first call I made was to Chili to inform him and the second call was to Joe Giordano, at Wells Fargo. He was taken aback that I was making this inquiry, but for a little while, he played along. He confirmed that the woman who was conducting the inspections was, in fact, a member of the original loan team and further admitted that she had very little experience in her new field. I'm sure that just by the changing tone of my voice he could sense my outrage. It continued to grow as we spoke. Not that it's the fault of this young lady, but rather she was placed in a position of certain failure . . . or that was the plan from the start.

This gal knows nothing about construction, but she is thrown into a pit of animals by her superiors, probably because they knew she was familiar with the loan and could better ascertain the "percentage of completion" when payment applications are submitted. What her superiors didn't consider was that the Moline kids have a keen sense of smell and when there is a weak, or injured, animal in their midst they know it. I have been in several meetings with these people and seen them work within their pack, so I can speak with some sense of authority.

I also know several sub-contractors who worked for Moline Construction on the Sun Devil Baseball Stadium. I was told by one individual that, due to a loophole in their contract, they were never paid and were still in litigation with them, but I don't want to get off the subject. If I do then I'll never come back to this, my Ritalin will wear off and my concentration will be shot. Once the Ritalin wears off and I lose concentration on a subject, there are only a few words that describe what happens in my head: pandemonium, bedlam, mayhem, and complete chaos. If you don't believe it, just ask someone who knows me.

Anyway, bank inspectors don't tell the contractor when they're coming to make inspections; they just show up, conduct their inspections, and report to the bank. Additionally, the bank will submit their request for inspection to the third party inspection service, in this case Swinerton, and be given a "window" of time (sometimes a couple of days) that the inspection will take place.

Rarely does the superintendent know the inspector is ever on site unless they announce themselves and they normally do not.

I mused that this poor gal probably showed up to the site, one morning and announced she was there to inspect "whatever" and when she did, a quick assessment of her knowledge was made. Once it was determined her knowledge was extremely limited and she was out of her league; Cha-ching! The Pavlov effect took place and salivary glands became over-active, as she was led away from the construction trailer, to the site itself, for her "inspection."

One of the degenerate hillbillies would speak up, "Now what was it you was here to 'spect, sweetheart?"

In her meek, squeaky little voice she would mutter, "Well, uh, I'm supposed to look at, uh, a 'column', or is that a bunch of 'columns'? Oh I don't know. Just. . . uh. Forget it. Where are they? You know? The word 'column' is spelled weird. Why is there an 'n' at the end of that word when you don't even pronounce it? That's stupid. Oh well. Anyway. Um. Whatever. OK, where is the column? Columns. Just show me."

"Well, honey," she would be led to the perimeter of the building where the concrete panels were standing and with the slap of his hand, her guide would smack the side of the tilt-up and say, "This here. . . . . . .is a column." His eyes darted back and forth as he waited for a response from her, but none came. He had her.

"Ya can tale bah the way it stands in a line with the other ones. See here? Putchyer face up near hear and ya can see where they all line up. Like a column!"

As she put her face near the concrete panel she would hear, "See there? Now ya can jus' write 'er down in that there report, just like you seen it."

Giggling, she would admit how dumb she is and thank everyone for their help.

"Now, next time y'all come around you jus' come to that there single-wide, over yonder, and I'll help ya again. Ya cain't never be too careful 'round here, honey. Ya hear?"

She smiles shyly and walks off.

The closest analogy to this I can come up with is when a cat kills a mouse, or bird, or other small creature, many times they'll play with it before either eating it or leaving it to rot in the hot sun. With this young lady, Moline was just batting around the "kill" for a little while and their "meal" would be when she signed off the building for "substantial completion."

Once that was done, according to the contract, Moline would be paid in full without ever actually completing the project. At that point, one could only hope the building would be completed in its entirety. As it would turn out and in my opinion (I want to make it very clear this is my OPINION), Woodruff Construction completed a great deal of work that Moline, neglected, failed, or refused to do, but was already paid for that same work.

As my questioning continued, Joe Giordano was less and less cooperative in his answers and where he was once very candid with them, he started to talk around my questions and not really answer them. Once I delved far enough into the subject, I used a couple of terms that no one in his industry likes to hear. When I suggested that this woman being involved in project inspections, for Wells Fargo Bank, was a "conflict of interest" and had a "serious stench of unethical business practices," he became insulted that I would have ever questioned him. Our conversation had now become labored and anything he said following, was very vague and ambiguous; Joe Giordano was giving up no more information.

Even though our conversation ended shortly after my "conflict of interest" statement, I followed up with an e-mail to him that outlined our conversation and everything that was said. I also demanded that "due to the conflict of interest," the bank inspector/former-Wells-Fargo-employee "be relieved of her duties immediately and without delay" and for good measure, I carbon-copied everyone and their mother on that e-mail. Ironically, the following day, she was reassigned and another inspector was assigned to our project. This one was no better, but at least they knew someone was watching, whereas before I came around, they were running amok.

Candice Kopple was very clear in letting everyone know she, "didn't give a damn about the quality of the work, as long as it was done." She also added that if she, "was paid to oversee quality control I would do something about it, but they don't pay me enough for that, so I just don't care." Amazingly, her comments were in front of several people, including Chili himself.

I could go on and on for about twenty pages, but I don't want to completely bore you. I basically came in and cleaned that house by pointing out all of the degenerates to Chili and they were picked off one by one, until we had a smooth-running operation again. The tenant improvement still needed to be done, on the inside, and it turned out that Woodruff Construction would do it. At least it would be done by a responsible and ethical company and I would be the one overseeing the work for my friend.

The initial tenant improvement would be a brutal eight weeks of work, in which a Starbucks Coffee was built in one of the spaces within the shell. The construction went pretty well considering the mediocre drawings we had to work with. Incomplete details, or details that were missing entirely, complement of an architectural firm in Phoenix, by the name of Archicon (pronounced 'ark-eh-con'). Another one of those groups of people who looked at Chili Davis and saw a big fat checkbook. In all my years in this industry, I have never known an architect to charge for a contractor sending them an RFI (Request For Information). RFI's are dispatched for two main reasons; 1) request a change in material for another, such as, for cost savings, using aluminum feeders to bring electrical power inside the building as opposed to copper (as was our case), and 2) to clarify a discrepancy in the drawings. It is the second type of RFI with which I had a huge problem.

As is the case with every single set of drawings I have ever seen, there were many discrepancies and the need for clarification; a missing door size, a conflicting, or missing gauge in steel stud detail, missing walls, etc. When I see these types of things, to cover my ass, I send an RFI to the architect. In this case, it was Archicon. After getting a call from Chili saying he wanted me "slow down on the RFIs." When I asked why, he informed me that he'd just received a bill "for answering RFI's."

"What the hell are you talking about, Chili? No one charges for RFI's, unless they have a set amount of RFIs they answer in their contract before they start charging."

"Eric, all I'm telling you is that I got a bill from Archicon and it says they're charging me to answer your RFI's."

"That's bullshit, Chili. They can't do that. We need to have a sit down with these assholes. Can you set it up?"

A week later we were sitting in front of Vince Dalke (pronounced doll-kee) and Mark Barbour in the offices of Archicon. It was Vince who stamped and signed our drawings. I jumped into the RFI issue immediately and started firing questions at the two of them, as they sat there with their and listened.

"Tell me why it is that you charge for answering RFI's when the RFI's are due to the inadequacies of your drawings," I demanded.

I didn't even let them answer, "I have never heard of such bullshit, hillbilly, cockroach move in my life. You guys leave something out or the drawing and when someone questions it, you charge them for it? What a racket you guys have here! Why not just submit a bill for a bunch of blank pages, get paid for NOT drawing them and when someone asks where the drawings are, you can present them with another huge bill for asking about it? Once you fill the pages you can charge them again!"

Vince is the type of guy that gets insulted when his practices are questioned and what he said stunned me.

"It was written in the contract, that Mr. Davis signed, we would be charging for all RFI's."

"What?" I asked. "You mean to tell me you *wrote* it into the contract that way? Why the *hell* would you do that, Vince?" Again, I didn't let him answer. "There is only one reason why I would do something like that and that would be to make a little extra cash off of a guy who doesn't know what he was signing."

Yeah, I know, it was a little harsh, but I didn't care. These guys were taking advantage of my friend and I was pissed. Vince was now pretty pissed off and as Mark just sat there with a doe-eyed stare, Vince went on a tirade about how difficult this particular job was.

I agreed that it *was* difficult since we had a pile of shit that was passed off as a working set of drawings. My comments didn't help Vince's blood pressure, but when he realized I wasn't backing down, he agreed to make some of the costs go away. I would not write another RFI for the remainder of the project.

We had several more meetings with Vince and in one of the final meetings I let him know that on a personal level, I liked him, but from a business standpoint, he was "a piece of shit" and his "business practices were suspect and bordering on unethical."

I let him know about something else, as well; I told him that if anyone ever asked me if I knew of a good architect, my response would be this: "Don't use Archicon, they'll charge you to answer RFI's." I told Vince, also, that if I was asked if I had heard of Archicon, I would not have anything positive to say about them. I also cautioned him not to use me or Woodruff Construction as a reference, that it wouldn't be in the best interest of his firm.

Building the Starbucks Coffee space was an experience, in and of itself. I'm not going to bore you with a long drawn-out and verbose diatribe about building the space, other than to give a brief rundown of a few people who made the project possible; and also say I had never before dealt with so many arrogant individuals in one place before.

They seemed to have colonized themselves in the upper northwest; Seattle to be exact. Home of the tree huggers. I won't go into trashing and bagging on these people, but I will say that they were very difficult to work with, on many levels. Of the many frustrating episodes in this project, there were three people with whom, I admit, I thoroughly enjoyed working. They were Wayne McIntosh, Bill Felton, and Nancy Becerra, not necessarily in that order.

Wayne was the head of the construction end of building these Starbucks spaces and with a background in architecture, he understood what it took to read a shitty set of plans and actually try to convert theory into application. It was never easy to do and when dealing with an architect, such as Archicon, who was "never wrong," the task became more difficult. Wayne would quell many of those disagreements for us. Another area in which he was helpful, was when dealing with the dreaded designers. Designers are probably the most arrogant and self-indulgent people alive. Well, come to think of it, they may fall behind Tiffany in that department, but they're way up there on the list.

When disagreements with the design team surfaced, or a decision had to be made where the designer insisted on having something done, which was virtually impossible, Wayne would be the mediator and make a final decision, taking on any repercussions from that decision. In this day and age, it was a remarkable trait for an individual to possess. I am grateful for his presence and help throughout this project.

Bob Felton was a crusty old salt who headed the installation of all the stainless steel sinks, coolers, coffee equipment, interior signage, and everything else that goes into a Starbucks. To give a Readers Digest condensed version, Bob had previously worked for a contractor who built these spaces, as contract work for another construction company, but when that company began having money problems, Bob stepped in and took over the operation, working exclusively for Starbucks in this capacity. Chili Davis' was his seven-hundred-forty-eighth store overall. I was impressed.

Like many others in the construction field, he wasn't a by-the-book guy and didn't follow installation protocol, as if it were an assembly instruction sheet from IKEA and he certainly would not install anything like the design team wanted it installed. That is if they were to actually step down from their little thrones on high, set aside their tiaras, and "lower" themselves to the level of installing something. Naw, these people are finger pointers and nothing more. Bob was a man's man who took his job seriously and if something, outside the parameters of protocol, needed to be done, he would make the decision that was best for all involved. He was efficient and a proper commander of the troops, once he got on site.

Through Chili, I had met Nancy Becerra several months prior to the start of the Starbucks project at a golf tournament Chili and I attended near the Arizona State University campus. The tournament was to raise money for the high school baseball team her son plays on and her husband, Filipe, coaches in Tempe. Nancy is the western regional something-or-other and holds a great deal of power within Starbucks. I liked her immediately. She is affable and easy to speak with and possesses a great sense of humor. Nancy was instrumental in smoothing out the finishing touches of the project and lobbied for us, with the corporate office in Seattle, to assure them we were in compliance.

As I had said, we completed the space in eight weeks and according to Wayne McIntosh, who conducted the punch walk, ours was the shortest punch list in the fourteen, or so, years Wayne had been in charge of this division. I give all the credit to Woodruff's little Bulldog, Dave Geruso, who was the project's superintendent and head perfectionist. Dave Geruso and I remain friends today.

A SMALL DEGREE OF VINDICATION

"When you shoot at a king, make sure you kill him"
– Unknown

January 22, 2009

Back in September of 2008, I had filed a motion to have the child support modified, but with the court being so busy, I received a court date of January 22, 2009. Due to the amount of child support I had to pay and by that, the limited funds I had live on, I was not happy about having to wait so long to get into court. I was hoping I could get an early date so the financial bleeding would stop, but I guess it didn't matter much at this point; I had been surviving until now. More importantly, at least I would be heard.

The laws in the State of Arizona afford a modification of support "if there is a substantial change in income by either party." The "substantial change" is now considered anything that exceeds fifteen percent of one, or both parties' income combined. For example, if a guy is making five thousand dollars a month and then changes jobs, but must accept a compensation package of four thousand dollars a month, his income just dropped by twenty percent and could have his child support reduced accordingly. It's a weird and jacked-up system, but I guess it works; one of the many spokes on the wheel of justice.

I had attempted to get my child support reduced two years prior due to an almost forty percent change in income, but Commissioner Brnovich refused to look at the numbers and would only rule that "not enough time had passed" since the original order was set. My attempt to have the support lowered was due to Tiffany claiming, at our Resolution Conference, in the office of that scarecrow, Cuccarullo that she was "unemployable as a paralegal in the State of Arizona," so her income was set at a paltry $2,500 per month as a "real estate expeditor." It was bullshit and everyone knew it, but at the time there was nothing anyone could do. The following month Tiffany ended up getting a job, in a Scottsdale law firm, making what I can only estimate as nearly fifty to sixty thousand dollars a year. That equation alone adds up to nearly a sixty-percent increase in pay and would constitute a "substantial change in income," but due to the good commissioner's ruling, I was pretty much screwed for the time being and had to suffer through having to pay an unfair amount of support. If you factor in *my* wages that, at the time, had been dropped by nearly twenty percent, you had the making of a perfect financial storm. I assure you; it sucked.

Now, more than two years had passed since that day in Commissioner Brnovich's Court and I had a solid case to have the support modified. My pay dropped considerably and the comfortable pay the histrionic "love of my life," was making, had not changed. There was, once again, another perfect storm, however now the winds of change had filled my sails, and I was traveling comfortably.

Our appearance, in front of a court administrator, was set at 5:00PM.

As I pulled into the parking lot, I noticed Tiffany's car already parked and empty. She was always early for these things, trying to carry the demeanor of a real cockroach, with a law degree. I pulled into a space, put the car in park, and set the brake. I sat there for a moment and even though I knew there was nothing the Courts could do to change the facts, I still wondered how it would go. One just never knows what is going to happen in a courthouse filled with sleazy vipers wearing suits and black robes.

I got out of my car, walked across the parking lot and through the double doors to the metal detectors. I emptied my pockets and walked through. I noticed that Tiffany was sitting off to the left pouring over papers in a manila folder. For what, I wasn't sure. This conference was pretty basic, although I had a few hand-grenades I was planning to lob Tiffany's way, once we were inside and everything was leaning toward a profitable outcome for her.

I approached the window of the court administrator's office and was handed the usual forms to fill out, which I did and handed back. Within five minutes, or so, a woman named Gail came out and called out my name and then Tiffany's name. We followed her through the front door. I followed Gail who held the door open for me as she passed through. Behind me was The Love of My Life and as I passed through the door, I let the door swing back into Tiffany. Yes, that was an asshole move, but considering the past few years...

I normally open doors for women, no matter what, but this was no ordinary woman and I wasn't about to show her any respect. She didn't deserve any. Not after all I had been through. It may have been an asshole thing to do, but I was at a point where I just didn't care anymore. I was jaded and "institutionalized" by the court system and just didn't care about much beyond myself, and my girls. Tiffany hadn't cared much about anything much beyond her bank account for years. She had dragged everyone down around her and she never so much as hinted that she cared one little bit. I always cared before, but not now. Not ever again.

"Fuck her," I thought, "She can use the weight of her own sagging ass to muscle the door open." I wasn't about to.

We entered "Gail's" office and I was directed to sit in a chair in front of her desk, Tiffany next to her desk, partially blocking the only exit available in the event of an emergency.

"Perfect," I thought. She was away from me, but if any of these two women turned rabid, I would have to get through them to get out. Pray for calm.

Gail advised us that we were going to try to come to an agreement on support and if we could not, it would be necessary to go before the judge and hash it out in the courtroom. I was ready and I'm sure that Tiffany thought she was, as well. She was again sitting up, straight-backed and trying to look as stoic as she could. Knowing how arrogant Tiffany was, I was sure at that very moment in time, she would have liked to end up taking her chances in front of a judge. However, she had no idea what I had for ammunition.

For the first time, I noticed Tiffany had a stack of papers that rivaled a Kinko's stock room. Every few pages in the stack had little blue tabs as markers for her reference.

"Holy Christ Almighty!" I thought. "That's a shit load of trees sitting in her lap." She was holding what amounted to a small section of the Amazon rainforest. No wonder the air is so bad in the world. Aside from the foul stench that emanates from her jowls when she belches and spews out her thoughts and commands, what Tiffany had sitting across her slushy lap was responsible for a good portion of it.

Tiffany started first and wanted to get out of the fact that she only worked thirty hours a week in a position that was "allotted twenty-four hours." As she spoke her voice soon became the breathy little whisper she uses to gain sympathy, from those with whom she is speaking. Knowing that I was probably going to use the fact that she was capable of working five days a week, she was trying to drive home the fact that she only works four days, because she was such a giving mother.

". . .and the other day of the week," she whispered, "I donate to the girls' school and volunteer in their classroom." She was so proud of herself. She was also full of shit. She never "donated" more than an hour of her time, once, or twice a month. Ever.

"So you only work thirty hours a week?" Gail, our court administrator, asked.

In her breathy voice, Tiffany responded, "Yes, ma'am."

I just sat there, quietly. I'm sure they were wondering why I just sat there mute and that I wasn't putting up a fight. They just shot glances across the desk at each other, as I sat there with the slightest, maybe even undetectable, smirk on my face.

Gail suggested she plug in the numbers to see where we were sitting with respect to support according to the numbers on Tiffany's worksheet. Once the computer was done calculating the figures, she threw a ridiculous number out at me.

"Father, do you agree with that?" Gail asked me.

My turn!

"I agree with the fact that it's obvious she *says* she works thirty hours a week, but if you look at her pay stubs, it's easy to see her math skills are somewhat deficient. Each of her pay stubs shows a number far greater than that of a thirty-hour work-week."

Gail just stared at me and Tiffany looked as if she was searching her memory bank for some cool legal terms, with which to respond, but she was having trouble retrieving one. No one said anything, so I continued.

"She has several months of pay stubs and not one of them will reflect a thirty-hour work-week. In fact, only one shows a work week close to thirty hours and all the others would suggest she is working far more than she is claiming." I pulled one of her bi-weekly paystubs out from the file I was given and held one up, "This one shows eighty-two hours." I held up another, "This one here, show seventy-six hours in two weeks." And another, "Here's one that shows she worked a total of seventy-nine hours for a two-week period."

"OK, OK, OK." Gail interrupted. "Mother?"

It always bugged the shit out of me when they responded to us with the "Father" and "Mother" thing. The use of these terms was rampant in the court system and rarely did these people refer to anyone differently. The only time I ever heard my real name was when I was speaking to my own attorney and that was over two years prior. Oh, and also when I was being arrested by the courthouse deputies, at the direction of Judge Ballinger, for not paying for medical insurance which never existed in the first place. As the good deputies led me out of the courtroom in handcuffs and down the hall, they referred to me by my real name then, too.

In court, once a motion was made, the judge would address the attorneys with things like, "Does Mother have a job?" "That's wonderful, so both Mother and Father are employed, but Mother doesn't have the money for childcare and needs more money from Father to pay for childcare while she works."

"Hmmm. Father is already paying more child support than is allowed by law and I can't really clip the guy for more money without raising eyebrows."

"What does Father want to do with this development?"

"Can Father take the minor children while Mother is working?"

"Is Mother willing to give up some time with the minor children, so she can pursue her career in prostitution?"

I hate to keep beating a dead horse, but the system is a joke.

"Is Judge going to stop talking? Because I'm getting a rash on my ass from listening to him."

Like a marriage counselor or, therapist, presiding over a counseling session, Gail was going back and forth between *The Love of My Life* and me. I imagined her at a tennis match. Whack! The ball has been hit. She would look at me, "Father?" I would give my argument. Whack! It's hit again and her head would whip the other way. "Mother?" Tiffany would argue her point. Whack! Head whip. "Father?" Whack! Head whip. "Mother?" Whack! Whack! Whack! Whack! Whack! Whack! Whack! Whack! The visual was tremendously funny.

In that breathy voice she normally saved for the male judges and attorneys, Tiffany laid it on thick trying to make Gail understand that she was just a victim of an irresponsible father, trying to get out of paying child support. She bemoaned every point I made about her bi-weekly pay stubs showing more than thirty hours worked in that pay period.

Gail looked at me and asked, "Well, Father, what do you want to do with this?"

My argument and the forcefulness of the same, took both Gail and Tiffany by surprise. I was tired of the bullshit Tiffany had gotten away with, to this point, and didn't hold back.

"What do I want to do with this? I'll tell ya what I want to do with this. I want you to factor in a forty-hour work week and see where we come out."

"Well, she says she only works thirty hours a week."

"Jesus! Whose side is this broad on?" I thought to myself.

"I know what she said, but the fact is her pay stubs tell a different story. But let's just say, for shits and giggles, that she *does* only work thirty hours a week."

Tiffany smirked and wiggled her ass to the back of the seat she was in and sat up straight as if she had finally made her point and even *I* saw the light, but I wasn't even remotely finished.

"That's fine, but the problem I have with it, is that she is *capable* of working forty hours a week, but she *chooses* not to. Here's the caveat to that. The law allows child support to be factored in as what the parent is *capable* of working on and not what the parent *is* working. If this weren't true, I could go get a part-time job and only work two days a week, and Tiffany here would be paying *me* child support. But the court doesn't see it that way. They figured the support payment off of me working forty hours a week and nothing less.

"What bothers me, Gail, is that during the R and C (Resolution and Conference) Tiffany claimed she was un-employable in the State of Arizona as a paralegal (Tiffany worked for thirteen years in this field in California) and the only job she could find was a 'real estate expeditor,' making $2,500 per month. I didn't have the energy, or the money, to fight it and stipulated what she claimed her earnings were. The following month she landed a job with a law firm in Scottsdale making fifty-thousand a year. Shocker! I immediately filed for a modification and was summarily turned down because 'not enough time had passed' since the order was entered by Judge Ballinger. Even though the law allows a modification 'if a substantial change in income has occurred,' which it did, Commissioner Brnovich turned my request down. I was screwed and had to continue to pay a child support amount that was grossly overstated. It was complete bullshit!"

I quoted the law to the two of them. "A 'substantial change in income is one that exceeds fifteen percent in earnings."

"He's right. The law does reflect this percentage," Gail interrupted.

"Having said that," I continued. "With her being capable of working forty hours, it would raise her percentage of income by more than fifteen percent and I want it factored in."

"Mother?"

I think *The Love of My Life* was finally starting to have her doubts, "How much would the support be, if forty hours as factored in?" She knew she was about to get a lesson in *new math*.

"Let's see." Gail started tapping away on the keyboard and within a few seconds she said, "Father would owe Mother, seventy-three dollars a month."

"Um, OK. I guess that'll work," Tiffany said. "But what about the other income he has?"

"What income?" I asked.

"Well, what about Elite Vineyards of New Zealand? You have an LLC and you've been published. How much are you making from that company?"

Gail asked, "What kind of a company is it?"

I laughed, "It's a wine distribution company."

I turned to Tiffany, "You need to get a new hobby, honey. Don't you get tired of wondering what I'm doing, all the time? Doesn't sitting in front of your computer and typing my name in the "Google," browser get boring? That business has not even started yet. It's just an LLC and I don't even have a liquor license. You can't sell wine without a license, or you go to jail." I laughed again at Tiffany's suggestion that I had a secret income and that she spends time checking up on me. To spend that much energy on me, I think she still digs me! Kidding. Truly.

"OK what about the income you're getting from Chili Davis."

"Huh?" I laughed again. If I didn't already cover this, I'll do it again; Chili Davis played professional baseball for nearly twenty years, starting out with the San Francisco Giants, he was traded to the California Angels in the late eighties, where I had first noticed his name, due to the oddity of it. I had followed his career for several years, through the time he was released to the Minnesota Twins and won a World Series Championship in their 1991 "Worst to First" season.

Chili was instrumental in Minnesota winning that Championship Series. The following year, he went back to Anaheim, California and played several more years with the Angels, until he left and made a pit stop with the Kansas City Royals, where he played for a year. The year following that one, he would get his biggest payday following a phone call from, George Steinbrener, who owned the Yankee organization. They wanted him and were willing to extend a very nice contract offer. He accepted the offer and went on to win two more World Series Championships with that organization until he retired in 1999. Had he stayed on for another few years, he would have a total of five World Series Trophies.

This was absurd. Tiffany was always trying to work an angle to get more out of whoever she was trying to clip for money. The fact was, Chili Davis was, and still is, a very good friend of mine and I was building a tenant improvement for him in Peoria, Arizona. The Chili Davis Premier Baseball Training Facility was to be opened in March of 2009 and I was responsible for making sure it was built on time and came in under budget, which it did, on a grand scale. Due to other contractual and financial issues that surfaced scores of missing funds, it had not yet opened, as anticipated. Tiffany, of course, was convinced that I was getting paid on the side and those monies should be factored in, as well. It's always been all about the money, with this woman.

"I have no other income than what I am getting paid from Woodruff Construction."

Gail was satisfied with my responses. "OK, Father, how does the new child support amount sound to you?" Gail looked at me and when she saw me smiling, she wadded up her brow.

I was about to drop a bomb on the two of them. "That would work for me, too, but there's another issue we need to discuss that would bring that figure down even further."

Tiffany's head whipped toward me, as I said those words. Even though the amount had dropped considerably, she still thought she had scored by garnering at least something from my pocket. Now she looked worried.

I pulled from the manila folder I was carrying, two sheets of paper that had the Woodruff letterhead on them. One was a letter signed by my immediate supervisor, Jake Beauchman and the other was an agreement signed by me and Wade Woodruff, vice president of Woodruff Construction. I handed them both over to the administrator.

The agreement stated that I was being removed as a project manager and relocated within the company as a superintendent. It also showed a wage far lower than I had been making. The letter was explaining that due to the economy, the only way to keep me employed at Woodruff Construction was to relocate me at a lower wage; otherwise, I would have to be laid off completely. I was kind enough to bring extra copies for the occasion, so they both had their own documents to peruse. I think I may have been smiling while they were quietly reading to themselves.

"I want this verified!" Tiffany shot at Gail.

"Uh, well I don't normally do things like that," Gail said. "I mean we *do* have the letterhead of Father's employer and it *is* signed by his supervisor . . . ."

"I don't believe these documents to be authentic and I want them verified." Tiffany was seething by now.

Gail was now very cautious, "Well?"

In looking up at the clock on the wall I saw it was about 5:30PM. I interrupted, "You know I think that Jake may still be in the office, let's give him a call."

Tiffany had a smug response. "Let's."

Gail put the call on *speaker* and dialed the number on the letterhead and one of our secretaries answered the phone, "Woodruff Construction."

"Hi, Jeremy," I said. "It's Eric. Is Jake, or Mary, available?"

"Dude!" She said, "It's like 5:30 or something and everyone's gone." She gave a little chuckle as if I was insane for making the inquiry. And yes, she had a guy's name.

"Jeremy, we're in the middle of a court hearing and you're on speaker. The court administrator would like to ask you a few questions."

In an instant, she became very professional. "Yes?"

Ma'am," Gail asked. "How much money does Mr. Di Conti make?"

I interrupted, "She wouldn't know that."

Jeremy concurred.

"OK, then, does Mr. Di Conti do any work for Chili Davis, through Woodruff Construction?" Gail asked.

"Yes, he does," she said.

"OK. Thank you very much."

By now, Tiffany was fidgeting in her seat and it was obvious she was fumed. I noticed a little vein on her forehead was bulging. I immediately thought of Salvador Dali and that if he were there he would paint her melting into her chair, spilling over the armrest and onto the carpet. I chuckled out loud again.

"Thanks, Jeremy," I called out before the line was disconnected.

"OK," I said. "Let's punch *those* numbers in, folks." I was overly and openly, ecstatic and exuded a manner of arrogance myself, but by now, I didn't care. I was driving the bus now.

Gail punched in the new numbers and the computer spat out its calculations.

"Uh. Hmmmmm." Gail had her chin resting in the palm of her hand as she looked at the results of her inquiry. I was smiling the whole time. "Well, Mother, it looks like you would owe Father a little over $25 a month."

"What?" Tiffany asked. "That's not right! He should be paying me!"

Tiffany, right in line with her histrionic world, started crying.

To be honest, I almost burst out laughing, although I did make a childish comment to rub it in her face. I'm not really even sorry about making it, because of all the bullshit poor, abused Tiffany put me through. The simple little comment I made was, "Cha-Ching!" It also drew a vicious glare from *The Love of My Life*.

She and Gail went back and forth while Tiffany was trying to figure out a way where I would still owe her child support but just couldn't come up with anything. I was howling with laughter inside.

Tiffany offered up a pathetic bill, signed by a young girl who watched Katie and Magen, while Tiffany was at work, saying she paid her ten dollars an hour. When she was done, I directed Tiffany and Gail to the Divorce Decree that stated both "parents were responsible for their own respective childcare." She then tried to get her out-of-pocket medical expenses entered into the equation. Nope.

"You'll have to petition for those costs," Gail told her. I hoped she would petition for those reimbursements because I had about $2,000 worth of reimbursements she had been ignoring for the past three years and I would love to have them examined again. Each time I had requested these to be paid by Tiffany, via formal invoicing, the court and the good judge, Eddward P. Ballinger III, would ignore them, after getting a dose of the breathy Tiffany and fall all over himself, while giving his ruling.

Tiffany was hitting roadblock, after roadblock and was becoming increasingly frustrated by it. She finally conceded that she had no more ammunition to fire. She was beaten. It was at this time I took the opportunity to toss one last hand grenade into her lap.

"Lastly," I said. "I want this final number to be effective and retroactive to back when I filed."

Tiffany almost vaporized right where she sat. "No! This is NOT acceptable! I will NOT agree to this!" That vein in her forehead was bulging again.

When I told her that she didn't really have much of a choice, she turned to Gail who gave her the bad news.

"Well, there is a statute that allows for this, Mother."

"Huh?" Tiffany looked as if were going to start crying again.

Gail looked at Tiffany and as sympathetically as she could, said "There's a statute that says the payments can be paid 'retroactively back to the first day of the month following service.' That means, uh, let's see here." Gail was looking for the date Tiffany was served.

"Oh, here it is! You were served in September, so that would mean that, by law, all of the money Father has paid, from October 1, 2008, will be applied toward the attorney's fees."

"Cha-Ching!" It slipped out again! Now Gail was glaring at me, as well, but I still chuckled inside. I knew I was being childish but just didn't care.

I said, "Hey, she has duped the court and everyone else for three years and I'm tired of it. She is a liar and a cheat of the worst kind."

Gail interrupted me, "Father, no sniping. That is not productive in this proceeding."

"I'm angry, ma'am. Have someone tell the world that you molested your children, then have yourself as the main focus of a police investigation, have that investigation stay on your record for the rest of your life, and see how pleasant you can be. I'm not 'sniping.' I'm speaking the truth."

"Excuse me?" Gail responded.

"Yeah!" I was pissed. "That's right! I was accused by this woman of molesting my girls. Nice, huh?"

"Well, that's not good." Was all she could say.

"No, it's 'not good.' And that's why I'm pissed. That's why I'm fighting this. I'm tired of her bullshit."

Tiffany spoke up, "God, Eric, you're so sensitive!"

All I could do is laugh at her. You can't reason with someone, who, in my opinion, is so completely out of touch that she would make a comment such as that. All the lies that she told about me destroyed my world and I had to struggle for the past three years, financially and within the community. I lost many of what I thought to be friends over her accusations. I couldn't find housing because the investigation into child molestation kept appearing. And she thinks I'm being *"sensitive"* about it? Jesus Christ!

Tiffany turned her focus back to the money she felt she would be losing and was outraged. She couldn't believe this was happening and she lashed out again. "I will NOT agree to this! As I said before, this is unacceptable and needs to be refigured." I truly wish there was a transcript of this because her words and behavior were beyond unimaginable. I did, however, secretly record this meeting and referred back to the recording, for exact verbiage during this exchange.

Poor Gail just sat there and not knowing what to say, fumbled through the papers in front of her.

I broke the silence, "Let's go talk to the judge then," I said. They both were now looking at me.

"Let me tell you something, Tiffany, your problem here is that I just don't care anymore, because I'm tired of you bullying me with your manipulation of this system. I've been in the right ever since this whole process started three years ago and you have exploited everything to get what you want; which is money, because that's really all that's truly important to you. Now I'm driving the bus and I'm not afraid to walk into the court and roll the dice. Another problem you have is that I'm not intimidated by the courts anymore, either. I actually *want* to go in there and watch this play out. I would *enjoy* going in there. So I'll tell you both right now; **this** is what is *going* to happen, or we can go before the judge, cuz I just don't give a damn about anything anymore. You got me?"

I then turned my body toward her and looking directly in her eyes, used a favorite line of hers, "I'm sure you understand."

I turned to Gail, "Her hours will be set at forty hours a week at her hourly wage. The payments that she has been given will be retroactive back to October 1st, 2008, and applied to her attorney's fees. If she can't agree to that and it's too 'unacceptable,' we can go see the judge."

Pointing at Tiffany, I said, "I'm done with her, I'm done with this negotiation, I'm done you and I'm done with this meeting. The next thing I will do here is to sign the papers showing we've agreed on what I just laid out. That's it! I'm done!"

I sat back in my chair and just stared at the two of them. First at Tiffany and then at Gail.

"Well?" I asked.

By this point, *The Love of My Life* and Gail were well aware of the fact I was no longer willing to play nicely in the sandbox. For three years I had been having to bow down to this smug woman, I had married ten years before and with whom I was so deeply in love for so long.

Tiffany was sniveling again and this time Gail broke the silence. "You know, the amount of money is so small, have you thought about just forgetting about child support altogether?" Tiffany never looked up.

I have no idea what the hell I was thinking when I said, "You know what? You're right. Screw the child support. Twenty-five bucks? In the grand scheme of things twenty-five bucks is fly shit," I said to Gail. "I'll waive the money owed to me. What do I need twenty-five bucks for? If it'll get me outta this dump, let her keep it." God knows Tiffany would have **never** forgiven **anything** when it came to money.

Gail looked as if she had found a diamond earring she had lost. Wide-eyed and grinning, she looked at Tiffany, "Well? That sounds pretty good, doesn't it?"

Tiffany just stared at her, so Gail continued, "I mean, is twenty-five dollars' worth the aggravation of going before the judge?"

"That's what I'm trying to figure out," Tiffany said. "Can I see the statute?" She ***actually*** said that!

"Are you fucking kidding me?" I thought to myself. She doesn't stop!

"You better figure it out soon," I said. "Because I'm about ready to pull my offer off the table, honey."

"Well?" Gail asked Tiffany.

Tiffany finally squeaked out the word, "Fine."

Gail gathered up all the papers, punched the numbers into the computer, and printed the agreement we had just made. After going over the figures and having us confirm the same, she asked us both to sign at the bottom, which we did, but before signing I noticed that Gail had returned the child support figure owed to seventy-three dollars that *I* would owe *Tiffany*.

"Uh, hold on a minute," I said. "You put Tiffany's hours back to thirty hours a week? Why?"

Gail made it a point to show me that the total owed is zero and the amount owed is pretty much moot. It made sense, but in my selfishness I wanted it to show that *Tiffany* owed *me*. With the language reading the "Father owes Mother," it looked as if Tiffany was gifting *me* and not the other way around, as it should have been and actually was.

After thinking about it, I let it go. It just wasn't that important to continue to be petty and demand that the language and figures be corrected, so as to reflect what was truly agreed upon.

What was important was that the child support was set correctly. Anyone who knows Tiffany knows there would be no way in hell she would EVER allow someone, especially me, to get away with not paying what she felt she was entitled to. If they saw the language and figures on the court order, they would know something was amiss. If Tiffany was owed seventy-three cents, she would demand she be paid exactly seventy-three cents, unless she could get more out of me. She will have a tough time explaining away why she would waive seventy-three dollars when it just isn't in her character to do so.

If Tiffany and I were to tell our respective sides to this episode, it would be very clear to everyone who would be telling the truth.

Unless, of course, we were telling our stories to a bunch of law students or actual attorneys or judges or, hell, just about any man who doesn't know Tiffany and her histrionics. Anyone who knows me knows how generous I am and it would be more like *me* to gift *Tiffany*. Hell I may have even waived the seventy-three dollars if it were in my favor. . . .or maybe I wouldn't have.

Money is a very important thing to Tiffany. Sadly, it always has been and always will be. Money will be a large part of her ultimate demise; I'm sure of it.

When Gail left to make copies, as condescendingly as I could, I said to Tiffany, "Think of it as a gift. You're saving a whole twenty-five bucks a month." Tiffany never looked up and as she sat there, stewing in her own vomit, I smiled to myself.

Gail returned and asked us to follow her; she needed to get the judge's signature on the order and once it was signed, she would give us each a copy. We walked out into the expansive hallway that was now relatively empty, as it was well after six o'clock and the bustling of the daytime crowd was absent.

It was actually pretty peaceful in the place considering what misery takes place within the confines of this joint. Tiffany stopped at the entrance of the building, by the metal detectors, and made a phone call. I continued to follow Gail down the hall and before she disappeared into the secured area where only court personnel have access, I sat down. I was so tired from the bullshit I had just been through,

I slumped down in my seat. In the quiet, I could hear Tiffany whimpering into her phone. I'm not sure exactly who it was she was speaking to. A family member would be my guess, but it was nice to hear, after all the crap I had been through in the past several years. She was probably telling them how unfair the courts are and wondering if there's anything that could be done.

Gail finally emerged from the secured hallway, handed me my copy, and thanked me for working with Tiffany saying, "Not many men would have done what you did." I said nothing to her, I just smiled, took my copy of the stipulation, and started for the front door.

As I walked out of the courthouse, and into the evening air, I pulled out my BlackBerry and began to compose a text message. As childish as it was, I wanted to get in one last dig. The text message read: *"You're welcome for the very generous gift I have given you by not making you pay me child support. Are you going to pick up that extra day at the office, now?"* I know that it may have been an asshole move, on my part, but I chuckled as I hit the "SEND" button. Quite frankly, I just didn't give a damn.

I left the parking lot, pulled onto the freeway, and headed for the home of a friend, where my girls were waiting for me. All I could think of was holding Kathryn and Megan in my arms and kissing their beautiful faces. For the first time, in a very long time, I felt a small degree of vindication.

The only other time I felt some sort of vindication was when I received an e-mail, in a thread between me and Tiffany. By the time this was received, it was too late to do anything about it. The manner in which most laws are written, I'm sure there's some kind of Statute of Limitations in place and Tiffany, who probably did her homework, knew she was in the clear. Most likely anyway.

The following is the e-mail described above. It is exactly as it was written and sent between us. Nothing has been altered or changed.

Eric Di Conti wrote:

Tiffany,

To confirm our conversation at 5:49am this morning; Megan is running a fever and will not be going to school today. You stated that you would inquire with Natalie as to whether, or not, Megan can stay with her for the day and would let be know, "in an hour." Presumably, this would be around 7:00am. If she is unable to assist you, I would be notified, at which time I would rearrange my work schedule and take Megan for the day.

This arrangement is contingent upon "Natalie's" availability to be with Megan. I trust that your honesty (as well as the best interest of Megan) will be at the forefront of this arrangement and Jim will NOT be the caregiver for the day.

I will be awaiting your call to be updated on your arrangements for Megan.

Best,

Eric

Tiffany wrote:

I do not lie. Megan is in the capable hands of her beloved Aunt Natalie and resting comfortably today. I will advise as I get closer to Gilbert the time at which I will be able to pick up Katie in front of Panda Express.

TN

Eric Di Conti wrote:

. . . . . her "beloved Aunt Natalie and resting comfortably today?" Sounds like she's in the hospital. LOL. You make me laugh. Megan has a fever, Tiffany. Good Lord, you don't ever stop, do you? Always on stage.

By the way, YES you DO lie. A great deal of the time and it's all for the attention. Let's not forget the vicious lies you told about me molesting the girls and how you told so many people that I beat you all the time. I certainly haven't forgotten and neither have many others. You should really get off that stage you're on because you're not a very good actress.

Is it really that important for you to continue to tell these lies to garner the attention you need? Yes, "continue to tell these lies." Your theatrics, for the little bubble you live in, can only go so far, Tiffany. It's incredible how far-reaching your lies were . . . and are. I spoke to a person this past Tuesday who had never met you, OR me, but they knew who I was from the stories that were told at Risen Savior Church and School. The response was, "Oh my God. That was you?" I was pretty embarrassed at first, but after a while, the tension eased and we both had a chuckle over it. I actually hope I don't see them again.

I guess what I'm trying to say, AGAIN is; Just stop the theatrics, Tiffany and concentrate on Katie and Megan. They need healthy parents.

Best,

Eric

Tiffany ██████████████████ wrote:

I have NEVER accused you of beating me as you have never laid a hand on me. I have NEVER accused you of molesting the children, I simply pointed out issues of concern raised by both myself AND the pediatrician, a disinterested third party.

TN

Date: Fri, 16 Feb 2007 13:16:37 -0800 (PST)
From: "Eric Di Conti" ██████████████████
Subject: Re: 021507-Megan Sick-Confirmation of Conversation
To: "Tiffany" ██████████████████

WOW! This response is a keeper!!!!! You state that there were "issues of concern raised by [you] and the pediatrician, a disinterested third party." Funny. I have ALL of the (subpoenaed) notes from the girls' medical file of Matsumoto and there is NOTHING in there about ***her*** having concerns, but there is a notation that **YOU** said you wanted her to check for signs of molestation. I'm sure you know the rest of the story, don't you?

With regard to you "NEVER" accusing me of beating you. OK, I have a question. What shall I call your testimony at my Order of Protection hearing? Oh! I know! Could it be Perjury? I have it on video ***with*** audio!

Or, what about your false police report? That's perjury, too, when you file these things when they're not true. You might want to check the soles of your shoes; I think you just stepped in something.

Yep. This one's a keeper, Tiffany.

Best,

Eric

Yeah. Just a small degree of vindication, but at least she finally admitted it. Now all I could hope for is an apology—one that will never come. Tiffany apologizes for *nothing*. Ever.

"JUST ONE TIME, YOU COULD STAND INSIDE MY SHOES"

> "Education is when you read the fine print. Experience is when you do not." – Pete Seeger, American Folk Singer

I have had several people tell me they wouldn't be surprised if I still had feelings for Tiffany. A few of those assumed I did. The thought of this completely floors me.

Their feeling is that since we had children together, we will always have a special bond between us. The thought actually nauseates me when I think of ever getting close to this woman again. If I ever had the inkling to do such a stupid thing, my main worry, after her accusations and what I call a catastrophic event, wouldn't be that we'd break up again, but rather, the next time (and it would come) she would do it the *right way*. What I mean is, when this whole thing started, she didn't have an exit strategy, or if she did, she certainly didn't plan it very well.

She made up these vicious lies, told an attorney whom I feel should be disbarred for her actions during the course of her representation of my ex-wife, and her husband fired from his job at the Phoenix Police Department for his. She then went to the Chandler Police Department and wanted me to be arrested for what she claimed were true stories, but never took into consideration what my reaction may have been. She never ran the "what if" scenario through her malcontented brain. She never asked herself what she would do if I stayed and fought, but rather she just assumed I would disappear to the Cayman Islands, to live with my friend Wally Clark, and never return.

Next time, and I believe in my heart the following isn't far from what would happen since she now knows the workings of the court system far better than she did several years prior. In a meeting between she and I alone if it were to happen, some very visible "abrasions" and "bruising" would appear afterward. She would then go to the police and say I assaulted her. I believe this woman (and it's just a ***belief***) is quite ill and *nothing* is beyond her ambit of devious, malicious, perverse, or demented creativity.

This is exactly what I believe her plan was when she dressed so seductively in a little, see-through, terry cloth outfit and showed up at my front door that day. I believe, in my heart-of-hearts that, had I let her into my home that day, even if I didn't fall for her wicked seductiveness, I would not be here today. I would undoubtedly be writing my memoirs from the inside of a jail cell and claiming my innocence to people who just don't care about "rapists."

To those people, who believe a relationship can be rekindled after one of the partners did what this woman did to me (and there have been several), I tell them this: The 1960s icon, Bob Dylan, wrote a song called *Positively Fourth Street*. It's about a guy who finally sees through the person he had been involved with and with whom he was apparently very close. It has been many years since I heard the words of this song, but that last verse has stayed with me since the first time I heard it. The song, as it relates to the person Dylan is singing about, describes the nerve of this particular individual to continue to attempt to be in his life and call him a friend, when Dylan knows what is inside this person's ugly heart. The last verse in the song is the following;

> ***I wish that for just one time you could stand inside my shoes, and I wish that for just one time I could be you.***
>
> ***Yeah, I wish that for just one time you could stand inside my shoes, then you'd know what a drag it is to see you.***

No, people, I have no feelings for what used to be The Love of My Life. When I lay my eyes upon her, it truly is a *drag to see her*.

For the most part, people are good and hold that good in their hearts, allowing some of it to seep out and touch those around them; I truly know this. But there are also people with evil in their hearts. These few are the ones who create strife and discord in our lives and in the world, as a whole. This contention is exacerbated by a switch somewhere in the brain that says, "Get that guy!" And for whatever reason, bad thoughts manifest themselves into a discernible agony for the recipient of the attack, physical, or otherwise. I hope I'm making as much sense to you as I am to me, but then I'm on Ritalin and EVERYTHING makes sense when Ritalin is on board (in its full potency) and I'm on a roll.

I reflected back on what may have been the motivation behind everything Tiffany had done over the past few years and even further back. I thought about why she had been skimming money from our bank accounts for several years. I thought about why she had claimed, to a judge, that I had molested my children. I wondered why she went so far as to file the police report, with the Chandler Police Department, and said that I molested my children and why, when it was found to be a lie, it would remain on my record for the rest of my life. I wondered why she thought she needed an attorney to determine simple child support. I wondered about all the times she hauled me into court to answer half-baked accusations, some of which landed me in handcuffs for questioning the authority of The Court.

Of all the things Tiffany did while we were married and those which she spearheaded, after we were apart, I have been able to come up with only one thing that may have explained her actions.

In the movie, "As Good As It Gets," Melvin Udall, played by Jack Nicholson, summed it up perfectly when he was asked how he was able to write about women so well.

His response to the receptionist, at the office of his publisher, **"I think of a man and then take away reason and accountability,"** was classic. Melvin Udall's response would also hold so true in this case; Tiffany was a woman who acted without ever using *reason*, when plotting her actions and she was certainly never held accountable for anything she did. She just strolled through this fiasco relatively unscathed, her world untarnished, for she is a woman who, by using her good looks and fair amount of theatrics, was able to tweak the system in her favor.

As unfortunate as it may be, our society allows both men and women, who are fortunate enough to be graced with above-average looks, to excel and move through our world with little resistance. Those who have a little bit of money travel even further. However, if a woman who is above average in looks saunters into any setting, any town, USA, she is immediately paid an enormous amount of attention, regardless of circumstance. Some women know how to use their God-given beauty to their advantage, but most use it sparingly. Then there are those who exploit it to the point that anyone around them is affected in the worst ways. Conversely, those of us who have not been graced with extreme beauty and merely fall into the average category, travel to average lengths and through their looks, garner less in life. The smart ones will use other avenues to get what they want out of life and attain greatness through their hearts.

I pray all four of my daughters, who were also graced by God with external beauty, as well as beautiful hearts, stay connected with who they are as people and use the beauty they were graced with sparingly, as they travel through their life, touching those around them with that same beauty in their hearts.

I look back on all I have accomplished and I don't see any true greatness at this point in my life. To be honest, I really haven't accomplished much at all. And although I don't see a great deal that would "wow" anyone, there *are* four accomplishments that I feel are noteworthy in my personal life; my daughters.

Though this may be scoffed at by many others, they are my personal accomplishments, which no one can take from me. Within those four accomplishments, there is another. In everything that made Tiffany, *who* and *what* she was, charismatic, vain, opportunistic, egotistical, self-serving, sanctimonious, egocentric, self-righteous, and arrogant, I was a fighter who finally faced his demons and refused to be beaten. That, and finally standing up and being the father I was to two little girls, is my greatest accomplishment.

RESPONSE TO "NEW PATH"

"Having faith is believing in things that common sense tells you not to." – Unknown

At about 10AM on Friday the 13th, five days after Tiffany's original "New Path" e-mail from the first chapter, I walked into the law offices of Fennemore-Craig, in downtown Phoenix. I took the elevator to the twenty-sixth floor, and walked to the receptionist's desk. I made sure that Tiffany was working that day and when, by a phone call to her desk, it was determined she was, I handed my "New Path" response to the receptionist and told her the envelope was for Tiffany.

As I turned to leave, the lady spoke, "Sir? Tiffany is on her way up. Would you like to wait for her?"

I stopped and pivoted back on one foot toward the receptionist. I'm sure I had a small smirk on my face when I said to her, "Tiffany is my ex-wife. If you were in my shoes, would *you* wait?"

When it was clear the receptionist wasn't going to respond, I gave a short little nod that told her, "I thought so." The doors of the elevator opened, as if on cue and when they did I turned away and stepped inside, making my descent back to the street level.

As I walked out onto Central Avenue and into the sunlight, I'm sure I had a smile on my face. As I walked, I wondered just how long it would be before Tiffany responded to my letter, if ever.

To my absolute astonishment that question would be answered in less than an hour. The following is her response, in its entirety and exactly as she wrote it. Nothing has been changed.

I am in receipt of the 7-page letter you hand-delivered to my office this morning. Clearly, the intent of my email was not as easily understood as I thought it would be. The idea was for BOTH to put aside EVERYTHING and move on. I'm not interested in the regurgitation of facts as you view them, nor am I willing to entertain a list of demands upon me as outlined in your letter.

"Put aside" and "move on" is as base as I can make it. I'm disappointed you were unwilling to do so.

TN

Obviously, she completely dismissed everything I wrote as a "demand," that she wasn't willing to oblige for her children. I, too, was disappointed by this response, as I had wished with scant optimism, but it was just another line of BS she was shoveling with the hope that I accept it; smoothing out the high spots for her, as she shoveled.

For a few hours, I absorbed the words I read, and then at 3:25PM that same day, I responded with the following, in its entirety and exactly as it was sent. Nothing has been changed.

TN,

Mother Of The Year! I figured it wasn't about the girls, but I was hoping beyond hope, I was wrong. Oh well, at least I'm on record with what it'll take for us to be civil.

The Bible clearly states that you cannot move on until you can rectify the wrongs you've committed and, with that, you have a helluva job ahead of you if you can't complete a few little tasks for the girls.

Nothing has been "regurgitated" because you have not dealt with one single, solitary thing. I KNOW you would rather make it all go away and I completely I understand why you would. If it goes away you don't have to be held accountable. I understand, truly I do!

However, it is so unfortunate for the girls that your offer really wasn't about them; it was about you. I expected as much but hoped for so much more.

Read the Bible and keep reading it. One day you can stop pulling excerpts from it to benefit you and your feelings. Once you do that, maybe you can put the girls at the top of your list of priorities.

Funny how, out of all times I begged you to do this, you've never been able to put those you claimed you were "blessed" with on top of that list.

Until the day you can face your demons and deal with them, you'll never be able to have peace that "resonates deep within" you. You'll just be another miserable soul; searching for yourself and that is truly sad. I hope you get well and get right with yourself soon.

Best,

Eric

She never responded and quite frankly, I was not at all surprised. Whenever Tiffany is confronted with an undeniable truth, or a factual statement pulled from a Court document, a statement she made under oath, or any other source where she may have to admit wrongdoing, she will completely ignore it. What she *will* do is, pull inert bits and pieces from the text where she thinks she can expound and exploit those items; just as she did in her response to my requests. Tiffany's real intention is to not only draw the focus away from the crux of the issue but rather find what she thinks is a chink in the armor and attempt to make those minutiae the main focus.

Other times, when there is nothing to find, or draw from, to divert the issue, she will take the, "I-don't-know-what-you're-talking-about" line of defense, i.e.; Eric – "Why did you go to the police and tell them I molested the girls?" Tiffany – "I don't know what you're talking about."

What I mean to say is this: Imagine Tiffany sitting on a couch. Next to her is a massive elephant and emanating from the animal's skin, the gamey pong of urine and filth hanging sticky in the damp and dead air; its presence and stench undeniable. Imagine also, when no one was looking, Tiffany was the one responsible for bringing this putrid-smelling animal into the room.

If someone pointed it out, her response would be, "Elephant? I don't know anything about an elephant, but your shoe is untied, your hair isn't combed, and there's a stain on your shirt. By the way, did you break wind? There's a horribly musty smell in this room and it's quite nauseating. Can you please make it go away? And oh! Why do you ask me about an elephant? What an odd question to ask."

That is what I mean. That is Tiffany. And it only took me about twenty years to realize that is what she has always done.

EPILOGUE

I'm not sure where we will go from here, but I can say this; I will carry on, as I have been, with the two youngest of my beautiful daughters, Katie and Megan. I will stay on the same course that I set on the day the Order of Protection was lifted. I still hold onto the hope that Tiffany will, one day, get well and accept what she has done, ask for forgiveness and complete the tasks, she needs to in order to gain forgiveness and acceptance back into a civil relationship. God willing, one day she will; however, given her desperate need to appear the guiltless victim in everything she does, I highly doubt it.

As I completed this work I was inexplicably drawn back in time; pulled by some unknown force to a crisp and clear winter morning in 2002. On this morning, in Newport Beach, California, I knelt before two tiny little girls who had their eyes fixed on the vast Pacific Ocean. With the waves crashing on the shore behind me, I burrowed my knees into the sand. I looked into their eyes and told them that I loved them more than life itself. Two pairs of eyes stared back at me: one dark brown and the other a pair of green eyes. Though they probably didn't understand what I said to them that day, I made a promise that I would always take care of and protect them. That I would be the best father that any little girl could ever wish for.

My life has been spent taking care of the people I loved most, at whatever cost. Even though I may have never really amounted to much in the eyes of most people, in that I never really made a name for myself in anything I have ever done in my life, one thing I did accomplish is being the best Dad I could be to my two loves, Katie and Megan. The other thing I continue to do is keep the promise that I made to them on that cold winter morning in Newport Beach. Of that promise, I have never faltered. I have and always will, keep that promise.

> *"No matter what pinnacle of success you might reach, children don't take that into consideration. With their honest little hearts, they see you for what you are." – Jimmy Buffett*

FINAL THOUGHTS

"Time is the judge of all offenders." – *William Shakespeare*

On February 17, 2009, with the exception of the "Afterward," I completed this book. It had taken me six months, and a week, to complete it and I did so by using the time between 3:30AM and 5:30AM each morning as my time to reflect back on the many events of my life and try to re-digest them, with the hope of a better understanding of everything.

As my two little girls slept in the beds of and our very modest, little home was at its quietest, I would sit at my computer and write about what had happened. I wanted some closure to everything that transpired and hoped that tapping away at my little laptop, and getting it print, would help me put all the bad memories to rest forever. I'm not sure that I accomplished that, but it sure felt good writing it.

One thing that may never be answered is why it was that Tiffany felt so compelled to allow a hubris-wracked heart out, into the open, to be unleashed on our two daughters and me. For whatever reason, she may have felt I deserved it. Katie and Megan were so innocent in her attack, but they were hit with the full force of that attack. Hubris may sound like a harsh word, to describe Tiffany's actions, but when one looks at the definition of the same, it fits well; "excessive pride, or arrogance, and ambition that usually leads to the downfall of a hero in a classical tragedy." Another one reads, "The infliction of unrealistic pain on innocent people."

In an ancient Greek tragedy, hubris was believed to offend the gods, and lead to vengeance-laden retribution. I think it fits well here and it tears my heart out to know that Katie and Megan had to endure what they did.

I will end this by saying that each one of us, as individuals, is not immune to making poor choices. As people, we are guilty of deceit, slander, theft, immorality, greed, laziness, gluttony, or any other wage of sin against each other, and God. Though the words above are horrible in their own right, any or all can be forgiven. Not *forgotten*, but forgiven.

I gave Tiffany that opportunity and instead of putting her children first, as she claimed was her main focus, she chose for whatever reason, to ignore my plea. She may attempt to tell her own story of how I was as a human being, husband, or father, and quite frankly, her interpretation of how I was, maybe just as horrific to some . . . if you're listening to her version of "her" truth. In my heart, I know I wasn't a bad person then, nor am I now. In fact, I am a far better person by the events that changed my life, so dramatically, on March 2, 2006.

In all the back-and-forth arguing she and I have done over the past several years, there is one thing that Tiffany cannot change; she cannot change *the truth*.

Each and every one of the stories, with regard to police reports, court proceedings, motions, etc., in this book is the absolute truth and each can be verified through public record, in Maricopa County, State of Arizona. For the rest of this book, you'll just have to take my word for it though, it too, is the truth. The truth is something Tiffany cannot deny, but rather just wishes would go away.

At the moment, and sadly, she refuses to step up and accept responsibility for what she has done to another human being and to her daughters, but rather coyly claims the events either never happened, I am exaggerating the facts, I'm being overly sensitive, or I am outright lying. Certainly, when these subjects come up in her presence, she will change the subject rather quickly, but the "facts" can be verified and that is one thing she cannot change.

We are all offenders of some kind. Some are worse offenders than others, but we all will commit offenses against mankind; it's our nature. Just as I have quoted Shakespeare above, I do so again; "Time will judge all offenders." We will all have to face and admit to our wrongdoing sooner, or later, and as soon as we do we can move on in our lives instead of vacillating and floundering in our own private misery.

Dreams? Yeah, I had a bunch of them, but they died on the evening of March 2, 2006. I have some new ones now. The dreams I have now are for a healthy future with Kathryn and Megan. As a father, I also have some making up to do for those I left behind. Though I cannot fix the damage that has been done or change anything in my flawed and broken past, I *can* start over. That's my plan anyway.

Another thought teases my senses and has since this whole ordeal started. It is the thought of filing a lawsuit against Fernando D. Vargas, Esq., forever making the phone call to inform me that Tiffany Nelson was trying to reach me. If it wasn't for him, I may be far better of than I have ever been. Because of that phone call I was made to endure the travesties of the court system in Arizona and will have to live with the fact that from now on, background checks will show I was investigated for "sex crimes against a child."

If only he hadn't made that call, I may have more money in the bank than I have now. I can blame him because he's not around to defend himself and if I did follow through, all Fernando would do is laugh that big booming laugh that always disarmed me. It would be good to see my old friend again. It would be good to speak with him again; to hear that laugh again.

Conversely, if he never made the call that day, in August 1997, then I would have never had the opportunity of the beautiful relationship I have with the two ***true*** loves of my life in this story, Kathryn and Megan. Would I go through it again, knowing that in the end, I would again have my daughters by my side? Absolutely, I would. All things considered, I'm glad he made the call. Truly, I am. Thank you, Counselor.

Eric Di Conti

February 2009

AFTERWARD

A New Judge, With a New Set of Judicial Jokes, a Reuniting, a New Beau, and an Anxious Prayer to Saint Rita

In early 2009, a judicial rotation occurred and the Hon. Eddward P. Ballinger was sent packing to the Juvenile Division to preside over cases of smallish criminals who will, in all probability, occupy the cells of the big boy prisons somewhere down the line. The incoming judge, assigned to Case FC 2006-050978, Nelson vs. Di Conti, was Carey Snyder-Hyatt. At first, I was fairly thrilled to finally have a woman on the bench. One of whom, I figured, couldn't be swayed by the theatrics of my former wife. What I found was that she didn't *seem* to be swayed, but she certainly had her own set of rules, which she enforced as she saw fit. Typical of most every Judge, or Commissioner, I stood before.

As all judges do, in their respective courtrooms, they will take the law and interpret the same; however, it applies to their particular mood on any given day. I imagine they walk into their chambers and decided what their mood is before they enter the actual courtroom. It's up to them who they will vilify; "Am I pissed off at something today? Hmmm. Let's just look at my list and see who I should crucify today."

In a scene from the movie "French Kiss," Meg Ryan said it best when speaking to her co-star, Kevin Kline, "Happy-Smile. Sad-

Frown. Use the corresponding face for the corresponding emotion." Catch a judge on a bad day and one will easily understand what the above means.

Minute Entries will be written, with Orders that The Court expects all to follow, and dispersed to respective parties, via the United States Postal Service. These orders will say things like, "Parties will bring with them any documents, or evidence, that will support their respective arguments, pertaining to income, financial stability, living expenses, etc."

Sounds easy enough to any layman reading it, but walk into court, as I did on January 28, 2010, at 9:00AM, with all the necessary documents supporting my financial state, when the good judge has an "angry face" attached to her nasty "emotion," you'll never get the chance to present any of it.

As I explained before, these proceedings are videotaped, so all one has to do is, provide a crisp new twenty-dollar bill to the court for a copy, to verify the following:

It didn't matter that I had bank statements showing one account overdrawn by nearly three hundred dollars and another account with less than one hundred dollars. It didn't matter that my unemployment was reduced by eighty dollars a week for child support arrearages. It didn't matter that my "income" was such that if I reached the "poverty level," it would greatly improve my standard of living. It didn't matter that my bills and cost of living exceeded my income.

What *did* matter and quite frankly, I believe pissed her off was that I was paying my bills and feeding my girls before making sure that Tiffany was being paid. It also *really* irritated her that my rent/mortgage was being forgiven and being paid by a close friend until I got back on my financial feet. You read that correctly; Judge Hyatt was irritated that, by the generosity of a friend, I had been relieved of the burden of having to pay to keep a roof over our heads. She glared at me from her seat, on high, and stated in a most condescending manner, "You sure have some nice friends."

She demanded to know my weekly expenses, which I recited back with only the major items necessary to maintain a minimal existence; electric bill, cell phone (I had no home phone), gas for my car, minimal groceries, and an absolute minimum for extras, like buying a *used* DVD for the girls and me to watch. She neglected to calculate my monthly car payment of three hundred dollars and refused to calculate the arrearages being taken from my unemployment, which dropped my income to one hundred eighty dollars a week.

I'm not certain what kind of device she was using to calculate my expenses, but the Honorable Carey Hyatt somehow decided that from the seven hundred and eighty dollars, I collected each month from unemployment, I had "about five hundred dollars in disposable income." Instead of using a calculator, she may have been using an abacus and didn't have a strong command of its function. With her "findings" she ruled that I was to pay Tiffany two hundred fifty dollars a month towards, what she figured to be, some four thousand eight hundred dollars in attorney's fees. She was puzzled by my audacity to keep my children fed before paying Tiffany what she was owed. All Tiffany did during this exchange was smirk as the good judge was admonishing me for my *indiscretions*.

The Honorable Carey Snyder Hyatt stated, in her courtroom, before *anything* is paid, my debt to Ms. Nelson must be paid first. She stated, "That's what I care about. Since these attorney's fees were generated from a child support issue, they are treated as child support arrearages and must be paid before anything else is paid." Bottom line was it was my obligation to pay the arrearages and *then* pay my bills, which included caring for my daughters. Yes, you read that correctly, as well. It's in the transcripts.

That day, nothing mattered beyond the surly mood of Honorable Carey Snyder Hyatt and the fact that she wanted Tiffany to be paid in full.

When I again attempted to show the Court what I had to bolster my financial state, the good judge said, "I'm really not interested in seeing what you have, Mr. Di Conti." She was more concerned with making sure the attorney's fees Tiffany had generated, were going to be paid at a rate of $250 per month. It didn't matter that my bills nearly exceeded my income. It didn't matter that due to the police report, identifying me as a pedophile, surfaced with each background check and, as such, made it extremely difficult to find a job of any consequence.

I guess Honorable Carey Snyder Hyatt felt I was exaggerating and being overly pushy when I brought up the police report and employment background checks, for the second time because she snapped at me, "Where is it? Give me a copy of it. I want to see it!"

I explained that these reports are not *handed out*, but rather prospective employees are *informed* of the findings in the background check. Her response was something to the effect of, "Well if you can't produce a report, then I don't believe you."

Toward the end of the hearing, the good judge asked me if there was any way I could pay this debt and close the books on it. If I had any friends that could loan me the money.

I said, "Your Honor, if there was *any* way I could pay this right now, I swear on my daughter's life I would do so, just to make her (Tiffany) go away, but even if I did, as she has proven in the past, next month it'll be something new, she'll want the Court to address. I truly wish I had the money to pay her, but even if I had the means to pay this debt right now, it wouldn't matter. I would be dragged back into court next month and your time would be wasted further. She did this in Judge Ballinger's Court and she'll do it in this Court."

My statement didn't seem to move her at all. Her final ruling was that I pay Tiffany two hundred fifty dollars a month and a follow-up hearing was set for a date in May to confirm that I was, in fact, making the payments as ordered. The Honorable Carey Snyder-Hyatt cautioned that if I was late, or missed making any of the payments, before the next hearing, I would be incarcerated until the balance was paid, in full. She informed me that, if incarcerated, I would "be given a job and paid minimum wage. The money [I] earn would go toward paying [my] debt and [I] would stay there until the debt is paid. So don't miss any payments."

Of course, she demanded I be in court on the day of review, in the event she needed to have me taken into custody.

Now there's a great way for the Court to force someone to be a good parent! Sit in jail for a couple of months to make sure an attorney's pockets are lined. And this is coming from a judge that claims the laws are geared to protect the interests of minor children. It has nothing to do with the children at all and everything to do with making sure her fellow attorneys are cared for.

It is amazing how much power a judge has in his, or her, courtroom. In their respective ecosystems, no rules govern judges other than the manner in which *they* interpret the law and how *they* rule according to that interpretation. It's actually quite scary how easily a judge can decide to hold an individual in contempt and have that individual taken into custody for the most minor of offenses. And the law protects the judge for nearly any decision he, or she, makes while sitting on the bench, no matter how unreasonable, or incompetent, the judge may be. Either way, you're pretty much screwed and there is absolutely nothing anyone can do to fight it without lots of money for yet, another attorney.

The following month, just as I had warned, "next month it'll be something new," Tiffany wanted the court to rule on another matter. She filed an "Emergency Request to Force Father to Medicate Minor Daughter."

This little snap was the offspring of a long-running conviction of Tiffany's that Katie, now eleven years old, is afflicted with bipolar disorder. Before that, she was convinced Katie had Asperger's Syndrome. Before that, it was Obsessive Compulsive Disorder. Then it was Autism. Prior to that, it was some sort of mental illness "caused by eating foods with partially hydrogenated oils." The list went on and on, channeled by some random soul commenting on some random characteristic of a random family member, or some random person. As soon as Tiffany heard this description, her response would be, "Oh my God! Katie does that!" And a new campaign for a new diagnosis is started.

By far, the most laughable claim Tiffany made was after she returned home from a long day of running errands and heard a four-year-old Katie yell, "Aw, Fuck!" while she played in her bedroom. Though I tried to explain to Tiffany, without any success, Katie had spent the entire day with me, while I was working on a project in the house. It didn't matter that my language is normally extremely colorful during these projects and expletives fly unrestrained; Tiffany was convinced that Katie was afflicted with Turret's Syndrome.

Though that may seem funny now, the sad part is that with each affliction Tiffany claimed Katie had, she actually spent the time to seek out a doctor to confirm each "illness" and oftentimes I never knew about the appointment with the doctor until it was over. Even more heartbreaking is each time the little voice in Tiffany's head claimed a new malady, poor little Katie was hauled around town and to endure another evaluation. Sadder still is that over the years Tiffany's convictions escalated and by the summer of 2008, she stepped over the line.

Tiffany had gone to the girls' pediatrician, Dr. Edward Madrid, in Chandler, Arizona, and claimed that Katie was bipolar. Though it was an outright lie, she also claimed to Dr. Madrid that I knew she was there and I was completely on board with ruling out bipolar disorder.

She claimed that her father had "terrible mood swings and was bipolar." In diagnosing his mood swings, his doctor said they were actually caused by a hydrocephalic ailment, or, in layman's terms, water on the brain. She also used the fact that I am afflicted with a severe form of ADHD to bolster her claim and somehow got Dr. Madrid bought into it.

Before I get into this, I want to begin by saying that I believe, in my heart, Edward Madrid is an excellent doctor, for whom I have an incredible amount of respect, however on this occasion he was caught up in Tiffany's theatrics.

On this visit, after explaining her "fears," Tiffany was given a checklist of signs and symptoms of bipolar disorder, which numbered around twenty-four. Amazingly, Tiffany checked off nearly everyone. I would think that if an individual really did show all of these symptoms, they might be institutionalized. Even more amazing is that Dr. Madrid, without directing Tiffany to a mental health professional, diagnosed Katie, on the spot and prescribed a medication to treat bipolar disorder.

A day, or two, afterward I received an e-mail from Tiffany outlining the appointment, the "diagnosis," and the medication that was prescribed for Katie. I was incensed at Tiffany's brazen act of malevolence and the unbelievable irresponsibility on the part of both, Tiffany and Dr. Madrid. After reading the e-mail on my BlackBerry and as soon as I had calmed down, I called the "exchange" and left an urgent message for Dr. Madrid to call me. He returned my call within fifteen minutes.

He could tell that I was livid with what Tiffany had done and that I was profoundly frustrated with his ridiculous diagnosis, based solely on a checklist provided by his office. I told him I was further disappointed by the fact that Tiffany had claimed I *knew* about the appointment when I had actually just learned of it. In his defense, Dr. Madrid had no way of knowing if I was aware of the appointment and I had to allow some latitude there.

I told Dr. Madrid that I wanted Katie to be taken off the medication immediately, but much to my consternation I was told that he "couldn't legally take her off of the medication, once she started to take it" that I would now "need a court order" to do so. I'm sure my blood pressure was spiking at this point, but there was nothing that could be done; Ed Madrid was hanging over a barrel and I think he knew he had put himself there by his own mistake.

Tiffany, on the other hand, couldn't be happier. She was now able to look at herself as a poor mother, whose child is afflicted with a mental illness and she made damned sure Katie was medicated each, and every, day. She made it a point, whenever she got the chance, to let people know, "My daughter is bipolar."

When the girls were with me, I refused to give Katie this medication, but rather left it up to Katie if she felt the need to "take a pill"; the entire time she was with me, she never once asked to take a pill.

The caveat to this is that it took several months, after Katie's "diagnosis," to get the matter in front of a judge. I described how it came to be that Katie was now taking the medication she did not need and pleaded with the Court (at the time it was the ever-Honorable, Eddward P. Ballinger) to order the medication be stopped. I was told if I wanted it stopped I would have to get Katie evaluated by an expert, in the field of psychiatry, and I was to do so at my own expense. The medication would continue to be dispensed.

Once again, the judicial system stepped up to show how completely ineptly some of these sitting judges rule on certain matters while continuing to claim the children are at the center of their world. As hideously pathetic as Judge Ballinger's ruling was, there was an upside; it was on the record that I could seek a second opinion.

It would take over a year before I would finally get Katie into seeing a psychologist named Jane deBrown, who, in turn, directed me to a true expert in the field of psychiatry and mental disorders; his name is Dr. Lauro Patino.

That I was finally able to get Katie into seeing a real mental health *expert*, instead of just accepting the diagnosis of a general practitioner in pediatrics. And this is what caused the sword to be drawn by Tiffany and before a more accurate diagnosis happened, she was going to make damned sure that she maintained some kind of control.

This action was the catalyst for Tiffany's request that the Court intervened, and "force" me to medicate Katie. Tiffany's action was also predicted with incredible accuracy and I reminded the Court (Hon. Carey Hyatt) of that very prediction in my "response" to Tiffany's request for the Court's intervention. I'm not so sure that the good judge took any pleasure in being reminded that Tiffany did exactly what I said she would do, and in the time frame I predicted.

On a side note: I went back and counted each filing over the past twenty-four months, in which Tiffany submitted for review, requesting the Court to act, or rule, on; they numbered twenty-six; Slightly more than one a month.

In my response to Tiffany's "Emergency Request," I gave the Court a very detailed account of how I was moving forward, in accordance with Judge Ballinger's ruling, in seeking "a second opinion." After reading that Katie had seen Dr. deBrown and Dr. Patino and was scheduled to undergo an EEG, to determine an exact diagnosis of her mental state, the Honorable Carey Snyder-Hyatt did what is a normal and common practice within the court system, when there is no desire to address something; she ignored it.

Instead of keeping the "wellbeing of the children" at the forefront of her rulings, Judge Hyatt ordered a Parenting Coordinator to intervene. She wanted no involvement in ruling to force me to medicate my daughter, or to have Tiffany stand down until all the tests had been completed, but she damned sure wanted that two-hundred fifty bucks paid to Tiffany every month. The Honorable Carey Snyder-Hyatt is just another laughably biased judge, who is as pitiful and ineffective on anything beyond making sure those attorney's fees are paid. But we shouldn't lose sight of the fact that she vehemently claims, "What matters most in my courtroom, is the children." She couldn't give two shits about children in her courtroom.

The results of the EEG were read and explained to me, on March 11, 2010.

Not surprisingly, Dr. Patino accurately diagnosed Katie, not with bipolar disorder, but rather a "very mild form of ADHD," passed down from me. Dr. Patino also informed me he would be letting Edward Madrid know that from that point forward, he (Dr. Patino) would be addressing any matters concerning Katie's ADHD and that Dr. Madrid should stick to any medical concerns. Dr. Patino also said he would be filing a report with the Court on the matter, as well.

It was a long battle, with Tiffany fighting the whole way to keep an accurate diagnosis from being realized, but it was one that was important for me to fight; for Katie. No one else seemed to care what was happening to my daughter and it is my belief that the people involved would rather have it just go away, so it didn't have to be addressed. I forced the issue and made it something that couldn't be ignored. I made sure no one could ignore what was being done to Katie and though I'm not sure I made very many people happy about it; I don't really give a damn.

*NOTE: With regard to the following, it is very important to note that Tiffany has never been formally diagnosed of having any mental illness whatsoever. The following text is not intended to infer she **is** afflicted with the same, but rather it is merely giving an account of my conversations with mental health professionals regarding Tiffany, and the manner in which I have viewed and conveyed her behavior to them. Please keep this in mind as you read on.*

I have personally recounted, to mental health professionals, Tiffany's history of claims that Katie has been afflicted with a vast array of mental illnesses. From those professionals, a couple of terms, in reference to Tiffany, have surfaced. Two of the terms I have heard multiple times are Histrionic Personality Disorder and Munchausen Syndrome by Proxy. Of course, they have been used in my description of Tiffany's claims and actions. I want to be clear that she has never been formally diagnosed with these maladies, but *my opinion* is much different.

My Old Friend

Fernando D. Vargas, Esq. – The Count and the Counselor

Katie, Me and Megan at the home of Fernando Vargas

As is obvious from the photographs in this book, I was finally reunited with Fernando Vargas. It was important for me to speak to him again to inform him of this book and to make sure he had no problem with me including our story. He was a huge part of it and without him, this story would have never happened. Had he protested his being included, I'm quite certain I would have ignored him. I had to include him. I had no choice.

After about ten years, with no contact, I called Fernando one afternoon. His voice hadn't changed a bit. We reminisced for a while, laughed, and talked about the times we shared when we were much younger and a lot more naïve than we were today. We laughed about the color of our hair fading from the luster of browns to a dismal gray. Well, I laughed; Fernando bellowed that very familiar laugh of his.

We made jokes about our hairlines having receded to the point that when standing in the direct sunlight, the glare would cause airplanes to veer off course and sunscreen was now necessary when outdoors. We laughed about the fact that my girls think it is funny that I have gained so much weight. And I told the girls that what *I* thought was funny, is infanticide. They looked at me sideways when I made them look it up in the dictionary, but when they absorbed and understood the definition, they didn't think I looked so fat anymore.

After the initial backslapping and bantering, Fernando asked, "So, how ya been, Count? Really."

"Well, Counselor," I started. "I wrote a book."

I gave Fernando a brief rundown about the past several years and with those years, the misery they carried. He listened in silence, his booming laugh gone. I told him the content of the book I had written and that due to his phone call, so many years before he was a big part of the story. I also told him I would be traveling to California, to see my mother; with me, would be my girls. I wanted Katie and Megan to meet Fernando. He immediately said he had a deposition the morning we were passing through Ranch Cucamonga, but would clear his schedule for the remainder of the day, so we could get together. Fernando, as always, did exactly as he promised.

We had dinner at his home and reunited with his lovely wife Sylvia, his son Fernando D. Vargas, Jr., whom I hadn't seen since his second birthday, and his youngest; a very precocious little girl named Delila, pronounced Dee-lie-lah.

We also met his true German Sheppard "attack dog." Fernando said he wanted to make sure his family was safe at all times. That would be an understatement. The dog, whose name, due to the deep scarring of my psyche escapes me, had a problem with anyone breaching the perimeter of the family compound; that included the gardeners. There were times, if the beast wasn't locked away in its wrought iron cage, the gardening was not done. Once the gardeners grasped the fact the animal was loose, they pretty much broke the land speed record to get off the property. What made this apparent were the sounds of snarling and foamy spit spraying through the cracks of the wooden fence. The dog's viciousness was even more convincing once he began chewing away (and consuming) large chunks of the back fence. I'm not sure how many times Fernando had the fence replaced and I dared not ask.

This unnatural specimen did not understand a word of English and responded only to commands in German; and even then, he didn't listen very well. Fernando asked if I'd like to see his dog and when I agreed, I saw firsthand what he was trying to tell me.

The animal was in an enclosure measuring twelve feet by six feet and I thank God that the wrought iron was thick enough that this beast couldn't chew through it because that is exactly what he tried to do. With the exception of the foul, rabid dogs portrayed on TV, I have never before seen an animal so angry, with such a yearning for human flesh, as this beast. It truly *did* try to chew through the metal enclosure and the whole time Fernando was screaming at him in German to calm down. The dog didn't care; he wanted some meat. We retreated back into the house, where we stayed until we left.

The three, or four, hours we spent together disappeared in a flash. It was Thursday, so Court Cases and depositions were waiting for Fernando in the morning. We said our goodbyes and Fernando walked us to the car. I gave him a hug and told him I hoped it wouldn't be too long before we saw each other again. He agreed, but we both knew it may be longer than we would like. Though the sun had set, the sky was still a beautiful blue, but I knew in time it would fade to black. Like the ending of the day, it was as if our reuniting was finally ending a chapter in both our lives; one which should have been closed long ago. As I did for so many years, I will miss my old friend and think of him often until we meet again.

Another "New" Man and Another New Desire

Another development in this story is that Tiffany has found, yet another man to share her life. Little Jimmy Norton, the guy who, in the words of Tiffany, "is a better man than I will ever be," was put on waivers and finally sent down the road.

In late 2009, an "old friend from school," Ted Bessa, was picked up as a free agent and brought in as his replacement. Ted resides in North Carolina and makes the trip to Arizona as often as he can, so they can spend time together. They ended up getting married (I think) in 2013 and then divorced in 2018.

Toward the end of March 2010, Katie and I stayed up late one night; just talking. Megan was tired and went to bed. It was so nice to have a conversation with my little girl who, at just ten and a half years old, was quickly becoming a young woman. It could be the fact that she has seen much more than other girls her age, but she is well beyond her years in maturity. I am both delighted and frightened by this. The fact remains that we can converse on a level far above most kids her age. Come to think of it, I have conversations with my girls that exceed the intellect of many much older than they are.

During our conversation, Katie asked me where I would live if I could move anywhere away from Arizona. My answer was an unequivocal "Back to California."

"Hmmm. Mom wants to move to North Carolina. Would you ever want to live there?"

I chuckled at the notion because I knew where this was going.

"No, honey. North Carolina is not a place I would choose to live."

She then said, in a random manner, that her mother told her and Megan that she wants me to be happy. She also said that her mother told the two of them that I could also sell wine in North Carolina.

"Happy?" I asked. "That's pretty funny."

"Why is that funny?" Katie responded.

I said, "Because if someone wants another person to be 'happy', they would do things to *make* the other person happy. Considering all that has gone on, I just can't see where that statement would be true."

In retrospect, I had never seen Tiffany do anything to bolster the happiness of anyone, other than that of her own.

Nonetheless, Tiffany told Katie she only wants me to be happy, but for some reason cannot understand why I would not want to move to North Carolina. Me, follow her so she can be with her boyfriend and I can start over in another state? She makes me laugh.

While Ted lives in North Carolina he served in a branch of the military and is employed by the United States Army. I thank him for his service. In that respect, *this* guy is a better man than I am, because I couldn't do his job. Wouldn't *want* to do his job.

Though she swears up and down she has always wanted to move to North Carolina, in all the years I have known her, I have never heard that state mentioned, as a place she wanted to live. Why now? She had told the girls the move was completely for them and it would be a better place for them to grow up, but for even a mildly intelligent individual, I think it's a pretty easy question to answer.

There is no other reason to randomly pick North Carolina, as a place to live, other than she wants to be closer to her newest beau. I get that. If I had a new gal in my life and I wanted to be with her all the time, I too would want to move where she was. I get it. I do. No need for conjugal visits.

Tiffany just doesn't want to admit it to the girls and I *don't* get *that*. After all that has gone on, she still cannot be honest. She wants them to believe the move is "for them" and it that is just a remarkable coincidence that her beau, Ted, resides there. Remarkable indeed.

The fact that she wants to move to North Carolina is one thing, but the fact she wants to take the girls with her has proved a little problematic. It's pretty sad that she has enlisted the help of the girls to coax me into moving out of Arizona and to North Carolina. And for no other reason than it is a "place for the girls to be raised." In order to make a move like that, she must first get me to do one of two things; get me to follow her, or get me to relinquish custody of my daughters. Neither of which will ever happen.

The way she is going about it, it's as if she thinks I have no idea that Ted lived there. What makes this quest even more laughable is that Tiffany actually believes I would buy her story and just mindlessly follow her to North Carolina, because it is "in the best interest of the girls" and has absolutely nothing to do with Ted Bessa. It has even less to do with the fact that the city in which she wishes to move is the very same city in which Ted Bessa resides. Of all the cities, in all the states, in this great country, she throws a dart at a map and the point of that dart pierces the very place where her new beau lives. How Ironic is *that*?

I think it is quite apparent that her suggested move to North Carolina, has absolutely nothing to do with anything, but her own desires. It has always been this way and always will be this way.

The following week Katie reported back to her mother and relayed our conversation. Though I did not hear the statement myself, the following is what Katie told me her mother said; "If your father wants to stay in this Sugar Honey Ice Tea hole of a state then fine, but he's just being stupid. Mom said the other word, though." I chuckled at that.

Of course, I was being stupid for not wanting to go. Why *wouldn't* anyone want to follow his, or her, ex-spouse wherever they may go? Especially after the misery I was put through. Where do I sign up?

During our follow-up conversation, I reminded Katie that it wasn't me who moved to this "Sugar Honey Ice Tea hole of a state" in the first place, that it was her mother who picked this place. She did so by spiriting her and Megan out of California while I was at work. And quite frankly, if it wasn't for her mother, we wouldn't even be here............"in this Sugar Honey Ice Tea hole of a state."

I mused that in two years, when she finds another man she wants to be with, (historically, her time with a man had been about two years – I crushed any record previously set record for longevity in a relationship) she will undoubtedly have the innate urge to move again. And if by some warped and perverse reason I *did* follow her to North Carolina, when she found someone else and wanted to move, she would want me to follow. Nope. I'm a California guy.

She has since moved on, yet again, to a man she was seeing off and on, when we first met in 1992 and even after we were dating exclusively. She has come full circle . . .

A Prayer To Saint Rita

Saint Rita of Cascia, an Italian, Augustine saint who was canonized by Pope Leo XIII became a saint in 1900. Rita is the Patron Saint of Hopeless and Impossible Causes, but ironically, on her list of patronages, are the words "marital problems." I laugh every time I think of it.

A Catholic priest said that if I wanted to pray for my seemingly impossible situation, Saint Rita is my gal; so I did, though not every day. With the most recent Court Order to see a Parenting Coordinator, my situation seems to be getting more and more "impossible." Rita must be busy working on another grim project more dreadful than my own, but every now and then I throw a shout-out to old Rita with the hope of hearing her yell back at me. Nothing yet.

I do hope this ends soon and I hope it ends with Tiffany facing her demons and defeating them. I did it and, next to my girls, it was the best thing I have ever done.

Eric Di Conti

April 2010

FEDERAL TRIAL OF PAXTON ANDERSON AND JOEY PLANY

END OF THE LINE......FOR THE NEXT 15 YEARS, OR SO

June 2014

Paxton Anderson and Joey Plany were finally indicted and on May 8, 2014, brought to trial for Bank Fraud, Conspiracy to Commit Bank Fraud, Forgery, and a plethora of other charges; 31 in all. The government dropped three of those charges before the trial got underway. Bruce Feder accepted money from Paxton for representation and Tom Hoidal was taking money from Joey, for one of the most inept showings in legal defense I've ever seen. Not that I'm an expert, but because I think I could have done a better job of representing these two guys.

With the Honorable Susan Bolton on the bench, Feder, a high-dollar attorney, fumbled through his questioning on every witness. His questioning was disjointed and illogical. He didn't seem to know where he was going with any of his questions and most were overruled by Bolton on the objection from Federal Prosecutor, Kevin Rapp. Hoidal was no better. This guy looked so old, his first "selfie" was done on canvas, in oil. Some thought he would die before the trial concluded. I did, anyway.

The one word he used more than anything was, "Uh" and could be heard as many as ten times in each sentence—no exaggeration.

"Well, uh, Miss Gutierrez, uh, uh, when did you, uh, go, uh to the, uh, bank with, uh, Mr. Plany, to uh, drop of the, uh, paperwork?" If this guy ever decided to go skydiving, where you have to count to ten, then pull the ripcord, Hoidal, because he would make himself a part of the terrain by the count of "ten," would be told to count to "One."

It took an eternity for him to get a question out. As these guys floundered through this trial I wondered how anyone ever hired these two attorneys. They failed miserably and laughably.

One thing Feder and Hoidal attempted to do, was pin the whole conspiracy and theft of millions of dollars from three banks, on Shawna Gutierrez and me. Shawna, whom I met and worked with at Nitti Brothers Construction and personally brought over to Dynamite Custom Homes, was the Office Manager. She witnessed most of the illegal activity going on in the office and was one of the government's star witnesses and basically buried both Anderson and Plany with her testimony alone. The detailed information I gave them was merely gravy.

Their theory was that Shawna Gutierrez and Eric Di Conti conspired to take the homebuilding business from Paxton in a hostile takeover. Why? Because they said we were supposedly having a torrid affair and each of us had a gluttonous love of and desperate need for money.

Of course they could not provide any proof of a relationship between Shawna and I, because we weren't having one. When asked pointedly if she and I had a relationship, her response was, "Ew.... He's like my Dad's age." In 2006 Shawna was 29 years old; I was 47. Shawna's father was 48. She was right. I was *like* her father's age. It's safe to say there was no interest from either of us.

Another thing they couldn't explain away were the numerous thoroughbred horses that were purchased with the bank's money, nor could they explain away the many forged documents that were submitted to the banks, on behalf of Dominique and Mark Acre and Tasha Henstein. It just wasn't possible.

One forgery that Feder and Hoidal swore up and down, was a legitimate signature of Tasha Henstein turned out to be a pretty humorous spectacle. He claimed he had several people he was willing to call to the stand and testify they *personally* watched Tasha Henstein sign her name. The problem was when Hoidal cross-examined Tasha and demanded she tell the Court she had, in fact, signed her name on the contract, she claimed she never signed the document.

Hoidal demanded, "How do you expect this court and this jury to believe you never signed this document? Can you prove you never sign it?"

Her response was a dagger in Hoidal's heart and the entire defense team.

"I wouldn't misspell my own name."

Tasha's name was, in fact, misspelled on the document. Both defense attorneys stood, red-faced in the federal courtroom, with no way to make that signature and their blunder in open court, disappear. Even Judge Susan Bolton smirked.

During the closing arguments, two things really stick out and are so preposterous, I was floored when the defense team addressed the jury. The first one, from Bruce Feder, caused me to snort out loud. It brought the eyes of Judge Bolton my way. I sunk down in my seat.

Feder pleaded with the jury saying, "Look at him over there. Little Paxton Anderson. A high school dropout, with little education, who's had menial jobs his whole life. It's just not possible for him to think up a scheme like this all by himself. He's a good guy. I mean, I love the guy."

It was difficult not to laugh out loud. I thought to myself, "Wow! Don't tell Bill Gates of Steve Jobs that." Kevin Rapp would mirror my thoughts in his rebuttal of the defense's closing.

Hoidal's comments caused me to almost swallow my tongue. In all of his rhetoric, the one statement that Hoidal made in his closing that I believe drove the knife right into their clients' hearts was the belief that because the contractor can request pay application from the bank, "the forgeries don't matter." He truly said that.

Then he said it again. "Ladies and Gentlemen of the jury, it doesn't matter that they forged documents. They were well within their right to ask for pay applications from the bank. You need to forget about the forgeries. They just don't matter."

Um, correct me if I'm wrong, but isn't it always illegal to forge the name of another person for personal gain? Was this guy serious? I couldn't believe it and neither could anyone else in the courtroom, but it was out there and everyone heard it. Hoidal thought he did a tremendous job. Yeah, of sealing the fate of your clients.

Kristena Hansen, of the Phoenix Business Journal, wrote two articles on the trial. The first was published on May 23, 2014; *Federal Jury Trail Underway for Arizona Home Builder's Mortgage Fraud Scheme*. The other was published, June 5, 2014, the day of the verdicts.

Considering the amount of money from which Paxton Anderson and Joey Plany defrauded banks (M & I Bank had, by far, the biggest loss), it's hard to believe that this didn't draw more attention from other media sources. Though it was an excellent article and it delighted me that Anderson and Plany have finally been *outed* publicly, for their indiscretions, there is so much more about these two, Ms. Hansen couldn't possibly have put to paper. Unfortunately, she must state only the facts of this case and doesn't have the latitude to offer up her opinion of what she saw in court, but I can.

I was in the courtroom when the verdicts were read. Paxton Anderson and Joey Plany were originally charged with conspiracy to commit bank fraud, bank fraud, forgery, and a plethora of other unlawful activities. As Anderson and Plany listened to the verdicts, the emotions and expressions of these two men spoke volumes of who they are; especially Anderson. He had his eyes locked on the court clerk. I had my eyes on the defendants.

The court clerk read each count in succession, "As to Count One in the indictment, defendant Paxton Anderson, Guilty. Defendant Joey Plany, Not Guilty."

Anderson's lips parted slightly as he turned his gaze from the court clerk to the jury. He had a smirk on his face. His look was that of disbelief. Plany, whose eyes were fixed on the table in front of him, immediately looked up to the court clerk, also in disbelief.

"As to Count Two in the indictment, Paxton Anderson, Guilty. Joey Plany, Not Guilty."

Anderson's eyes were still on a jury in further disbelief. Plany glanced at his attorney, Thomas Hoidal, as if to ask, "Really?" He then returned his attention to the court clerk. He was visibly relieved; bordering on excited.

Count Three was another "Not Guilty" verdict for Plany, who adjusted himself in his seat. Anderson caught his third "Guilty" verdict and his eyes narrowed. His smirk was gone.

I, too, was bordering on disbelief. I couldn't believe Plany had three straight "Not Guilty" verdicts. I was thinking to myself that this could not be happening. Where is the justice? Is he going to get off on these crimes? Then Plany caught his first "Guilty" verdict and then another and another and another and another. They started rolling in. Plany's eyes went back to staring at the tabletop in front of him.

With the exception of saying a few words to his attorney, Bruce Feder, Paxton Anderson never stopped looking toward the jury, as if to ask how they could possibly find him guilty. By now, he was glaring at them, in fact. They were both initially charged with 31 various counts. A few were dropped.

Paxton Anderson believes he should have never been charged in the first place. How do I know this? Because I know Paxton Anderson and Joey Plany. I know them both very well. I was the Licensed Contractor and Qualifying Party for Dynamite Custom Homes during the time they were defrauding banks and I had first-hand knowledge of their business dealings.

I was also the person who brought a stack of evidence to the Federal Government, as proof they were defrauding many people of their respective life savings and dreams of building a home in which, they could retire.

The dream homes of these people were never built. Instead, the millions of dollars people put up for homes were replaced with racehorses named Darlin, Gold Hearted, KO Kitty, House Of Soviet's, Magic Alphabet, Miracle Worker, Cap and Gown, Rah Rah Bertie, Shin Fein, Brave Broco, Quiet Celebrity, Water Walker, Sweet Melody, and many, many others. I still have the Bill of Sale for these horses as well as, copies of wire transfers from the account of Dynamite Custom Homes to numerous horse breeders in Lexington, Kentucky. They are the same copies the FBI used to arrest and the Federal Government used to convict Anderson and Plany.

Paxton Anderson owed me just under $10,000 for work I had done for him on some custom homes and after a conversation with some church officials at Risen Savior Lutheran Church in Chandler, regarding misappropriated funds, Paxton decided he was no longer obligated to pay me what I was owed. When I warned him that I had a lot of very incriminating evidence that could put him away for a long time, his response was not surprising. He told me that he is untouchable and had the best lawyers in the land. "You can't touch me," he said.

His recklessness and disregard for the law became so out of control that I felt I, too, was in grave danger of going down with Anderson and Joey in a hail of federal charges. I went to the FBI and told my story. That was in July of 2007 and seven long years later, I was finally sitting in the gallery of a Federal Courtroom, listening to the jury hand down "Guilty" verdict after "Guilty" verdict, for their offenses against the banking industry, numerous subcontractors, who were never paid for their work and several other people, including Dominique and Mark Acre and Will and Tasha Henstein. They lost literally everything they had when Paxton Anderson promised to build their dream home and then vanished with all the money. I wish now, that I had gone to the authorities much sooner. Had I done so, perhaps the monetary losses of Mark and Dominique and Will and Tasha would have been less. To them, I offer my sincerest apologies.

I am no psychologist, nor do I have any education in psychology, but I am well read enough to have an opinion on Paxton Anderson; he is (in my uneducated opinion) a sociopath with little or no remorse for anything he's ever done. In fact, he was very clear in telling me, "if someone isn't smart enough to know they're being taken, then they deserve to lose everything they own." Paxton Anderson has no moral compass. He lacks any moral responsibility. He is completely devoid of any social conscience and his assertions were chilling.

He truly did believe this and his reaction, as the verdicts were being read further bolster my belief he is a sociopath. He was in complete disbelief and utter shock that he was hearing the word "Guilty" over and over and over again. Twenty-five times "Guilty" echoed in the courtroom for Paxton Anderson and twenty-two times for Joey Plany. Anderson sat there, lips slightly parted, and asked his attorney, "What the hell is going on?" What is going on? Indeed.

I think Joey Plany saw the writing on the wall during closing arguments and perhaps sooner, but he was too far gone; sucked in by a promise from the wizard, Paxton Anderson. A promise that no one could touch them and they would eventually walk.

I feel for Anderson's wife and kids, as well as, the family of Joey Plany, but I have little regard for the two convicted felons. They received exactly what was due.

In a very pleasant turn of events, the two were remanded to the custody of United States Marshals at the conclusion of the trial. The Honorable Susan Bolton placed them in custody, due to never having any secured bond in place while they were released prior to trial. With a cash bond, they'll be free, awaiting sentencing in August. They will remain in custody until then.

Again, in typical Paxton Anderson fashion, when the US Deputy Marshal approached him, he had difficulty understanding why she wanted his belongings; his belt, tie, personal effects, backpack, etc. He was still having trouble digesting the fact that he had just been convicted of twenty-five major offenses. He asked the deputy, "Why are you here? What do you want?" When she told him, he asked "Why?"

Truly amazing for a man to have so little understanding, or to ignore his culpability, for what he's done to so many people.

And to think that, upfront, they were both offered a sweet plea deal; plead guilty and receive a five-year sentence. They have to now be thinking they should have taken the deal, but knowing how immensely arrogant Paxton Anderson is, it would have never happened anyway. Instead, they relied on two lawyers, who handled their defense in the most maladroit manner one could imagine, blaming everyone else on earth but their clients.

I continue to think to back his closing argument for Plany, when Hoidal claimed, "The forgeries don't matter in this case." And Hoidal is a licensed attorney in Arizona!

I'm sure that Joey is remorseful that he got caught up in Paxton's web, but Paxton Anderson will go to his grave believing he's never done anything wrong. I am certain of this because I know Paxton Anderson well and with the exception of their sentencing, on August 18th, I'm glad it's finally over. Anderson and Plany had their day in court and now they'll spend many more in federal prison.

Shortly after the verdicts were read, I spoke to Ms. Hansen via telephone. She wanted to know how I was doing.

"How do you feel? Now that it's over. I mean, you being the one who originally brought this whole thing to the FBI. What are you feeling right now?"

I didn't know how to answer. I hadn't thought about it and I don't remember how I answered her. I can say this; knowing these two individuals as well as I do and being a witness to them being told their freedom was about to be taken away was exhilarating. To know that Paxton *didn't* have the best lawyers in the land and *could* be touched was as invigorating, as it was rejuvenating.

Knowing that Federal Prosecutor, Kevin Rapp and Brandon Lopez with the IRS did an amazing job in securing a conviction for Anderson and Plany, reassured me that our judicial system, although flawed in so many ways, does work to some degree.

After our short conversation, I pushed the "END" button on my cell phone. I sighed, stared at the phone, pondered the past ten years of my life, and realized the reflection of my face on the dark screen of my phone showed the perils of stress; more gray hair than I remembered having. It was a crazy ten years.

I also thought about my life up to that point in time and reflected on each *accomplishment* in my life. I realized, once again, that I hadn't really accomplished much in life. I was just some average guy, doing average stuff, trying to get through my own forest and hopefully, toward the end of my life, find a clearing for myself. No, I really hadn't accomplished anything that would make a person truly envious of me. I haven't done anything so remarkable that people took notice. But I did keep a promise to two little girls. I didn't walk away from them. I stayed and fought for them.

And after all the misery we were forced to endure, I believe I saved them from a different life, had I not stood up to their mother, Tiffany; at one time, the love of my life. I believe I provided a healthier upbringing, rather than one of materialism and the constant search for what they can gain from others around them.

Instead, they value themselves. They value friendships. They value family. And they value the relationship we have. I believe they are better human beings, with higher moral standards than they may have had, had I not stayed and fought for them. They are now grown and on their own and I couldn't be more proud of them. They are without a doubt, exactly what I wanted them to be as human beings and as it is for all four of my daughters, I love them more than life itself.

Have I had a remarkable and successful life? Not at all. Not even close. But I'll take what I have and when my life ends, I'll be able to go to my grave knowing I did the right thing and no matter how little of an impact I had on anyone. Through my daughters, I know I was a success in some small way.

Through the turmoil, I also believe I had some success in reclaiming my existence, because for several years, that existence was destroyed, and all I wanted to have was a piece of myself that wasn't tainted by the lies spread about me.

Through this journey and among the many things I learned from my *teachers*, two stand out the most; when you lie about someone, be ready, because that *someone* may just decide to fight back and expose you for who and what you are.

The other thing I learned, after all the bullshit the girls and I went through, at the hands of Tiffany, is that I have my girls and they have me. Not that this is a game, but Tiffany didn't break me. I won . . . and I have my existence back.

Everything you've read in this book is the absolute truth, and it can be proven. It is far more than what Tiffany can say.

And I have finally told my story.

Katie, Me and Megan – Newport Beach 2017

Katie and Megan 2019

MY FOUR LOVES – Kathryn, Analiese, Megan, Caitlin

NOT THE LOVE OF MY LIFE

Carmel, California 2020

CPSIA information can be obtained
at www.ICGtesting.com
Printed in the USA
JSHW021743020223
37101JS00001B/9